CAMBRIDGE GREEK AND LATIN CLASSICS

BACCHYLIDES
A SELECTION

EDITED BY

H. MAEHLER

Emeritus Professor of Papyrology
University College, London

CAMBRIDGE
UNIVERSITY PRESS

PUBLISHED BY THE PRESS SYNDICATE OF THE UNIVERSITY OF CAMBRIDGE
The Pitt Building, Trumpington Street, Cambridge, United Kingdom

CAMBRIDGE UNIVERSITY PRESS
The Edinburgh Building, Cambridge, CB2 2RU, UK
40 West 20th Street, New York, NY 10011–4211, USA
477 Williamstown Road, Port Melbourne, VIC 3207, Australia
Ruiz de Alarcón 13, 28014 Madrid, Spain
Dock House, The Waterfront, Cape Town 8001, South Africa

http://www.cambridge.org

First published 2004

Printed in the United Kingdom at the University Press, Cambridge

Typefaces Baskerville 10/12 pt. and New Hellenic   *System* LATEX 2ε   [TB]

A catalogue record for this book is available from the British Library

Library of Congress Cataloguing in Publication data
Bacchylides.
[Selections]
Bacchylides : a selection / edited by H. Maehler.
p.   cm. – (Cambridge Greek and Latin classics)
Based on the editor's Die Lieder des Bakchylides.
Includes bibliographical references and index.
ISBN 0 521 59036 1 (hardback) – ISBN 0 521 59977 6 (paperback)
1. Athletics – Greece – Poetry.   2. Athletes – Greece – Poetry.
3. Mythology, Greek – Poetry.   4. Games – Greece – Poetry.   5. Laudatory
poetry, Greek.   I. Maehler, Herwig.   II. Bacchylides. Works.
German & Greek. 1997.   III. Title.   IV. Series.
PA3943.A2   2003
881′.01 – dc22   2003055397

ISBN 0 521 59036 1 hardback
ISBN 0 521 59977 6 paperback

In memory of W. S. Barrett

CONTENTS

Preface   *page* ix
List of abbreviations   x

Introduction   1
  1 *Choral lyric poetry and its public*   1
  2 *Festivals and games*   4
  3 *Bacchylides' life and works*   9
  4 *Language and prosody*   10
  5 *Metre*   14
  6 *Style*   18
  7 *Alexandrian scholarship and the fate of the text*   25
  8 *The surviving papyri*   28
  9 *Sigla and editorial conventions*   31

ΒΑΚΧΥΛΙΔΟΥ ΕΠΙΝΙΚΟΙ   33
  3 ΙΕΡΩΝΙ ΣΥΡΑΚΟΣΙΩΙ ΙΠΠΟΙΣ [ΟΛΥ]Μ̣ΠΙΑ   33
  4 ΤΩΙ ΑΥΤΩΙ <ΙΠΠΟΙΣ> ΠΥΘΙΑ   37
  5 <ΤΩΙ ΑΥΤΩΙ ΚΕΛΗΤΙ ΟΛΥΜΠΙΑ>   38
  6 ΛΑΧΩΝΙ ΚΕΙΩΙ <ΠΑΙΔΙ> ΣΤΑΔΙΕΙ ΟΛΥΜΠ[ΙΑ   46
  11 ΑΛΕΞΙΔΑΜΩΙ ΜΕΤΑΠΟΝΤΙΝΩΙ ΠΑΙΔΙ ΠΑΛΑΙΣΤΗΙ
     ΠΥΘΙΑ   47

ΒΑΚΧΥΛΙΔΟΥ ΔΙΘΥΡΑΜΒΟΙ   53
  15 ΑΝΤΗΝΟΡΙΔΑΙ Η ΕΛΕΝΗΣ ΑΠΑΙΤΗΣΙΣ   53
  16 [ΗΡΑΚΛΗΣ (vel ΔΗΙΑΝΕΙΡΑ ?) ΕΙΣ ΔΕΛΦΟΥΣ]   55
  17 ΗΙΘΕΟΙ Η ΘΗΣΕΥΣ <ΚΗΙΟΙΣ ΕΙΣ ΔΗΛΟΝ>   57
  18 ΘΗΣΕΥΣ <ΑΘΗΝΑΙΟΙΣ>   62
  19 ΙΩ ΑΘΗΝΑΙΟΙΣ   64
  20 ΙΔΑΣ ΛΑΚΕΔΑΙΜΟΝΙΟΙΣ   67

ΠΑΙΑΝ   68
  fr. 22 + fr. 4 [ΑΠΟΛΛΩΝΙ ΠΥΘΑΙΕΙ ΕΙΣ ΑΣΙΝΗΝ]   68

ΠΡΟΣΟΔΙΟΝ   71
  fr. 11 + fr. 12   71

ΕΓΚΩΜΙΑ (?)   72
    fr. 20A   72
    fr. 20B [ΑΛΕΞΑ]Ν[ΔΡΩΙ ΑΜΥΝΤ]Α   73
    fr. 20C [Ι]ΕΡΩΝΙ [ΣΥ]ΡΑΚΟΣΙΩΙ   74
    fr. 20D   75

Commentary   77
Appendix: *Vases referred to in the Commentary*   260
Works cited   264
Indexes   273

PREFACE

The poetry of Bacchylides, Simonides' nephew, was unfavourably compared to that of his contemporary, Pindar, by Ps.Longinus (περὶ ὕψους 33.5), and even after the publication of the great London papyrus by F. G. Kenyon in 1897 modern commentators have tended to criticize Bacchylides for not being sufficiently like Pindar. In truth, however, the two poets are very different stylistically, even in their victory odes where they necessarily conform to the same set of conventions; comparison of their dithyrambs is scarcely possible, as none of Pindar's are preserved complete. In fact, the first five of Bacchylides' dithyrambs are the only complete (or nearly complete) specimens of this important genre from the first half of the fifth century BCE.

To do justice to the qualities of Greek choral lyric poetry, one has to bear in mind the function of the respective literary genre (victory ode, praise poem, cult song, etc.) and the aims which the poet was expected to achieve within each genre. An unbiased approach to Bacchylides' poems will show him not as a lesser Pindar, but as an imaginative, original and highly accomplished poet in his own right.

The present selection is based on my complete edition with commentary in two parts: *Die Lieder des Bakchylides:* I *Die Siegeslieder* (1982), II *Die Dithyramben und Fragmente* (1997). That commentary has here been revised and adapted to the interests and needs of an English-speaking academic but non-specialist readership.

It is a pleasure to thank Professors P. E. Easterling and R. Hunter, whose guidance and constructive comments have greatly improved my draft and whose meticulous scrutiny of my typescript has cleansed it of many inaccuracies and inconsistencies. Thanks are also due to Dr Michael Sharp and especially to my copy-editor, Ms Muriel Hall, whose watchful eye has spotted many oversights. My greatest debt of gratitude is to the late W. S. Barrett, who communicated the results of his own unpublished research into problems of text or interpretation to me and allowed me to make use of them in the most generous way. I dedicate this volume to his memory.

H. Maehler

ABBREVIATIONS

ABL	C. H. E. Haspels, *Attic black-figured lekythoi* (Paris 1936)
ABV	J. D. Beazley, *Attic black-figure vase painters* (Oxford 1956)
Add.	T. H. Carpenter, *Beazley Addenda* (2nd edn., Oxford 1989)
ARV²	J. D. Beazley, *Attic red-figure vase painters* (2nd edn., Oxford 1963)
BKT IX	G. Ioannidou, *Catalogue of Greek and Latin Literary Papyri in Berlin* (*Berliner Klassikertexte* IX, Mainz 1996)
Coll.Alex.	J. U. Powell, *Collectanea Alexandrina* (Oxford 1925)
CPG	*Corpus Paroemiographorum Graecorum* ed. E. L. von Leutsch and F. G. Schneidewin, 2 vols. (Göttingen 1839 and 1851)
CVA	*Corpus Vasorum Antiquorum*
FGrHist	F. Jacoby, *Die Fragmente der griechischen Historiker* (Berlin–Leiden 1923–58)
G.–P.	B. Gentili and C. Prato, *Poetae elegiaci*, 2 vols. (Leipzig 1979 and 1985)
IEG	M. L. West, *Iambi et elegi graeci ante Alexandrum cantati* (2nd edn., Oxford 1992)
IG	*Inscriptiones Graecae*
Jebb	R. C. Jebb, *Bacchylides, The poems and fragments* (Cambridge 1905)
Kenyon	*The poems of Bacchylides* ed. F. G. Kenyon (London 1897)
K–B	R. Kühner–F. Blass, *Ausführliche Grammatik der griechischen Sprache, 1.Teil: Elementar- und Formenlehre*, 2 vols. (3rd edn., Hannover 1890–92)
K–G	R. Kühner–B. Gerth, *Ausführliche Grammatik der griechischen Sprache, 2.Teil: Satzlehre*, 2 vols. (3rd edn., Hannover 1898)
LIMC	*Lexicon Iconographicum Mythologiae Classicae*

LSJ	H. G. Liddell–R. Scott–H. S. Jones, *A Greek-English Lexicon* (Oxford 1940)
OCD³	*Oxford Classical Dictionary* 3rd edn. by S. Hornblower and A. Spawforth (Oxford 1996)
Ox.Pap.	*The Oxyrhynchus Papyri*
Para	J. D. Beazley, *Paralipomena* (2nd edn., Oxford 1971)
PCG	*Poetae Comici Graeci* ed. R. Kassel and C. Austin (Berlin 1983–98)
PEG	*Poetae Epici Graeci*, vol. 1 ed. A. Bernabé (Leipzig 1987)
PLF	*Poetarum Lesbiorum fragmenta* ed. E. Lobel and D. Page (Oxford 1955)
PMG	*Poetae Melici Graeci* ed. D. L. Page (Oxford 1962)
PMGF	*Poetarum Melicorum Graecorum fragmenta* ed. M. Davies (Oxford 1991)
PSI	*Papiri della Società Italiana*
RE	*Pauly's Realencyclopädie der classischen Altertumswissenschaft*
SH	*Supplementum Hellenisticum* ed. H. Lloyd-Jones and P. J. Parsons (Berlin 1983)
SLG	*Supplementum Lyricis Graecis* ed. D. Page (Oxford 1974)
TrGF	*Tragicorum graecorum fragmenta*, 1 ed. B. Snell (*Didascaliae etc., fragmenta tragicorum minorum*, Göttingen 1971, 1986), 11 ed. R. Kannicht and B. Snell (*Adespota*, 1981), 111 ed. S. Radt (Aeschylus), 1v ed. S. Radt (Sophocles, 1985, 1999)

Abbreviated titles of periodicals, where not self-explanatory, are cited as in *L'année philologique*.

INTRODUCTION

1. CHORAL LYRIC POETRY AND ITS PUBLIC

'Greek poetry differed profoundly from modern poetry in content, form, and methods of presentation. An essentially practical art, it was closely linked to the realities of social and political life, and to the actual behaviour of individuals within a community. It rendered the poet's own experience as well as that of others, but was not private poetry in the modern sense. It drew regularly for its themes on myth, which was at once the sole subject matter of narrative and dramatic poetry and a constant point of paradigmatic reference in lyric.'[1] In the Greek world from the second millennium to the fourth century BCE, poetry was characterized by two essential features: it was sung, and it was transmitted orally. Poetry was sung from memory, not from written texts, and listened to, not read. Although systems of writing existed, they were not essential to the performance or to the reception of song; what role, if any, writing played in the composition of poetry in Homer's time and in the subsequent three centuries, we cannot tell; it was, of course, vital for the preservation of the texts, without the music. The oral character of Greek poetry down to the 'classical' age is a fundamental feature of Greek culture.

To Homer, all poetry is 'song' (ἀοιδή or μολπή). In the *Odyssey*, ἀοιδή also means 'singing': to the epic bards, the song and the activity that creates it are the same; typically for the culture of 'oral poetry', the song only exists as it is being sung. Alkman and Archilochos (seventh century BCE) are the first to use μέλος to designate the 'song' as distinct from its performance. It seems that by this time only μέλη, i.e. poems in metres which we call 'lyric' (see below, pp. 14–17), were sung, while epic and iambic poetry was recited. The composers of *sung* poetry were called μελοποιοί or μελικοί (sc. ποιηταί). The term 'lyric', derived from 'lyre' (λύρα), is not found before the Hellenistic age; it is imprecise, since 'lyric' songs were sung not only to the lyre but to a variety of instruments, including the double oboe (αὐλοί).

'Lyric' poetry is performed either by a solo singer ('monodic lyric'), or by a choir ('choral lyric'). The distinction is determined by the function of

[1] Gentili, *Poetry and its public* 3.

1

the song and the circumstances of its performance. In very general terms, monodic songs tend to be addressed to a restricted, private audience, or to one person, or to the poet's own self, whereas choral songs are aimed at a wider public, often the local community which has gathered either for a religious festival, or to celebrate an athletic or hippic victory of one of its citizens. While monodic songs often purport to convey the poet's own experiences, thoughts and feelings to persons close to him or her, choral songs give voice to the collective views, aspirations, and feelings of the community for which they have been composed. Many of them are cult songs, performed in honour of a god or hero as an expression of the community's veneration; the singers of a dithyramb or paean, whether in their home city or at Delphi or on Delos, sing as representatives of their city. This is true not only for songs composed for religious celebrations (εἰς θεούς), but also for those celebrating a fellow citizen (εἰς ἀνθρώπους). Such compositions, which included victory odes (ἐπίνικοι or ἐπινίκια), songs of praise (ἐγκώμια), or dirges (θρῆνοι), are also addressed to a public audience in the sense that a success, for example, at one of the panhellenic festivals (which were, of course, also religious festivals) added to the pride and prestige of the whole city and was celebrated not only by the victor's family and friends but by the whole citizen body. This explains why Bacchylides' and Pindar's victory odes often combine praise of the victor with a mythical narrative linked to his city, or to the place of his victory. The victory thus appears as proof that the victor has shown himself worthy of the great deeds of his mythical ancestors. Bacchylides' ode 11 is a particularly clear illustration of the interrelation of the victor's praise and mythical narrative.

The intrinsically public character of the victory ode also explains why the poet's general statements (γνῶμαι), which normally provide transitions from one section of the ode to the next, are to be understood as general truths handed down from past generations to which everyone present can subscribe. In that respect, their function is comparable to that of the choruses in Handel's *Messiah* or Bach's *St. Matthew Passion*.

All choral lyric poetry, from Alkman to Pindar and B., is public and representative poetry, comparable in that respect to statues and other monuments dedicated in the sanctuaries of Delphi or Olympia, in the sense that they are public and representative art. Both poetry and art strive to create images that will be recognized by the citizens as ideal representations. In the sixth and early fifth centuries, the statue of an athlete is not an individual portrait but a young Athenian's or Aiginetan's ideal image that will immortalize his achievement (ἀρετή), enhancing his city's prestige (κῦδος); similarly, a dithyramb that narrates the exploits of its principal hero will be perceived as an image of the city's greatness.

The society on whose behalf statues and choral odes were commissioned was the educated and wealthy upper class of the aristocratic city states. Not only was their wealth based, as it had been in the feudal society reflected in Homer, on land ownership and agriculture, but it was created increasingly by overseas trade and the introduction of a monetary economy. As Gentili has argued, 'the new wealth favored the arts in general, painting and sculpture as well as poetry, though not so much for their own sake as out of a desire for prestige and power. For the rich nobleman or city aristocrat and, above all, for the tyrant, the artist's work was a means of increasing status and consolidating political position.'[2] If one of them commissioned a victory ode, the poet had to take his requirements into account in deciding what myth would be appropriate to the occasion and acceptable to his patron, and what would be the most successful way of presenting it – successful, that is, in terms of public appreciation by the community which his patron represented.

Cult songs, such as dithyrambs, hymns, or paeans, are different. They were commissioned not by individuals but by communities; Pindar's *Paeans* are addressed 'To the Delphians', 'To the Thebans' etc., which implies that these communities had commissioned them. However, the poet's situation was essentially the same; he had to consider what would appeal most to his audience. This was particularly important if the performance was part of a competition, as was the case with the dithyrambs performed at the Dionysiac festivals in Athens. It seems that the great festival of Apollo on Delos, the Δήλια or Ἀπολλώνια, also included a competition of choral poetry, as the end of B.17 suggests. Even though in Athens, at any rate, festivals had changed, after the constitutional reforms of Kleisthenes in 509 BCE,[3] from occasions for celebrating a tyrant's greatness to occasions for celebrating the city's glory, and in that sense had become more inclusive and 'democratic', the dithyrambs and paeans of Pindar and Bacchylides remained 'élitist'; both poets composed for a well-educated, knowledgeable and discerning audience, and their choral songs were designed to appeal to quite sophisticated tastes.

[2] Gentili, *Poetry and its public* 115.
[3] Cf. Hignett, *Athenian constitution* 124ff.

After the middle of the fifth century, however, when most of the Greek city states became democracies, their societies also changed. The class of wealthy and ambitious noblemen, which had dominated the political and cultural life of Greece in the sixth and the early part of the fifth century and produced 'tyrants' like Polykrates of Samos, Peisistratos of Athens and Hieron of Syracuse, gradually lost its political power and cultural influence. Its demise meant that the traditional form of choral lyric poetry lost its patrons and its scope. The athletes who gained victories at Olympia or Delphi now came from different backgrounds; increasingly, the 'upper class' amateur was replaced by the professional champion who travelled from one festival to another, collecting prizes, rather like professional tennis players today. In Athens, the traditional dithyramb gave way to tragedy and comedy, which appealed to a wider public.

2. FESTIVALS AND GAMES

(a) Festivals

Everyday life in Greece was articulated by recurring festivals. These were the occasions when a community would come together to celebrate a god or hero with whom it had a particular link. The celebration often involved a procession (πομπή) and the presentation of an object, such as the *peplos* which was carried in the Panathenaic procession and presented to Athena on the Acropolis (see introd. to ode 15, p. 157), or of sheaves of wheat-stalks presented at the *Apollonia* on Delos (cf. Herodotos 4.33.1).

Dancing in groups and hymns sung by choruses are basic elements of Greek festivals, and taking an active part in them 'was part of community life, a way of learning a city-state's religious traditions and expressing one's devotion to the recognized gods.'[4] The hymn is also, like the Panathenaic peplos or the Delian wheat-sheaf, a votive offering, intended to please the god or goddess and win his/her favour toward the chorus and the community. Walter Burkert describes its function in these terms: 'The hymn must always delight the god afresh at the festival; therefore for dance and hymn there must always be someone who makes it, the poet, *poietes*. The literary genre of choral lyric, which can be traced from the end of the seventh century, accordingly develops from the practice of the cult and culminates

---

[4] Furley and Bremer, *Greek hymns* I 21; see also Cartledge 1985.

in the first half of the fifth century in the work of Pindar. The invocation of the gods, the enunciation of wishes and entreaties, is interwoven ever more artfully with mythical narratives and topical allusions to the festival and chorus. Already in the seventh century, several choruses are competing for the honour of performing the most beautiful hymn – with the costuming of the chorus then also playing its role. The religious function, the relationship with the gods, is in danger of being lost in the rivalry; but all are well convinced that the gods, like men, take a delighted interest in the contest.'[5]

Paeans and dithyrambs are particular types of hymns. Traditionally, paeans are hymns addressed to Apollo, Artemis or Leto, while dithyrambs are hymns addressed to Dionysos. The earliest description of a paean being performed is in *Iliad* 1.472–4, where the young Achaians, after the priest's prayer to Apollo for an end to the plague, 'propitiated the god all day long by singing a beautiful paean; they sang of the far-reacher, and he was pleased in his mind as he listened.' Three typical elements are evident here: (1) all the warriors are singing together as a chorus, (2) they are young (κοῦροι Ἀχαιῶν) and (3) they sing for the sake of protecting or saving their community.[6] According to a recent survey of the genre,[7] performing paeans had three main social functions: (1) articulating a sense of community among the members, (2) training for hoplite warfare, and (3) transmitting civic values from one generation to the next. Whether Bacchylides' Paean (frs. 4 + 22), composed for performance at the old sanctuary of Apollo Pythaieus at Asine in the Argolid, followed the traditional pattern, we cannot tell, as its beginning and end are lost. There is, however, a distinct possibility that the wonderful praise of peace (lines 61–80) was relevant to the circumstances of its performance: if the ten lines missing at the end contained another address to Apollo, it may have been a prayer for peace to be preserved or restored.

The dithyramb, first mentioned by Archilochos (fr. 120 W.) as a 'song of Dionysos', seems to have been given its definitive form towards the end of the sixth century, apparently by Lasos of Hermione.[8] As far as its content is concerned, there is evidence to suggest that in the sixth century its main characteristic was an extended mythical narrative, for Ibykos is said to have told in a dithyramb how Helen fled into the temple of Aphrodite and from

---

[5] Burkert, *Greek religion* 103.   [6] Cf. Furley & Bremer I 90–1.
[7] Rutherford, *Paeans* 61–2.   [8] Cf. D'Angour 1997: 346–50.

there spoke to Menelaos, whereupon he, conquered by love, threw away his sword (*PMG* 296). The mythical narrative is the main feature of the extant dithyrambs of Pindar and B., which all have titles indicating their subject matter. Such titles were an innovation of the sixth century, attributed to Arion (about 625–585 BCE) by Herodotos, who claimed that Arion was 'the first of men whom we know to have composed the dithyramb and named it and produced it in Corinth' (καὶ διθύραμβον πρῶτον ἀνθρώπων τῶν ἡμεῖς ἴδμεν ποιήσαντά τε καὶ ὀνομάσαντα καὶ διδάξαντα ἐν Κορίνθωι, 1.23); the controversial term ὀνομάσαντα is interpreted by the Suda as 'he named what the chorus sang' (λέγεται . . . ὀνομάσαι τὸ ἀιδόμενον ὑπὸ τοῦ χοροῦ).[9] One of Simonides' dithyrambs (*PMG* 539) had the title 'Memnon'.[10] In Pindar and B., some of the extant titles also name the community or city which had commissioned the dithyramb: [Κ]ατά[βασις] Ἡρακλέου[ς] ἢ Κέρβερος Θηβαίοις (Pindar, fr.70b), Ἰὼ Ἀθηναίοις (B. 19), Ἴδας Λακεδαιμονίοις (B. 20).

   The most obvious difference between the dithyrambs of Pindar and B. is that Pindar's, as far as we can tell from the extant fragments, refer to Dionysos and his cult, whereas those of B. do not – the only exception being B. 19 which gives a very brief genealogy of Dionysos at the end. One must, however, beware of generalizations, as none of the Pindaric dithyrambs survives complete and the number and extent of the fragments is quite limited. As for B., it is not clear why his dithyrambs omit the cletic invocations and other references to Dionysos and consist almost entirely of narrative or, in ode 18, of strophic dialogue. One might speculate that in the odes B. composed for Athens (15, 17, 18, 19)[11] he was following the example of Attic tragedy which had loosened its original connection with the cult of Dionysos and widened its scope to narrate myths that could help create an Athenian civic identity. Be that as it may, the difficulties which some Alexandrian scholars experienced in classifying these odes (see below on papyrus **B** in Section 8, and introd. to ode 17, p. 173) stem from their lack of distinguishing formal features. Ode 17, for instance, classified as a dithyramb, may in reality have been conceived as a paean, even though it

   [9] Cf. Pickard-Cambridge, *Dithyramb* 12; van der Weiden, *Dithyrambs* 2–3; Ieranò, *Ditirambo* 189.
   [10] Cf. Pickard-Cambridge, *Dithyramb* 17; Ieranò, *Ditirambo* 195.
   [11] Whether 16, the ode with the closest affinity to Attic tragedy, was composed for Athens is uncertain; see p. 165.

lacks the ritual refrain ἰὴ παιάν. The disagreement between Kallimachos and Aristarchos (see p. 27) about the 'Kassandra' (see below, Section 8) shows that Aristarchos had identified mythical narrative as the defining feature of the dithyramb.

(b) Games

Athletic competitions are described in Homer. The funeral games in honour of Patroklos (*Iliad* 23.250–897) and the contests held by the Phaeacians to entertain their guest, Odysseus (*Odyssey* 8.109–233), have no direct connection with religious festivals, but seem to be inspired simply by the Greeks' desire to compete for 'first prize', which is so tellingly summed up by Peleus' advice to his son, Achilles: αἰὲν ἀριστεύειν καὶ ὑπείροχον ἔμμεναι ἄλλων ('always to be the best and pre-eminent among all others', *Iliad* 11.784). The oldest Greek hexameter inscription, thought to be contemporary with Homer,[12] sets out a prize for a dancing competition. Competitors not only hope to win, but want to be seen winning, so it was natural to hold these competitions at places and on occasions where a crowd of people would come together. In Greece, such occasions were primarily the numerous festivals in honour of gods or heroes, which attracted all kinds of contests: beauty-contests for girls, athletic contests for men and boys in different age-groups, musical contests for oboe- and kithara-players and singers, and in Athens stage-productions of dithyrambs, tragedies and comedies.

From the sixth century BCE, the four most prominent festivals became known as 'Panhellenic' festivals because they attracted visitors from all over the Greek world. They were the *Olympia*, held in honour of Zeus at Olympia in the north-western Peloponnese; the *Pythia* at Delphi in honour of Apollo; the *Isthmia* near Corinth, for Poseidon; and the *Nemeia* in honour of Zeus, held at Nemea, about half-way between Argos and Corinth. In Greek mythology, these games are also linked to funeral games honouring a local hero, such as Pelops or Oinomaos at Olympia, Archemoros at Nemea, or Palaimon on the Isthmus; the mythical origin of the Pythian games is traced back to the killing of the dragon, Python, by Apollo.[13]

---

[12] Athens, Nat. Mus. 192; *IG* I² 919; Jeffery, *Local scripts* 76 no.1 and pl.1; Immerwahr, *Attic script* p. 7 no.1 and pl.1,1.
[13] W. Burkert, *Greek religion* 106.

The *Olympia* and *Pythia* were held every four years (Greek chronology reckoned in 'Olympiads', i.e. the numbered four-year periods which were counted from the year when the *Olympia* were thought to have been founded, 776 BCE; the *Pythia* began in 582). The *Isthmia* and *Nemeia* were held every two years, from 582 and 573 respectively. At Olympia, the festival of Zeus lasted for five days, but the preparations took the best part of a year. The ten organizers and judges, called *Hellanodikai* ('Judges of the Greeks' – only ethnic Greeks were allowed to compete), were chosen by lot; during the last month before the festival, they supervised the competitors in a strict regime of training. After the swearing-in of the competitors and judges on the morning of the first day, the festival programme included the following events:[14]

> Contests for heralds and trumpeters held near the stadium entrance. Boys' running, wrestling, and boxing contests. Prayers and sacrifices in the Altis, including the official sacrifice of one hundred oxen at the altar of Zeus; consultation of oracles. Orations by well-known philosophers and recitals by poets and historians. Chariot- and horse-races in the hippodrome. Pentathlon (discus, javelin, jumping, running, and wrestling). Funeral rites in honour of the hero Pelops. Parade of victors and singing of victory odes. Foot-races and races in armour, wrestling, boxing, pankration (a combination of boxing and wrestling). On the last day, the victors were crowned with wreaths of wild olive by the *Hellanodikai* in the temple of Zeus.

The programme of the *Pythia* originally consisted of just one contest: the singing of a hymn to Apollo; after its reorganization in 582 BCE it included other musical contests: singing to the kithara, kithara-playing, and aulos(oboe)-playing. The athletics programme was similar to that of the *Olympia* (the chariot- and horse-races were held in the plain below Delphi, at Krisa). The prize was a crown of bay-leaves. The *Isthmia* and *Nemeia* also included musical and poetic competitions, athletics programmes similar to those of the *Olympia* and *Pythia*, and chariot- and horse-races. The prize was a crown of celery-leaves.

---

[14] Adapted here from Swaddling, *Olympic Games* 37; see also Lee, *Olympic Games*.

3. BACCHYLIDES' LIFE AND WORKS

Very little is known about B.'s life and dates. His home town was Iulis on the island of Keos off the south-eastern tip of Attica. His mother was a sister of the poet Simonides (557/6–468/7 BCE); even if she was up to ten years younger than her brother, she would have been unlikely to have had children after about 516. In fact, B. may have been born around 520, given that two of his poems, ode 17 and the *enkomion* for the young prince Alexandros, son of King Amyntas of Macedonia (fr. 20B), can be dated to the early 490s; this would make him closely contemporary with Pindar, who was born in 518. The assumption, made in some late Byzantine sources but not shared by the earlier biographies, that he was younger than Pindar is therefore unfounded, as is the entry in Eusebios' *Chronicle* for 431 BCE that B. 'became known' in that year, which may be based on confusion with a flute-player of that name (cf. Fatouros 1961: 147–9). B.'s latest securely dated victory ode (6) was composed for a boy's victory at the 82nd Olympic Games (452 BCE). Nothing is known of the poet's life after this date, which makes it seem likely that he died not much later.

When B. was born, his uncle, Simonides, already enjoyed a high reputation as a poet of dithyrambs and other choral songs as well as of epigrams. Peisistratos' son, Hipparchos, who ruled Athens between 527 and 514, invited Simonides to his court, as did Hieron of Syracuse half a century later. Simonides was also on friendly terms with aristocratic families in Thessaly. It is quite likely that B. benefitted from his uncle's many connections in his career, which seems to have taken off soon after 500 BCE with commissions from Athens for the great Delian festival (ode 17) and from Macedonia of a song for the young prince Alexandros, to be sung at a *symposion* (fr. 20B). In the 480s he competed with Pindar for commissions from the leading families of Aigina, and in 476 he celebrated Hieron's first success at the Olympic Games (ode 5), again in competition with Pindar, who composed his first *Olympian* for the same victory. In 470, when Hieron's chariot won the race at the Pythian Games in Delphi, B. sent a short victory ode (4), while Pindar composed his elaborate first *Pythian* for Hieron's victory celebration at Syracuse. B.'s most prestigious commission was the victory ode (3) for Hieron's success in the chariot race at Olympia in 468. B. also composed victory odes for athletes from Keos (1, 2, 6, 7, and 8), Phleious (9), Athens (10), Metapontion in Southern Italy (11), Aigina

(12 and 13), and Thessaly (14), as well as an ode (14B) celebrating not a victorious athlete but a magistrate's election to office, possibly as hipparch, at Larisa in Thessaly; this ode may well have concluded the book of B.'s victory odes.[15] As Pindar's poems were assembled and arranged in 17 books by Aristophanes of Byzantion (see p. 27 below), he may well have done the same for B.

Of the poems collected in the book of dithyrambs, odes 17, 18, and 19 were doubtless composed for Athens, probably also 15 and just possibly 16, while 20 was almost certainly performed at Sparta. B. also wrote hymns (frs. 1–3), paeans (one of which, frs. 4 + 22, contains a wonderful eulogy of peace), procession songs (frs. 11–13), maiden songs, dancing songs (*hyporchemata*, frs. 14–16), songs about love (*erotika*, frs. 17–19), and songs of praise or reproach for living persons (*enkomia*?, frs. 20–20F).

The only other event in the poet's life for which there is evidence outside his poems can be gleaned from a remark in Plutarch's *On exile* (14, 605C), who claims that the 'ancients' (παλαιοί) often created their best and most famous works while they were in exile, quoting, among others, B. who spent some time in exile in the Peloponnese. This seems credible in view of the fact that Pindar composed a paean for the Keans at the time when he was also writing his *Isthmian* 1. The Keans would presumably have commissioned the paean from B., had he been available: so he may have been in exile then. When this was is not known, because the date of Pindar's *I.* 1 and *Paean* 4 cannot be established.

4. LANGUAGE AND PROSODY

(a) Language

Greek choral songs must have been sung in many cities and islands for many centuries before Homer (eighth century BCE), and long before they were first recorded in writing and transmitted under poets' names. The first Greek poets known to have composed choral songs of which fragments

---

[15] Similarly, the book of Pindar's *Nemeans*, which was the last book of his victory odes in the Alexandrian edition, also has at the end three odes that have nothing to do with the *Nemeia*, the last one (*N.* 11) being an ode honouring a civic official (*prytanis*) upon taking office. The last three odes were appended to the last book of *epinikia* apparently because there was no other book into which they would have fitted better.

have survived are Eumelos of Corinth (later eighth century)[16] and Alkman of Sparta (*c.* 650–600). The dialect spoken in Corinth and Sparta was Doric, and as a result of their poetry being fixed in writing, Doric became the predominant dialect of all subsequent choral lyric song, whatever the poet's origin.

The language of B., like that of Simonides, is an artificial 'literary' Doric with many words, forms and formulas borrowed from epic, including some Aeolic forms. The following epic forms are found in B.: the genitive singular ending in –οιο (ἀπλάτοιο 5.62, διωξίπποιο 11.75, δυστάνοιο 11.102), uncontracted forms (Ἰαόνων 17.3, ἀμφακέα fr. 4.72, δυσμενέων 5.133), the omission of augment in past tenses (σάμαινεν 15.38, θίγεν 17.12, ἴδεν 17.16, etc.), the 3rd person singular subjunctive in –ησι (λάχησι 19.3, θάλπησι fr. 20B.7), the Aeolic infinitive endings in –μεν (ἴμεν 19.12, ἔμμεν 5.144) and –μεναι (ἔμμεναι 18.14) and the dative plural endings in –σσι (ποσσί(ν) 5.183, πόδεσσι 6.2). B.'s language is very similar to Pindar's, except that forms of Ionic, B.'s native dialect, are occasionally found in the text where one would expect their Doric equivalents, and frs. 19 and 20A are almost entirely in Ionic.

The Doric colouring is due mainly to the long *alpha* in place of the Ionic *ēta*, even though ᾱ is not consistently preserved in the papyri. For example, the scribes always write –ζη, not -ζᾱ: πολύζηλος, πολυζήλωτος, ἐπίζηλος (but ζαλωτός in Pindar, *O.* 7.6: papyri and later manuscripts of Pindar do not share this tendency to substitute η for α), Τροιζηνία B. 17.58; they often write η instead of ᾱ where an ᾱ follows (φήμα, but φαμί; κυβερνήτας, but κυβέρνασεν; ἀδμήτᾱ 5.167, but ἄδμᾱτοι 11.84), but regularly have Ἀθάνα, Ἀθᾶναι, Ἀθαναίων, προφάτας, ἀλάταν, αἰχματάν, σελάνα. In some cases one might wonder whether an 'Ionic' η in a papyrus is due to the scribe's carelessness and should be changed to ᾱ: so in 5.187 αληθειας, also perhaps in 11.45 παράπληγι (read –πλῆγι?), where Blass preferred παραπλᾶγι (cf. πλᾶξεν, πλάξιππος). It is possible that B. himself was not consistent in his spelling: cf. ἐπισκήπτων 5.42, but σκᾶπτρον 3.70; ἠλύκταζον 11.93, but ἆγον 15.37; λῃσταί 18.8, but λαΐδος 16.17; παιήων 16.8 (so also in Simonides and Pindar), but παιάνιξαν 17.129; παρηΐδων

[16] Pausanias (4.4.1) says that Eumelos composed a procession song (*prosodion*) for the Messenians, for performance at the Apollonia on Delos, from which he quotes two lines (*PMG* 696), and that this was the only work correctly ascribed to Eumelos. Other works sometimes ascribed to him appear to belong to a much later period, cf. West 2002: 109–133.

17.13 (but cf. χαλκοπάραιος Pind. *P.* 1.44 and *N.* 7.71). Original η appears in ἥβα, στῆθος, μῆλος 'sheep', and εἰρήνα.

The Doric infinitive ending in -εν, instead of the more frequent ending in -ειν, appears where the metre requires a short syllable, i.e. before vowel (ἐρύκεν 17.41; ἴσχεν 17.88, where the papyrus has ισχειν; φυλάσσεν 19.25), but also before consonant (θύεν 16.18 and probably φάμ]εν 3.65). Other verb endings show similar inconsistencies: Doric -οντι (for -ουσιν) appears after σ or ξ: πτάσσοντι 5.32.

In compound verbs, *apokopé* of ἀνά, κατά, παρά, common in Homer and a regular feature of all Doric and Aeolic dialects, appears in ἀμπαύσας 5.7, ἄμπαυσεν fr. 20D.11, ἀντείνων 11.100, ἀγκομίσσαι 3.89, ἀμμειγνυμένα fr. 20B.9, κάππαυε fr. 20B.2, also in compound adjectives (πάρφρονος 11.103).

Other Doric features are the articles τοί (5.149, fr. 4.22) and ταί (11.43) for οἱ and αἱ, used as demonstrative; the genitive singular masc. in –ᾱ (Ἀΐδᾱ 5.61), the genitive plural fem. in –ᾶν (τᾶν ἱερᾶν Ἀθανᾶν 18.1), the future and aorist forms in –ξ– of verbs in -ζειν: εὐκλεΐξας 6.16; δοίαξε 11.87; παιάνιξαν 17.129, but after –κ– B. prefers –σσ– to –ξ–: ἀγκομίσσαι 3.89.

The Doric accusative of the pronoun νιν (Ionic μιν) is regularly used by B., mostly for the singular (= αὐτόν or αὐτήν), rarely for the plural (= αὐτούς).

Aeolic forms, apart from those familiar from Homer and other epic poetry, are rare: Μοῖσα 5.4, λαχοῖσαν 19.13, ἔλλαθι 11.8 (on epic ἔμμεν and ἔμμεναι see above).

(b) Prosody

In Greek, syllables with long vowels and double vowels (diphthongs) are long, those with short vowels are short. Vowels are either naturally long, such as η, ω and sometimes α, ι, υ, or short, such as ε, ο, and sometimes α, ι, υ. However, short vowels followed by two or more consonants are long, except that before certain combinations of *muta cum liquida*, i.e. plosive (π, τ, κ, β, δ, γ, φ, θ, χ) and liquid or nasal (λ, ρ; μ, ν), they *may* be treated as short. Vowels followed by 'mute and liquid' (plosive + liquid consonant, e.g. δρ, γλ, κμ) are measured long in three out of four cases; where they count as short, the following plosive + liquid consonants, marked by a loop (‿), are either (a) at the beginning of the next word (or at the beginning of the second element of a compound: λεπτόπρυμνον 17.119, ἀγλαόθρονοι 17.125, or after augment: ἔκλαγεν 17.127, or reduplication: πεπρωμέναν

17.26), or (b) in personal names (e.g. Ἴφικλον 5.128); there are (c) a few other cases, mostly with plosive + ρ (ὑγροῖσι 17.108, πατρί fr. 20A.6, etc.), also ἀφνεοῦ 17.34.

At the beginning of a word, ρ and σ can, if required by the metre, be treated as double consonants: ἐπὶ (ρ)ροδόεντι 16.34, ἀπὸ (ρ)ρίζας fr. 4.54 (also in ἀ(ρ)ραχνᾶν fr. 4.70), δόρυ· (σ)σόει (i.e. σϜόει) 17.90. Likewise, final ν can count as a double consonant: δόμον(ν)· ἔμολεν 17.100, ἀπωσάμενον(ν), εἴ τις 5.189, πόλιν(ν) Ἀχαιοῖς 11.114, also in συν(ν)εχέως 5.113.[17]

Combinations of vowels which do not normally form a diphthong but remain separate are marked by *diairesis* (ἐΰκτιμέναν 15.10); when they are contracted into one syllable, this is marked by a loop (ἠϊθέων 17.43 and 93, χέον 17.96)

Long vowels and diphthongs at word-ends are usually shortened before another vowel ('correption'), most often κᾰί and -τᾰι, but also other endings: ἄλσος τέ τοῐ ἱμερόεν 11.118, παρθένοͅι Ἀθάναι 16.21, ἐπιδέγμενοͅι ἀνάγκαν 17.96, τόν ποτέ ὅͅι ἐν γάμωι 17.115. Correption within a word occurs where a short syllable is required by the metre: Μίνῳι 17.68, Ἀθανᾰίων 17.92, πᾰιάνιξαν 17.129. Conversely, Doric forms with short first syllable are sometimes replaced by epic forms with long first syllable for metrical convenience ('epic lengthening'): κόρα/κούρα, μόνος/μοῦνος, νόσος/νοῦσος, ξένος/ξεῖνος, but the regular ῡ in χρῡσο– is shortened in 16.2 (χρῠσέαν).

As in Homer, hiatus (the 'gap' between vowels at word-juncture, where the first vowel or diphthong is neither elided nor 'correpted') is obviated by 'invisible' digamma in words which originally began with this consonant (Ϝ = v, as in οἶνος ~ *vinum*). Although this letter, used in Doric but unknown to the Ionic of B.'s time, was certainly not pronounced or written by him, its presence is assumed where it serves to avoid hiatus: (Ϝ)ιοστέφανον 3.2 (but without Ϝ in 5.3, and in ἰόπλοκοι 17.37); (Ϝ)οπί 17.129; εὖ (Ϝ)έρδων 5.36 (but without Ϝ in 18.43), cf. εὖ (Ϝ)έρξαντα *Il.* 5.650. Assumed Ϝ avoids contraction of vowels within a word: μεγιστο(Ϝ)άνασσα 19.21. A *wrong* digamma is assumed in εἵλετο ἰόν 5.75: B. was unaware that only (Ϝ)ἴον 'violet' and (Ϝ)ιός 'poison' begin with Ϝ, not ἰός 'arrow'. Hiatus is sometimes admitted before names: Ἱέρων 3.64 and 92, Ἕβρωι 16.5, as in Pindar, *I.* 1.16 ἢ 'Ιολάοι(ο).

---

[17] The lengthening of the final ε in 3.64 ὦ μεγαίνητε Ἱέρων is very strange, although there are parallels in Homer (χρυσέωι ἐν δέπαϊ ὄφρα *Il.* 24.285).

5. METRE

The metrical structure of B.'s odes is either triadic or monostrophic. A triad consists of strophe, antistrophe, and epode; of these, the first two are metrically identical, while the epode has a different pattern, though usually in a related metre. Odes 16 and 19 consist of only one triad, longer odes are in two or more triads. Monostrophic odes, such as the victory odes 4 and 6, the dithyramb 18, and the *enkomia* frs. 20A–D, repeat the metrical pattern of a strophe twice or several times. As we do not have the poet's autograph, we can not know how he arranged his text on a papyrus roll; the earliest texts of Greek lyric poetry that have survived on papyrus, written in the later fourth and early third century BCE, are set out as prose in long lines, not divided into strophes or verses. The division into triads or strophes, and their subdivision into short verses, was made by the Alexandrian scholar Aristophanes of Byzantion in the second half of the third century BCE.[18] The most important criteria for the division of the text into strophes, and of these into shorter units, were probably his observation of (1) the recurrence ('responsion') of identical patterns of sequences of short and long syllables at regular intervals, and (2) of 'pauses' between identical patterns; 'pauses' are indicated (a) by hiatus, (b) by a short syllable in the position of a long one (*brevis in longo*), i.e. where the corresponding identical sequences have a long syllable and where after a short syllable a pause is needed to fill the time of a long one. Pauses often coincide with the end of a sentence or phrase, which the editors usually indicate by punctuation. Within a strophe or epode, the metrical sequences between pauses are called 'periods'. As these are often quite long, Aristophanes divided them into shorter units (*cola*, κῶλα), guided by word-ends recurring regularly in the same place within a 'period'. This seems to be the rationale behind the 'colometry', i.e. the division into short verses, or 'cola', in the ancient manuscript tradition as represented by the papyri.

This division into 'periods' and 'cola' is clearly not arbitrary, as identical or closely related patterns, such as the 'hemiepes' ('half-hexameter', $-\smile\smile-\smile\smile-$) or the 'glyconic' ($\overset{\smile}{\times}\hspace{-0.3em}{\times}-\smile\smile-\smile-$) tend to recur in different contexts and combinations. The frequent coincidence of regular word-end or sentence-end with the end of a 'colon' or 'period' suggests that the poets themselves arranged the words in accordance with these metrical units. The metres of B.'s odes, like Pindar's, fall into one of two groups, dactyloepitrite or ionic-aeolic.

[18] See Irigoin, *Histoire du texte de Pindare* 45–8.

(a) Dactyloepitrite

B.'s longer victory odes, such as 5 and 11, as well as the dithyrambs 15, 19, and 20, and the paean fr. 4 are composed in dactyloepitrites, as are the praise poems (*enkomia*) frs. 20B, 20C and 20D.

Dactyloepitrite[19] metre combines dactylic cola, chiefly the 'hemiepes' (‒ ⌣ ⌣ ‒ ⌣ ⌣ ‒), with iambic (⌓ ‒ ⌣ ‒) or trochaic (‒ ⌣ ‒ ⌓) cola. Maas, *Metre* §55, introduced the following symbols to analyse them:

‒ ⌣ ⌣ ‒ ⌣ ⌣ ‒	*D*	‒ ⌣ ‒	*e*
‒ ⌣ ⌣ ‒	*d¹*	‒ ⌣ ‒ ⌓ ‒ ⌣ ‒	*E*
⌣ ⌣ ‒	*d²*		

Maas stated that these cola are often preceded, followed or 'linked' by one *anceps* (a syllable that can be either long or short, marked ⌓) which is usually long. Most of B.'s poems in dactyloepitrites can indeed be analysed in Maas's terms, but one needs to remember that the 'link-syllable', or *anceps interpositum*, was not part of the original concept of this metre, which seems to have evolved out of a free combination of the *hemiepes* (‒ ⌣ ⌣ ‒ ⌣ ⌣ ‒ or *D*) with trochaic or iambic elements (‒ ⌣ ‒ ⌓, ⌓ ‒ ⌣ ‒, or ‒ ⌣ ‒ ⌓ ‒ ⌣ ‒): 'Greek poets compose with cola and need no mortar to join them' (West, *Metre* 70).

The fact that poems of praise, such as *enkomia* and victory odes, are often composed in dactyloepitrites is not surprising, given that this metre developed out of the *encomiologicum* (ἐγκωμιολογικόν: ‒ ⌣ ⌣ ‒ ⌣ ⌣ ‒ ⌣ ‒ ⌣ ‒ ‒, or *D ⌣ e*–), which was used already by Alkaios 383 and Anakreon *PMG* 393, both quoted in Hephaistion's *Encheiridion* (handbook on metre) 15.10: as the term indicates, this verse was employed primarily in poems of praise. Simonides, too, used it in the famous opening line of his victory ode for Anaxilas of Rhegion: Χαίρετ᾽ ἀελλοπόδων θύγατρες ἵππων ('Hail, daughters of storm-swift mares', i.e. mules, *PMG* 515).[20]

The metres of the dithyrambs 19 and 20 are essentially dactyloepitrites with certain innovative elements. The metre of B.19 differs from conventional dactyloepitrites, e.g. those of B.15, in that (a) the 'link-syllable' is

[19] The term, coined by R.Westphal in 1854, assumes the long to be equal in length to two short, so that an ἐπίτριτος πούς (‒ ⌣ ‒ ‒ or ‒ ‒ ⌣ ‒) represents a proportion of 3/4 or 4/3; cf. West, *Metre* 70.

[20] Aristotle, *Rhet.* 1405b23 reports that Simonides initially refused to compose a victory ode for mules, but when the victor, Anaxilas the tyrant of Rhegion, offered him a more substantial fee he did, though without referring to them as 'mules'.

always short, (b) a trochaic/iambic colon (– ◡ – ◡ – –) appears that can be interpreted as a variant of the *E* (or *e͡e*) colon without its last short syllable, and (c) the *D* colon appears several times without its first short syllable (– ◡ – ◡ ◡ –), which makes it look similar to glyconics, giving it an 'aeolic' appearance (on 'aeolic' metres see below). B.20 seems to have a strophe of eight verses, each beginning with a *D* colon preceded by one syllable, except that the *D* colon of the 8th verse appears in a shortened form (– ◡ ◡ – ◡ –, i.e. replacing the second double-short by a single short), which seems to slow the rhythm down, giving it the character of a *clausula* (see 19.7–8n.).

(b) *Iambic-aeolic*

Iambic and aeolic metres are found in dithyrambs 17 and 18, in the *prosodion* (procession song) fr. 11 + 12, the *enkomion* fr. 20A, and in the victory odes 3, 4 (combined with dactyls), and 6; of these, ode 3 is unique in B. in that the strophe/antistrophe is aeolic while the epode is in dactyloepitrites.[21] Dithyramb 16 combines iambic and aeolic cola with dactyls.

Iambic metres are: the iambic (⌄– ◡ –) and trochaic (– ◡ – ⌄) metron, the cretic (– ◡ –), the paeon (= cretic with resolution: ◡ ◡ ◡ – or – ◡ ◡ ◡), the baccheus (◡ – –), the 'lekythion' (– ◡ – ◡ – ◡ –), and the ionic dimeter ⟨◡ ◡ – – ◡ ◡ – –), also with 'anaclasis' (i.e. long and short syllables reversed: ◡ ◡ – ◡ – ◡ – –, noted *anacl*) or 'catalexis' (i.e. shortened: ◡ ◡ – – ◡ ◡ –); all three of these occur in B. fr. 20A.1–3.

The principal forms of aeolic cola[22] are the 'glyconic' and its variations:

⌄⌄– ◡ ◡ – ◡ –	glyconic,	*gl*
⌄– ◡ ◡ – ◡ –	telesilleion,	∧*gl* (shortened *gl*)
⌄⌄– ◡ ◡ – –	pherecratean,	*pher*
⌄– ◡ ◡ – –	reizianum,	∧*pher* (shortened *pher*)
⌄⌄– ◡ ◡ – ◡ – –	hipponactean,	*hipp*
⌄– ◡ ◡ – ◡ – –	hagesichorean,[23]	∧*hipp* (shortened *hipp*)

The aeolic cola can be expanded from within; dactylic or choriambic expansion means that the internal sequence – ◡ ◡ or – ◡ ◡ – is repeated,

---

[21] A similar mixture of different metrical genres occurs in Pindar's *O.* 13.

[22] They are called 'aeolic' because they first occur in the poems of Sappho and Alkaios, written in the aeolic dialect.

[23] Term coined by West, *Metre* 30 n.3, after Alkman 1.57 Ἀγησιχόρα μὲν αὔτα.

as e.g. in B.3, strophe 2:⏒ – – ‿ ‿ – ‿ ‿ – ‿ – – is a 'hagesichorean' (= shortened 'hipponactean') with dactylic expansion (ᵥ*hipp*ᵈ).

A closely related metre is the choriambic dimeter, which consists of a flexible 'base' of four *ancipitia* (syllables which can be either long or short) followed by a choriamb (⏒ ⏒ ⏒ ⏒ – ‿ ‿ –); B. even splits or 'resolves' one long into two shorts (4.9~19 ‿ ‿ ‿ – ‿ – ‿ ‿ –).

Dithyramb 17 is composed in an unprecedented metrical form which has been interpreted in different ways and with divergent results. It may therefore be useful to analyse its metrical structure in some detail in an attempt to identify its underlying principle. This ode tells the story of Theseus's voyage to Crete, and it is probably significant that the metre is predominantly 'Cretan', consisting mainly of cretics and paeons, often combined with seemingly iambic or trochaic cola. Observation of regular word-ends shows that B. experiments with cretics, rather as Pindar does with dactyloepitrites: by expanding the cretic by ‿ –, he creates a new colon (– ‿ – ‿ –) between cretic (– ‿ –) and 'lekython' (– ‿ – ‿ – ‿ –). This 'long cretic' (– ‿ – ‿ –, or ⏓‿ – ‿ –, or – ‿ – ‿ ⏓) appears again and again in the strophe/antistrophe: twice in verse 1, then again in 2, 3, 12, 13, 14, 16, 17, 18, 19, 20 and 23, and in the epode: 2, 3, 9, 15 and 18, combined with straight or 'resolved' cretics (= paeons) and 'linked', preceded, or followed by 'link-syllables', as in the dactyloepitrites discussed above. This 'link-syllable' tends to be short, apart from the beginning or end of a period; at period-start it can also be double-short (strophe: 8,12,18, 20). Likewise, paeons at the beginning of a period appear as ⏓‿ ‿ – (strophe: 1) and ⏓‿ – (strophe: 21). Given the predominance of cretics in this 'Cretan' ode, it seems more logical to interpret the lines seemingly beginning with iambics (strophe: 2, 5, 7, 8, 14, 18, 20, 22; epode: 1, 2, 5, 8, 12, 13, 17, 20) as cretics with preceding syllable rather than iambics, and the apparent 'lekython' (strophe: 9, epode: 10, 14) should be seen as *cr* ‿ *cr*, not as *cr ia*. There is just one passage, from verse 9 to 11 of the strophe, where the cretics appear briefly to change into 'dactyls', but these, too, can be understood as a variation of the 'lekython':
9 – ‿ – ‿ – ‿ –, → 10 – – ‿ ‿ – ‿ – ‿, → 11 – ‿ – ‿ ‿ – ‿ ‿ –.

However, the labels we give to individual verses or cola are relatively unimportant; what matters much more is to understand what metrical units the poet employed to structure his strophes and epodes, and how he then developed these units into new rhythmical forms through the constant use of variation.

6. STYLE

Whether there was a style of choral lyric poetry in the same sense as there is a style of epic or of tragic poetry, and whether all choral lyric poetry had certain characteristic features in common, is still an open question. It is true that the discoveries of papyrus texts of Alkman, Ibykos and in particular Stesichoros have significantly enlarged our knowledge of early choral lyric poetry in the seventh and sixth centuries BCE. And yet, there are still so many gaps, and the discrepancy between what little we can know and what has been lost is still so great, especially as far as Pindar's and B.'s immediate predecessor, Simonides, is concerned, that it is hardly possible to describe the style of the genre as a whole. It is therefore often difficult to decide whether a particular stylistic feature observed in B.'s or Pindar's poetry was shared by their predecessors and can be regarded as traditional, or whether it is an innovation peculiar to either or both of them. Moreover, even though B. and Pindar were contemporaries, they are so different from one another in terms of their manner of narrative and structure that comparisons from a stylistic perspective of their poems, even in the same category such as victory odes, tend to reveal differences rather than features common to both.

Despite the limitations of our knowledge of the earlier stages of the genre, there can be no doubt that the poetry of B. and Pindar represents the maturest and most sophisticated form of Greek choral lyric. Both poets witnessed a period of momentous political and social upheaval, which also saw the emergence in Athens of another great and powerful poetic genre, Attic drama. As tragedy gradually replaced the dithyramb as the leading genre of poetry, it inherited in its choral songs the dialect ('literary Doric', see above, p. 11), the metres (and so, presumably, the music), and the poetic language of choral lyric with its imagery, its metaphors and its manifold rhetorical devices. In turn, tragedy has left its mark on some of B.'s dithyrambs. The way in which the myth of Deianeira is presented in ode 16 is so elliptical that the audience can hardly have followed it without knowledge of Sophocles' *Women of Trachis*, with which it shares a sense of foreboding, of impending disaster, and the tragic twist of the heroine's fate. The situation assumed in 18 recalls the opening scenes of Aeschylus' *Persians* and *Suppliants* and that of Sophocles' *King Oedipus*.

The stylistic peculiarity of choral lyric poetry can be understood as a result of its reaction to and emancipation from epic poetry. Although

B. marks the end of a long process of evolution, the influence of epic is still conspicuous in his style. He uses and combines Homeric words, word-groups, and formulas, and varies them freely. A substantial part of his vocabulary is derived from Homer, either unchanged or with slight modifications. Where he coins new words, most of them are either variants of Homeric words, or compounds. About 230 words are found uniquely or for the first time in B., of which by far the largest number are compound adjectives; only 14 are nouns, another 14 are verbs, and one an adverb; six of the verbs, and the adverb (εἰσάνταν 5.110, cf. epic ἐσάντα), are just slight variations of Homeric forms. Likewise, many of his compound adjectives are modifications of Homeric compounds in that they combine one element taken from the Homeric model with another that is a variation of the Homeric one, as in πολύκριθος 11.70 ~ πολυλήϊος *Il.* 5.613, or γλυκύδωρος 11.1 ~ ἠπιόδωρος *Il.* 6.251.

While variation of Homeric compounds is a feature which B. shares with Pindar and most of the earlier choral lyric poets, one characteristic of B.'s personal style seems to be his preference for graphically descriptive compounds, many of which refer to colour: ἰοβλέφαροι Χάριτες 19.5, καλυκῶπις Μάρπησσα fr. 20A.17, Προίτου κυανοπλόκαμοι θύγατρες 11.83, μελαμφαρὴς σκότος 3.13, πορφυρόζωνος θεά (Hera) 11.49, πυριέθειρα ἀστραπά 17.56, πυρσόχαιτον κάρα 18.51, βοῦς φοινικόνωτοι 5.102, χρυσόπαχυς Ἀώς 5.40, also other visual aspects: εὐδαίδαλος ναῦς 17.88, εὐρυνεφὲς Κήναιον 16.17, δολιχαύχην κύκνος 16.6. Others emphasize sound: βαρυαχὴς ταῦρος 16.18, βαρύβρομον πέλαγος 17.77, λιγυκλαγγὴς νευρά 5.73; or power: εὐρύαναξ Ζεύς 5.19, πῶλος ἀελλοδρόμας 5.39, ἐρειψιπύλας (Herakles) 5.56, θελξιεπὴς γᾶρυς 15.48, θελξίμβροτος Κύπρις 5.175, θρασύχειρ Εὐᾱνός fr. 20A.16, ἱμεράμπυξ θεά 17.9; or location and/or extent: ἀμφικύμων ἀκτά 16.16, δελφῖνες ἁλιναιέται 17.97, δεξίστρατος ἀγορά 15.43, εὐρυδίνας Ἀλφεός 3.6 and 5.38. Several unique compounds refer to feelings: θυμάρμενον τέρας 17.71, τλαπενθὴς Νιόβα fr. 20D.4; or to mental attitudes: μενέκτυπος (Theseus) 17.1, ἀδεισιβόας 5.155 and 11.61, ἀναιδομάχας 5.105, ἀταρβομάχας 16.28, φρενοάρας 17.118.

The function of epithets is not merely decorative. B. often employs them, as the above selection illustrates, in order to evoke in the audience's imagination certain aspects or qualities of key figures in his narrative.[24] That explains the frequency of colour epithets and compounds, such as

[24] On B.'s use of epithets, see Segal 1976: 99–130.

those beginning with ξανθο–, κυανο–, πορφυρο–, φοινικο–, χαλκ– and χρυσ–, and such boldly evocative phrases as πρόπεμπ' ἀπ' οὐρανοῦ θοὰν πυριέθειραν ἀστραπάν (17.55–6). Moreover, B. selects his epithets carefully in order to accentuate contrasts, as he does in 3.31–2 where the 'brazen-walled courtyard' of Kroisos' palace (χαλκοτειχέος αὐλᾶς), an image of safety and strong protection, faces the pyre on which the hapless king is to be burnt alive, and again some lines below (3.44–5) where Kroisos himself describes how the 'gold-eddying' (χρυσοδίνας) Paktolos is reddened with blood as the women are led from their 'well-built halls' (ἐξ ἐϋκτίτων μεγάρων) – all his gold could not prevent disaster. Strong contrasts dominate also the end of the Deianeira dithyramb (16.23–35): Fate has 'woven' a 'plan that is to cause her many tears' (πολύδακρυν μῆτιν), 'shrewd' (ἐπίφρονα) though it seemed to her, when she received the 'painful' (ταλαπενθέα) message that Herakles, the 'fearless fighter' (ἀταρβομάχας), was sending 'white-armed' (λευκώλενον, see 16.27–8n.) Iole to his 'rich home' (λιπαρὸν ποτὶ δόμον). The chorus's immediate reaction (ἆ δύσ-μορος, ἆ τάλαινα etc.) hints at the impending doom for both Iole and the 'home', and reveals its cause in powerful and dark terms: φθόνος εὐρυβίας and δνόφεον κάλυμμα of things to come.

Contrasts are also emphasized by epithets in 5.151–8, where the 'fear-less fighter' (ἀδεισιβόας) Herakles weeps compassionate tears for the 'grief-stricken' (ταλαπενθής) Meleagros, who had to leave his 'sweet life' and 'splendid youth' behind; similarly in 17.12–18, where Eriboia's 'white cheeks' suggest vulnerable female beauty, protected by 'bronze-clad' (χαλκοθώραξ) Theseus in his 'black' rage, and in 19.17–18, where 'wide-powered' Zeus causes Io, turned into a 'golden heifer', to flee from Argos, the 'rose-fingered maiden', whose tender fingers have just turned into hard hooves: the epithets underline the cruel irony of her fate. Niobe's fate, how-ever, provokes Zeus' compassion, fr. 20D.4–11. The common denominator of nearly all these contrasts in B. is their emotional appeal. In this respect, the way in which B. evokes compassion in his presentation of Kroisos, Meleagros, Deianeira and Io comes close to the spirit of Attic tragedy.

The appeal to strong emotions, particularly pity, is created even more effectively by constant reference to the protagonists' feelings, which appear as the driving force behind their actions. The narrative of ode 17 is a good example: Aphrodite's gifts 'stirred' (κνίζεν, 8) Minos' heart, Theseus feels 'wild pain' (σχέτλιον ἄλγος, 19), the crew are amazed at his boldness (48–50), which angers Minos (50), yet he is baffled by his courage (86), the young

Athenians tremble with fear and weep (92–6), the tears from their 'tender eyes' contrast vividly with their 'new-found joy' (126) when they rejoice at the sight of their saviour; even Theseus feels frightened by the sight of the Nereids (102); when he unexpectedly emerges from the sea, what will Minos feel (120–1)?

A scene full of heroic pathos and high emotion is that of Kroisos on the pyre (3.29–52): Kroisos himself has the pyre heaped up, which he mounts with his wife and the daughters who 'wail inconsolably'; when it is lit, they scream and cling to their mother (see 3.49–51n.): against their uncontrolled despair, Kroisos' heroic resolve to die rather than to experience slavery, and his highly emotional speech (3.37–47), which culminates in the paradox 'to die is sweetest' (θανεῖν γλύκιστον) is all the more impressive. Like Kroisos, Proitos, too, feels driven to suicide by despair (11.85–8); for him, it is the sight of his 'dark-tressed virgin daughters' fleeing from their home in their mad frenzy.

In addition to the element of pathos, B.'s narrative can create displays of increasing dramatic tension. He tends to begin the narration in the middle of a myth, at a point from where its progression to the dramatic climax can already be anticipated. This technique can also be seen in ode 17: Minos' harassment of Eriboia prompts Theseus' sharp reaction, their confrontation leads to Theseus' leap into the sea (a first climax) and to his surprising reappearance, the main climax. Likewise, the trumpet-call at the beginning of 18 immediately creates a dramatic situation: the news of the amazing deeds of an unknown young hero keeps king and people in suspense and in contrasting moods and expectations (see 18.60n.) as the hero is approaching Athens; the dramatic climax is not, as one might have expected, the revelation of his identity – that would have been an anticlimax, as the audience can infer from the second strophe that he is Theseus, the king's son – but the king's last announcement (18.57–60) that he, 'with war and bronze-clanging battle' on his mind, is heading for 'splendour-loving Athens'. In ode 15, the narrative begins with the encounter between Theano and the Achaean delegates and culminates in Menelaos' warning that *hybris* destroyed even the Giants – an abrupt ending, which has puzzled critics who did not understand that B., instead of telling the whole story as an epic poet might have done, just wants to exploit its dramatic potential up to the point from where the outcome can be foreseen. In the narrative sections of victory odes the same technique can be seen, as they tend to begin with an exciting event: in 3, it is the sack of Sardis by the Persians, in 5 Herakles' descent into Hades, in 11 the flight of Proitos' deranged daughters. However, the 'elliptical' storytelling which gives just an outline of a section of the myth, focussing on its significant elements, and leaves the audience to fill in the rest, appears to be more typical of the dithyrambs.

Another peculiarity of B.'s style, and one which he does not share with Pindar, is his choice of literary 'models', which he follows sometimes so closely that his reworking almost amounts to a quotation. In some cases we are lucky enough to have both the 'model' and B.'s version of it, so that we can compare the two, such as the story of Meleagros in ode 5. In the fifth century, every educated Greek will have known the story of the Kalydonian boar hunt from the *Iliad* (9.529–99); someone like Hieron, the ruler of Syracuse and a patron of poetry and art (see 3.85n. and 5.3–6n.), will have appreciated B.'s sophisticated adaptation of Homer's account, his elaboration of dramatic highlights, its emphasis on pathos, and possibly also the balance and symmetry of its careful formal structure (see below). In the same ode, not only the Meleagros story but three other passages can be recognized, and were probably meant to be recognized, as adaptations of well-known literary models: (1) The eagle simile (5.16–30) appears to have been inspired by a passage in the homeric *Hymn to Demeter* (*h.Dem.* 375–83), which must have been particularly well known in Sicily; (2) the comparison of human life to autumn leaves (5.65–7) 'quotes' a very famous passage in *Iliad* 6.146–9, and the melancholy statement 'for humans it is best not to be born' (5.160) is also found among the epigrams ascribed to Theognis (425–8) but may have been considerably older. At the end of the same ode (5.191–4), another 'quotation' is explicitly attributed to Hesiod (but is not found in Hesiod's extant works). In 3.78–82, B. quotes a saying allegedly given to Admetos, the mythical ruler of Pherai in Thessaly, which is also known from the Sicilian poet Epicharmos, a contemporary of B. who lived in Syracuse under Hieron (478–467 BCE). Other intertextual references may remain undetected because the passages on which they are modelled are lost to us. The ones mentioned above are all adaptations or even quotations of well-known passages or statements, aimed at an audience who would recognize them as such and appreciate the poet's art of variation.

Formal structure is another interesting aspect of B.'s style. From this point of view, the dithyrambs are less complex than the victory odes, because they are essentially narrative accounts, often allusive and elliptical, of myths, or rather selected sections of myths. B., like Homer, makes ample use of direct speech and dialogue in both dithyrambs and the longer victory odes, but while the epic poet tends to tell a story from beginning to end at a leisurely pace, B. selects that part which offers the greatest potential for dramatization (see above), where he then focuses on key elements which will produce the strongest emotional appeal. Essentially, however, his dithyrambs are straightforward, linear narratives. Of the dithyrambs, 15, 16 and 19 have a proem, while 17 and 18 plunge straight into the story (the fragmentary 20 may have resembled 16 in that it begins with a reference to a different song, see 20.2–3n.). Only 17 (which appears to be a paean rather than a dithyramb, see p. 173) has a conclusion which refers to the performance and the performing chorus. The proem of 19 is unique in that it is presented as an invitation by the chorus to the poet (see 19.11n.) to 'weave something new', namely the story of Io and her descendants to the birth of Dionysos. It has an interesting symmetrical structure in two halves. The first half (to ὕμνοισιν, 8) is a general statement: a gifted poet knows countless 'paths' of songs, if the Muses inspire him and the Graces bestow respectability on his songs; the second half, an address to the poet (8–14), takes this up (with *asyndeton*: see 19.8n.) and specifies what the poet's 'purposeful planning' (μέριμνα: see 19.11n.) is to focus on. The two halves are linked by the pun on the popular 'etymology' which derived ὕμνος from ὑφαίνειν, and by the correspondences of Μουσᾶν (4) with Καλλιόπας (13), and the recurrence of the ideas of 'obtaining gifts' (λάχησι δῶρα 3/4, and λαχοῖσαν . . . γέρας 13/14) and of the song as 'path' (μυρία κέλευθος 1 and φερτάταν ἴμεν ὁδόν 12/13). The main part of the ode (15–51) is rapid and selective narrative, slowed down only by speculation on who might have caused the death of the giant, Argos (see 19.29–36n.), and gathering pace again in the last section.

    The narrative sections of dithyrambs 16, 17 and 18 are also linear. In 16 the narrative is in two halves: the first (13–22) describes Herakles' last triumph, the second (23–35) his destruction. The structure of 17 is straightforward, with its most dramatic moments highlighted by speeches (20–46, 52–66, 74–80) which become progressively shorter as the story approaches its first climax, Theseus' leap into the sea (94). Ode 15 is, as far as its fragmentary state allows us to guess, structured in three parts, each containing a speech (by Theano, Odysseus, and Menelaos, see introd. to ode 15, pp. 158–9). Ode 18 is unique in having no narrative, as it is entirely a dialogue in two pairs of question-and-answer stanzas, rounded off by the last line (δίζησθαι δὲ φιλαγλάους Ἀθάνας) echoing the first (Βασιλεῦ τᾶν ἱερᾶν Ἀθανᾶν).

The structure of victory odes is generally, and by their very nature, more complex, given that the poet had to incorporate and combine a number of disparate elements without creating an impression of disjointedness and incoherence. Victory odes are praise songs; they all have to have a 'praise' section mentioning what the herald will have announced after the victory: the victor's name, his father's name, his home town, and the contest. Short odes performed at the site of the festival after the games often contain not much else beyond this basic 'programme', or they may link the victory to previous successes by the victor, his relatives, ancestors, or co-citizens: see, for instance, introd. to ode 6, pp. 129–30 (ode 4 is a special case; for its structure, see p. 102). Most of the longer victory odes, performed at celebrations in the victor's home town after his return from the festival, have as their centre-piece a mythical narrative section, preceded and followed by 'praise' sections which normally relate to each other, as do the proem and conclusion. The interrelation of corresponding parts can be emphasized and made audible by repetitions of key words, names, themes or ideas. In the final section of ode 5, for example, the repetition of the victor's name (197 Ἱέρωνι ∼ 16 Ἱέρωνα) and of the reference to poets as servants of the Muses and to their willingness to praise (192–3 πρόπολος Μουσᾶν ∼ 13–14 Οὐρανίας θεράπων) will have audibly signalled to the audience that the ode is nearing its conclusion. The overall structure of this ode, like that of odes 3 and 11, is symmetrical in that the central narrative section is framed by praise passages, each followed by general statements or *gnomai*, whose principal function is to link sections of a different nature (e.g., praise and myth, or proem and praise, etc.). Its narrative section (5.56–175) shows a similarly symmetrical structure, analogous to that of the ode itself: the centre-piece is Meleagros' monologue, framed by Herakles' questions, which are in turn framed by Meleagros' address and answer (see introd. to ode 5, pp. 109–10). Ode 11 also illustrates B.'s technique of marking off sections from one another within the ode by repeating key phrases or themes. Its first part, the proem and main praise (1–39), begins and ends with the theme of 'victory' (1 Νίκα γλυκύδωρε ∼ 39 νίκαν ἔδωκε); its central part, the mythical narrative (40–112), begins and ends with the key word 'altar' (40–2 τᾶι ... βωμὸν κατένασσε ∼ 110–12 οἱ τέμενος βωμόν τε τεῦχον), and its concluding part is framed by references to 'Achaeans' (113–14 ἀρηϊφίλοις ... Ἀχαιοῖς ∼ 126 ἀλκὰς Ἀχαιῶν). The central part itself, the narrative of the daughters of Proitos, is structured as a multiple 'ring-composition' (see introd. to ode 11, pp. 136–8).

The analysis of the formal structure of B.'s longer odes reveals his endeavour to balance their constituent parts and to weld them into symmetrical structures that create an aesthetically pleasing formal unity, comparable to that of the figures assembled in the pediments of a classical Greek temple, like those of the temple of Zeus at Olympia.

7. ALEXANDRIAN SCHOLARSHIP AND THE FATE OF THE TEXT

During Bacchylides' lifetime, his songs do not seem to have been widely known. The patrons who commissioned odes for victory celebrations, and other songs for convivial entertainment, such as *enkomia* (frs. 20A–D), and the communities for which he had composed cult songs such as dithyrambs and paeans to be performed at religious festivals, must have preserved these songs (at least the texts, if not the music) in private or public archives – otherwise, they would not have survived long enough to be collected and edited by Alexandrian scholars (see below). Some may have circulated among friends in private copies, though this cannot be proved. Unlike some of the songs of Simonides or Pindar, which were known in Athens and sung at parties, parodied by Aristophanes and quoted by Plato, B.'s songs have left no traces in Greek literature of the later fifth and fourth centuries – not even those dithyrambs which had been composed for Athenian festivals. His early dithyramb (or paean) 17, composed for performance at the *Delia*, the festival for Apollo on Delos, appears to have inspired at least one Attic vase painter, Onesimos, who brilliantly captured one of the key scenes of the narrative, the young Theseus' encounter with Amphitrite in her palace at the bottom of the sea (see introd. to ode 17, pp. 174–5), but later vase painters seem to have taken no notice of public performances of his odes.[25]

It was not before the Hellenistic age that B.'s poems were edited, read and commented on. After a long period of oblivion, Kallimachos (third century BCE) seems to have been the first author and scholar whom we know to have read B.'s odes again. The Oxyrhynchus papyrus 2368 (pap. **B**), a commentary possibly compiled by Didymos at Alexandria in the first

---

[25] Theseus' encounter with Amphitrite (and Poseidon) appears once again much later, on a calyx crater of the Kadmos painter (*c.* 420 BCE) in Bologna, see Appendix no. 19. It may reflect a recent performance of a tragedy or a new dithyramb, hardly a repeat performance of B. 17.

century BCE (Pfeiffer, *History* 222), quotes Aristarchos (*c.* 217–145, the successor to Aristophanes of Byzantion as head of the Mouseion at Alexandria) as having classified one of B.'s odes as a dithyramb and given it the title '*Kassandra*', whereas Kallimachos had classified it as a paean, presumably in his *Pinakes*, the great catalogue of the royal library at Alexandria which Kallimachos compiled in 120 book rolls.[26] It is very likely that the first classification of B.'s odes was due to him, since he is also known to have classified at least the victory odes of Simonides and Pindar (frs. 441 and 450 Pfeiffer). Moreover, he may have 'borrowed' themes and motifs from B., such as the story of Herakles' encounter with Molorchos in the third book of his *Aitia* (frs. 54–9 Pfeiffer), which may have been inspired by B.'s dramatic account of Herakles' struggle with the Nemean lion in 13.44–57.

Acquaintance with B.'s works at Alexandria in the early third century is also documented by *P.Hibeh* II 172 = *SH* 991, a list of poetic compounds culled from epic, choral lyric, and tragic poetry, of which about one third are not attested elsewhere. Four of these compounds are found only in B.: αἰολόπρυμνος (1.114), μελαμφαρής (3.13), ἱπποδίνητος (5.2), and the feminine form κυανόπρωιρα (17.1; Homer has the masculine form in –ος with a feminine noun, ναῦς). His text must therefore have been available to scholars from at least the middle of the third century BCE, together with the texts of many other poets and prose authors of classical Greece who were considered 'canonical', or models in their respective literary genres: the three tragedians, the three poets of (old) comedy, the nine lyric poets, the ten Attic orators,[27] etc. King Ptolemy I Soter, the founder of the great Alexandrian library, had ordered all the works of Greek classical authors, 'as far as they were worth serious study' (ὅσα γε σπουδαῖα ὑπῆρχεν, Eusebios, *Hist. eccles.* 5. 8.11), to be collected for his new library (Pfeiffer, *History* I 98–103; Fraser, *Ptol. Alex.* I 320–30), where Kallimachos and others catalogued and classified them. There is no evidence to suggest that at this time poems of B. circulated also in any other part of the Hellenistic world, with the exception of one epigram on stone from Pergamon, datable to *c.*280–270 BCE (Ebert no. 59; Moretti no. 37), which celebrates a chariot victory in terms strongly reminiscent of the description in ode 5.37–49 of the race won

---

[26] Pfeiffer, *History* I 125–7; Fraser, *Ptol. Alex.* I 452 and II 655 n.46.

[27] Although not always the same ten, and sometimes only six, are listed; cf. P. E. Easterling, *OCD*[3] 286.

by Hieron's horse at the Pythian games of 476. If this epigram does indeed reflect that passage, B.'s victory ode must have been known at Pergamon; such textual similarities may, however, not be conclusive proof of familiarity with B.'s ode, because it is also possible that the author created his epigram out of his own imagination, having watched the chariot race.

After the sorting and cataloguing of the many thousands of book rolls that were delivered to the royal library at Alexandria, the next task for the scholars employed there by the king was to produce critical text editions. It was Aristophanes of Byzantion (*c*.260–180 BCE) who edited the texts of Alkaios, Alkman, Pindar, and probably B. and other lyric poets. It is very likely that he divided the texts, which he found written like prose, into strophes and triads which repeat identical metrical patterns, and the strophes into short verses or *cola* (see Section 5 above, p. 14), and that he used metrical 'responsion' as a guideline for correcting the text. He is said to have divided Pindar's odes into 17 books (i.e. papyrus rolls), and to have ordered the odes within each book; it seems likely therefore that he did the same for the odes of B., given that their arrangement, colometry, and presentation with critical signs, such as *paragraphos* (dividing strophes), *coronis* (dividing triads) etc., are essentially the same as those found in Pindaric papyri of the late Ptolemaic and Roman periods. It may also have been Aristophanes who established the selection of nine lyric poets as models of their genre (*Anth. Pal.* 9 184 and 571; Pfeiffer, *History* 205); if so, he probably made text editions of all nine of them. From this time, the early second century BCE, copies of their works, no doubt derived from texts in Alexandria, were available, fragments of which have been found in various parts of Egypt. On the papyri of B., see Section 8 below, pp. 28–31.

Remains of two ancient commentaries on papyrus have also been preserved (pap. **B** and **M**). While pap. **M** contains mainly paraphrases of victory odes, pap. **B** preserves an interesting discussion about the classification of a poem: regarded as a paean by Kallimachos, it was reclassified as a dithyramb and labelled '*Kassandra*' by Aristarchos (see p. 26 above). The author of this commentary may well be Didymos, who is known to have discussed problems of classification in a monograph '*On lyric poets*' (Περὶ λυρικῶν ποιητῶν, cf. Pfeiffer, *History* 277). His commentary on B.'s victory odes is explicitly attested (Ammonios 333 Nickau), but this can hardly be the commentary partly preserved in pap. **M**, which is very pedestrian and on a quite modest level. One line of B. is quoted in a papyrus fragment of unidentified prose, possibly a commentary (see 15.56n.).

The chronological spread of the papyrus fragments shows that B.'s works were fairly widely read in Egypt during at least the first three centuries of Roman rule. Strabo and Horace may have known them directly from text editions, possibly also Plutarch and Pausanias, but the great majority of references are found in commentaries (scholia) on other poets and in grammarians and lexicographers. A fair number of passages were selected for anthologies, which have preserved them independently of the main manuscript tradition. Quotations in authors of the later Roman and Byzantine periods seem to be derived from anthologies, which also explains the erroneous attribution of four quotations to other poets (Pindar, Alkman, Ibykos). Ammianus Marcellinus reports that the emperor Julian (331–363 CE) used to quote a saying of B., 'whom he enjoyed reading' (25. 4.3) – probably in anthologies, because it seems unlikely that text editions could still be found in the middle of the fourth century.

8. THE SURVIVING PAPYRI

Of B.'s works, only a handful of lines were known from quotations and anthologies when the great papyrus **A** was discovered in 1896 and acquired for the British Museum, where F. G. Kenyon published it in 1897, together with a splendid facsimile of the entire papyrus. Kenyon reassembled it from some 200 fragments, helped by many scholars, among them Sir Richard Jebb and Friedrich Blass; in his edition, all but 42 small fragments had been inserted into their proper places, 40 of which have since been placed, nearly all of them by Blass. Two more fragments of papyrus **A**, now in Florence, were bought by Medea Norsa in Cairo in 1938, one of which belongs in ode 4 (see 4.7–10n.).

Papyrus **A** (British Library, P.Lond. inv. 733 found at Meir, some 40 km south of Mellawi, west of al-Qussiyah) preserves parts of two rolls, written by the same hand. The first 35 columns contain the book of victory odes (*epinikia*) more or less complete, the next ten columns the first half of the book of dithyrambs, which are arranged in alphabetical order by the first letter of their titles (A to I). From the way ancient authors quote lines from these books, it is clear that there was only one book of epinikia and one of dithyrambs (see below on pap. **O**). A papyrus published in 1956 (pap. **L**) has shown that the first book roll contained at least two more odes after column 35 of pap. **A**, the second of which (ode 14B) was very probably the last one of this book. The book's total length can be estimated at *c.* 1300 lines – slightly less than Pindar's *Pythians* and *Olympians*, but slightly more than his *Nemeans*.

As with Pindar's Olympian and Pythian odes, B.'s victory odes are arranged according to the prominence of the victor, except that the first two celebrate a young athlete from Keos, and ode 1 tells the mythical 'history' of his and B.'s native island. Odes 3–5 were composed for Hieron's chariot victories at Olympia (in 468: 3) and Delphi (in 470: 4) and that of his racehorse at Olympia (in 476: 5). Odes 6 and 7 relate to Olympian victories, odes 8–13 to various other 'panhellenic' (Pythian, Isthmian and Nemean) victories, ode 14 to a victory at a local festival; 14B is not really a victory ode: its occasion, like that of the last ode in Pindar's book of *Nemeans*, seems to have been the appointment of a civic official.

The handwriting of pap. **A** is a beautifully clear and regular upright bookhand characterized by the contrast between broad and narrow letters; it can be dated to the late second or early third century CE. There are numerous corrections and several additions by contemporary or slightly later hands. The bulk of the corrections and additions is due to hand **A**[3]; this corrector has also added most of the titles, as well as five lines omitted by the main scribe (**A**): 11.106 and 18.55–7 in the top margin, 19.22 in the bottom margin. **A**[3] must have collated the text either against the exemplar from which it had been copied, or against another copy. Even so, he left quite a few mistakes uncorrected and even produced some of his own (see on 3.47; 5.179; 19.9).

Papyrus **B** (*P.Oxy.* XXIII 2368; second century)[28] preserves two columns of a commentary, apparently on dithyrambs; from col. i.8ff. it discusses a poem which Kallimachos classified as a paean, whereas Aristarchos regarded it as a dithyramb and gave it the title '*Kassandra*' (see p. 26 above). As B. is known to have composed an ode in which Kassandra foretold the outcome of the Trojan War (Porphyrio on Horace, ode 1. 15), this was probably the ode in question, = B. 23.

Papyrus **C** (*P.Oxy.* XXIV 2364 + *P.Oxy.* XXXII p. 160 'addendum' + *P.Oxy.* IV 661 fr. 2 + P.Oxon.Ashmol. inv.20; second century) seems to contain fragments of dithyrambs, which E. Lobel attributed to B.: B.24–7 and 29.

---

[28] All dates are CE.

Papyrus **D** (P.Berol 16139 + 21209, found at Dîmeh in the Fayûm; early second century) partly overlaps with papyrus **C** fr. 2, but with slightly divergent colometry: B. 24.

Papyrus **H** (*P.Oxy.* XXIII 2366; second century) contains remains of Doric verses on the back of a document; the editor, E. Lobel, attributed the fragment to B.'s hymns, frs. 1A and 1B.

Papyrus **L** (*P.Oxy.* XXIII 2363; late second/early third century) contains the end of a poem (B. 14A) and the first eleven lines of the next (B. 14B), with which two fragments of pap. **A** overlap. On the nature of this poem, which may have been the last in the book of B.'s victory odes, see above, p. 10.

Papyrus **M** (*P.Oxy.* XXIII 2367; second century) belongs to a roll made up of various documents, which has parts of a commentary on B.'s victory odes on the reverse. On the nature of this commentary, see above, p. 27.

Papyrus **O** (*P.Oxy.* VIII 1091 = British Library, inv. 2056; second and third centuries) was part of a book roll of B.'s dithyrambs. A parchment label (*sillybos*) was attached to the top margin, giving the title of the roll: the original title,[29] Ἀντηνορίδαι ἢ Ἑλένης ἀπαίτησις (the title of B. 15), was washed out and replaced by Βακχυλίδου διθύραμβοι in a third-century hand. The label confirms that B. 15 was the first ode in his book of dithyrambs. The papyrus itself preserves B. 17.47–78 and 91–2 in the same colometry as pap. **A**; verse 63, left out in **O** and misplaced in **A** (between 61 and 62), may have been left out but added in the margin of the exemplar from which both **A** and **O** are derived: the scribe of **A** inserted it in the wrong place, the scribe of **O** overlooked it (unless he added it in the bottom or left-hand margin, now lost).

Papyrus **P** (*P.Oxy.* XI 1361 + XVII 2081e = British Library, inv. 2443; first century) comes from a roll with some marginal notes (scholia) but no *paragraphoi*: their absence in this otherwise carefully annotated papyrus is strange. A quotation by Athenaios (second century) of eleven lines, which he attributes to B., overlaps with part of column 5; the poems represented (frs. 20A–C) may be *enkomia*, see pp. 238–9.

Papyrus **Q** (*P.Oxy.* XXIII 2362; late second/early third century) preserves six fragments of a roll written by the same hand as papyrus **U**. Some of the fragments of pap. **P** overlap with pap. **Q**, and a scholion of pap. **P** (*P.Oxy.* 2081e fr. 2) relates to a passage in pap. **Q** (see introd. to fr. 20D, pp. 255–6).

---

[29] Deciphered by Edmonds (1922) 160.

Papyrus **T** (*P.Oxy.* III 426 = Victoria University, Toronto 5; early third century) was published by B. Snell (*Hermes* 67,1932,1–13) who had seen that the last ten verses on the back of a documentary text partially overlap with the first ten verses of a passage quoted by Stobaios (4. 14.3) from B.'s paeans, = B. fr. 4.61–80.

Papyrus **U** (*P.Oxy.* XXIII 2361, by the same hand as pap. **Q**) contains verses which overlap with a quotation in Hephaistion, = B. fr. 19, apparently from a book of love poetry (*erotika*), from which Hephaistion also quotes fr. 17.

9. SIGLA AND EDITORIAL CONVENTIONS

ạ	uncertain letter	κρ	'mute and liquid' not counting as double consonant (i.e. not lengthening the preceding vowel)
[α]	letter lost in the papyrus		
⌊α⌋	letter lost but transmitted in another source		
<α>	letter added by editor		
{α}	letter deleted by editor	ρ̇, σ̄	letter treated as double consonant (i.e. lengthening the preceding vowel)
⟦α⟧	letter deleted in the papyrus		

A	scribe of papyrus London 733 and PSI 1278	**D**	P. Berol. 16139 + 21209
		H	P. Oxy. 2366
A[1]	corrections by this scribe	**L**	P. Oxy. 2363
A[2]	first corrector	**M**	P. Oxy. 2367
A[3]	second corrector	**O**	P. Oxy. 1091
A[4]	third corrector	**P**	P. Oxy. 1361+2081 (e)
A[1]?	= **A**[1] rather than **A**[2] or **A**[3]	**Q**	P. Oxy. 2362
A[3]?	= **A**[3] rather than **A**[1] or **A**[2]	**T**	P. Oxy. 426
B	P. Oxy. 2368	**U**	P. Oxy. 2361
C	P. Oxy. 2364		

⊗	beginning or end of a poem
⦀	end of a strophe
‖	end of a period
|	end of word recurring in the same position throughout the poem
⋮	end of word in most instances

⋮ - ⋮ or ⋮ - ⋮   end of word either before or after the syllable.

Examples illustrating the principle of the critical apparatus:

πεδίωι (in the text)

1. ΠΕΔΙΟΝ: A¹ i.e. ΠΕΔΙΟΝ A, ΠΕΔΙѠΙ A¹ (correct reading)
2. ΠΕΔΙΟΝ: Bl. i.e. ΠΕΔΙΟΝ A, πεδίωι Blass (correct reading)
3. ΠΕΔΙΟΝ A¹ i.e. ΠΕΔΙѠΙ A, ΠΕΔΙΟΝ A¹ (wrong reading)
4. πεδίον Bl. i.e. ΠΕΔΙѠΙ A, πεδίον proposed by Blass but not adopted in this edition.

ΒΑΚΧΥΛΙΔΟΥ ΕΠΙΝΙΚΟΙ

3

ΙΕΡΩΝΙ ΣΥΡΑΚΟΣΙΩΙ
ΙΠΠΟΙΣ [ΟΛΥ]ΜΠΙΑ

ΣΤΡ metra iambica et aeolica (v. p. 16) A′−Z′

⏓—◡ ⏒ ⏓ ⏖ ◡—◡—— ‖ *trim iamb catal* ‖

⏓—◡◡—◡◡—◡—— ‖ $_\wedge hipp^d$ ‖

⏓ —◡◡—◡◡—◡—◡ :

—◡—⏓— : ◡◡—◡—— ‖‖ $_\wedge g_l^{pl}\ ia\ _\wedge hipp$ ‖‖

ΕΠ dactyloepitr. (v. p. 15)

⏓ —◡◡—◡◡ ——

—◡— ⏓ —◡— ‖ ⏓ D – E ‖

—◡— ⏓ —◡—

——◡ ⏖ ——◡— ‖ E – E ‖

⏖ ◡—⏓—◡— ⏓ —◡—

—◡— ⏓ —◡— ‖‖ E ⏓ e E ‖‖

A′ Ἀριστο[κ]άρπου Σικελίας κρέουσαν
 Δ[ά]ματρα ἰοστέφανόν τε Κούραν
 ὕμνει, γλυκύδωρε Κ̣λεοῖ, θοάς τ᾽ Ὀ—
 λυμ]πιοδρόμους Ἱέρωνος ἵππ[ο]υς.

⸻

5 σεύον]το γὰρ σὺν ὑπερόχωι τε Νίκᾱι
 σὺν Ἀγ]λαΐᾱι τε παρ᾽ εὐρυδίναν
 Ἀλφε̣ό̣ν, τόθι] Δεινομένε̣ο̣ς ἔθηκαν
 ὄλβιον τ̣[έκος στεφάνω]ν κυρῆσαι·

⸻

θρόησε δὲ λ[αὸς ◡——·

3 **9** λ[αὸς Ἀχαιῶν Kenyon, ἀπείρων Blass, ἀγασθείς Jebb

10   ἇ τρισευδαίμ[ων ἀνήρ,

col. 7   ὃς παρὰ Ζηνὸς λαχὼν
            πλείσταρχον Ἑλλάνων γέρας
            οἶδε πυργωθέντα πλοῦτον μὴ μελαμ-
                φαρέϊ κρύπτειν σκότωι.
)—

Β′ 15   βρύει μὲν ἱερὰ βουθύτοις ἑορταῖς,
            βρύουσι φιλοξενίας ἀγυιαί·
            λάμπει δ᾽ ὑπὸ μαρμαρυγαῖς ὁ χρυσός,
                ὑψιδαιδάλτων τριπόδων σταθέντων

            πάροιθε ναοῦ, τόθι μέγιστον ἄλσος
  20   Φοίβου παρὰ Κασταλίας ῥεέθροις
            Δελφοὶ διέπουσι. θεὸν θ[εό]ν τις
                ἀγλαϊζέθω γὰρ ἄριστος ὄλβων·

            ἐπεί ποτε καὶ δαμασίππου
                Λυδίας ἀρχαγέταν,
  25   εὖτε τὰν πεπ[ρωμέναν
                Ζηνὸς τελέ[σσαντος κρί]σιν
            Σάρδιες Περσᾶ[ν ἁλίσκοντο στρ]ατῶι,
                Κροῖσον ὁ χρυσά[ορος
)—

Γ′   φύλαξ᾽ Ἀπόλλων. [ὁ δ᾽ ἐς] ἄελπτον ἆμαρ
  30   μ[ο]λὼν πολυδ[άκρυο]ν οὐκ ἔμελλε
            μίμνειν ἔτι δ[ουλοσύ]ναν· πυρὰν δὲ
                χαλκ[ο]τειχέος π[ροπάροι]θεν αὐ[λᾶς

            ναήσατ᾽, ἔνθα σὺ[ν ἀλόχωι] τε κεδ[νᾶι
            σὺν εὐπλοκάμοι[ς τ᾽] ἐπέβαιν᾽ ἄλα[στον

---

12 ΓΕΝΟΣ: **Α¹**   **13** ΜΕΛΛΗ· **Α¹**?   **25** Palmer   **26** τελέσσαντος Wacker-
nagel | κτίσιν Kenyon, κρίσιν Weil   **27** ἁλίσκοντο Wackernagel, ἐπόρθηθεν
Maas   **28** χρυσά[ορος Palmer, χρυσά[ρματος Kenyon   **31** δουλοσύναν Jebb

35 θ]υ̣[γ]ατράσι δυρομέναις· χέρας δ᾽ [ἐς
    αἰ]πὺν̣ αἰθέρα σφετέρας ἀείρας

    γέ]γωνεν· "ὑπέρ[βι]ε δαῖμον,
      πο]ῦ θεῶν ἐστιν χάρις;
      πο]ῦ δὲ Λατοίδας ἄναξ;
40   ἔρρουσ]ι̣ν Ἀλυά[τ]τα δόμοι
    —ᴗ— ᴗ̲ —ᴗ— ᴗ̲] μυρίων
    —ᴗ— ᴗ̲ —ᴗ—]ν·

)—

Δ′ ᴗ̲ —ᴗ ᴗ̲ᴗ ᴗ̲ᴗ ᴗ—ᴗ]ν ἄστυ,
    ἐρεύθεται αἵματι χρυσο]δίνας
col. 8 45 Πακτωλός, ἀεικελίως γυναῖκες
      ἐξ ἐϋκτίτων μεγάρων ἄγονται·

    τὰ πρόσθεν [ἐχ]θρὰ φίλα· θανεῖν γλύκιστον."
    τόσ᾽ εἶπε, καὶ ἁβ[ρο]βάταν κ[έλε]υσεν
    ἅπτειν ξύλινον δόμον. ἔκ[λα]γον δὲ
50   παρθένοι, φίλας τ᾽ ἀνὰ ματρὶ χεῖρας

    ἔβαλλον· ὁ γὰρ προφανὴς θνα-
      τοῖσιν ἔχθιστος φόνων·
    ἀλλ᾽ ἐπεὶ δεινοῦ πυρὸς
      λαμπρὸν διάϊ[σσεν μέ]νος,
55   Ζεὺς ἐπιστάσας [μελαγκευ]θὲς νέφος
      σβέννυεν ξανθὰ[ν φλόγα.

)—

Ε′ ἄπιστον οὐδέν, ὅ τι θ[εῶν μέ]ριμνα
    τεύχει· τότε Δαλογενὴ[ς Ἀπό]λλων
    φέρων ἐς Ὑπερβορέο[υς γ]έροντα

44 Kenyon, cf. Hesych. ε 5756 ἐρεύθεται· πίμπλαται   47 ΘΕΝΔ: Fraccaroli |
ἐχθρὰ Palmer | ΝΥΝ supra ΑΦΙΛ add. A³   56 Palmer

60   σὺν τανισφύροις κατ[έν]ασσε κούραις

δι᾽ εὐσέβειαν, ὅτι μέ[γιστα] θνατῶν
ἐς ἀγαθέαν <ἀν>έπεμψε Π[υθ]ώ.
ὅσϙ[ι] <γε> μὲν Ἑλλάδ᾽ ἔχουσιν, [ο]ὔτι[ς,
ὦ μεγαίνητε Ἱέρων, θελήσει

65   φάμ]ε̣ν σέο πλείονα χρυσὸν
        Λοξί]ᾶι πέμψαι βροτῶν̣.
εὖ λέγειν πάρεστιν, ὅσ-
    τις μ]ὴ φθόνωι πιαίνεται,
    . . . .]λη φίλιππον ἄνδρ᾽ ἀρήϊον
70   . . . .]ίου σκᾶπτρον Διός
)—

F′   ἰοπλό]κων τε μέρο[ς ἔχοντ]α Μουσᾶν·
    . . . .]μαλεαι ποτ[ε . . . . . .] ῾.ιων
    . . . .]νος ἐφάμερον α[. . . . . .]·
    . . . .]ᾳ σκοπεῖς· βραχ[ύς ἐστιν αἰών·
    —

75   πτερ]όε̣σσα δ᾽ ἐλπὶς ὑπ[ολύει ν]όημα
        ἐφαμ]ερίων· ὁ δ᾽ ἄναξ [Ἀπόλλων
    . . . . .]᾽.λος εἶπε Φέρη[τος υἷι·
col. 9   "θνατὸν εὖντα χρὴ διδύμους ἀέξειν

γνώμας, ὅτι τ᾽ αὔριον ὄψεαι
80   μοῦνον ἁλίου φάος,
χὤτι πεντήκοντ᾽ ἔτε̣α
    ζωὰν βαθύπλουτον τελεῖς.
ὅσια δρ̣ῶν εὔφραινε θυμόν· τοῦτο γὰρ
κερδέων ὑπέρτατον."
)—

62 <ἀν> Blass   **63** <γε> Blass   **65** φάμεν Blass   **66** Blass   **68** ὅστις
μὴ Palmer   **69** εὐθαλῆ Sandys   **70** ξεινίου Nairn, τεθμίου vel δαμίου Blass
71 Blass   **74** καίρι]α σκόπει{ς} Lloyd-Jones cl. schol. pap. **Μ** fr.3 | βραχ[ύς ἐστιν
αἰών Blass   **77** ἑκαβόλος Jebb | υἷι Platt, Wackernagel

Ζ′ 85 φρονέοντι συνετὰ γαρύω· βαθὺς μὲν
αἰθὴρ ἀμίαντος· ὕδωρ δὲ πόντου
οὐ σάπεται· εὐφροσύνα δ᾽ ὁ χρυσός·
ἀνδρὶ δ᾽ οὐ θέμις, πολιὸν π[αρ]έντα

——

γῆρας, θάλ[εια]ν αὖτις ἀγκομίσσαι
90 ἥβαν. ἀρετᾶ[ς γε μ]ὲν οὐ μινύθει
βροτῶν ἅμα σ[ώμ]ατι φέγγος, ἀλλὰ
Μοῦσά νιν τρ[έφει.] Ἱέρων, σὺ δ᾽ ὄλβου

——

κάλλιστ᾽ ἐπεδ[είξ]αο θνατοῖς
ἄνθεα· πράξα[ντι] δ᾽ εὖ
95 οὐ φέρει κόσμ[ον σι]ω-
πά· σὺν δ᾽ ἀλαθ[είᾱι] καλῶν
καὶ μελιγλώσσου τις ὑμνήσει χάριν
Κηΐας ἀηδόνος.

4

ΤΩΙ ΑΥΤΩΙ
<ΙΠΠΟΙΣ> ΠΥΘΙΑ

metrum: aeolica et dactylica (v. p. 16)

1 ∪∪∪–∪∪–∪–	*gl*
∪∪∪–∪∪––– |	*hipp* |
3 –∪∪–∪∪–∪∪– |	*4 da* |
∪–⏓⏑–∪∪––∪– |	*decasyllab (= ∪–gl) cr* |
5 –∪∪–∪∪–∪∪ |	
–∪∪–∪∪–|∪–– |	*6 da ba* |
7 ∪∪∪–∪∪–<∪>–	*gl*
∪––∪–∪∪–∪– |	*ba hipp = chodim ba* |
9 ∪∪∪–∪–∪∪– |	*chodim* |
–∪–∪∪–∪–– ‖	*hipp* ‖

Α′ 1 Ἔτι Συρακοσίαν φιλεῖ
πόλιν ὁ χρυσοκόμας Ἀπόλλων,

3 ἀστύθεμίν θ᾽ Ἱέ[ρω]να γεραίρει·
τρίτον γὰρ παρ᾽ [ὀμφα]λὸν ὑψιδείρου χθονός
5 Πυ[θ]ιόνικος ἀ[είδε]ταῖ
ὡ[κυ]πόδων ἀρ[ετᾶι] σὺν ἵππων.
7 ἐ[. . . .] ἁδυεπὴς ἁ[να-
ξιφόρ]μιγγος Οὐρ[αν]ίας ἀλέκτωρ
9 . . . . . .]εν· ἀλλ᾽ ἐκ[όν]τι νόωι
10 . . . . . ο]υς ἐπέσεισ[εν] ὕμνους.

———

Β′   1 ἔτι δὲ τέ]τρατον εἴ τις ορ-
. . . . . (.)] εἷλκε Δίκας τάλαν[τ –,
col. 10   3 Δεινομένεός κ᾽ ἐγερα[ίρ]ομεν υἱόν·
†παρεστίαν† ἀγχιάλοισι Κ̣[ί]ρρας μυχοῖς
15   5 μοῦνον ἐπιχθονίω̣ν τ̣άδε
μησάμενον στεφάνοις ἐρέπτειν
7 δύο τ᾽ ὀλυμπιονικ<ί>ας
ἀείδειν. τί φέρτερον ἢ θεοῖσιν
9 φίλον ἐόντα παντο[δ]απῶν
20 λαγχάνειν ἄπο μοῖρα[ν] ἐσθλῶν;

5

<ΤΩΙ ΑΥΤΩΙ
ΚΕΛΗΤΙ ΟΛΥΜΠΙΑ>

metrum: dactyloepitr. (v. p. 15) Α′—Ε′
ΣΤΡ   — — ◡ ◡ — ◡ ◡ —
— ◡ — — — ◡ — —   — D E –‖
3 — — ◡ ◡ — ◡ ◡ —
— — ◡ ◡ — ◡ ◡ — ⏓ — ◡ —   – D – D ⏓ e |
5 — ◡ ◡ — ◡ ◡ —
— — ◡ ◡ — ◡ ◡ —   D – D ‖
7 — ◡ — — — ◡ — —
— ◡ — ⏓ — ◡ —   E – E – ‖

4 **7** Ἐ[, ἔ[λακε δ᾽] Snell   **7–8** Maas   **10** ἐπέσεισεν Lobel cl. schol. pap. **M**
11 ἔτι δὲ Pfeiffer, τέ]τρατον Gallavotti | **11–12** ὀρ[θὰ θεὸς] . . . τάλαν[τα Snell   **14**
ΠΑΡΕΣΤΙΑΝ: πάρεστίν νιν Blass, πάρεστιν δ᾽ ἐν Maehler

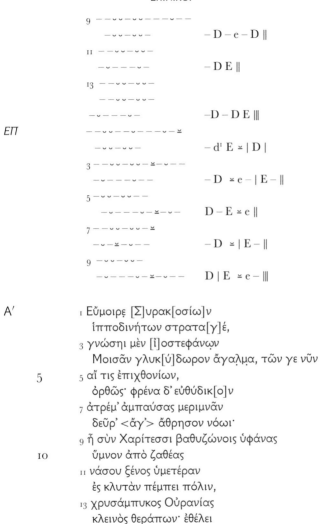

9 ‒ ‿ ‿ ‒ ‿ ‿ ‒ ‒ ‿ ‒
  ‒ ‿ ‿ ‒ ‿ ‿ ‒   ‒ D ‒ e ‒ D ‖
11 ‒ ‒ ‿ ‿ ‒ ‿ ‿ ‒
  ‒ ‿ ‒ ‒ ‒ ‿ ‒   ‒ D E ‖
13 ‒ ‒ ‿ ‿ ‒ ‿ ‿ ‒
  ‒ ‒ ‿ ‿ ‒ ‿ ‿ ‒
  ‒ ‿ ‒ ‒ ‒ ‿ ‒   ‒D ‒ D E ‖‖

ΕΠ   ‒ ‒ ‿ ‿ ‒ ‿ ‒ ‒ ‿ ‒ ‿
     ‒ ‿ ‿ ‒ ‿ ‿ ‒   ‒ dᴵ E ≍ | D |
3 ‒ ‒ ‿ ‿ ‒ ‿ ‿ ‒ ≍ ‒ ‿ ‒ ‒
  ‒ ‿ ‒ ‒ ‒ ‿ ‒   ‒ D ≍ e ‒ | E ‒ ‖
5 ‒ ‿ ‿ ‒ ‿ ‿ ‒ ‒
  ‒ ‿ ‒ ‒ ‒ ‿ ‒ ≍ ‒ ‿ ‒   D ‒ E ≍ e ‖
7 ‒ ‒ ‿ ‿ ‒ ‿ ‿ ‒ ≍
  ‒ ‿ ‒ ≍ ‒ ‿ ‒ ‒   ‒ D ≍ | E ‒ ‖
9 ‒ ‿ ‿ ‒ ‿ ‒
  ‒ ‿ ‒ ‒ ‒ ‿ ‒ ≍ ‒ ‿ ‒ ‒   D | E ≍ e ‒ ‖‖

Α′   1 Εὔμοιρε [Σ]υρακ[οσίω]ν
        ἱπποδινήτων στρατα[γ]έ,
      3 γνώσηι μὲν [ἰ]οστεφάνων
        Μοισᾶν γλυκ[ύ]δωρον ἄγαλμα, τῶν γε νῦν
   5 5 αἴ τις ἐπιχθονίων,
        ὀρθῶς· φρένα δ᾽ εὐθύδικ[ο]ν
      7 ἀτρέμ᾽ ἀμπαύσας μεριμνᾶν
        δεῦρ᾽ <ἄγ᾽> ἄθρησον νόωι·
      9 ἦ σὺν Χαρίτεσσι βαθυζώνοις ὑφάνας
   10   ὕμνον ἀπὸ ζαθέας
      11 νάσου ξένος ὑμετέραν
        ἐς κλυτὰν πέμπει πόλιν,
      13 χρυσάμπυκος Οὐρανίας
        κλεινὸς θεράπων· ἐθέλει

5   8 <ἄγ᾽> Maehler   11-12 ΠΕΜ ⋮ ΠΕΙ ΚΛΕΕΝΝΑΝ ΕΣ ΠΟΛΙΝ Α: Maas
14 ΕΘΕΛΕΙ ΔΕ Α: δὲ secl. Walker

15   γᾶρυν ἐκ στηθέ͜ων χέων

      1 αἰνεῖν Ἱέρωνα. βαθὺν
      δ' αἰθέρα ξουθαῖσι τάμνων
      3 ὑψοῦ πτερύγεσσι ταχεί-
      αις αἰετὸς εὐρυάνακτος ἄγγελος
20   5 Ζηνὸς ἐρισφαράγου
      θαρσεῖ κρατερᾶι πίσυνος
      7 ἰσχύϊ, πτάσσοντι δ' ὄρνι-
      χες λιγύφθογγοι φόβωι·
      9 οὔ νιν κορυφαὶ μεγάλας ἴσχουσι γαίας,
25   οὐδ' ἁλὸς ἀκαμάτας

      11 δυσπαίπαλα κύματα· νω-
      μᾶι δ' ἐν ἀτρύτωι χάει
      13 λεπτότριχα σὺν ζεφύρου πνοι-
      αῖσιν ἔθειραν ἀρί-
30   γνωτος ἀνθρώποις ἰδεῖν·

      1 τὼς νῦν καὶ <ἐ>μοὶ μυρία πάντᾶι κέλευθος
      ὑμετέραν ἀρετάν
      3 ὑμνεῖν, κυανοπλοκάμου θ' ἕκατι Νίκας
      χαλκεοστέρνου τ' Ἄρηος,
35   5 Δεινομένευς ἀγέρωχοι
      παῖδες· εὖ ἔρδων δὲ μὴ κάμοι θεός.
      7 ξανθότριχα μὲν Φερένικον
      Ἀλφεὸν παρ' εὐρυδίναν
      9 πῶλον ἀελλοδρόμαν
40   εἶδε νικάσαντα χρυσόπαχυς Ἀώς,
)—

Β'   1 Πυθῶνί τ' ἐν ἀγαθέᾱι·
      γᾶι δ' ἐπισκήπτων πιφαύσκω·

26–27 ΝΩΜΑΙ ⋮ ΤΑΙ **A**: ΝΩΜΑ ⋮ ΤΑΙ **A¹**: Walker   **30** ΜΕΤ ΑΝΘΡΩΠΟΙΣ
A: μετ' secl. Walker

3 οὔπω νιν ὑπὸ προτέ[ρω]ν
ἵππων ἐν ἀγῶνι κατέχρανεν κόνις

45   5 πρὸς τέλος ὀρνύμενον·
ῥιπᾶι γὰρ ἴσος βορέα
7 ὃν κυβερνήταν φυλάσσων
ἵεται νεόκροτον
9 νίκαν Ἱέρωνι φιλοξείνωι τιτύσκων.

50   ὄλβιος ὧτινι θεός
11 μοῖράν τε καλῶν ἔπορεν
σύν τ' ἐπιζήλωι τύχαι
13 ἀφνεὸν βιοτὰν διάγειν· οὐ
γά⌊ρ τις⌋ ἐπιχθονίων
55   π⌊άντ⌋α γ' εὐδαίμων ἔφυ.

——

1 τ[ὸν γὰρ π]οτ' ἐρειψιπύλαν
παῖδ' ἀνίκ]ατον λέγουσιν
3 δῦναι Διὸς] ἀργικεραύ-

col. 12   νου δώματα Φερσεφόνας τανισφύρου,

60   5 καρχαρόδοντα κύν' ἄ-
ξοντ' ἐς φάος ἐξ Ἀΐδα,
7 υἱὸν ἀπλάτοι' Ἐχίδνας·
ἔνθα δυστάνων βροτῶν
9 ψυχὰς ἐδάη παρὰ Κωκυτοῦ ῥεέθροις,

65   οἷά τε φύλλ' ἄνεμος
11 Ἴδας ἀνὰ μηλοβότους
πρῶνας ἀργηστὰς δονεῖ.
13 ταῖσιν δὲ μετέπρεπεν εἴδω-
λον θρασυμέμνονος ἐγ-

70   χεσπάλου Πορθανίδα·

——

1 τὸν δ' ὡς ἴδεν Ἀλκμή<ν>ιος θαυμαστὸς ἥρως
τ[ε]ύχεσι λαμπόμενον,

56 Τ[potius quam Υ[, suppl. Maehler   **70** ΘΑΝΙΔΑ: ΘΑΟΝΙΔΑ **A**²

3 νευρὰν ἐπέβασε λιγυκλαγγῆ κορώνας·
χαλκεόκρανον δ' ἔπειτ' ἔξ

75 5 εἵλετο ἰὸν ἀναπτύ-
ξας φαρέτρας πῶμα· τῶι δ' ἐναντία

7 ψυχὰ προφάνη Μελεάγρου
καί νιν εὖ εἰδὼς προσεῖπεν·

9 "υἱὲ Διὸς μεγάλου,

80 στᾶθι τ' ἐν χώραι, γελανώσας τε θυμόν
)—

Γ' 1 μὴ ταύσιον προΐει
τραχὺν ἐκ χειρῶν ὀϊστόν

3 ψυχαῖσιν ἔπι φθιμένων·
οὔ τοι δέος." ὣς φάτο· θάμβησεν δ' ἄναξ

85 5 Ἀμφιτρυωνιάδας,
εἶπέν τε· "τίς ἀθανάτων

7 ἢ βροτῶν τοιοῦτον ἔρνος
θρέψεν ἐν ποίαι χθονί;

9 τίς δ' ἔκτανεν; ἦ τάχα καλλίζωνος Ἥρα

90 κεῖνον ἐφ' ἁμετέραι
11 πέμψει κεφαλᾶι· τὰ δέ που

col. 13 Παλλάδι ξανθᾶι μέλει."

13 τὸν δὲ προσέφα Μελέαγρος
δακρυόεις· "χαλεπὸν

95 θεῶν παρατρέψαι νόον

———

1 ἄνδρεσσιν ἐπιχθονίοις.
καὶ γὰρ ἂν πλάξιππος Οἰνεύς

3 παῦσεν καλυκοστεφάνου
σεμνᾶς χόλον Ἀρτέμιδος λευκωλένου

100 5 λισσόμενος πολέων
τ' αἰγῶν θυσίαισι πατήρ

7 καὶ βοῶν φοινικονώτων·
ἀλλ' ἀνίκατον θεά

9 ἔσχεν χόλον· εὐρυβίαν δ' ἔσσευε κούρα

105 κάπρον ἀναιδομάχαν

11 ἐς καλλίχορον Καλυδῶ-
ν', ἔνθα πλημύρων σθένει
13 ὄρχους ἐπέκειρεν ὀδόντι,
σφάζε τε μῆλα, βροτῶν
110 θ' ὅστις εἰσάνταν μόλοι.

___

1 τῶι δὲ στυγερὰν δῆριν Ἑλλάνων ἄριστοι
στάσαμεθ' ἐνδυκέως
3 ἕξ ἄματα συνεχέως· ἐπεὶ δὲ δαίμων
κάρτος Αἰτωλοῖς ὄρεξεν,
115 5 θάπτομεν οὓς κατέπεφνεν
σῦς ἐριβρύχας ἐπαΐσσων βίᾱι,
7 Ἀ[γκ]αῖον ἐμῶν τ' Ἀγέλαον
φ[έρτ]ατον κεδνῶν ἀδελφεῶν,
9 οὓς τέ]κεν ἐν μεγάροις
120 . . . . .]ς Ἀλθαία περικλειτοῖσιν Οἰνέος.
)—

Δ'   1 τοὺς δ' ὤ]λεσε μοῖρ' ὀλοὰ
πάντα]ς· οὐ γάρ πω δαΐφρων
3 παῦσεν] χόλον ἀγροτέρα
col. 14   Λατοῦς θυγάτηρ· περὶ δ' αἴθωνος δορᾱς
125 5 μαρνάμεθ' ἐνδυκέως
Κουρῆσι μενεπτολέμοις·
7 ἔνθ' ἐγὼ πολλοῖς σὺν ἄλλοις
Ἴφικλον κατέκτανον
9 ἐσθλόν τ' Ἀφάρητα, θοοὺς μάτρωας· οὐ γὰρ
130 καρτερόθυμος Ἄρης
11 κρίνει φίλον ἐν πολέμωι,
τυφλὰ δ' ἐκ χειρῶν βέλη
13 ψυχαῖς ἔπι δυσμενέων φοι-
τᾶι θάνατόν τε φέρει

___

106 ΟΣ: ὪΣ A³?: ἐς Palmer   **113** ΣΥΝΕ A: ΣΥΝΝΕ A³   **117** ΑΓΓΕΛΟΝ:
Kenyon   **120** πατρὸς Kenyon, παῖδας Schadewaldt   **122** πλεῦνας Housman, πάντας Ludwich

135   τοῖσιν ἂν δαίμων θέληι.

          ——

       1 ταῦτ' οὐκ ἐπιλεξαμένα
         Θεστίου κούρα δαΐφρων
       3 μάτηρ κακόποτμος ἐμοὶ
         βούλευσεν ὄλεθρον ἀτάρβακτος γυνά,
140   5 καῖέ τε δαιδαλέας
         ἐκ λάρνακος ὠκύμορον
       7 φιτρὸν ἐξαύσασα· τὸν δὴ
         μοῖρ' ἐπέκλωσεν τότε
       9 ζωᾶς ὅρον ἁμετέρας ἔμμεν. τύχον μὲν
145   Δαϊπύλου Κλύμενον
       11 παῖδ' ἄλκιμον ἐξεναρί-
         ζων ἀμώμητον δέμας,
       13 πύργων προπάροιθε κιχήσας·
         τοὶ δὲ πρὸς εὐκτιμέναν
150   φεῦγον ἀρχαίαν πόλιν

          ——

       1 Πλευρῶνα· μίνυθεν δέ μοι ψυχὰ γλυκεῖα·
         γνῶν δ' ὀλιγοσθενέων,
       3 αἰαῖ· πύματον δὲ πνέων δάκρυσα τλά[μων,
         ἀγλαὰν ἥβαν προλείπων."
155   5 φασὶν ἀδεισιβόαν
col. 15   Ἀμφιτρύωνος παῖδα μοῦνον δὴ τότε
       7 τέγξαι βλέφαρον, ταλαπενθέος
         πότμον οἰκτίροντα φωτός·
       9 καί νιν ἀμειβόμενος
160   τᾶδ' ἔφα· "θνατοῖσι μὴ φῦναι φέριστον
)—
Ε'   1 μηδ' ἀελίου προσιδεῖν
         φέγγος· ἀλλ' οὐ γάρ τίς ἐστιν
       3 πρᾶξις τάδε μυρομένοις·
         χρὴ κεῖνο λέγειν ὅτι καὶ μέλλει τελεῖν.

142 ΕΓΚΛΑΥΣΑΣΑ: Wackernagel   **151** ΜΙΝΥΝΘΑ (cf. Il. Α 416): Wilamowitz

165 5 ἦρά τις ἐν μεγάροις
        Οἰνῆος ἀρηϊφίλου
     7 ἔστιν ἀδμήτα θυγάτρων,
        σοὶ φυὰν ἀλιγκία;
     9 τάν κεν λιπαρὰν <ἐ>θέλων θείμαν ἄκοιτιν."
170   τὸν δὲ μενεπτολέμου
     11 ψυχὰ προσέφα Μελεά-
        γρου· "λίπον χλωραύχενα
     13 ἐν δώμασι Δαϊάνειραν,
        νῆϊν ἔτι χρῦσέας
175   Κύπριδος θελξιμβρότου."

      ———

     1 λευκώλενε Καλλιόπα,
        στᾶσον εὐποίητον ἅρμα
     3 αὐτοῦ· Δία τε Κρονίδαν
        ὕμνησον Ὀλύμπιον ἀρχαγὸν θεῶν,
180 5 τόν τ' ἀκαμαντορόαν
        Ἀλφεόν, Πέλοπός τε βίαν,
     7 καὶ Πίσαν, ἔνθ' ὁ κλεεννὸς
        πο]σσὶ νικάσας δρόμωι
     9 ἦλθ]εν Φερένικος <ἐς> εὐπύργους Συρακόσ-
185   σας Ἱέρωνι φέρων
     11 εὐδ]αιμονίας πέταλον.
        χρὴ] δ' ἀλαθείας χάριν
col. 16 13 αἰνεῖν, φθόνον ἀμφ[οτέραισιν
        χερσὶν ἀπωσάμενον,
190   εἴ τις εὖ πράσσοι βροτῶ[ν.

      ———

     1 Βοιωτὸς ἀνὴρ τάδε φών[ησεν, γλυκειᾶν
        Ἡσίοδος πρόπολος
     3 Μουσᾶν, ὃν <ἂν> ἀθάνατοι τι[μῶσι, τούτωι
        καὶ βροτῶν φήμαν ἔπ[εσθαι.

———

184 ἦλθεν . . . <ἐς> Blass, Housman   **187** ΑΛΗΘ: Blass

195   5 πείθομαι εὐμαρέως
        εὐκλέα κελεύθου γλῶσσαν οὐ[— ◡ —
      7 πέμπειν Ἱέρωνι· τόθεν γὰ[ρ
        πυθμένες θάλλουσιν ἐσθλ[ῶν,
      9 τοὺς ὁ μεγιστοπάτωρ
200   Ζεὺς ἀκινήτους ἐν εἰρήν[αι φυλάσσοι.

6

ΛΑΧΩΝΙ ΚΕΙΩΙ
\<ΠΑΙΔΙ\> ΣΤΑΔΙΕΙ ΟΛΥΜΠ[ΙΑ

metrum: aeolicum (v. p. 16) Α′-Β′

1	◡ — ◡ — ◡ — | ◡ ◡ — ◡ — ◡ — — ‖	*ia ba | anacl* ‖
3	— ◡ ◡ — — ◡ ◡ — ◡ — | ◡ — ◡ ◡ — ◡ ‖	*2 cho ba | ∧pher* ‖
5	— ◡ — ◡ — ◡ — ‖	*lec* ‖
6	◡ — — ◡ ◡ — ◡ — — ◡ ◡ — ◡ — — |	*gl hipp |*
8	◡ ◡ — ◡ — — ‖‖	(∧*pher* ‖‖)

Α′   Λάχων Διὸς μεγίστου
            λάχε φέρτατον πόδεσσι
            3 κῦδος ἐπ᾽ Ἀλφεοῦ προχοαῖσ[◡ — —
            δι᾽ ὅσσα πάροιθεν
     5   ἀμπελοτρόφον Κέον
            6 ἄεισάν ποτ᾽ Ὀλυμπίαι
               πύξ τε καὶ στάδιον κρατεῦ[σαν
             στεφάνοις ἐθείρας
)—
Β′   νεανίαι βρύοντες.
10   σὲ δὲ νῦν ἀναξιμόλπου
            3 Οὐρανίας ὕμνος ἕκατι Νίκ[ας,
            Ἀριστομένειον
            ὦ ποδάνεμον τέκος,

196 οὐκ ἐκτὸς δίκας Jebb   **200** Blass alii
6   **3** ΛΑΦΕΙΟΥ: ΑΛΦ **Α**[3]: -φεοῦ Kenyon \| ἀέθλων Housman, προχοαῖσ[σιν ἴσον
Schwartz, -αῖσ[ι τοῖον (vel ῥέξας) Maehler

₆ γεραίρει προδόμοις ἀοι-
15   δαῖς, ὅτι στάδιον κρατήσας
Κέον εὐκλέϊξας.

II

ΑΛΕΞΙΔΑΜΩΙ ΜΕΤΑΠΟΝΤΙΝΩΙ
ΠΑΙΔΙ ΠΑΛΑΙΣΤΗΙ ΠΥΘΙΑ

metrum: dactyloepitr. Α′–Γ′

12 — ◡ ◡ — ◡ ◡ —

— — ◡ ◡ — ◡ ◡ —

— ◡ — — — ◡ — —   – D – D E – ‖

A′

1 Νίκα γλυκύδωρε· [μόναι γὰρ
σοὶ πατ[ὴρ — — ◡ — — —
3 ὑψίζυ[γος — ◡ ◡ —
ἐν πολυχρύσωι <τ'> Ὀλύμπωι
5   5 Ζηνὶ παρισταμένα
κρίνεις τέλος ἀθανάτοι-
σίν τε καὶ θνατοῖς ἀρετᾶς·
8 ἔλλαθι, [βαθυ]πλοκάμου
κούρα Σ[τυγὸς ὀρ]θοδίκου· σέθεν δ' ἕκατι
10   10 καὶ νῦ[ν Μετ]απόντιον εὐγυίων κ[ατέ]χουσι νέων
12 κῶμοί τε καὶ εὐφροσύναι θεότιμον ἄστυ·
ὑμνεῦσι δὲ Πυθιόνικον
παῖδα θαητ[ὸ]ν Φαΐσκου.

15   1 ἵλεώι νιν ὁ Δα[λ]ογενὴς υἱὸς βαθυζώνο[ιο] Λατοῦς
3 δέκτ[ο] βλεφά[ρω]ι· πολέες
δ' ἀμφ' Ἀλεξ[ίδα]μον ἀνθέων
5 ἐν πεδίωι στέφανοι
20   Κίρρας ἔπεσον κρατερᾶς
ἦρα παννίκοι<ο> πάλας·
8 οὐκ ε[ἶ]δέ νιν ἀέλιος
κείνωι γε σὺν ἄματι πρὸς γαίαι πεσόντα.
10 φάσω δὲ καὶ ἐν ζαθέοις
25   ἁγνοῦ Πέλοπος δαπέδοις

---

11   **1** μόναι γὰρ Ed. Fraenkel, κλυτὰν γὰρ Snell   **2** σοὶ πατὴρ τιμὰν ἔδωκεν Hense, τεθμὸν δέδωκεν Maehler   **3** ὑψ. Οὐρανιδᾶν Jebb, Οὐρανίδας Snell   **4** <τ'> Snell <δ'> Neue   **8** ἔλληθι Wackernagel | βαθυπλ. Jebb   **9** Blass **10–11** ΕΙ : ΓΥΙΩΝ: **A**¹   **11** Blass alii   **21** ΝΙΚΟΙΠΑΛ: Kenyon | ΠΑΛΛΑΣ: **A**³

12 Ἀλφεὸν πάρα καλλιρόαν, δίκας κέλευθον
εἰ μή τις ἀπέτραπεν ὀρθᾶς,
παγξένωι χαίταν ἐλαίαι

1 γλαυκᾶι στεφανωσάμενον
30 πορτιτρόφον ['Ιταλ]ί[αν πάτ]ραν θ'ἱκέσθαι.
3 [– ‿‿ – ‿‿ –]
col. 24 παῖδ' ἐν χθονὶ καλλιχόρωι
ποικίλαις τέχναις πέλασσεν·
6 ἀ]λλ' ἢ θεὸς αἴτιος, ἢ
35 γ]νῶμαι πολύπλαγκτοι βροτῶν
ἄ]μερσαν ὑπέρτατον ἐκ χειρῶν γέρας.
9 νῦν δ' Ἄρτεμις ἀγροτέρα
χρυσαλάλατος λιπαράν
Ἡμ]έρα τοξόκλυτος νίκαν ἔδωκε.
40 12 τ]ᾶι ποτ' Ἀβαντιάδας
β]ωμὸν κατένασσε πολύλ-
λ[ι]στον εὔπεπλοί τε κοῦραι·
)—
Β' 1 τὰς ἐξ ἐρατῶν ἐφόβησε<ν>
παγκρατὴς Ἥρα μελάθρων
45 3 Προίτου, παραπλῆγι φρένας
καρτερᾶι ζεύξασ' ἀνάγκαι·
5 παρθενίαι γὰρ ἔτι
ψυχᾶι κίον ἐς τέμενος
πορφυροζώνοιο θεᾶς·
50 8 φάσκον δὲ πολὺ σφέτερον
πλούτωι προφέρειν πατέρα ξανθᾶς παρέδρου
10 σεμνοῦ Διὸς εὐρυβία.
ταῖσιν δὲ χολωσαμένα
12 στήθεσσι παλίντροπον ἔμβαλεν νόημα·

30 Platt   31 ἢ τινα γὰρ ποτὶ γᾶι e.g. Maehler   39 Blass   45 ΠΑΡΑΠΛΗΓΙ:
Kenyon, παραπλᾶγι Blass   54 ΒΑΛΕΝΟΜΜΑ: Kenyon

55   φεῦγον δ᾽ ὄρος ἐς τανίφυλλον
      σμερδαλέᾱν φωνὰν ἱεῖσαι,

      —

      1 Τιρύνθιον ἄστυ λιποῦσαι
        καὶ θεοδμάτους ἀγυιάς.
      3 ἤδη γὰρ ἔτος δέκατον
60   θεοφιλὲς λιπόντες Ἄργος
      5 ναῖον ἀδεισιβόαι
        χαλκάσπιδες ἡμίθεοι
        σὺν πολυζήλωι βασιλεῖ.
      8 νεῖκος γὰρ ἀμαιμάκετον
65   βληχρᾶς ἀνέπαλτο κασιγνήτοις ἀπ᾽ ἀρχᾶς
col. 25   10 Προίτωι τε καὶ Ἀκρισίωι·
        λαούς τε διχοστασίαις
      12 ἤρειπον ἀμετροδίκοις μάχαις τε λυγραῖς,
        λίσσοντο δὲ παῖδας Ἄβαντος
70   γᾶν πολύκριθον λαχόντας

      —

      1 Τίρυνθα τὸν ὁπλότερον
        κτίζειν, πρὶν ἐς ἀργαλέαν πεσεῖν ἀνάγκαν·
      3 Ζεύς τ᾽ ἔθελεν Κρονίδας
        τιμῶν Δαναοῦ γενεὰν
75   καὶ διωξίπποιο Λυγκέος
      6 παῦσαι στυγερῶν ἀχέων.
        τεῖχος δὲ Κύκλωπες κάμον
        ἐλθόντες ὑπερφίαλοι κλεινᾶι π[όλ]ει
      9 κάλλιστον, ἵν᾽ ἀντίθεοι
80   ναῖον κλυτὸν ἱππόβοτον
        Ἄργος ἥρωες περικλειτοὶ λιπόντες,
      12 ἔνθεν ἀπεσσύμεναι
        Προίτου κυανοπλόκαμοι
        φεῦγον ἄδματοι θύγατρες.

)—

Γ′ 85 1 τὸν δ᾽ εἷλεν ἄχος κραδίαν, ξεί-
         να τέ νιν πλᾶξεν μέριμνα·

3 δοίαξε δὲ φάσγανον ἄμ-
φακες ἐν στέρνοισι πᾶξαι.
5 ἀλλά νιν αἰχμοφόροι
90   μύθοισί τε μειλιχίοις
καὶ βίᾳ χειρῶν κάτεχον.
8 τρισκαίδεκα μὲν τελέους
μῆνας κατὰ δάσκιον ἠλύκταζον ὕλαν
10 φεῦγόν τε κατ' Ἀρκαδίαν
95   μηλοτρόφον· ἀλλ' ὅτε δή
12 Λοῦσον ποτὶ καλλιρόαν πατὴρ ἵκανεν,
ἔνθεν χρόα νιψάμενος φοι-
νικοκ[ραδέμνο]ιο Λατοῦς

1 κίκλη[ισκε θύγατρ]α βοῶπιν,
col. 26 100   χεῖρας ἀντείνων πρὸς αὐγάς
3 ἱππώκεος ἀελίου,
τέκνα δυστάνοιο λύσσας
5 πάρφρονος ἐξαγαγεῖν·
"θύσω δέ τοι εἴκοσι βοῦς
105   ἄζυγας φοινικότριχας."
8 τοῦ δ' ἔκλυ' ἀριστοπάτρα
θηροσκόπος εὐχομένου· πιθοῦσα δ' Ἥραν
10 παῦσεν καλυκοστεφάνους
κούρας μανιᾶν ἀθέων·
110 12 ταὶ δ' αὐτίκα οἱ τέμενος βωμόν τε τεῦχον,
χραῖνόν τέ μιν αἵματι μήλων
καὶ χορὺς ἵσταν γυναικῶν.

1 ἔνθεν καὶ ἀρηϊφίλοις
ἄνδρεσσιν <ἐς> ἱππότροφον πόλιν Ἀχαιοῖς

---

94 ΚΑΤΑΚΑΡΔΙΑΝ: Palmer   **98–99** Kenyon   **106** om. **A**, add. **A**³ in margine
superiore   **114** <ἐς> Jebb | de πόλιν cf. p. 13

115   3 ἕσπεο· σὺν δὲ τύχᾳι
        ναίεις Μεταπόντιον, ὦ
        χρυσέα δέσποινα λαῶν·
     6 ἄλσος δέ τοι ἱμερόεν
        Κάσαν παρ' εὔυδρον †προγο-
120   νοι ἐσσάμενοι† Πριάμοι' ἐπεὶ χρόνωι
     9 βουλαῖσι θεῶν μακάρων
        πέρσαν πόλιν εὐκτιμέναν
        χαλκοθωράκων μετ' Ἀτρειδᾶν. δικαίας
     12 ὅστις ἔχει φρένας, εὑ-
125   ρήσει σὺν ἅπαντι χρόνωι
        μυρίας ἀλκὰς Ἀχαιῶν.

ΒΑΚΧΥΛΙΔΟΥ ΔΙΘΥΡΑΜΒΟΙ

15 = dith. 1

ΑΝΤΗΝΟΡΙΔΑΙ Η ΕΛΕΝΗΣ ΑΠΑΙΤΗΣΙΣ

metrum: dactyloepitr. Α′ – Γ′

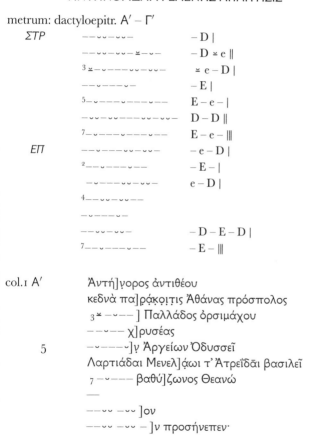

col.1 Α′   Ἀντή]γορος ἀντιθέου
       κεδνὰ πα]ρᾴκοιτις Ἀθάνας πρόσπολος
       3 ⌣ – ⌣ – –] Παλλάδος ὀρσιμάχου
       – – ⌣ – – χ]ρυσέας
    5 – ⌣ – – – – ⌣]ν Ἀργείων Ὀδυσσεῖ
       Λαρτιάδαι Μενελ]ᾴωι τ' Ἀτρεΐδᾱι βασιλεῖ
       7 – ⌣ – – – βαθύ]ζωνος Θεανώ
       —
       – – ⌣⌣ – ⌣⌣]ον
       – – ⌣⌣ – ⌣⌣ –]ν προσήνεπεν·

15   **7** ὥς ποτ' ᾔντησεν β. Koerte

10   3 —‿—‿ ἐ]ΰκτιμέναν

         —‿—‿—]

         —‿—‿—]δων τυχόντες

         —‿‿ —‿‿ —‿‿]. σὺν †θεοῖς

         7 —‿ —‿ —‿ —]δους

         ___

         (deest epod. α′)

Β′   —‿‿ —‿‿]

23   —‿‿ οὐ γὰρ ὑπόκλοπον φορεῖ

         βροτοῖσι φωνάεντα λόγον σοφία

         (desunt vv. XI)

ΕΠ. Β′ 36   —‿ —‿‿ —‿‿]

col. 2   ἆγον, πατὴρ δ' εὔβουλος ἥρως

         πάντα σάμαινεν Πριάμωι βασιλεῖ

         4 παίδεσσί τε μῦθον Ἀχαιῶν.

40   ἔνθα κάρυκες δι' εὐ-

         ρεῖαν πόλιν ὀρνύμενοι

         Τρώων ἀόλλιζον φάλαγγας

)—

Γ′   δεξίστρατον εἰς ἀγοράν.

         πάνται δὲ διέδραμεν αὐδάεις λόγος·

45   3 θεοῖς δ' ἀνίσχοντες χέρας ἀθανάτοις

         εὔχοντο παύσασθαι δυᾶν.

         Μοῦσα, τίς πρῶτος λόγων ἆρχεν δικαίων;

         Πλεισθενίδας Μενέλαος γάρυϊ θελξιεπεῖ

         7 φθέγξατ', εὐπέπλοισι κοινώσας Χάρισσιν·

50   "ὦ Τρῶες ἀρηΐφιλοι,

         Ζεὺς ὑψ[ιμέδων ὃ]ς ἅπαντα δέρκεται

         3 οὐκ αἴτιος θνατοῖς μεγάλων ἀχέων,

         ἀλλ' ἐν [μέσ]ωι κεῖται κιχεῖν

         πᾶσιν ἀνθρώποις Δίκαν ἰθεῖαν, ἁγνᾶς

55   Εὐνομίας ἀκόλουθον καὶ πινυτᾶς Θέμιτος·
7 ὀλβίων π⌊αῖδές⌋ νιν αἱρεῦνται σύνοικον.

  ἁ δ' αἰόλοις ϙέρδεσσι καὶ ἀφροσύναις
  ἐξαισίοις θάλλουσ' ἀθαμβής
3 Ὕβρις, ἃ πλοῦτ[ο]ν δύναμίν τε θόως
60   ἀλλότριον ὤπασεν, αὖτις
   δ' ἐς βαθὺν πέμπει φθόρον·
  κε]ίνα καὶ ὑπερφιάλους
  Γᾶς] παῖδας ὤλεσσεν Γίγαντας."

16 = dith. 2

[ΗΡΑΚΛΗΣ (vel ΔΗΙΑΝΕΙΡΑ ?) ΕΙΣ ΔΕΛΦΟΥΣ]

metrum: dactyli

ΣΤΡ   1 — — ◡◡ — ◡ — ‖   ∧*gl* ‖
    — ◡◡ — ◡◡ — ◡◡ — | *4da*∧ |
  3 — ◡◡ — ◡◡ — ◡◡ — ◡◡ —   *5da*∧
    ◡? ◡◡ — ◡ — ◡ — — | *2tr* |
  5 — ◡◡ — ◡◡ — ◡◡ — � — — | *4da* ∧ *ba* |
    — ◡◡ — ◡◡ — ◡◡ — ◡◡ — — | *5da* |
  7 ◡◡ — ◡◡ — ◡◡ — ◡◡ —   ◡◡ *4da*∧
    — ◡◡ — — — ◡ ⏓ | *cho ia* ‖
    — ◡◡◡ — — ‖   *cr* ◡◡*sp* ‖
  10 — ◡◡ — — | *adon* |
    ◡◡◡ — — — | ◡◡*cr sp* |
    — ◡◡ — — | ◡◡ — ◡◡ — ⏓ ‖‖‖   *adon* ∧*pher* ‖‖‖

ΕΠ   1 — ◡◡ — ◡◡ —
    ◡◡ — ◡◡ — ◡◡ — — ‖   *6da* ‖
  3 ◡◡ — ◡◡ — — ◡ — | ◡◡ *cho cr* |
    ◡◡ — ◡◡ — ◡◡ —   ◡◡ *5da*∧ |
    ◡◡ — ◡◡ — | ◡◡◡ — — — ‖   ◡◡*cr sp* ‖
  6 — — ◡◡ — ◡ — — ◡◡ — ◡ — | ∧*gl* — ◡◡ — ◡ — |
    ◡◡ — ◡◡ — ◡◡ — ◡ — | ◡◡ *3da*◡ — |

62–63 suppl. Kenyon

8 ‿‿—‿‿—‿—   ∧gl

   —‿‿—‿‿—

‿‿—‿‿—‿‿—— | 6da |

11 —‿‿—— |‿‿—‿‿—‿— ||| adon | ∧gl |||

    . . .]ιου . ιọ . . . ἐπεὶ
    ὁλκ]άδ᾽ ἔπεμψεν ἐμοὶ χρῦσέαν
    Πιερ]ίαθεν ἐ[ΰθ]ρονọς [Ο]ὐρανία,
    πολυφ]άτων γέμουσαν ὕμνων
5   . . . . .]νεịτịς ἐπ᾽ ἀνθεμόεντι Ἕβρωι
    . . . . . ἀ]γάλλεται ἢ δολιχαύχενι κύ[κνωι
    . . . . .]δεϊα[[ν¹]] φρένα τερπόμενος
    . . . . . .]δ᾽ ἵκηι παιηόνων
col.3   ἄνθεα πεδοιχνεῖν,
10   Πύθι᾽ Ἄπολλον.
    τόσα χοροὶ Δελφῶν
    σὸν κελάδησαν παρ᾽ ἀγακλέα ναόν.

    1 πρίν γε κλέομεν λιπεῖν
    Οἰχαλίαν πυρὶ δαπτομέναν
15   3 Ἀμφιτρυωνιάδαν θρασυμηδέα φῶ–
    θ᾽, ἵκετο δ᾽ ἀμφικύμον᾽ ἀκτάν·
   5 ἔνθ᾽ ἀπὸ λαΐδος εὐρυνεφεῖ Κηναίωι
    Ζηνὶ θύεν βαρυαχέας ἐννέα ταύρους
   7 δύο τ᾽ ὀρσιάλωι δαμασίχθονι μέ[λ-
20   λε †κόρᾱι τ᾽† ὀβριμοδερκεῖ <δ᾽> ἄζυγα
    παρθένωι Ἀθάνᾱι
  10 ὑψικέραν βοῦν.
    τότ᾽ ἄμαχος δαίμων
    Δαϊανείρᾱι πολύδακρυν ὕφα[νε

---

16   **5**]Ν vel]Αἰ: ἐς θεὸ]ν Jebb, εὔχομ]αι D. A. Schmidt   **7** μελια]δε<ῖ> D. A. Schmidt, ἰᾶι Kuiper   **8** πρὶν τό]δ᾽ ἵκηι Maehler   **19–20** μέ[λ]λ᾽, ὀβριμοδερκεῖ <δ᾽> ἄζυγα Maas, Barrett (κόραι τ᾽ del. Maas)

25   ι μῆτιν ἐπίφρον' ἐπεὶ
         πύθετ' ἀγγελίαν ταλαπενθέᾳ,
       3 Ἰόλαν ὅτι λευκώλενον
         Διὸς υἱὸς ἀταρβομάχας
         ἄλοχον λιπαρὸ[ν] ποτὶ δόμον πέμ[π]οι.
30   6 ἇ δύσμορος, ἇ τάλα[αι]ν', οἷον ἐμήσατ[ο·
         φθόνος εὐρυβίας νιν ἀπώλεσεν,
       8 δνόφεόν τε κάλυμμα τῶν
         ὕστερον ἐρχομένων,
         ὅτ' ἐπὶ ῥοδόεντι Λυκόρμαι
35   ιι δέξατο Νέσσου πάρα δαιμόνιον τέρ[ας.

17 = dith. 3

ΗΙΘΕΟΙ Η ΘΗΣΕΥΣ <ΚΗΙΟΙΣ ΕΙΣ ΔΗΛΟΝ>

metrum e iambis ortum (v. p. 17)

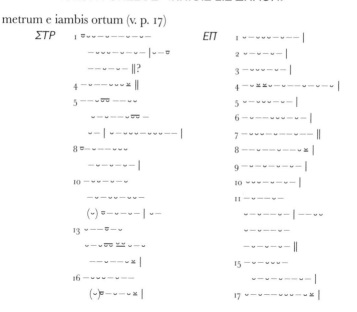

34 ΕΠΙ ΠΟΤΑΜΩ[Ι] ΡΟΔ.: ποταμῶι del. Ludwich, Wilamowitz

18 ‒᪶‒ ‒ ‒ ‒ ‒ ‒ ‒   18 ‒ ᪶᪶ ‒ ‒ ‒ ‒

‒ ᪴ ᪴ ᪴ ‒ ‒ ‒ ᪶ | ᪴ ᪴ ᪴ ‒ ‒ |

20 ᪶‒ ‒ ᪴ ⏤⏤ ᪶᪶ ᪴ ‒ ‒ ‒ ‖   20 ᪴ ‒ ‒ ᪶᪶ ‒ ‒ ‒ ‒ ᪴ ‒ ⫶

21 ᪶⏤᪴ ᪴ ‒ ‒ ‒ ‒ ‒

᪴ ‒ ᪴ ‒ ‒ ‒ ᪴ |

23 ‒ ᪴ ‒ ᪴ ᪴ ᪴ ‒ ᪴ ᪶᪶ ‒ ᪴ ᪶ ⫶

A΄   Κυανόπρωιρα μὲν ναῦς μενέκτυ[πον
          Θησέα δὶς ἑπτ[ά] τ᾽ ἀγλαοὺς ἄγουσα
          κούρους Ἰαόνω[ν
          Κρητικὸν τάμνε πέλαγος·
5   τηλαυγέϊ γὰρ [ἐν] φάρεϊ
          βορήϊαι πίτνο[ν] αὖραι
          κλυτᾶς ἕκατι π[ε]λεμαίγιδος Ἀθάν[ας·
col. 4   κνίσεν δὲ Μίνω<ϊ> κέαρ
          ἱμεράμπυκος θεᾶς
10   Κύπριδος [ἄ]γνὰ δῶρα·
          χεῖρα δ᾽ οὐ[κέτι] παρθενικᾶς
          ἄτερθ᾽ ἐράτυεν, θίγεν
          δὲ λευκᾶν παρηΐδων·
          βόασέ τ᾽ Ἐρίβοια χαλκο-
15   θώρα[κα Π]ανδίονος
          ἔκγ[ο]νον· ἴδεν δὲ Θησεύς,
          μέλαν δ᾽ ὑπ᾽ ὀφρύων
          δίνα[σ]εν ὄμμα, καρδίαν τέ οἱ
          σχέτλιον ἄμυξεν ἄλγος,
20   εἶρέν τε· "Διὸς υἱὲ φερτάτου,
          ὅσιον οὐκέτι τεᾶν
          ἔσω κυβερνᾷς φρενῶν
          θυμ[όν]· ἴσχε μεγάλαυχον ἥρως βίαν.

        ὅ τι μ[ὲ]ν ἐκ θεῶν μοῖρα παγκρατὴς
25   ἄμμι κατένευσε καὶ Δίκας ῥέπει τά-
          λαντον, πεπρωμέν[α]ν

17   **23** ΜΕΓΑΛΟΥΧΟΝ: Kenyon

4 αἶσαν [ἐ]κπλήσομεν, ὅτ[α]ν
5 ἔλθηι· [σ]ὺ δὲ βαρεῖαν κάτε-
χε μῆτιν. εἰ καί σε κεδνὰ
30 τέκεν λέχει Διὸς ὑπὸ κρόταφον Ἴδας
8 μιγεῖσα Φοίνικος ἐρα-
τώνυμος κόρα βροτῶν
10 φέρτατον, ἀλλὰ κἀμὲ
Πιτθ[έ]ος θυγάτηρ ἀφνεοῦ
35 πλαθεῖσα ποντίωι τέκεν
13 Ποσειδᾶνι, χρυσεόν
τέ οἱ δόσαν ἰόπλοκοι
†καλυμμα† Νηρηΐδες.
16 τῶ σε, πολέμαρχε Κνωσίων,
40 κέλομαι πολύστονον
18 ἐρύκεν ὕβριν· οὐ γὰρ ἂν θέλοι-
col.5   μ' ἀμβρότοι' ἐραννὸν Ἀο[ῦς
20 ἰδεῖν φάος, ἐπεί τιν' ἠϊθέ[ων]
21 σὺ δαμάσειας ἀέκον-
45 τα· πρόσθε χειρῶν βίαν
23 δε[ί]ξομεν· τὰ δ' ἐπιόντα δα[ίμω]ν κρινεῖ."

———

1 τόσ' εἶπεν ἀρέταιχμος ἥρως·
2 τά]φον δὲ ναυβάται
3 φ]ωτὸς ὑπεράφανον
50 4 θ]άρσος· Ἁλίου τε γαμβρῶι χόλωσεν ἦτορ,
5 ὕφαινέ τε ποταινίαν
6 μῆτιν, εἶπέν τε· "μεγαλοσθενές
7 Ζεῦ πάτερ, ἄκουσον· εἰ πέρ με νύμ[φ]α
8 Φοίνισσα λευκώλενος σοὶ τέκεν,
55 9 νῦν πρόπεμπ' ἀπ' οὐρανοῦ θοάν
10 πυριέθειραν ἀστραπάν
11 σᾶμ' ἀρίγνωτον· εἰ
δὲ καὶ σὲ Τροιζηνία σεισίχθονι
φύτευσεν Αἴθρα Ποσει-

---

38 ΚΑΛΥΜΜΑ ΝΗΡ: κάλυμμ' ἄ<δυ> Ludwich; estne κάλ. glossema?

60   δᾶνι, τόνδε χρύσεον
15 χειρὸς ἀγλαὸν
ἔνεγκε κόσμον ἐκ βαθείας ἁλός,
17 δικὼν θράσει σῶμα πατρὸς ἐς δόμους.
18 εἴσεαι δ' αἴκ' ἐμᾶς κλύηι
65   Κρόνιος εὐχᾶς
20 ἀναξιβρέντας ὁ πάντω[ν με]δ[έω]ν."
)—

Β'   1 κλύε δ' ἄμεμπτον εὐχὰν μεγασθενὴ[ς
Ζεύς, ὑπέροχόν τε Μίνωϊ φύτευσε
τιμὰν φίλωι θέλων
70   4 παιδὶ πανδερκέα θέμεν,
5 ἄστραψέ θ' · ὁ δὲ θυμαρμένον
ἰδὼν τέρας χεῖρα πέτασε
κλυτὰν ἐς αἰθέρα μενεπτόλεμος ἥρως
8 εἶρέν τε· "Θησεῦ, τάδε μὲν
75   †βλεπεις† σαφῆ Διός
10 δῶρα· σὺ δ' ὄρνυ' ἐς βαρύβρομον πέλαγος· Κρονί[δας
col. 6   δέ τοι πατὴρ ἄναξ τελεῖ
13 Ποσειδὰν ὑπέρτατον
80   κλέος χθόνα κατ' ἠΰδενδρον."
ὡς εἶπε· τῶι δ' οὐ πάλιν
16 θυμὸς ἀνεκάμπτετ', ἀλλ' εὐ-
πάκτων ἐπ' ἰκρίων
18 σταθεὶς ὄρουσε, πόντιόν τέ νιν
85   δέξατο θελημὸν ἄλσος.
20 τάφεν δὲ Διὸς υἱὸς ἔνδοθεν
21 κέαρ, κέλευσέ τε κατ' οὖρον ἴσχεν εὐδαίδαλον
23 νᾶα· μοῖρα δ' ἑτέραν ἐπόρσυν' ὁδόν.

———

70 ΠΑΝΔΕΡΚΕΑ Α, ΠΑΝΤΑΡΚΕΑ Ο   72 ΧΕΙΡΑΣ ΠΕΤΑΣΣΕ Α, ΧΕΙΡΑ⟦Σ⟧
ΠΕΤ[Ο   75 ΒΛΕΠΕΙ Ο, ΒΛΕΠΕΙΣ Α: βλέπεις glossema esse (pro ἔδρακες ?)
videtur   87–88 ΚΑΤΟΥ : ΡΟΝ Α, i.e. κατ' οὖρον

90

1 ἵετο δ' ὠκύπομπον δόρυ· σόει
νιν βορεὰς ἐξόπιν πνέουσ' ἀήτα·
τρέσσαν δ' Ἀθανᾱίων
4 ἠϊθέων <—> γένος, ἐπεὶ
5 ἥρως θόρεν πόντονδε, κα-

95

τὰ λειρίων τ' ὀμμάτων δά-
κρυ χέον, βαρεῖαν ἐπιδέγμενοι ἀνάγκαν.
8 φέρον δὲ δελφῖνες {εν} ἁλιναιέται μέγαν θοῶς
10 Θησέα πατρὸς ἱππί-

100

ου δόμου· ἔμολέν τε θεῶν
μέγαρον· τόθι κλυτὰς ἰδὼν
13 ἔδεισ' ὀλβίοιο Νη-
ρέος κόρας· ἀπὸ γὰρ ἀγλα-
ῶν λᾶμπε γυίων σέλας

105

16 ὧτε πυρός, ἀμφὶ χαίταις
δὲ χρυσεόπλοκοι
18 δίνηντο ταινίαι· χορῶι δ' ἔτερ-
πον κέαρ ὑγροῖσι ποσσίν.
20 εἶδέν τε πατρὸς ἄλοχον φίλαν

110

21 σεμνὰν βοῶπιν ἐρατοῖ-
σιν Ἀμφιτρίταν δόμοις·
23 ἅ νιν ἀμφέβαλεν ἀϊόνα πορφυρέᾱν,

—

1 κόμαισί τ' ἐπέθηκεν οὔλαις

col. 7

2 ἀμεμφέα πλόκον,

115

3 τόν ποτέ οἱ ἐν γάμωι
4 δῶκε δόλιος Ἀφροδίτα ῥόδοις ἐρεμνόν.
5 ἄπιστον ὅ τι δαίμονες
6 θέωσιν οὐδὲν φρενοάραις βροτοῖς·
7 νᾶα πάρα λεπτόπρυμνον φάνη· φεῦ,

120

8 οἴαισιν ἐν φροντίσι Κνώσιον
9 ἔσχασεν στραταγέταν, ἐπεί

---

97 ἘΝᾹΛΊ: Palmer   **102** ΕΔΕΙΣΕ ΝΗΡΕΟΣ ΟΛΒΙΟΥ ΚΟΡΑΣ A: Ludwich,
Richards   **108** –ΟΙΣΙΝ ΕΝ ΠΟΣΙΝ: Kenyon   **118** ΘΕΛΩΣΙΝ: Crusius

10 μόλ᾽ ἀδίαντος ἐξ ἁλός
11 θαῦμα πάντεσσι, λάμ-
   πε δ᾽ ἀμφὶ γυίοις θεῶν δῶρ᾽, ἀγλαό-
125   θρονοί τε κοῦραι σὺν εὐ-
      θυμίᾳ νεοκτίτῳ
15 ὠλόλυξαν, ἔ-
   κλαγεν δὲ πόντος· ἠΐθεοι δ᾽ ἐγγύθεν
17 νέοι παιάνιξαν ἐρατᾷ ὀπί.
130 18 Δάλιε, χοροῖσι Κηΐων
      φρένα ἰανθείς
      20 ὄπαζε θεόπομπον ἐσθλῶν τύχαν.

18 = dith. 4

ΘΗΣΕΥΣ <ΑΘΗΝΑΙΟΙΣ>

metrum: aeolicum

$$\text{1} \cup\cup - -\cup\cup-\cup-- \mid \; \cup\!\!-\cup\cup-\cup-\cup-\cup \mid \qquad hipp \,{}_{\wedge}gl \; ba \parallel$$

$$\text{3} \cup\cup\cup - \cup\cup-\cup-\vdots - \vdots \; \cup\!\!-\cup\cup-\cup-\cup-- \mid \qquad hipp \,{}_{\wedge}gl \; ba \parallel$$

$$\text{5} \cup\!\!-\cup \; -\cup\cup-\cup-\vdots - \vdots \; \cup\!\!-\cup\cup-\cup--\mid\cup\!\!-\cup-\cup- \mid \quad gl \; hipp \; ia\cup- \mid$$

$$\text{8} -- \; -\cup\cup-\cup \; \cup \parallel \qquad gl \parallel$$

$$\text{9} -\cup \; -\cup\cup-\cup- \mid \; --\cup\cup-\cup \cup \parallel \qquad hipp \,{}_{\wedge}gl \parallel$$

$$\text{11} -\cup\!\!- \; -\cup\cup-\cup- \mid \; \cup\!\!-\cup\cup-\cup-\cup-- \parallel \qquad hipp \,{}_{\wedge}gl \; ia \parallel$$

$$\text{13} -\cup\!\!- \; -\cup\cup-\cup-- \qquad \cup-\cup-\cup- \mid \qquad gl \; lec \mid$$

$$\text{15} -- \; -\cup\cup-\cup- \qquad \cup--\parallel\parallel\parallel \qquad gl \; ba \parallel\parallel\parallel$$

Α′ <ΧΟΡΟΣ> Βασιλεῦ τᾶν ἱερᾶν Ἀθανᾶν,
        τῶν ἁβροβίων ἄναξ Ἰώνων,
     τί νέον ἔκλαγε χαλκοκώδων
        σάλπιγξ πολεμηΐαν ἀοιδάν;
5   ἦ τις ἁμετέρας χθονὸς
        δυσμενὴς ὅρι᾽ ἀμφιβάλλει
        στραταγέτας ἀνήρ;
        ἦ ληισταὶ κακομάχανοι
        ποιμένων ἀέκατι μήλων

10   σεύοντ' ἀγέλας βίᾳι;
        ἦ τί τοι κραδίαν ἀμύσσει;
        φθέγγευ· δοκέω γὰρ εἴ τινι βροτῶν
        ἀλκίμων ἐπικουρίαν
        καὶ τὶν ἔμμεναι νέων,
15   ὦ Πανδίονος υἱὲ καὶ Κρεούσας.

Β' <ΑΙΓΕΥΣ> 1 Νέον ἦλθε<ν> δολιχὰν ἀμείψας
col.8   κᾶρυξ ποσὶν Ἰσθμίαν κέλευθον·
        3 ἄφατα δ' ἔργα λέγει κραταιοῦ
        φωτός· τὸν ὑπέρβιόν τ' ἔπεφνεν
20   5 Σίνιν, ὃς ἰσχύϊ φέρτατος
        θνατῶν ἦν, Κρονίδα Λυταίου
        σεισίχθονος τέκος·
        8 σῦν τ' ἀνδροκτόνον ἐν νάπαις
        9 Κρεμ<μ>υῶνος ἀτάσθαλόν τε
25   Σκίρωνα κατέκτανεν·
        11 τάν τε Κερκυόνος παλαίστραν
        ἔσχεν, Πολυπήμονός τε καρτερὰν
        13 σφῦραν ἐξέβαλεν Προκό-
        πτας, ἀρείονος τυχών
30   15 φωτός. ταῦτα δέδοιχ' ὅπᾶι τελεῖται.

Γ' <ΧΟ.>   1 Τίνα δ' ἔμμεν πόθεν ἄνδρα τοῦτον
        λέγει, τίνα τε στολὰν ἔχοντα;
        3 πότερα σὺν πολεμηΐοις ὅ-
        πλοισι στρατιὰν ἄγοντα πολλάν;
35   5 ἦ μοῦνον σὺν ὀπάοσιν
        στ<ε>ίχειν ἔμπορον οἶ' ἀλάταν
        ἐπ' ἀλλοδαμίαν,
        8 ἰσχυρόν τε καὶ ἄλκιμον
        9 ὧδε καὶ θρασύν, ὃς τ<οσ>ούτων

18 **9** Δ' ΕΚΑΤΙ: Palmer **35** ΟΠΛΟΙΣΙΝ: Weil **39** ΤΟΥΤΩΝ: <τε>
τούτων Palmer, τ<οσ>ούτων Platt, τ<οι>ούτων Kenyon

40   ἀνδρῶν κρατερὸν σθένος
11 ἔσχεν; ἦ θεὸς αὐτὸν ὁρμᾶι,
      δίκας ἀδίκοισιν ὄφρα μήσεται·
13 οὐ γὰρ ῥάιδιον αἰὲν ἔρ-
      δοντα μὴ 'ντυχεῖν κακῶι.
45   15 πάντ' ἐν τῶι δολιχῶι χρόνωι τελεῖται.

            ——

Δ' <ΑΙΓ.>   1 Δύο οἱ φῶτε μόνους ἁμαρτεῖν
      λέγει, περὶ φαιδίμοισι δ' ὤμοις
      3 ξίφος ἔχειν <ἐλεφαντόκωπον>,
      ξεστοὺς δὲ δύ' ἐν χέρεσσ' ἄκοντας
col.9 50   5 κηΰτυκτον κυνέαν Λάκαι-
      ναν κρατὸς πέρι πυρσοχαίτου·
      χιτῶνα πορφύρεο̯ν
      8 στέρνοις τ' ἀμφί, καὶ οὔλιον
      9 Θεσσαλὰν χλαμύδ'· ὀμμάτων δὲ
55   στίλβειν ἄπο Λαμνίαν
      11 φοίνισσαν φλόγα· παῖδα δ' ἔμ<μ>εν
      πρώθηβον, ἀρηΐων δ' ἀθυρμάτων
      13 μεμνᾶσθαι πολέμου τε καὶ
      χαλκεοκτύπου μάχας·
60   15 δίζησθαι δὲ φιλαγλάους Ἀθάνας.

19 = dith. 5

ΙΩ ΑΘΗΝΑΙΟΙΣ

metrum: v. pp. 15–16

48 suppl. Desrousseaux   **51** ΥΠΕΡ: Blass   **60** Δ *vacat* ΦΙΛ. **A**, ΙΖΗΣΘΑΙ ΔΕ suppl. **A**³

5 ‿–‿‿–‿‿–?

‿–‿‿–‿‿– |

‿–‿–‿–– |

8 –––‿‿–‿‿-

– ‿‿–‿–‿‿ |

–‿–‿–– |

11 ––‿‿–‿–‿–? |

‿–‿–‿–‿ᵕ |

13 ‿–‿‿–‿‿–‿

–‿–‿–‿– ‖?

15? ᵕᵛ–‿‿–‿–‿–‿ |

–‿–‿–– ‖

17 ––‿‿–‿–‿–‿–ᵕ |

–‿–‿‿–‿–‿– ‖‖

––‿–‿–[

‿‿‿–‿[

7 ‿–‿–‿[‿–

‿‿‿–‿–[

‿––‿–[

10 ‿–‿‿–‿‿[–

‿–‿‿–[

––‿‿[–

13 –‿–‿–[

––‿‿–‿[

–‿–‿‿[– . . . ‖‖‖

       Πάρεστι μυρία κέλευθος

       ἀμβροσίων μελέων,

       ὃς ἂν παρὰ Πιερίδων λά-

       χησι δῶρα Μουσᾶν,

5   ἰοβλέφαροί τε κ<όρ>αι

       φερεστέφανοι Χάριτες

       βάλωσιν ἀμφὶ τιμάν

       ὕμνοισιν· ὕφαινέ νῦν ἐν

       ταῖς πολυηράτοις τι καινὸν

10   ὀλβίαις Ἀθάναις,

       εὐαίνετε Κηΐα μέριμνα.

       πρέπει σε φερτάταν ἴμεν

       ὁδὸν παρὰ Καλλιόπας λα-

       χοῖσαν ἔξοχον γέρας.

15   †τιην† Ἄργος ὅθ᾽ ἵππιον λιποῦσα

       φεῦγε χρυσέα βοῦς,

19   **5** ΤΕ ΚΑΙ: Erbse   **9** ΚΑΙΝΟΝ **A**: ΚΛᴱΙΝΟΝ A³   **15** ΤΙΗΝ dubium: ἦεν Headlam, ἦν ποτ᾽ Kenyon, ἦ ποτ᾽ Maehler

εὐρυσθενέος φραδαῖσι φερτάτου Διός,
Ἰνάχου ῥοδοδάκτυλος κόρα,

—

1 <τ>ότ᾽ Ἄργον ὄμμασι βλέποντα

20   πάντοθεν ἀκαμάτοις

3 μεγιστοάνασσα κέλευσε
    χρυσόπεπλος Ἥρα

5 ἄκοιτον ἄϋπνον ἐόν-
    τα καλλικέραν δάμαλιν

25   φυλάσσεν· οὐδὲ Μαίας

8 υἱὸς δύνατ᾽ οὔτε κατ᾽ εὐ-
    φεγγέας ἀμέρας λαθεῖν νιν

col.10   οὔτε νύκτας ἀγγ[άς.

11 εἴτ᾽ οὖν γένετ᾽ ε[◡—◡—◡

30   ποδαρκέ᾽ ἄγγελο[ν Διός

13 κτανεῖν τότε [Γᾶς ◡◡—◡
    ὀβριμοσπόρου λ[ίθωι

15 Ἄργον· ἦ ῥα κᾶι ο[◡—◡—◡
    ἄσπετοι μέριμν[αι·

35   17 ἢ Πιερίδες φύτευ[σαν —◡—◡×
    καδέων ἀνάπαυσ[ιν —◡×

1 ἐμοὶ μὲν οὖν
    ἀσφαλέστατον ἃ προ[
    ἐπεὶ παρ᾽ ἀνθεμώ[δεα

40   4 Νεῖλον ἀφίκετ᾽ ο[ἰστροπλὰξ
    Ἰὼ φέρουσα παῖδ[α . . .
    Ἔπαφον· ἔνθα νι[ν

7 λινοστόλων πρύτ[ανιν . . .
    ὑπερόχωι βρύοντ[α τιμᾶι

45   μεγίσταν τε θνατ[. . .

19 ΟΤ: Kenyon   **31** Γᾶς Jebb, τέκος αἰνόν Snell   **32** λ[ίθωι Deubner
35 ἀδύμωι μέλει Jebb   **36** ἀνάπαυσ[ιν ἐσχάταν e.g. Maehler   **38** ΑΠΡΟ[
(vel Ε[): ἃ πρέ[πει λέγειν e.g. Maehler   **40** ο[ἰστροπλάξ Blass, Festa
44 Blass   **45** θνατ[ῶν ἔφανεν γενέθλαν Jebb

10 ὅθεν καὶ Ἀγανορί[δας
ἐν ἑπταπύλοισ[ι Θήβαις
Κάδμος Σεμέλ[αν φύτευσεν,
13 ἃ τὸν ὀρσιβάκχα[ν
50 τίκτε<ν> Διόνυσον [ἀγλαῶν ἀγώνων
καὶ χορῶν στεφαν[αφόρων ἄνακτα.

20 = dith. 6

ΙΔΑΣ ΛΑΚΕΔΑΙΜΟΝΙΟΙΣ

metrum: dactyloepitr.

Σπάρτᾱι ποτ' ἐν ε[ὐρυχόρωι
ξανθαὶ Λακεδα[ιμονίων
τοιόνδε μέλος κ[ελάδησαν παρθένοι,
ὅτ' ἄγετο καλλιπά[ρᾱιον
5 κόραν θρασυκάρδ[ιος Ἴδας
Μάρπησσαν ἰότ[ριχα νύμφαν
φυγὼν θανάτου τ[. . . .
ἀναξίαλος Ποσ<ε>ι[δὰν . . . .
? —
ἵππους τέ οἱ ἰσαν[έμους
10 Πλευρῶν' ἐς ἐϋκτ[ιμέναν
χρυσάσπιδος υἱὸ[ν Ἄρηος
(desunt reliqua)

47-48 Jebb   **50** West, ἀγλαῶν τε κώμων Jurenka   **51** Wilamowitz
20   **1** Rossbach, Platt   **2** Wilamowitz   **3** κ[ελάδησαν Maas   **4** Blass,
Platt   **5** Kenyon   **6** ἰότ[ριχα Jebb   **9-10** Kenyon   **11** Sandys,
Reinach

ΠΑΙΑΝ

fr. 22 + fr. 4

[ΑΠΟΛΛΩΝΙ ΠΥΘΑΙΕΙ ΕΙΣ ΑΣΙΝΗΝ]

metrum: dactyloepitr.

ΣΤΡ

——◡——◡—	
——◡◡—◡◡——	−E–D– |
3 —◡——◡——◡—	E– e ||
—◡◡—◡◡——	D – |
—◡——◡——◡—	E – e ||
6 —◡———◡——	E– |
—◡◡—◡◡—	D|
——◡——◡—	– E|
9 —◡◡—◡——◡——	D– e – |
—◡——◡——	E – |||

ΕΠ

—◡◡—◡◡—	
——◡——◡◡—◡—	D – e – D||
3 —◡◡—◡◡—	D |
——◡——◡———◡——	– E – e – |
—◡——◡——	E – |
6 —◡◡—◡◡—	
——◡————◡—[–]	D – E[–] |
[——]◡◡—◡◡—[	[–] D [
9 [——]◡◡—[◡◡– ?	[–] D [
[———◡]———[◡– ?	[–] E [|||

Α'?   (desunt stropha et antistropha = vv.1–20)

(Ἡρακλῆς) ἦλθεν ἐπὶ τὸν Κήυκος οἶκον,

21   στᾶ δ' ἐπὶ λάϊνον οὐ-
  δόν, τοὶ δὲ θοίνας ἔντυον, ὧδέ τ' ἔφα·
3 "αὐτόματοι δ' ἀγαθῶν
  <ἐς> δαῖτας εὐόχθους ἐπέρχονται δίκαιοι

22+4 21–25 Athen. 5.178b (= fr.22)   **21** ἔστη: Barrett   **22** ἔντυνον: Neue |
ἔφασ': Neue   **24** <ἐς> Barrett

25 φῶτες.'' — — — ◡ — —
    (desunt epodi versus 6–10,
    incertum an desit trias tota,
Β´?   desunt strophae versus 1–8)
    9 — ◡ ◡ — ◡]τα Πυθω[— ◡ — —
40 — ◡ — —]ε̣ι̣ τελευτ̣[–

    ———

(.) ......]κέλευσεν Φοῖβος [Ἀλ-
κμήνας] πολεμαίνετον υ[ἱόν
3 στέλλεν] ἐκ ναοῦ τε καὶ παρ[— ◡ — ·
ἀλλ' ὅ γε τᾶ]ιδ' ἐνὶ χώρᾱ<ι>
45 (.) ....]χισεν ταν φυλλο.[
    6 (.) .... στ]ρέ̣ψας ἐλαίας
    (.) ....]φ' Ἀσινεῖς
    (.) ....]λεσσ̄' · ἐν δὲ χρόν[ωι
    9 (.) ......]ες ἐξ αλικων τε.[— ◡ — —
50 μάντι]ς ἐξ Ἄργευς Μελάμ[πους

    ———

    ἦλ]θ' Ἀμυθαονίδας
    βω]μόν τε Πυθα<ι>εῖ κτίσε[— ◡ ◡ —
    3 καὶ] τέμενος ζάθε̣ον·
    τοί]ας ἀπὸ ῥίζας τόδε χρ[— — ◡ — —
55 ἐξό]χως τίμασ' Ἀπόλλων
    6 ἄλσο]ς, ἵν' ἀγλαῖαι
    τ' ἀνθ]εῦσι̣ καὶ μολπαὶ λίγ[ειαι
    (.) ......]ονε̣ς, ὦ ἄνα, τ. .[
    9 (.) ......]τι σὺ δ' ὀλ[β
60 (.) ......].αιοισιν
)———

39–70 pap. **T**   **41** κείνους] Barrett, πάντας] Snell, ὡς τοὺς] Maehler   **41–42** Barrett   **42** υ[ἱόν Edmonds   **43** Παρ[νασσίας vel παρ' [ὀμφαλοῦ Barrett   **44** Snell   **46** Barrett   **47** ἠδ' ἐτέως Snell   **47–48** σ]φ' Ἀσινεῖς [εὖντας κά]λεσσ' Lobel   **50** Snell   **51** Edmonds   **52** βω]μόν Blass   **53** Blass   **54** τοί]ας Snell | χρ[ησμωιδὸν Barrett αὔξων Maehler   **55** ἐξό]χως Blass   **56** Snell   **57** in. Barrett | fin. Blass   **59** ὀλ[βον ὀπάζοις Snell

Γ′ ?

τίκτει δέ τε⌋ θνατ⌊οῖσιν εἰρήνα μεγαλ⌋άνορα ⌊πλοῦτον
3 καὶ μελιγλώ⌋σσων ἀ⌊οιδᾶν ἄνθεα
δαιδαλέων τ⌋ ἐπὶ βω⌊μῶν
65 θε⌊ρ⌋ῖσιν αἴθε⌋σθαι βο⌊ῶν ξανθᾶι φλογί
6 μηρί᾽ εὐ]μάλ⌋λων τε ⌊μήλων
γυμνασίω⌋ν τε νέοι⌊ς
αὐλῶν τε καὶ⌋ κώμω⌊ν μέλειν.
9 ἐν δὲ σιδαρο⌋δέτοις ⌊πόρπαξιν αἰθᾶν
70 ἀρ⌊α⌋χνᾶν ἱστ⌋οὶ πέλ ⌊ονται,

_____

ἔγχε⌊α⌋ τε λογχωτὰ ξίφε⌊α⌋
τ᾽ ἀμφάκεα δάμναται εὐρώς.
3 <−◡−−−◡−−−◡ −
      −◡◡−◡◡−−>
75 χαλκεᾶν δ᾽ οὐκ ἔστι σαλπίγγων κτύπος,
6 οὐδὲ συλᾶται μελίφρων
ὕπνος ἀπὸ βλεφάρων
ἀῶιος ὃς θάλπει κέαρ.
9 συμποσίων δ᾽ ἐρατῶν βρίθοντ᾽ ἀγυιαί,
80 παιδικοί θ᾽ ὕμνοι φλέγονται.
(deest epodus: versus 81–90)

61–80 Stob.*Flor.* 4.14.3 (= fr.4)   **66** μηρίταν εὐτρίχων Stob.: Barrett   **69–77**
Plut. *Num.* 20.6   **75** χαλκέων δ᾽ οὐκέτι Stob.: οὐκ ἔστι Plut.   **78** ἅμος (ἄμος)
Stob.: Blass

ΠΡΟΣΟΔΙΟΝ

fr. 11 + fr. 12

metrum: aeolicum

— ◡ — ◡ — ◡ — ◡ — ◡◡ — ◡ — |	*2 tr gl* |
— ◡ — ◡◡ — ◡ — — ◡◡ — |	*gl cho* |
◡ ◡ ◡ — ◡ ◡ — ◡ — ≍◡ — ◡◡ — ◡ — ||	*2gl* ||
5 ≍≍◡ — — ◡ <—>— ◡ — — — |	*3cr sp* ? |
◡ ◡ — ◡ ◡ — ◡ — |	∧*gl* ? |
◡ ◡ ◡ — ◡ ◡ — ◡ — |	*gl* |

(11)   εἷς ὅρος, μία βροτοῖσίν ἐστιν εὐτυχίας ὁδός,
        θυμὸν εἴ τις ἔχων ἀπενθῆ δύναται
    3 διατελεῖν βίον· ὃς δὲ μυ-
        ρία μὲν ἀμφιπολεῖ φρενί,
5   τὸ δὲ παρ' ἆμάρ τε <καὶ> νύκτα μελλόντων
    6 χάριν αἰὲν ἰάπτεται
        κέαρ, ἄκαρπον ἔχει πόνον.

      . . . .

(12)   3 τί γὰρ ἐλαφρὸν ἔτ' ἐστὶν ἄ-
        πρακτ' ὀδυρόμενον δονεῖν
        καρδίαν;

11 Stob. *Flor.* 4.44.5 \| **12** Stob. *Flor.* 4.44.46

ΕΓΚΩΜΙΑ (?)

fr. 20A

metrum: glyconei et ionici (v. p. 16)

```
1 ᵕᵕ—–ᵕᵕ——          ion ion
   ᵕᵕ–ᵕ–ᵕ——          anacl
3   ᵕᵕ——ᵕᵕ— |        ion ion∧ |
4 ———ᵕᵕ—ᵕ—ᵛ—ᵕ—       gl ia |
5 ———ᵕᵕ—ᵕ—            gl
   ———ᵕᵕ—ᵕ——ᵕ——— ||   gl ia ||||
```

A′?

```
      ᵕᵕ——ᵕᵕ——

      ᵕᵕ–ᵕ–ᵕ——

3     ᵕᵕ——ᵕᵕ—
   ———ᵕᵕ—ᵕ—      κ]αθημένη
5    ].ọ[.]..[      ᵛ]μας
   –––] καὶ ὑπέρ[μορ᾿ ἄχθε]ται πατρί,
   <—>
```

col.2? B′?

```
       ἰκ[ε]τεύει δὲ καμ[ — —
       χ[θ]ονίας τάλαι[ν᾿ Ἀρὰς] ọ-
       ξ[ύ]τερόν νιν τελ[έσαι
10     γῆρας καὶ κατάρατ[ον . . . . . . . . . . ]ν
       μούνην ἔνδον ἔχω[ν ᵕ —
       λε]υκαὶ δ᾿ ἐν [κ]εφαλ[ῆι . . . . . . . . τ]ρίχες.
   <—>
```

Γ′

```
       Ἄρ]εος χρυσολόφου παῖ[-
       δα] λέγουσι χαλκ{ε}ομίτραν
15     τα]νυπέπλοιο κόρης
       Εὐ]εạνὸ[ν] θρασύχειρα καὶ μιαι[φόνο]ν
       Μ]αρπήσσης καλυκώπιδος
       τοι]οῦτον πατέρ᾿ ἔμμεν᾿· ἀλλά γ[ιν] χρόνος
   <—>
```

20A   5 δέ]μας Snell   6 Snell   7 κα[μόντων vel κα[λοῦσα Maas, κα[μοῦσα
Snell   8–9 Maas   13 Ἀρ]εος Snell   13–14 Maas, Snell   15–16 Hunt

Δ' ἐδά]μασσε κρατερά τ' ἐκ-
  20 δόμεν ο]ὺ θέλοντ' ἀνάγκη.
    ⏑⏑ — —]ελίου
    — — —⏑⏑]εν Ποσειδαωνίας
    ἵππους ὠκυδρόμ]ας ἐλαύ-
    νων Ἴδας Ἀφάρ]ητος ὄλβιον τέκος.
    <—>
Ε' 25 ἐθέλουσαν δ]ὲ κόρην ἥρ-
    πασεν εὐέθει]ραν ἥρως·
    (sequuntur XXVI versuum fragmenta)

fr. 20B

col.5? [ΑΛΕΞΑ]Ν[ΔΡΩΙ ΑΜΥΝΤ]Α

metrum: dactyloepitr.

  — —⏑⏑ —⏑⏑ —⏛—⏑⏑ — —   —D ⏛ e— ‖
  —⏑⏑ —⏑⏑ —⏛—⏑ — —   D ⏛ e — |
3 —⏑⏑ —⏑⏑ —⏛—⏑⏑—   D ⏛ e — |
  —⏑ — — —⏑ — — —⏑ —   E— e ‖‖

Α' Ὦ βάρβιτε, μηκέτι πάσσαλον φυλάσ̣ [σων
    ἑπτάτονον λ[ι]γυρὰν κάππαυε γᾶρυν·
    δεῦρ' ἐς ἐμὰς χέρας· ὁρμαίνω τι πέμπ[ειν
    χρύσεον Μουσᾶν Ἀλεξάνδρωι πτερόν
    <—>
Β' 5 καὶ συμποσ[ίαι]σιν ἄγαλμ' [ἐν] εἰκάδεσ[σιν,
    εὖτε νέων ἁ[παλὸν]ˌ γλύκει' ἀˌνάγκα
    σευομενᾶν κˌυλίκων θάλπηˌσι θυμˌόν
    Κύπριδός τ' ἐλπˌ ὶς δ<ι>αιθύσσηι φρέˌνας,
    <—>

19 ἐδά]μασσε Hunt **19–20** ἐκ[δόμεν Maehler **22** τέλλοντος
πέλασ]εν Snell **23–24** ἵππους ὠκυδρόμ]ας ἐλαύ[νων Snell Ἴδας
Ἀφάρ]ητος Maas **25** Maas **26** ἥρ[πασε Hunt εὐέθει]ραν Maas
20B **6–16** Athen. Epit. 2.39e–f **6** Maas **8** δ' αἰθύσσει Athen.: Blass

Γ′
      ἀμμειγνυμέν⌊α Διονυσίοισι⌋ δώροις·
10   ἀνδράσι δ᾽ ὑψο⌊τάτω πέμπει⌋ μερίμν⌊ας
      αὐτίκ⌊α⌋ μὲν π⌊ολίων κράδ⌋εμνα ⌊λύει,
      πᾶσ⌊ι δ᾽ ἀνθρώποις μοναρ⌋χήσ⌊ειν δοκεῖ·
      <—>

Δ′
      χρυ⌊σ⌋ῶ⌊ι δ᾽ ἐλέφαντί τε μαρμ⌋αίρ⌊ουσιν οἶκοι,
      πυροφ⌊όροι δὲ κατ᾽ αἰγλάεντ⌋α πό⌊ντον
15   νᾶες ἄγο⌊υσιν ἀπ᾽ Αἰγύπτου μέγιστον
      πλοῦτον· ὡς ⌊πίνοντος ὁρμαίνει κέαρ.
      <—>

Ε′
      ὦ π[α]ῖ μεγαλ[. . . . .]υ[⌣ – Ἀμύντα
   . . .]ϙουπ[. . . . .]ον[
   . . . .]λάχ[ον·] τί γὰρ ἀνθρώ[ποισι μεῖζον
20   κέρδο]ς ἢ θυμῶι χαρίζε[σθα]ι κ[αλά
      <—>

      (sequuntur XII versuum fragmenta)

fr. 20C

col.7?   [Ι]ΕΡΩΝΙ [ΣΥ]ΡΑΚΟΣΙΩΙ

     metrum: dactyloepitr.

      — — ⌣ ⌣ – ⌣ ⌣ — —
      — ⌣ — — — ⌣ — — [– ⌣ — —   –D – E – [e –] |
3 — ⌣ — — — ⌣ ⌣ – [⌣ ⌣ –
      ⌣̣ — ⌣ — —   e – D ⌣̣ e – |
      — ⌣ ⌣ — ⌣ ⌣ —   D ‖
6 — — ⌣ — — — ⌣ – [–   – E [– ?] ‖‖

Α′
      Μήπω λιγυαχέ̣[α κοίμα
         βάρβιτον· μέλλ[ω πολυφθόγγων τι καινόν
      ἄνθεμον Μουσᾶ[ν Ἱ]έρων[ί τε καὶ
      ξα̣νθαῖσιν ἵπποις

20B **9** ἄ μειγνυμεν[P, ἀναμιγνυμένα Athen.: Dindorf   **17** μεγαλ[οκλεὲς]
ὑ[ψαυχέο̣ς Snell, Ἀμύντα Maas   **19–20** Snell
20C **1** Maas   **2** Snell   **3** τε καὶ Maas

5   ἱμ]ερόεν τελέσας
    κα]ὶ συμπόταις ἄνδρεσσι π[έμπειν
    <—>

Β′ Αἴ]τναν ἐς ἐΰκτιτον εἰ κ[αὶ
      πρ]όσθεν ὑμνήσας τὸν [ἐν Κίρρᾱι θ᾽ ἑλόντα
      πο]σσὶ λαιψ[η]ρο[ῖ]ς Φερ[ένικον ἐπ᾽ Ἀλ-
10   φ[ε]ῶι τε ν[ί]καν
    ἀν[δ]ρ[ὶ χ]αριζόμενος
    ει [. . . . . . .]εανερ[– ◡ – –
    <—>

Γ′ . ᾽[. . . σὺν] ἐμοὶ τότε κοῦραί [
      τ᾽ ἠΐθεοί θ᾽] ὅσσοι Διὸς πάγχρ[υσον ἄλσος
15 πᾶν βρύειν κώ]μο[ι]ς τίθεσαν μ[◡ ◡ –
    . . . . .]ερειπε[
    ὅστι]ς ἐπιχθονίων
    . . .]ω τὸ μὴ δειλῶι . υναι[–
    <—>

Δ′ τέχν]αι γε μέν εἰσ[ι]ν ἅπα[σαι
20   μυρία]ι· σὺν θεῶι δὲ θ[α]ρσήσας πιφαύσκω·
    οὔτι]ν᾽ ἀνθρώπων ἕ[τερον καθορᾶι
      λε[ύκι]ππος Ἀώς
    τόσσ[ο]ν ἐφ᾽ ἁλικία[ι
24 φέγγος κατ᾽ ἀνθρώπ[ους φέρουσα
    <—>

    (sequuntur xiv versuum fragmenta)

8 [ἐν Κίρρᾱι Barrett, θ᾽ ἑλόντα Snell   13–15 Snell   17 Maas   19 ΕΙΣ [Ι]Ν vel
ΕΙΕΝ possis   20 Maas   21 οὔτι]ν᾽ H.Fränkel, ἕ[τερον καθορᾶι Schadewaldt
24 Snell, κατ᾽ ἀνθρώπ[ων χέοντα Maas

fr. 20D

metrum: dactyloepitr.

—◡— —◡ ◡— [◡ ◡— (– ?)	e – D (–?)
— —◡— — —◡ [— —	– E [–]
3 — —◡ ◡—◡ ◡— [	– D [ ]
— —◡ ◡—◡ ◡— — —[	– D — — [
—◡— — —◡ ◡—◡ [◡—	e – D	
6—◡ ◡—◡ ◡— — —	
◡ ◡— — — —◡ ◡ —◡ ◡— —	D – dᴵ – D ◡	
—◡— — —◡— — [—◡— (– ?)	E – [e (–?) ||||

col.ι v.ι]   ].οις
            (desunt cetera huius columnae = vv. non minus
                xxvιιι)
col.2   .όθεν εὐειδὴς ἄλοχος .[◡ ◡— —
            λοισθίαν ὥρμασεν Οἰν[— —◡— (–)
            ⎯
            οὐδὲ τλαπενθὴς Νιόβα [◡ ◡— (–)
        5   τὰν ὤλεσαν Λατοῦς ἀγ[αυοὶ
            παῖδες δέκα τ᾽ ἠϊθέους δ[
            κο<ύ>ρας τανυάκεσιν ἰοῖς τᾱ[
            εἰσιδὼν ὑψίζυγος οὐραν[
            Ζεὺς ἐλέησεν ἀνακέστ[οις
        10 ἄχεσιν, θῆκέν τε νιν ὀκριόεντ[α
            λᾶαν ἄμπαυσέν τε δυστλάτ[—◡— (–)
            ⎯
            οὐδ[ ].ωπ[.] ε. [.] . . . γ ις
            (sequuntur vιι versuum fragmenta)

20D 2 Ι[, Π[, Μ[, Κ[sim. | 2–3 Π[άριος τὰν] λοισθίαν ὥρμασεν Οἰν[ώνα κέλευθον
Lobel, Μ[ελέαγρον] . . . Οἰν[είδαν Maehler   4 [γενεάν Lobel   5 ἀγ[αυοί
Snell   6 δ[έκ᾽ ἀγλαάς τε Maas, δ[αμάσαντες καὶ δέκα Snell   6–8 δ[έκα τ᾽
εὐπλόκους] . . . ἰοῖς·τὰ[ν δὲ πατὴρ] ἐ{ι}σιδὼν . . . οὐραν[όθεν Barrett   9 Lobel
ΙΙ δυστλάτ[ου πάθας Maas

COMMENTARY

VICTORY ODES

ODE 3: FOR HIERON OF SYRACUSE

1. Hieron's chariot victory at Olympia

The date is given by the *hypothesis* to Pindar's *First Olympian* (*Scholia* 1 p.16 Drachmann) as the 78th Olympiad = 468 BCE. After Hieron's death in the following year, his son, Deinomenes, dedicated a splendid monument consisting of a bronze four-horse chariot with charioteer, a work of the sculptor Onatas of Aegina, and of racehorses with jockeys on either side of it, made by the sculptor Kalamis (Paus. 8.42.9); the dedicatory inscription on the base reads:

Σόν ποτε νικήσας, Ζεῦ Ὀλύμπιε, σεμνὸν ἀγῶνα
τεθρίππωι μὲν ἅπαξ, μουνοκέλητι δὲ δίς,
δῶρ' Ἱέρων τάδε σοι ἐχαρίσσατο· παῖς δ' ἀνέθηκε
Δεινομένης πατρὸς μνῆμα Συρακοσίου.

Hieron won his first Olympic victory with his racehorse Pherenikos in 476, which was celebrated by Pindar's *Olympian* 1 and by B. 5, and his second in 472, attested in the list of Olympic victors *P.Oxy.* II 222 col. 1 32 for the 77th Olympiad: [Ιερ]ωνος Συρακοσιου κελης; but the crowning glory was his only Olympic chariot victory in 468.

Whether Hieron had travelled to Olympia in person to witness his chariot's victory seems doubtful, as he is said to have been suffering from some severe illness as early as 470, when Pindar, in his first *Pythian*, alludes to it by καμάτων ἐπίλασιν (*P.*1.46) and the example of Philoktetes (*P.* 1.50–1). The scholia (II p.17–18 Dr.) report, quoting Aristotle's *Constitution of Syracuse* fr. 587, that Hieron was suffering from a bladder or kidney disease (λιθουρία), cf. Plut. *Mor.* 403c Γέλων μὲν ὑδρωπιῶν, Ἱέρων δὲ λιθιῶν ἐτυράννησεν. This information is clearly not derived from Pindar's words; it must come from an independent source and therefore needs to be taken seriously. Kidney or bladder stones are painful, but they alone do not kill a man; there may have been another, more serious disease which was to kill Hieron in the following year, 467 BCE.

If this is correct, it seems reasonable to assume that Hieron probably knew about his condition and was aware that he might not have much

longer to live. This could be relevant to the question why B. chose the story
of the Lydian king Kroisos' calamity and salvation to be the centrepiece
of this ode, and why he made the parallel between Hieron and Kroisos so
obvious, for here the relevance of the mythical narrative to the person and
circumstances of the *laudandus* is made more explicit than anywhere else in
choral lyric.

2. The myth

The story of Kroisos on the pyre, which B. tells in this ode, was not – or
not entirely – his own invention. That it was known earlier is attested by
the amphora of Myson in Paris, dated 490–480 BCE (Louvre G 197; *ARV²*
238; Appendix no. 1) which shows the king on a richly decorated throne,
holding his sceptre and pouring a libation, on top of a large pyre which
is being lit by a servant. The bearded king wears a chiton, and a wreath
on his head; he is not represented as a captive, but seems to be fully in
control. He is certainly not characterized as an oriental or barbarian king;
his dress and hairstyle look Greek. On the amphora, the servant's name
is given as Ευθυμος. All these features match his characterization in B.
who seems to follow the same version as the vase-painter, Myson; the most
important element which they share is the king's autonomous decision to
commit suicide on the pyre, and the absence of the victorious Persians
from this scene. It is Kroisos himself who orders the pyre to be heaped, he
mounts it of his own free will and orders the servant to set fire to it. In B.,
as on the Myson amphora, the king's resolve to end his life with dignity
and before enduring slavery shows him in a heroic light; his gesture on the
amphora, where he holds the libation bowl in his right hand, suggests a
prayer, obviously not for his salvation but perhaps, on the contrary, for a
quick death (cf. B. 3.47 θανεῖν γλύκιστον).

The wife and daughters do not appear on the amphora. If they formed
part of the original story, the vase-painter may have omitted them in order
not to distract from the impressive figure of the king on his throne. Alternatively, they may have been invented by B. to provide a contrast between
their panic and despair and the king's heroic but selfish solitude. In either
case it is evident that Myson and B. reflect essentially the same story which
contrasts sharply with the later version, first found in Herodotos (1.86–7)
and repeated by many later authors (Xenophon, *Cyr.* 7.2; Ktesias *FGrHist*

688 F 9; Nikolaos Damasc. *FGrHist* 90 F 68; Diodoros 9.2 and 9.34, from Ephoros?).

In Herodotos' version, Kroisos has lost all visible insignia of royal power. 'Indeed, this stripping of external goods is the prerequisite to the loss of delusions and the acquisition of a truer ... inward wisdom' (Segal 1971: 42). He is in fetters and at the Persians' mercy; events are no longer controlled by him but by Kyros, who orders the pyre to be lit, because he wants to see whether a god will rescue his prisoner (1.86.2). In that situation Kroisos remembers what Solon once said to him, and with a deep groan calls his name three times. Kyros apparently believes this to be an invocation of some god and enquires, through interpreters, whom he is calling, where-upon Kroisos, after a long silence, tells him about his encounter with Solon, for he had realized that Solon's statement 'With all things one must consider the outcome; for having given a glimpse of happiness to many, god utterly destroyed them' (σκοπέειν δὲ χρὴ παντὸς χρήματος τὴν τελευτήν, κῆι ἀποβήσεται· πολλοῖσι γὰρ δὴ ὑποδέξας ὄλβον ὁ θεὸς προρρίζους ἀνέ-τρεψε, 1.32.9) applies to himself as much as it applies to all humans. Kyros, too, understands the implication for himself and changes his mind, when the flames are already licking at the edges of the pyre. This is the dramatic climax of the scene. Kyros orders his men to quench the fire and to bring Kroisos 'and those with him' (Κροῖσόν τε καὶ τοὺς μετὰ Κροίσου, 1.86.6) down; when they fail to put the fire out, Kroisos invokes Apollo, remind-ing him of the gifts he had sent him, with tears (δακρύοντα, 1.87.1) – his composure is gone, he is distraught as he sees the sudden glimmer of hope which Kyros' 'change of heart' (μετάγνωσις) had offered him, disappear.

Kroisos is saved by a god who puts out the flames with a sudden rain-storm – on this, and on the reference to Kroisos' gifts to Apollo, Herodotos' version agrees with that of B. But while in Hdt. he is saved by Apollo alone, in B. the whole scene is orchestrated by Apollo and Zeus, who jointly set it in motion (Ζηνὸς τελέ[σσαντος κρί]σιν ... Κροῖσον ... φύλαξ᾽ Ἀπόλλων, 26–9) and jointly rescue Kroisos: Zeus quenches the fire, Apollo takes Kroisos and his daughters away to the Hyperboreans (55–60).

In all other respects, however, the two versions are fundamentally dif-ferent, especially in the way Kroisos is portrayed. It therefore seems very unlikely that B. was the source of Herodotos' story, which conveys the mes-sage, familiar from Attic tragedy, that mortals learn through suffering (πάθει μάθος, Aesch. *Ag.* 177). In fact, it appears that in the first half of the fifth

century there was a tragedy about Kroisos which inspired the painter of
an Attic hydria of *c.* 470–450 BCE (Appendix no. 2), the fragments of which
were published by Beazley 1955 pl.85 (*ARV*² 571.74; cf. Page 1962: 47–9;
Snell 1973: 204). Its fragment A shows the upper part of a man in oriental
costume and a Persian headdress (κίδαρις) with a staff in each hand; the
lower part of his body is concealed by a burning pyre (flames are shown in
red). The hand and wrist are also visible of a second man who is apparently helping the first to rise. Fr. B shows part of the pyre, also with flames.
Frs. C, D, and E show other men dressed as Orientals, fr. E, moreover, a
young Greek flute-player 'in the full-dress costume worn by αὐληταί on
the concert-platform, at athletic contests, or in the theatre' (Beazley 1955:
308). Page convincingly concluded (1) that this scene represented a tragedy
of roughly Aeschylean date 'on the fall of the royal house of Lydia' and
(2) that it must be part of a trilogy on this subject, to which, presumably, the
fragment of a play on Gyges (*P.Oxy.* XXIII 2382 = Pack² 1707) also belonged:
'In a tragedy of that period, the crime of Gyges and the Queen will not have
been left unpunished: there must have been a sequel, in which retribution
overtook them or their family; and the obvious end of the story was the fall
of Croesus' (Page 1962: 49).

A 'Lydian' trilogy may well have been the source, or a source, of
Herodotos' account. The source that inspired the Myson amphora and
B. is, however, difficult to identify. Nothing is known about an epic version
of the story; there may have been an early (Ionic ?) prose version, but no
author can be named. The earliest known author of Λυδιακά is Xanthos
(*FGrHist* IIIC, 765) in the late fifth century; earlier ones must have existed,
because Hdt. repeatedly refers to οἱ Λυδοί for details of his account on
Lydian history (cf. Hdt. 1.87.1; 1.93.5; 1.94.1–3; 4.45.3, = *FGrHist* 768 F
5–8), but whether he is referring to oral or written accounts is disputed; see
F. Jacoby, 'Herodotos', *RE* Suppl.II 393–423. The first of those passages
where 'the Lydians' are quoted (λέγεται ὑπὸ Λυδῶν, 1.87.1) is the story of
Kroisos' rescue after invoking Apollo, which happens to be one of the few
details in which Hdt. and B. agree (cf. B. 3.38). This may suggest that a
prose version was in circulation in Athens at the time of the Persian Wars,
when this story would have been particularly relevant.

The message of the story is clear: as Apollo once saved Kroisos and took
him to the land of the Hyperboreans, so he will protect Hieron in his darkest
hour. It is possible that Hieron's views on life after death, the judgement
of the dead, and the Islands of the Blessed were similar to those of Theron

(cf. Pind. *O.* 2.68–83; see Zuntz, *Persephone* 85–7; Graf 1993: 239–58; on the close parallels between Orphic and Egyptian eschatology see Merkelbach 1999: 1–13 with bibliography). Whether or not Hieron shared these Orphic views and was hoping to be taken to the Islands of the Blessed, it is obvious from the way B. tells the story of Kroisos that he expected gratitude and help from Apollo in the face of death. If Hieron was conscious of death approaching, this story – as well as Apollo's advice to Admetos (78–84) and the prospect of lasting fame after death (90–8) – will have had a very personal significance for him.

3. Structure

The formal structure of this victory ode is simple. The mythical narrative, i.e. the story of Kroisos on the pyre, forms its central part in 40 lines; it is preceded by a relatively brief first passage of praise for Hieron and his victory (1–22) and followed by a longer second praise passage (63–99). Its parts, however, are constructed with great skill in such a way as to reveal a number of formal and conceptual correspondences between their individual elements, as the following analysis will explain.

The first part begins with an invocation of Kleio, the Muse who is most closely associated with praise (κλείειν, cf. Hes. *Th.* 67 and 77) and fame (κλέος). The first stanza, while formally distinct and characterized as a προοίμιον, is at the same time part of the first praise because it mentions, in Ὀλυμπιοδρόμους Ἱέρωνος ἵππους, the three most important data of the epinician 'programme': the place of the victory, the victor's name, and the contest; the fourth, the name of the victor's father, is added in the antistrophe (Δεινομένεος, 7). The first strophe and antistrophe consist of one sentence each, showing parallel structures in that each invokes two goddesses (Demeter and Kore, Nika and Aglaia), then the victory and the victor; they are linked by the last word of the strophe (ἵππ[ο]υς, 4), which is the subject of the antistrophe, thus achieving a smooth transition from the *prooimion* to the first praise.

There is also a conceptual link between the first three and the last three verses of the ode: the verb of the first stanza, ὕμνει, recurs in the *sphragis* at the end (ὑμνήσει, 97); also, the request addressed to Kleio to praise Hieron's horses is echoed by the statement at the end that the Muse 'nourishes' (τρέφει, 92) the fame of victory through the poet's song (χάριν, 97); the poet's epithet, μελιγλώσσου, echoes the Muse's, γλυκύδωρε (3).

These verbal and conceptual correspondences form a kind of frame for the ode.

The first epode begins with a statement (θρόησε δὲ λ[αός, 9) which, though formally still part of the description of the chariot race, introduces a new element which will form the transition to the second part of the first praise, i.e. the reaction of the spectators, or more generally the public. While line 9 refers to the spectators of the race at Olympia, lines 15–16 focus on the people of Syracuse and the public of the present performance. In between, and right in the middle of the first praise passage, stands the comment on the victor: ἃ τρισευδαίμων ἀνήρ (10), to whom Zeus has given power and who has used his wealth wisely. These two motifs, 'power' and 'wealth', relate to Zeus and Apollo who will then come into focus at the beginning and end of the mythical narrative, and again in the second praise passage, see below.

The transition from the first praise to the mythical narrative is made by the *gnome* θεὸν θ[εό]ν τις ἀγλαϊζέτω (21–2), which is echoed by Apollo's advice to Admetos (83–4). Both statements relate to the myth of Kroisos, which provides a particularly close parallel to the victor, Hieron.

The narrative section (23–62) has a symmetrical structure, analogous to the ode as a whole, its central part being Kroisos' speech (37–47), which is preceded and followed by the wailing of the daughters (33–5 and 49–51). The 'frame' of the Kroisos story is provided by the double intervention of the gods, which also shows a symmetrical structure in that Zeus' destruction of Sardis (25–7) is matched by his extinguishing the flames of the pyre (55–6), whereas Kroisos' rescue is attributed 'proleptically' to Apollo (28–9) and then presented as his transfer to the land of the Hyperboreans (58–60). The gods' intervention is thus neatly shared between Zeus and Apollo, and this is reflected in the prayer of Kroisos, who first addresses the 'almighty god' (ὑπέρβιε δαῖμον, 37–8) before he names Apollo (39). It seems likely that in the original version of the story Apollo was the dominant figure on the divine level, as he is in Herodotos' account, and that B. has reduced his role in order to give prominence to Zeus, who appears at the outset, in the centre and at the end of the story. This change was evidently dictated by the occasion of the ode, because the poet wanted to highlight the parallel between Kroisos and Hieron, whose Olympic victory was won in the games dedicated to Zeus.

The second praise passage, which occupies the last part of the ode, falls into three sections of unequal length. The first (63–71) takes up the themes of 'power' (Zeus) and 'generosity' (Apollo) from the first praise (10–14), but in reverse order, thus creating another symmetrical 'frame' for the narrative section. It is followed by a series of general statements or *gnomai* (72–84) which develop the idea that in view of the precariousness of the human condition, 'godfearing deeds' (in this context: generous donations to temples, such as Hieron's dedications to Delphi, and festivities in honour of the gods) yield the best 'profit' (κέρδος), being, so to speak, the most profitable investment (83–4). This is presented as a conclusion from the Kroisos story; it is also in line with the statement which introduced it, concluding the first praise (21–2). This idea ('generosity towards god pays dividends') thus provides the link between the first praise and the narrative section, which it connects with the second praise (61–6), from which it leads on to the final section (83–4). Here it is presented in direct speech, as Apollo's advice to Admetos, rather like the quotation from 'Hesiod' in 5.191–4: both quotations introduce the final dedication to the victor, Hieron.

The last triad contains the final section (85–98) which falls into two almost equal halves, the second of which (92 Ἱέρων . . .–98) recalls the *prooimion* through verbal repetitions. The two halves correspond in that the first combines the idea of wealth and generosity with that of lasting fame, which the second half then applies explicitly to Hieron. Here, too – as in the *prooimion* – the poet's skill in effecting smooth, 'gliding' transitions can be seen at its best: the final sequence of statements moves smoothly into the final *sphragis*; the ode, which the chorus had requested from the Muse (ὕμνει, γλυκύδωρε Κλεοῖ, 3) is here called the 'gift' (χάρις, 97) of the 'honey-tongued Kean nightingale' (μελιγλώσσου . . . Κηΐας ἀηδόνος).

4. Metre

Among the extant odes of B., this is the only one that combines an aeolic/iambic strophe with an epode in dactyloepitrites. (There is only one other example of such a combination in Greek choral lyric, Pindar's *O.* 13.) The strophe ends with ⏓–⏖–⏑⏑––, a 'hipponactean', and the epode begins with ⏓–⏑⏑–⏑⏑––, which at first appears as a slight variation (⏑⏑ for ⏑) of the preceding 'hipponactean'. But the following lines of the epode may be interpreted as dactyloepitrites, so that its first line will also be described as dactyloepitritic, i.e. as ⸗*D*– rather than *ₐpher^d*. However, lines 2–6 of the epode may also be analysed as 'iambic' (i.e., $^2cr\ ia$ ‖ $^3cr\ ia\ ^42ia$ ‖ $^5cr\ 2ia\ ^6cr$

ia ‖), so that the transition from the end of the epode to the first line of the strophe (*2ia ba* ‖) is not marked by any abrupt change in the metrical character. There is, however, a difference between strophe/antistrophe and epode as far as the rhythm is concerned: lines 2–6 of the epode contain no double *brevia* (apart from two cases of resolved *longum*, Ἀλυά[τ]τα 40 and ὅσια 83), their rhythm therefore appears to be slower and weightier, almost solemn, and this seems to be in keeping with the content of each of the seven epodes:

ep.1 address to Hieron, who received power and wealth from Zeus,

ep.2 Zeus destroys Sardis (beginning of narrative section),

ep.3 Kroisos' invocation of Zeus and Apollo (central part of narrative section),

ep.4 Zeus extinguishes the flames (dramatic climax),

ep.5 address to Hieron, who has wealth and power from Zeus,

ep.6 Apollo's advice,

ep.7 address to Hieron and *sphragis*.

In other words, each of the epodes either addresses Hieron, or refers to Zeus, Apollo, or both. The poet seems to have adapted the words to the rhythm of the music, not the other way round.

1–4 B. likes to begin his victory odes with invocations of the Muse or Muses (as he does in 1 and 12), to the Graces (9), Phema (2 and 10) and Nika (11). The Muse Kleio may also be addressed in 13.9. Her name implies her function (κλείειν, see West on Hes. *Th.* 76), which makes her particularly relevant to encomiastic poetry. In *AP* 9.504.2 she is even credited with the 'invention' (εὗρεν) of choral lyric: Κλειώ καλλιχόρου κιθάρης μελιηδέα μολπήν.

1 Ἀριστοκάρπου Σικελίας: the compound is found only here; it may have been coined by B., like ἀριστοπάτρα (11.106) and ἀρισταλκής (7.7), which are also ἅπαξ εἰρημένα. Sicily is praised for her abundance in grain by Pindar (ἀριστεύοισαν εὐκάρπου χθονὸς Σικελίαν πίειραν *N.* 1.14–15, cf. ἀγλαοκάρπου Σικελίας fr. 106.5–6 and εὐκάρποιο γαίας *P.* 1.30) and Aeschylus (τῆς καλλικάρπου Σικελίας *Prom.* 369).

2 ἰοστέφανον: goddesses are often called 'violet-garlanded', cf. B. 5.3 and Theognis 250 (the Muses), *h. Ven.* 175, *h. Hom.* 6.18 and Solon 19.4 (Kypris), B. 13.122 (Thetis); this may suggest that the compound originated in cult poetry.

3–4 θοάς . . . ἵππους: chariot horses tend to be stallions on vases and in sculpture, but mares in poetry. In Homer, however, both sexes compete in the funeral games for Patroklos (*Il.* 23.290 and 377 stallions, 295 mare and stallion, 376 and 392 mares); 'this . . . is a question not of sex but of <grammatical> gender (cf. esp. Soph. *El.*, where Orestes' team are fem. in the pl. (703f., 734f., 737f.) but its members masc. in the sing. (721f., 744)', Barrett on Eur. *Hipp.* 231. It is not clear why and how this convention has developed.

5–8   The formal correspondence between the first strophe and antistrophe is close: both name two goddesses, then refer to the victory and the victor (ʹΟ[λυμ]πιοδρόμους 4 ≈ [στεφάνω]ν κυρῆσαι 8); the connecting link is the horses, which are the object in 4 and the subject of 5–8.

5 σεύον]το (or ὄρνυν]το):   Kenyon preferred σεύοντο on account of the Pindaric parallels (*O.*1.20, *I.* 8.61, *Pai.* 9.5), but cf. B. 5.45 πρὸς τέλος ὀρνύμενον, of Hieron's racehorse Pherenikos.

γάρ: 'the explanatory particle . . . is a characteristic not only of prayer hymns . . . but also of hymns of praise', Bundy, *Studia Pindarica* 46, who also refers to B. 4.4 and Pind. *O.* 13.6.

σὺν ὑπερόχωι τε Νίκαι: the epithet implies that Victory grants 'supremacy' (ὑπερέχειν) over competitors. Instead of giving a vivid picture of the race, as he does in 5.37–49, B. quite briefly stresses the superiority of Hieron's horses. The sequence Νίκα – Ἀγλαΐα points to the link between the victory and the splendour of its celebration, which is also implied in the statement at the end, πράξα[ντι] δ᾽ εὖ οὐ φέρει κόσμ[ον σι]ωπά 94–96.

6 εὐρυδίναν: only here and 5.38, also of the Alpheios river. Three of B.'s compounds beginning with εὐρυ– are not found in other authors (εὐρυδίνας, εὐρυάναξ, εὐρυνεφής).

7–8 Δεινομένεος ἔθηκαν ὄλβιον τ[έκος στεφάνω]ν κυρῆσαι   'they made Deinomenes' son prosper, so that he won garlands'; the construction is not acc. + inf., but τιθέναι + double acc. (ὄλβιον is predicative) and consecutive inf. depending on ὄλβιος. For examples of consecutive infinitives depending on adjectives such as this, or ἐπιτήδειος, ἱκανός, τοῖος, οἷός τε etc., see Schwyzer ɪɪ 364; a close parallel to this construction is Pindar's statement in *P.* 9.6–8 that Apollo took Kyrene τόθι νιν . . . θῆκε δέσποιναν χθονὸς ῥίζαν ἀπείρου τρίταν . . . οἰκεῖν 'where he made her mistress of a land . . . to inhabit the . . . root of the third continent'.

9 θρόησε δὲ λ[αὸς ‿ – –: Blass' supplement ἀπείρων is based on 9.30 Ἑλλάνων δι᾽ ἀπ[εί]ρονα κύκλον, cf. *Il.* 24.776 ἐπὶ δ᾽ ἔστενε δῆμος ἀπείρων. Another possible supplement is Jebb's ἀγασθείς, cf. Pind. *P.* 4.238 ἴυξεν . . . δύνασιν Αἰήτας ἀγασθείς ('amazed', when Jason managed to yoke the bulls). B. refers to the spectators' reaction to the victory in 9.35 βοὰν ὤτρυνε λαῶν, following a detailed description of the contest; there, too, it is an element of the victor's praise.

10–14 ἅ τρισευδαίμ[ων ἀνήρ] . . . κρύπτειν σκότωι: is this passage (a) a comment by the chorus and/or the poet, or (b) by the admiring crowd? Line 9 might well serve as a formula introducing direct speech, for which [Hes.] fr. 211 would provide a close parallel. However, the calm description of the victor in lines 11–14 (ὃς . . . λαχὼν . . . οἶδε κτλ.) is very different from the noisy applause suggested by line 9, and lines 15–16 obviously refer to Syracuse where Hieron's success is being celebrated, which would seem odd if the preceding passage 10–14 were set at Olympia, in direct speech, as Führer, *Reden* 147 has pointed out.

11 παρὰ Ζηνός: again and again the poet emphasizes the roles of Zeus and Apollo: Zeus has given Hieron power, to Apollo Hieron has sent rich gifts (17–21), and this is reflected, in reverse order, in the second praise (64–71) which completes the 'frame' around the story of Kroisos on the pyre; on its structure, see above, pp. 83–5.

12 πλείσταρχον Ἑλλάνων γέρας 'the privilege of ruling over the greatest number of Greeks'; Kenyon drew attention to the language of the Greek envoys to Gelon, Hieron's elder brother and predecessor, in Hdt. 7.157 μοῖρά τοι τῆς Ἑλλάδος οὐκ ἐλαχίστη μέτα, ἄρχοντί γε Σικελίας. The epithet, πλείσταρχος, is found only here, although it occurs as a personal name in Hdt., Thuc. and later in inscriptions and papyri.

13–14 οἶδε . . . πλοῦτον μὴ . . . κρύπτειν: a variation of the 'generosity' motif, on which see Bundy, *Studia Pindarica* 89–90. Pindar, too, stresses the need to use wealth in order to secure fame, especially in victory odes for chariot races, cf. *N.* 1.31–2 and *I.* 1.67–8 and the parallels collected by Bundy 84–91. This motif recurs at the end of the ode where B. says that Hieron has displayed 'the most beautiful flowers of wealth, and when a man has prospered, adornment is not brought him by silence' (92–5).

μελαμφαρεῖ: only here and in the word-list *P.Hibeh* II 172.4 = *SH* 991, presumably from this line in B. (but cf. also *Hymn. Is.* 43–4 μελάμφαρόν τε βερέθρων . . . φυλακάν). Darkness (σκότος) is seen as wearing a black cloak; this is simply a metaphor for 'silence', 'being ignored' or 'forgotten', and has nothing to do with a shroud, as has been suggested (Townsend 1956: 75), for a φᾶρος used as a shroud is white, cf. *Il.* 18.353, *Od.* 24.148; the law on burials *IG* XII 5.593.2 requires θά[πτ]εν τὸν θανόντα ἐν ἐμ[α]τίο[ις τρ]ισὶ λευκοῖς, cf. Andronikos, *Totenkult* 9.

15–16 βρύει . . . ἀγυιαί: these two lines complete the description of the celebration in Syracuse; βρύειν + dat. = 'to teem with', + gen. = 'to be full of', as in fr. 4.79 συμποσίων . . . βρίθοντ᾽ἀγυιαί (on the meaning of ἀγυιαί, see on 11.58).

17–19 λάμπει δ(έ) . . . πάροιθε ναοῦ: this answers 15 βρύει μέν, marking the change of venue – the golden tripods are at Delphi, outside the temple. The bases of tripods dedicated by Hieron and his brothers are still *in situ* on the terrace near the entrance to the temple, *c.* 10 metres to the north of the altar (see Homolle 1897: 588–90; Courby, *La terrasse du temple* 249–51; Amandry 1987: 81–92 has seen that the base dedicated by Hieron's elder brother Gelon (from the spoils of the Deinomenids' victory over the Carthaginians at Himera in 480, = base A) cannot have carried a tripod but probably a bronze column which supported a plinth, or a capital, which in turn formed the base of a Victory with tripod. As Theopompos (quoted by Athen. 6.231f.) states that Hieron's monument was 'similar' (τοῦ δ᾽ Ἱέρωνος τὰ ὅμοια), it seems at least possible that his base (B) also supported a bronze column which carried a golden Victory statue and a tripod. The two bases are on the same level and closely aligned to one another; although their diameters differ slightly (base A: 144.6 cm, base B: 148 cm), the two monuments may have been of approximately the same height. That Hieron's tripod and Victory were made of pure gold (ἐξ ἀπέφθου χρυσοῦ) which his agents had acquired at Corinth is also attested by Theopompos (Athen. 6.232a–b); cf. Diod. 11.26.7.

17 ὑπὸ μαρμαρυγαῖς   is usually translated as a dative of attendant circumstances ('with flashing light'), but this seems unlikely: Kenyon rightly pointed out that 'it seems better to make τριπόδων dependent on μαρμαρυγαῖς than on χρυσός, since the former would stand rather awkwardly by itself'; his translation ('the splendour of gold flashes forth from the radiance of the . . . tripods') implies that 'under' the quivering gleam of the tripods which are reflecting the sunlight, the gold shines forth: the image would be similar to those evoked by Philostr., *VS* 2.1.14 χρυσοῦ ψῆγμα ποταμῶι ἀργυροδίνηι ὑπαυγάζον and Oppian, *C.* 1.420–1 πυρόεντες | ὀφθαλμοὶ χαροπαῖσιν ὑποστίλβοντες ὀπωπαῖς, cf. Ap.Rhod. 3.1300–1 φῦσαι . . . ἀναμαρμαίρουσιν | πῦρ . . . πιμπρᾶσαι (see Campbell 1982: 16).

18 ὑψιδαιδάλτων: not 'deep-chased' (Kenyon), as compounds beginning with ὑψ- tend to suggest something high or tall; so here perhaps 'high and richly wrought' (LSJ). Alternatively, it may mean 'decorated at the top': large bronze vessels, at any rate, of the late sixth and the fifth centuries tend to have sophisticated decoration, such as separately cast figures or friezes, on the shoulders or neck; the most spectacular of these is the crater from Vix, now in Châtillon-sur-Seine (Joffroy, *Le trésor de Vix*; Richter, *Handbook of Greek Art* 215–16, figs. 302 and 303; Appendix no. 3) see also the two craters from Trebenishte: Joffroy pll. 19–21.

21–2 θεὸν θ[εό]ν τις: the repetition was common in ritual invocations, cf. Diagoras *PMG* 738.1, Aesch. *Th.* 566, Eur. *HF* 772 and *Andr.* 1031; Hsch. θ 300 θεός, θεός· ἔθος ἦν, ὅτε κατάρχοιντό τινος, λέγειν θεὸν ἐπιφημιζομένοις.

ἀγλαϊζέθὼ = ἀγλαϊζέτω· ὁ: *synekphonesis*, as in Sappho 1.11 ὠράνωἴθερος = ὠράνω αἴθερος, cf. Schwyzer I 401–4; Lobel, Σαπφοῦς μέλη p. lxii.

22 ἄριστος ὄλβων: this kind of partitive genitive recurs at 3.52 and 83–4, cf. Eur. fr. 137 τῶν γὰρ πλούτων ὅδ᾽ ἄριστος γενναῖον λέχος εὑρεῖν.

23–62 The narrative section centres on the story of the fall and rescue of Kroisos, which B. presents as a close parallel to Hieron's relation with Delphi. On its structure see above, p. 84.

23–9 ἐπεί ποτε . . . φύλαξ Ἀπόλλων: the account of Kroisos' fall and rescue is presented as illustration of the statement that to honour god is the best <guarantee of> prosperity (ὄλβος). The events are set in motion by Zeus and Apollo, who also bring them to a conclusion (55–60), Zeus playing the more active part, while Apollo protects and eventually removes his protégé.

23–4 δαμασίππου Λυδίας: the compound stresses the parallel between the king of 'horse-taming Lydia' and Hieron's 'hippic' victory. The Lydians were famous for their horsemanship, cf. Mimn. 14.3 Λυδῶν ἱππομάχων and Hdt. 1.79.3 who says that in the time of Kroisos there were no better fighters on horseback in Asia Minor than the Lydians.

24–8 Λυδίας ἀρχαγέταν . . . Κροῖσον: this type of anticipated apposition occurs several times in Solon, cf. 1.21–2 θεῶν ἕδος . . . οὐρανόν, 1.57–8 Παιῶνος . . . ἔργον ἔχοντες | ἰητροί, 2.2 κόσμον ἐπέων ὠιδήν.

26 Ζηνὸς τελέ[σσαντος κρί]σιν: κρί]σιν (Weil) would be Zeus' 'decision' to destroy Sardis, cf. Aesch. Ag. 1288 ἐν θεῶν κρίσει (the destruction of Troy), Pindar, fr. 131b.4 τερπνῶν ἐφέρποισαν χαλεπῶν τε κρίσιν. τί]σιν (Sandys), which might fit marginally better into the lacuna, would imply the notion that Kroisos' fall was vengeance for Gyges' crime in the fifth generation after him, counting inclusively: ἐπεῖπε ἡ Πυθίη ὡς Ἡρακλείδηισι τίσις ἥξει ἐς τὸν πέμπτον ἀπόγονον Γύγεω Hdt. 1.13.2, cf. 1.91.1. Whether B. was aware of this version is uncertain, and Kenyon pointed out that 'as Croesus is here set forth as a favourite of the gods, it is perhaps more appropriate to represent him as suffering from the *fate* of Zeus than from his *vengeance*'.

28 χρυσᾳ[ορος 'of the golden (lyre)-strap'? The meaning of this compound was controversial; Schol. A on Il. 15.256 claims that the strap (ἀορτήρ) could hold either Apollo's quiver or his lyre, but not a sword, 'for the god is pure' (ἁγνός), and quotes Pindar's fr. 128c where the epithet is given to Orpheus, supporting the meaning 'of golden (lyre-) strap'. Cf. Janko on Il.15.254–9.

30–1 πολυδ[άκρυο]ν . . . δ[ουλοσύ]ναν 'tearful slavery'. The thought that death is preferable to slavery (also in Eur. fr. 245) is a variation of a topos, common in tragedy, that 'it is better to die than to live miserably or ignominiously'; many parallels have been collected by Pearson on Soph. frs. 488 and 952, to which Ion PMG 746 = TrGF 1 19 F 53 can be added.

ἔτι: in addition to the loss of his kingdom and the destruction of his city.

32 χαλκ[ο]τειχέος τ̣[ροπάροι]θεν αὐ[λᾶς 'in front of his bronze-walled courtyard'. Many mythical palaces have bronze or bronze-clad walls, like those of Hephaistos (Il. 18.369–71), Alkinoos (Od. 7.86), Aiolos (Od. 10.3–4), or a bronze floor, like the χαλκοβατὲς δῶ of Zeus (Il. 1.426 etc.), also of Alkinoos (Od. 13.4), cf. Pindar, Paean 8.68–9 (on the third temple at Delphi) and Antimachos fr. 187 Wyss (Ἀράων θάλαμοι).

34–5 ἄλα̣[στον] . . . δυρομέναις 'wailing inconsolably', cf. Od. 14.174 παιδὸς ἄλαστον ὀδύρομαι. B. seems to use the adverb in the sense of 'woefully', in accordance with the epic formula πένθος ἄλαστον (Il. 24.105; Od. 1.342; 24.423; Hes. Th. 467), not with the etymology ('unforgettable', ἀνεπιλήστως Schol. *Od.* 14.174, cf. Schol. bT on *Il.* 19.64). Hesych. α 2779 combines both meanings (ἀλάστοις· ἀνεπιλήστοις, χαλεποῖς, δεινοῖς). The wailing of the daughters, here and in 49–51, and their helpless gesture (see 49–51n.) form a contrasting frame around the defeated king's defiant and heroic speech (37–47).

35–6 χέρας . . . ἀείρας: raising both hands is a typical prayer gesture, quite distinct from stretching out one hand (17.72n.).

37 ὑπέρ[βι]ε δαῖμον: Zeus, the 'overwhelming power', who has implemented the fate of Sardis (25–6); certainly not Apollo (so LSJ *s.v.* ὑπέρβιος), who is referred to in 39.

38–9   According to Hdt. 1.90, Kroisos sent his fetters to Delphi and enquired 'whether the Greek gods were in the habit of being ungrateful'; the Pythia's response was that it was 'impossible even for a god to escape the apportioned fate' (1.91). This kind of indignant question is also found in tragedy: Aesch. *Cho.* 900–1; Eur. *Tro.* 428 ποῦ δ'Ἀπόλλωνος λόγοι;

40 Ἀλυά[τ]τα δόμοι: Hdt. 1.30 mentions Alyattes' palace and his treasuries. The American excavations at Sardis have uncovered what could be part of the supporting terraces of the Lydian royal palace; cf. Hanfmann 1977: 145–54 and pl. 41; id., *Sardis* 73–5 and figs. 79–80.

44–5 [χρυσο]δίνας Πακτωλός: the river Paktolos (Sart Çayı) was famous for its gold dust washed down from Mt.Tmolos (Boz Dağı); cf. Bean, *Aegean Turkey* 261. Soph. *Phil.* 394 calls it εὔχρυσος, cf. Hdt. 5.101.

45–6 ἀεικελίως γυναῖκες . . . ἄγονται: even though Xenophon claims that Kroisos persuaded the victor, Kyros, 'not to loot the city nor to take away children and women' (*Cyr.* 7.2.12), this is probably due to his tendency to idealize Kyros, rather than to historical fact. In B., by contrast, Kroisos' graphic description of the catastrophe that is unfolding before his eyes echoes the experience of Homeric heroes whose city is sacked: 'they kill the men, fire consumes the city; others lead off the children and the deep-bound women' (*Il.* 9.593–4).

47   The papyrus reads τα προσθεν δ [εχ]θρα^νυν φιλα: the δ' is against the metre, as is the νῦν above the line; both have to be deleted. The scribes are often puzzled by asyndeta and instinctively insert particles, particularly δ' or γ'; νῦν was added by **A³**, presumably off his own bat, in order to clarify the sentence. Both additions, apart from being unmetrical, destroy the grandiose pathos of this speech which comes exactly at the centre of the mythical narrative; its last line is the capping climax to a series of short, almost breathless, asyndetic statements. What matters to the poet here is not so much the dramatic build-up and climax of events (the sack of Sardis or Kroisos' rescue would have made a very effective climax), but the increasing intensity of the king's despair, and his heroic resolve to face death with dignity, rather than slavery (cf. 30–1).

48 ἀβ[ρο]βάταν 'soft-stepping': only here and Aesch. *Pers.* 1072, also as a noun (ἀβροβάται are the old Persians who form the chorus). As B. may have been in Syracuse at about the time of the play's second performance there at Hieron's request (cf. Schol. on Ar. *Ran.* 1028), it is conceivable that he witnessed that performance. If so, he may have borrowed the word for the Lydian attendant (whose name is Εὔθυμος on Myson's amphora, Louvre G 197).

49 ξύλινον δόμον: similarly, Pindar calls the pyre on which Koronis is cremated a ξύλινον τεῖχος, *P.* 3.38.

49–51 ἐκ[λα]γον . . . χεῖρας ἔβαλλον: the daughters wailed as they mounted the pyre (34–5), but now, as it is being lit, they 'shrieked and threw up their hands to their mother', a touching gesture which contrasts sharply with the king's heroic composure. As the daughters and their mother do not appear on the Louvre amphora, it seems possible that they were added by B. for the sake of contrast. Alternatively, one might assume that Myson left them out lest they should detract attention from the majestic figure of Kroisos.

51–2 ὁ γὰρ προφανὴς . . . φόνων 'the death that is seen coming is the most hateful to mortals'. Prometheus had taken the foreknowledge of their own death away from humans (Aesch. *Prom.* 248, cf. Plato, *Gorg.* 523d), which was one of his benefactions to mankind. The opposite view, that misfortune is easier to bear if it has been seen approaching, is first found in Euripides' fr. 964 N² (also quoted by Plut. *Mor.* 112d and translated by Cicero, *Tusc.* 3.13.28–9) and Aristotle, *NE* 3.1117a18–22, and (from Aristotle?) by Ach.Tat. 1.3 and Heliodoros 2.24.

53–4 δεινοῦ πυρὸς λαμπρὸν . . . [μέ]γος 'the bright strength of the grim fire'; the phrase may have been inspired by Homer's description of Chimaira, *Il.* 6.182 δεινὸν ἀποπνείουσα πυρὸς μένος αἰθομένοιο.

55–6 Ζεὺς . . . σβέννυεν ξανθὰ[ν φλόγα 'Zeus . . . quenched the yellow flame'. Zeus' intervention (the fall of Sardis) had set in motion the dramatic action (23–9n.) which is now coming to its conclusion. In Hdt. 1.87, by contrast, the saving rain-cloud appears to be sent by Apollo in answer to Kroisos' prayer. B. is careful to make Apollo and Zeus act in tandem, for reasons discussed in §3 above, p. 84.

57–8 ἄπιστον οὐδὲν . . . τεύχει 'nothing that the planning of the gods brings about is past belief', cf. 17.118n. In Pindar, this topos functions as a transition from the mythical narrative to the victor's praise (*P.* 9.69–70; *P.* 10.48–50) or vice versa (*N.* 10.49–54), whereas B. uses it as a dramatic climax, both here and in 17.117–18. Cf. also Sem. 1.2 Ζεὺς . . . τίθησ᾽ ὅκηι θέλει and Thgn. 142 θεοὶ δὲ κατὰ σφέτερον πάντα τελοῦσι νόον.

59 This is the only case of living mortals being taken to the 'Land of the Blessed' (Jebb). For B. and Pindar, the Hyperboreans were a kind of blessed people, and their land, thought to be somewhere in the North, a kind of Ἠλύσιον πεδίον (*Od.* 4.561–9) or 'Islands of the Blessed' (Hes. *Op.* 167–73) where Zeus settled dead heroes. The idea of Kroisos' and his daughters' rescue by Apollo may have been inspired by Stesichoros, who made Apollo take Hekabe to Lycia (Paus. 10.27.2 = *PMG* 198).

62 ἐς ἀγαθέαν . . . Π[υθ]ώ: the adjective ('holy') is usually given to places dedicated to the cult of a god, such as Delphi, as in *Od.* 8.80 and Hes. *Th.* 499.

<ἀν>έπεμψε 'had sent up'. Herodotos says ἀπέπεμψε (1.51–2), 'the fitting word from a Lydian point of view, as ἀνέπεμψε is from that of a Greek' (Jebb). The verb provides the cue for the second praise passage (πέμψαι 66).

63–99 The second praise passage; on its structure, see above, pp. 84–5.
63–6 ὅσợ [ι] <γε> μὲν Ἑλλάδ᾽ ἔχουσιν, [ο]ὔτι[ς] . . . βροτῶν: negative superlatives are not uncommon in epinicians, cf. B. 8.22–5 ('no-one among the Greeks . . . won more victories'), Pind. *O.* 2.93–5, *P.* 2.58–61, *N.* 6.24–6, also in B. fr. 20C.21–4. On adversative γε μέν see Denniston 386–7; of all people Kroisos had sent the most generous gifts to Delphi, and of all Greeks it was Hieron. The point here is not a distinction between Hellenes and non-Hellenes (Jebb), but the parallel between Kroisos and Hieron (see above, pp. 80 and 84).

64 ὦ μεγαίνητ ε̄ Ἱέρων: the hiatus before Ἱέρων is paralleled at 92, where the name stands in the same position in the verse; similar hiatuses before names occur in B. 2.7 (αὐχένι Ἰσθμοῦ) and in 16.5 (ἀνθεμόεντι Ἕβρωι). The lengthening of –τε is strange; cases like δόρυ· σόει (17.90n.) or δόμου· ἔμολεν (17.100) are not comparable because there the lengthening of the vowel can be accounted for by assuming 'duplication' of the following consonant.

65 χρυσόν: the golden tripods dedicated by Hieron and placed on the terrace on the east side of the temple; they have been discussed by Amandry 1987: 81–92 and Krumeich 1991: 37–62.

67–71 Formally, this sentence is the inversion of the preceding one: 'no-one of those who dwell in Greece . . .' >< 'anyone who does not fatten himself on envy'. For the φθόνος-motif, see 11.123–4n.

68 πιαίνεται: the correction (from ιαινεται) by A³ is confirmed by the scholion *P.Oxy.* 2367 (pap.**M**) fr. 2. The image is also used in a negative sense by Pindar (*P.* 2.55–6 and *N.* 8.21) and in *TrGF* 11 fr. 533 εἰσίν τινες νῦν οὓς τὸ βασκαίνειν τρέφει 'there are some now who feed on malice'.

70 [. . . .]ίου . . . Διός: Nairn's [ξειν]ίου is the most likely supplement, cf. Pind. *N.* 11.7–9 where the addressee's hospitality and fondness for music are praised in similar terms; see Bundy 25 nn.58 and 61.

72–4 The lines are paraphrased in the commentary *P.Oxy.* 2367 (pap.**M**) fr. 3.1–6 where ἐφ]ήμεροι [ὄντ]ες (line 3) refers to ἐφάμερον 73; lines 4–6 [δυ]νατὰ ἐρεύνα [*c.* 10 letters] ὅτι ὀλιγοχρό[νιος ὁ βίος ?] must therefore paraphrase 74, which may suggest reading [καίρι]α σκόπει{ς} there (cf. Lloyd-Jones, 1958:18).

74 βραχ[ύς ἐστιν αἰών (Blass) or βραχ[ὺ γὰρ τὸ τερπνόν (H. Fränkel); in any case, the phrase seems to be meant as an explanation of the preceding statement.

75–6 πτερ]όεσσα δ' ἐλπὶς ὑπ[ολύει ν]όημα | [ἐφαμ]ερίων 'winged hope undoes the thinking of mortals', paraphrased in pap. **M** fr.3: ἡ πτερ[όεσσα ἐλπὶς δι]αφθείρει τὸ [τῶν ἀνθρώπων ν]όημα. The verb paraphrased by διαφθείρει may have been ὑπολύει (Snell), cf. *Il.* 6.27 ὑπέλυσε μένος. The idea of the dangerous seductive force of 'hope' recurs in Thuc. 5.103.

77 ×–].'λος (or].'ϙος): the only convincing supplement so far suggested is [ἐκαβ]όλος (Jebb). This seems to be a reference to the 'Sayings for Admetos' (Ἀδμήτου λόγοι), a collection of maxims supposedly given to Admetos, the son of Pheres, by Apollo when he was in the service of the Thessalian king, cf. Pherekydes, *FGrHist* 3 F 35. They may have been similar to the 'Teachings of Chiron' (Χίρωνος ὑποθῆκαι, [Hes.] frs. 283–5); some Attic drinking songs, one of them ascribed to Praxilla (*PMG* 749), also refer to 'sayings for Admetos', cf. Bowra, *Greek lyric poetry* 377.

78–82 θνατὸν εὖντα . . . τελεῖς 'since you are mortal, you must foster two thoughts: that tomorrow will be the only day on which you see the sun's light, and that for fifty years you will live out a life steeped in wealth'. This has a close parallel only in Epicharmos: ὡς πολὺν ζήσων χρόνον χὤς ὀλίγον, οὕτως διανοοῦ 'think as if you would live for a long time and for a short while' (267 Kaibel = *CGF* 1 256 p.149; cf. also Stob. 3. 1.93). B. may have borrowed the statement either from a collection of 'sayings for Admetos' (see 77n.), or from Epicharmos: this could then be another example of an intertextual reference in an ode performed at Syracuse to poetry that must have been particularly well known in Sicily, like the Homeric *Hymn to Demeter* (see 5.16–30n.). The formal function of this quotation is similar to that of the quotation from Hesiod in 5.191–4 in that both provide the transition to the final section; both odes end with personal references to Hieron.

83–4 ὅσια δρῶν . . . κερδέων ὑπέρτατον   'gladden your heart by doing righteous deeds, for this is the highest of gains'. These lines clearly form part of Apollo's saying, as they are the conclusion to be drawn from the preceding lines; cf. 21–2 above, where θεὸν θεόν τις ἀγλαιζέτω follows in a very similar manner, also as asyndeton, the description of Hieron's tripods at Delphi.

ὅσια   'righteous deeds', such as generous offerings to the gods, and εὔφραινε θυμόν 'gladden your heart' anticipate 87 εὐφροσύνα δ' ὁ χρυσός in the sense that the offerings and festivities, paid for by Hieron, will be 'a good investment'.

85–98   The last triad falls into two parts of almost equal length: 85–92 τρ[έφει] are a series of general statements which prepare the way for the final address to Hieron and the personal dedication of the ode by the poet. The two halves of this last triad correspond in that the second (92–8) is the specific example, i.e. Hieron's victory and hence his fame in song, which illustrates the first; the series of *gnomai* (85–92) is capped by the vocative Ἱέρων (92), a 'name cap' in Bundy's terminology (Bundy 5 n.8), just as the second is capped by the reference to the poet, the 'Kean nightingale'. Hieron's name is in the same position here as in the first stanza (4), thus linking proem and conclusion and presenting the last sentence (τίς ὑμνήσει) as the fulfilment of the prayer to the Muse (ὕμνει . . . Κλειοῖ, 3); see 97n. The implication is that the ode is inspired by the Muse, Kleio, and will guarantee Hieron's fame. This assertion is no less proud than Ibykos' final statement in his song for Polykrates: 'And you too, Polykrates, will have fame forever, as far as poetry and my reputation can ensure it' (*PMG* 282.47–8); cf. Barron 1969: 119–49 (translation: p. 135).

85–92   The meaning of this sequence of *gnomai* has eluded most scholars. The argument of the passage moves between opposites in three stages: (a) heaven and sea are eternal, (b) joy and youth are transient, (c) only fame of achievements, 'nourished' by poetry, will last. Its first three lines (85–7) may 'copy Pindar's abruptness, and his splendour' (Jebb, with reference to the famous opening lines of Pindar's first *Olympian*: 'Best is water, while gold, like fire blazing | in the night, shines preeminent amid lordly wealth. But if you wish to sing | of athletic games . . .'). Pindar's ode was performed at Syracuse in 476; it is, of course, possible that it was known to B., but it does not necessarily follow that his verses are an 'open imitation of Pindar', as Jebb thought. In fact, B. introduces different elements (εὐφροσύνα, γῆρας/ἥβα), and those he shares with Pindar he uses differently. For him, the heavens (αἰθήρ) and the sea stand for the everlasting and unchanging elements; gold is not the best part of wealth, as in Pindar, but 'joy' or 'festivity' (εὐφροσύνα) – it is this statement which has always caused problems. Most commentators have taken gold, together with heaven and sea, as an eternal and incorruptible element (cf. Thgn. 449–52; Sim. *PMG* 541.4) and therefore εὐφροσύνα as 'a joy forever' (Kenyon, Jebb), ignoring the fact that gold, here as well as in Pind. *O.* 1.1–2 and *O.* 3.42, stands for wealth, and wealth is never considered as something stable and unchanging; on the contrary, wealth is often thought of as something short-lived and very precarious, cf. Solon 15 = Thgn. 315–18; Hes. *Op.* 320–6; B. 1.159–84; Eur. *El.* 941–4, *Phoen.* 555–7, frs. 354 and 618 N². In B., gold 'is' joy (εὐφροσύνα = ὧι τις εὐφραίνεται), something quite different from the eternal elements; it is in the same category as 'youth' (ἥβα) which will not last and, once gone, cannot be retrieved. The only thing that will last is ἀρετᾶς φέγγος, 'the light of excellence' (90–1), which lives on in song.

85 φρονέοντι συνετὰ γαρύω   'I say what will be intelligible to one who thinks'. The formula with which B. announces his statements is a variation of *Il.* 23.787 εἰδόσιν ὔμμ᾽ ἐρέω, cf. Pind. *P.* 4.142; Aesch. *Supp.* 742, *Ag.* 39 and 1402, *Prom.* 441–2. In all these passages the meaning is 'you know already what I am going to say', whereas B. says 'you have to reflect on what I am going to say', i.e. the implication of his words will not be immediately obvious to all, but Hieron will understand them (see 5.3–6n.). Pindar also emphasizes that his words are meant for those who can think (*O.* 2.85 φωνάεντα συνετοῖσιν); cf. Theocr. 24.71 and the 'riddle' stele from Egypt, *Sammelbuch* v 8026.20 συνιέντι θέλω λέγειν τι.

85–6 βαθύς . . . αἰθήρ: 5.16–17n.

88–9 πολιὸν . . . γῆρας: a common formula, cf. B. fr. 25.2–3; Pind. *I.* 6.15; Thgn. 174; Eur. *Supp.* 170, etc.

π[αρ]έντα   'passing by', i.e. retrieve youth instead of enduring 'grey' old age; for this usage, cf. Eur. *Alc.* 939 παρεὶς τὸ μόρσιμον: Admetos 'passed by' the death that was destined for him.

90 γε μ]έν: examples of adversative γε μέν in Homer and lyric poetry ('however', corresponding to γε μήν in Attic prose) have been collected by Denniston, *Particles* 387.

91 ἅμα σ[ώμ]ατι: in choral lyric, the expectation of death or, more generally, the limitation of the human condition is often contrasted with the immortality of fame, e.g. B. 1.181–4; Pind. *N.* 7.19–21; *P.* 1.92–4; see Bundy 87–8. Here, too, the motives of old age and death serve as a dark foil for the 'light of excellence' (ἀρετᾶς φέγγος). Hieron, who had probably been suffering for some time from the illness which was to kill him the following year (see above, p. 79), may have drawn comfort from this thought.

92–4 Μοῦσά νιν τρ[έφει]:   for the 'feeding' metaphor, cf. B. 13.58–62; Pind. *O.* 1.112; *O.* 10.95–6. On the hiatus before Ἱέρων, see 64n.

Ἱέρων, σὺ δ' ὄλβου . . . ἄνθεα: the 'name cap' (see 85–98n.) introduces the second half of the concluding triad, in which the general statements of the first half are applied to the occasion of the ode, the celebration of Hieron's victory (above, 85–98n.). Hieron's name (in the same position as in 4), combined with the ὄλβος motif, recalls the proem (1–8); these verbal and conceptual repetitions serve to make the audience aware that the ode is drawing to a close (see also 95n. and 97n.). The 'flowers' (ἄνθεα) are the visible manifestations of 'wealth' (ὄλβος), in Hieron's case both the golden tripods at Delphi (17–22) and the celebration of his Olympic victory (cf. 5.186 εὐδαιμονίας πέταλον), which he has 'displayed to mortals' (ἐπεδ[είξ]αο θνατοῖς 93).

95 [σι]ωπά: the function of the 'silence' motif in Pindar is discussed by Bundy 73–4. Used, as here, in a negative way it amounts to an exhortation to praise, cf. Pind. *N.* 9.6–7; *I.* 2.43–5; *P.* 9.93–4. It echoes the phrase in the first praise passage, 13–14 (Hieron 'knows how not to hide his wealth in darkness').

96–8 σὺν δ' ἀλαθ[είαι] . . . ἀηδόνος   'with the truth of your successes, men will sing the gift of the Kean nightingale'. The concluding sentence has been almost universally misunderstood ('men will praise also the charm of the melodious nightingale of Ceos', Jebb). H. Fränkel understood the meaning of this passage correctly: 'χάρις is much more likely to signify the ode itself as a pleasure and a gift of friendship, as so often in Pindar (*O*. 10.78; *P*. 11.12; *N*. 7.75 etc.; with possessive *P*. 10.64; with genitive *P*. 2.70); and just as the transitive κελαδέω can mean both 'sing about' (*N*. 9.54: ἀρετὰν κελαδῆσαι) and 'perform' (*O*. 11.14: κόσμον ἀδυμελῆ κελαδήσω; *N*. 4.16 ὕμνον κελάδησε καλλίνικον), so ὑμνήσει here must mean 'perform the ode' (cf. Ovid's *canar* in *Am*. 1.15.8). For the thought: 'someone will also sing this song of mine', cf. *N*. 4.13–16; *I*. 2.45 (also in conjunction with 'no silence')', Fränkel, *Early Greek poetry* 464 n.44. In fact, after 92–5, there can be no doubt that only Hieron can be the object of praise here, not B. (although B. will get praise as author of the song, see 97–8n.); τις ὑμνήσει 'men will sing' is the logical conclusion and climax of the sequence 'Hieron has been victorious – success must be praised', just as the sequence of 85–92 leads, also in three steps, to the statement 'song feeds fame'.

σὺν δ' ἀλαθ[είαι] καλῶν   'with the truth of your successes'. καλῶν must be gen. plur. of καλά 'successes' (as in 5.51 μοῖραν καλῶν), and in particular 'victories' (as in 2.6). The combination of the two nouns is, as Bundy 61 (with n.69) has seen, a variation of the idea of 'praise without stint and praise to match (σύν τε δίκαι) the worth of the laudandus'; see also Bundy 58 n.54. More specifically, the meaning of ἀλήθεια is, for most poets after Hes. *Th*. 233–6, determined by the etymology (α privative + λήθη, λανθάνειν), which suggests that they understood the word in the sense of 'not ignoring' or even 'revealing'; cf. Heitsch 1962: 26–33. That B. understood the word in this sense is confirmed by its opposition to οὐ φέρει κόσμον σιωπά (95) – great achievements must not remain hidden in obscurity or be forgotten, they must be brought out into the open and be displayed to the public. Prose authors use ἀλήθεια in the sense of 'what is manifest, for all to see': cf. Hdt. 2.119 τὴν ἀληθείην τῶν πρηγμάτων, 3.64 ὄνειρος (Kroisos' dream) ὅς οἱ τὴν ἀληθείην ἔφαινε τῶν μελλόντων γενέσθαι κακῶν, Thuc. 2.41.2 who speaks of ἔργων ἀλήθεια in contrast to λόγων κόμπος ('the facts speak for themselves'), and Demosth. *or*. 19.81 ἡ γὰρ ἀλήθεια καὶ τὰ πεπραγμέν'αὐτὰ βοᾶι, also Antiphon 2.4.1, Isocr. 2.46. Pindar, in his *Hymn to Zeus*, spoke of ἀληθέας Ὥρας because they, as Hesych. α 2733 explains, κυκλισμῶι πάντα <φανερὰ add. Bergk> ποιοῦσιν (fr. 30).

97 ὑμνήσει: the future is 'a conventional element of the enkomiastic style. It never points beyond the ode itself, and its promise is often fulfilled by the mere pronunciation of the word' Bundy 21, who has collected many examples from Pindar; cf. also Slater 1969: 86–94. In B., ὑμνήσει refers to the present performance of the ode at Syracuse; it recalls ὕμνει in the proem (3), suggesting that this performance is the result of the chorus' exhortation to the Muse, Kleio.

97–8 μελιγλώσσου . . . Κηΐας ἀηδόνος   'of the honey-tongued Kean nightingale', i.e. the poet. He is 'honey-tongued' because his song has been inspired by 'Kleio, giver of sweetness' (γλυκύδωρε Κλεοῖ, 3) – another link between the concluding and the opening sentence of the ode. The nightingale stands for the poet in Hes. *Op.* 202–12, and many later poets have adopted the image: Alkman *PMG* 10.6–7; Sappho 136; Alc. 307 I(c); Sim. *PMG* 586; Thgn. 939; *PMG* 964b; Simias of Rhodes 26.4 (*Coll. Alex.* p. 119 = *AP* 15.27) Δωρίας ἀηδόνος may be a direct imitation of B.; *AP* 7.44; 7.80, etc. In his self-presentation, or σφραγίς (lit. 'seal'), B. appears much less self-assured than Pindar who wishes 'to consort with victors, conspicuous in my skill everywhere throughout Greece' (*O.* 1.115–16).

ODE 4: FOR HIERON'S CHARIOT VICTORY AT DELPHI

1. The victory

The date of Hieron's victory in the chariot race at Delphi is given by the scholia on Pindar's *Pythians* (II p.3 Drachmann) as the 29th Pythiad = 470 BCE. This victory, like his victory with the racehorse at Olympia in 476 (see on B. 5, p. 107), was celebrated by both B. and Pindar; while B. composed a short ode for a performance in Delphi, presumably immediately after the race, Pindar produced a long and elaborate ode for a performance at Aitna, the former Katana, where Hieron's son, Deinomenes, had been introduced as ruler on his father's behalf (*Pythian* 1). Pindar claims that the herald had announced the victorious Hieron as ruler of Aitna (*P.* 1.29–33), whereas B. praises him as ruler of Syracuse. This is strange, given that Hieron evidently attached great importance to being praised by Pindar as 'founder' of Aitna – how could B. have ignored this?

If Hieron was indeed announced by the herald as Αἰτναῖος, then B. (who may not have been present at the games in Delphi) would probably have been unaware of this, and whoever was in charge of the performance of this ode at Delphi would not have been able to alter the text accordingly.

It is, however, questionable whether in these circumstances his ode could have been performed at all. The alternative scenario seems more probable: Hieron was officially announced as Συρακόσιος, so B.'s ode conforms to the announcement *at Delphi*, whereas Pindar's first *Pythian*, performed *at Aitna*, conforms to Hieron's wish to create the impression, at least in Aitna and probably all over Sicily, that he had been officially honoured as master of Aitna. This would be an interesting case of Pindar manipulating the facts in order to further his client's political ambitions. The official list of *Olympic* victors in *P.Oxy.* II 222 always lists Hieron as Συρακόσιος, col.i 19 (476), 32 (472), 44 (468), which would be strange if the records kept at Olympia had listed him as Αἰτναῖος. The scholia to *P.* 2 and 3 also refer to him as Συρακούσιος (II p. 30 and 61 Drachmann), only those to *P.* 1 as Αἰτναῖος (II p. 8 and 16 Drachmann) which is probably an inference from Pindar's verses, *P.* 1.27–32.

It therefore seems likely that Hieron had commissioned the long ode for his victory celebration in Aitna from Pindar with a request that he be referred to as founder and master of Aitna, whereas B. had either sent his short ode in advance of the race, expecting Hieron's chariot to win, or had travelled to Delphi to compose and perform it there immediately after the race, but in either case had not received instructions regarding Aitna.

Hieron's chariot victory of 470 was his third success at the Pythiads (B. 4.4); before this, he had twice won the horse race (κέλης), in the 26th and 27th Pythiads (482 and 478); at least the second of these victories was due to his outstanding stallion Pherenikos (see introd. to ode 5). B. even claims that Hieron's chariot victory could have been his fourth triumph here if a god (?, see on lines 11–13) had held the scales of Justice. The missing victory might have been in a horse race, or a chariot race at a previous Pythiad: at one of these, his younger brother Polyzalos won the chariot race and dedicated a splendid group of bronze statues, of which the famous charioteer, fragments of the horses, and an inscribed limestone block of the base have been recovered. Cf. Chamoux, *L'aurige* 51–82; on the base and inscription: 17–31. The surviving part of the inscription, the right-hand halves of two hexameters, has been altered, but the original text of the first line had not been completely erased; on the possibility that there may have been a link between the alteration and the fourth Pythian victory which Hieron failed to achieve (or chose to forgo ?), see Maehler 2002: 19–21.

2. Structure

Like odes 6, 7, and 8, this ode consists of only one pair of strophes. It was not until 1938 that Medea Norsa recognized and acquired from a dealer in Cairo two fragments of the great London papyrus **A**, the first of which, published as *PSI* xii 1278A, has been fitted into the bottom part of its ninth column; it contains the middle portions of B.4.4–12. The result of this addition has been that it can now be seen much more clearly how closely the two strophes are interrelated; there are close links between responding verses in terms of both metre and content. For example, lines 1–3 say that Apollo 'honours' (γεραίρει) Hieron, 'the city's righteous ruler'; the responding lines 11–13 say that 'we' (= the chorus) 'would honour him for the fourth time if a god (?) had held up the scales of Justice'. The central parts of both strophes (4–6 and 14–16) refer to the present victory that is now being celebrated (5 ἀείδεται ≈ 14–18 πάρεστι<ν> . . . ἀείδειν, and 6 ἀρετᾶι responds with 16 στεφάνοις. Indications of localities also correspond: 4 Apollo's temple ≈ 14 Kirrha. Finally, the opening sentence 'Apollo loves (φιλεῖ) Syracuse and honours Hieron' is echoed by the last one: 'What better than to be beloved by the gods (φίλον ἐόντα) and to share in good things.'

1–2 Ἔτι Συρακοσίαν φιλεῖ πόλιν . . . Ἀπόλλων: a god's special care for his or her favourite cult centre is often expressed as φιλεῖν, cf. [Hes.] fr. 240.5–6 Δωδώνη, . . . τὴν δὲ Ζεὺς ἐφίλησε, *h.Ap.* 138 (Φοῖβος) φίλησε δὲ κήροθι μᾶλλον (sc. Delos), Pind. *P.* 1.39 Φοῖβε . . . Κασταλίαν φιλέων. But Syracuse was not one of Apollo's principal cult centres (although there was a temple of Apollo Temenites); Apollo's care and protection, expressed as φιλεῖν, is devoted to Syracuse as the victor's city. This is in accordance with Homer's belief that some gods have a particular affinity not only to some outstanding mortals whom they help to protect, but also to peoples and their cities; he makes Achilles say (*Iliad* 16.94) that Apollo 'loves' the Trojans, and claims that the descendants of Tlepolemos of Rhodes 'are loved' by Zeus (*Il.* 2.668–9). In the same way, Apollo still (ἔτι) 'loves' Syracuse – 'still', after Hieron had been successful twice before.

2 χρυσοκόμας: golden hair is the privilege of gods and their horses, cf. West on Hes. *Th.* 947 and Kirk on *Il.* 4.2. This is particularly true of Apollo, who is often referred to as 'the golden-haired': cf. Alkman, *SLG* 1 (= 1 Calame) Χρυσοκόμα φιλόμολπε, Pindar, *O.* 6.41 and 7.32 ὁ χρυσοκόμας, also *Paean* 5.41 and *P.* 2.16, and later in the Attic drinking song *PMG* 886.2 and the *Paean PMG* 950b.

3 ἀστύθεμιν   'righteous ruler', only here; one of the rare compounds in B. made up of two nouns, and the only one having –θεμις as its second component, other than proper names like Χρυσόθεμις, Δαμόθεμις, etc.

Ἰέ[ρω]να γεραίρει: see below on 13.

4 τρίτον γάρ: Hieron's racehorse had won at Delphi twice before, in 482 and 478, so this chariot victory of 470 is his third hippic victory in the Pythian games. On the function of γάρ in such contexts, see on ode 3.5.

παρ' [ὀμφα]λόν: the stone 'navel' in the temple of Apollo at Delphi was thought to be the centre of the world, according to Pausanias (10.16.3), who may, however, have seen only the marble copy on the temple terrace. The original was found in 1913 at the south wall of the cella of the temple, cf. Courby, *La terrasse du temple* 69–78, figs. 64–9. Strabo refers this honour (τιμή) to the temple itself (τῶι ἱερῶι τούτωι, 9.3.6 p. 419), as does Pindar in *Paean* 6.17, see Radt ad loc.

ὑψιδείρου χθονός   'of the high-ridged land', a reference to the high cliffs of the Phaidriades which rise up to 300 metres above the sanctuary.

6 ἀρ[ετᾶι] σὺν ἵππων: σύν in the sense of 'thanks to', as often in Pindar (*N.* 1.9; 10.48; *P.* 11.48; ἀμφ' ἀρετᾶι *P.* 1.80 and 2.62).

7–10   The Florentine fragments of papyrus **A**, inserted here, have helped to elucidate these lines, making it clear that the cock (ἀλέκτωρ, 8) of the Muse, Ourania, represents the poet, as does the nightingale in ode 3.98 and the bee in ode 10.10. Even so, the loss of the beginnings of lines 7–12 is still a serious obstacle to the understanding of this passage. Although ἀλλ'(9) implies a contrast to the preceding statement, it cannot have been a negative one because at the beginnings of lines 7 and 9 no long syllables (such as οὐ or μή) can be supplied. Snell's supplements (7) ἔ[λακε δ'] . . . (9) φρενόθ]εν or ἔ[θελε δ'] . . . [παρέμ]εν are unsatisfactory, the first one because it does not provide a contrast to 9–10 ἀλλ' ἐκ[όν]τι νόωι . . . ἐπέσεισεν ὕμνους, the second because it does not say what 'Ourania's cock' would have wanted to 'leave out'. The contrast may have been between past and present: e.g., ἔ[λακε δ'] . . . [ποτὲ μ]έν· ἀλλ' ἐκ[όν]τι νόωι [αὖθ' ἁβρο]ὺς (or [νῦν νέο]υς) ἐπέσεισ[εν] ὕμνους. This would mean that the 'cock' had 'crowed' once before, i.e. in 476 when he celebrated Hieron's Olympic victory (see on ode 5), but now he has 'again' (?) showered him with praise ('hymns'). The first two stanzas of fr. 20C provide a close parallel, as does ode 6, where the present victory is similarly contrasted to the previous ones (6.6 ἄεισάν ποτ᾽ Ὀλυμπίαι . . . 10 σὲ δὲ νῦν . . .). A very similar contrast between 'before' (μέν) . . . and 'now again' (αὖτε) is used by Pindar in *I.* 6.3–5 ἐν Νεμέαι μὲν πρῶτον, ὦ Ζεῦ, τὶν ἄωτον δεξάμενοι στεφάνων, νῦν αὖτε Ἰσθμοῦ δεσπόται κτλ.; further parallels for contrasting μὲν . . . αὖτε can be found in Denniston 376.

7 ἐ[. . . .]: ἐ[λακε δ᾽] would fill the gap which corresponds to that of line 12 (see the facsimile in *PSI* xii pl.5), whereas ἐ[κλαγε δ᾽] would be too long. The verb λάσκειν (literally 'to scream') is used of other birds: a falcon (*Il.* 22.141), and a nightingale (Hes. *Op.* 207, and *SLG* 460.8 ἀηδονὶς ὧδε λέλακε); it is also used for mantic utterances, as in Aesch. *Cho.* 35. Cf. ἱμερόφων<ος> ἀλέκτωρ in Simonides (*PMG* 583 = Athen. 9.374d); although Athenaeus does not indicate the context, this image may also have referred to the poet; see also Gow on Theocritus 7.47f.

7–8 ἀ[ναξιφόρ]μιγγος: supplied by Maas, cf. Pindar, *O.* 2.1; all other compounds beginning with ἀναξι– in B. are ἅπαξ εἰρημένα, presumably coined by him.

10 ἐπέσεισεν: the commentary of papyrus **B**, *P.Oxy.* 2367 fr.5, seems to have explained the verb 'metaphorically . . . in the sense of "to shower with" ' (ἐπισκ[εδάσαι, or ἐπισκ[εδάννυσι ?). The idea behind this metaphor is that of the φυλλοβολία, see on ode 11.17–20.

11–13 ἔτι δὲ τέ]τρατον . . . κ᾽ ἐγερα[ίρ]ομεν is evidently the main clause following the conditional εἴ τις . . . εἷλκε: 'if someone . . . , we would praise Hieron for the fourth time', i.e. an unfulfilled (or 'contrary to fact', *irrealis*) conditional clause. Who is τις? Either (a) one of the judges who denied Hieron a fourth victory, possibly the one with the racehorse after he had already won the chariot race (so Gallavotti 1944: 4–6 with reference to c. 11.24ff.); or (b) a god: εἴ τις ὀρ[θὰ θεὸς] . . . τάλαν[τα] Snell; (b) is supported by all the early parallels of τάλαντα ἕλκειν: in *Il.* 8.69 = 22.209; 16.658; 19.223; *h.Merc.* 324; Archil. 91.30 and Theognis 157 it is always Zeus who holds up the scales, as in Triphiod. 506–7 and Nonnos, *Dion.* 2.553. Moreover, to say 'had a judge held up the scales' (or perhaps 'dragged them down', i.e. put weight on them, as in Hdt. 1.50.3 εἰκόνα . . . ἕλκουσαν σταθμὸν τάλαντα δέκα, cf. 1.51.2, i.e. in Hieron's favour) would imply that Hieron could have gained a fourth victory only through favouritism or bribery; such an allegation would have been completely out of place in an ode praising Hieron's success. It must be the other way round: 'If a god had lifted up the straight (= uncorrupted) scales of Dike', Hieron might have achieved a fourth victory. This seems to imply either an unfair decision, or a very close one, or possibly – if the alteration of the Polyzalos inscription is relevant here – a political deal by which Hieron ceded a victory to his younger brother for some favour; see Maehler 2002: 21. For whatever reason Hieron failed to win a fourth victory at Delphi, B. seems to have implied that as far as Dike was concerned, he would have deserved to win it.

13 Δεινομένεος κ' ἐγερα[ἱρ]ọμεν υἱόν˙   echoes ἱέ[ρω]να γεραίρει˙ in the responding verse of the first strophe (3), with punctuation in the papyrus after both, which makes it impossible to link 13 to the next lines.

14 †παρεστίν†:   παρεστίαν pap., παρ' ἑστίαν Kenyon. The text of the papyrus cannot be right, as (1) the metre requires ◡ – – ◡ (not ◡ – ◡ –), and (2) the infinitives in 16 and 18 require a finite verb which can only have stood at the beginning of 14. Therefore Blass' correction πάρεστιν is necessary (cf. ode 3.67), and since a contrast is implied between the 'lost' victory and the actual victory being celebrated here, πάρεστιν δ' ἐν seems preferable to Blass's πάρεστίν νιν.

14–16 <ἐν> ἀγχιάλοισι Ķ[ί]ρρας μυχοῖς . . . τάδε μησάμενον   'who has accomplished this in the seaside glens of Kirrha', i.e. three victories in the Pythian games, two with the racehorse and now one with the chariot. The 'seaside glens of Kirrha' correspond to παρ' [ὀμφα]λὸν ὑψιδείρου χθονός (4), the difference being that the victory celebration is taking place in the sanctuary above, while the chariot race and other contests, such as wrestling (see B. 1.19–20 and Pindar, *P.* 10.15–16), were held in the plain below near Kirrha, between Delphi and the Corinthian Gulf.

μησάμενον: for the meaning of μήδεσθαί τι 'to achieve something' cf. Pindar, *O.* 1.31–2 (Χάρις) ἄπιστον ἐμήσατο πιστὸν ἔμμεναι: in both passages, the derivation from μήδεα 'purposeful thoughts, planning' is clear; B. knew well that for success in the chariot race, careful planning and preparation were essential.

15 μοῦνον ἐπιχθονίων: a frequent topos in eulogies; cf. the epigram on Theogenes of Thasos whom the herald proclaimed twice ἐγ κύκλωι μοῦνον ἐπιχθονίων | πυγμῆς παγκρατίου τ' ἐπινίκιον ἤματι τωὐτῶι (Ebert no. 37.8–9; similarly Ebert nos. 31.2; 33.3; 45.4; 67.7; parodied in *A.P.* 11.84). Records set in the ancient games were not measured in metres or seconds but in numbers of victories, which meant that it became increasingly diffi-cult to match those won by the outstanding athletes of the sixth and early fifth centuries. However much poets of victory odes or epigrams might have liked to lavish superlatives on their clients, they had to keep to the truth, as such claims were easily verifiable from the victory-lists; they therefore either qualify their superlative statements (B. 8.22–5 'no one among the Greeks . . . won more victories in equal time'), or they add up the whole family's victories (Pindar, *N.* 6.25–6 and 58–63; Ebert no. 45.4), or they limit superlatives to contest (Ebert no. 67) or home town (Ebert no. 31.2). In claiming that Hieron was 'the only mortal' to have won three Pythian victories, B. refers to hippic contests but without explicitly qualifying his success, which he makes here *appear* as an absolute record (having made the qualification already in 6 ἀρ[εταῖ] σὺν ἵππων).

17 δύο τ' ὀλυμπιονικ<ί>ας: corrected by Maas, cf. ἀεθλονικία Pindar, *N.* 3.7. These two victories are those of Hieron's racehorse in 476, celebrated by B. 5 and Pindar's *O.* 1, and 472 for which – strangely – no victory ode appears to have survived.

18–20 τί φέρτερον ἤ . . . παντο[δ]απῶν λαγχάνειν ἄπο μοῖρα[ν] ἐσθλῶν;   'what better than to . . . win a share in all manner of blessings?' Pindar ends his ode for the same victory with a very similar statement: τὸ δὲ παθεῖν εὖ πρῶτον ἀέθλων· εὖ δ' ἀκούειν δευτέρα μοῖρ'· ἀμφοτέροισι δ' ἀνὴρ | ὃς ἂν ἐγκύρσηι καὶ ἕληι, στέφανον ὕψιστον δέδεκται, *P.* 1.99–100.

θεοῖσιν φίλον ἐόντα: the reference to the gods' favour harks back to the opening sentence, thus rounding off the ode and giving it a more general perspective: while it began by highlighting the Pythian chariot victory as tangible proof of Apollo's favour, it ends with a reference to 'a share in all kinds of blessings', which must mean wealth, power, and glory.

ODE 5: FOR HIERON'S VICTORY WITH THE RACEHORSE

1. Hieron's Olympic victory with the racehorse

The epigram preserved in Pausanias (8.42.9) and quoted on p. 79 was inscribed on the base of Hieron's victory monument, dedicated at Olympia after his death in 467 by his son, Deinomenes. It states that Hieron gained three victories there, one with the chariot and two with the racehorse. Accordingly, the monument consisted of a bronze chariot with charioteer and four horses, flanked on either side by bronze racehorses with jockeys (παῖδες, Paus. 6.12.1); the former was made by the Aiginetan sculptor

Onatas, the latter by Kalamis, renowned for his equestrian bronze statues. The fact that two racehorses were dedicated suggests that one of their
victories at Olympia was won by Pherenikos, the other by another horse.
Therefore, B.'s ode 5 and Pindar's *O.* 1 must celebrate the same victory.

The dates of Hieron's two racehorse victories are given in the victory
list *P.Oxy.* 11 222 col.i 19 and 32 as Olympiads 76 and 77, = 476 and 472
respectively. As neither B. nor Pindar refer to an earlier Olympic victory,
the date of the victory celebrated by them must be the earlier one, 476;
both attribute it to Hieron's famous stallion Pherenikos. B. 5.41 mentions a
victory by the same horse at Delphi, and as the scholia (11 p. 5 Drachmann)
mention Hieron's successes in the horse-races of the 26th and 27th Pythiads
(= 482 and 478), Pherenikos must have won at least the second of these.

2. The myth

The core of the mythical narrative in B. 5 is the report of Meleager's fate
(97–154), which is framed by the dialogue between Herakles and Meleager's
shade so as to make Meleager tell his own sad story, maximizing its emotional potential. Herakles' descent into Hades by order of Eurystheus, who
had demanded that he bring back Kerberos, is referred to in Homer (*Il.*
8.364–9; *Od.* 11.621–6) but his encounter there with Meleager is not attested
before B. and Pindar, fr. 249a. Pindar's version is paraphrased by the scholia ABDGe[1] on *Il.* 21.194: 'When Herakles descended to Hades to fetch
Kerberos, he met Meleager the son of Oineus, who begged him to marry his
sister, Deianeira. Having returned to the daylight, he hurried to Aitolia to
her father, Oineus. When he heard that the girl was betrothed to Acheloios,
the nearby river <god>, he wrestled with him, who had the shape of a
bull, and after breaking off one of his horns he took the girl. It is said that
this Acheloios received a horn from Amaltheia the daughter of Okeanos,
which he gave to Herakles and received his own back . . . The story is
in Pindar.' Apollodoros, in his account of Herakles' descent to Hades,
also briefly refers to it, 2.5.12: 'When the shades saw him, they fled, with
the exception of Meleager and Medousa the daughter of Gorgo.' While
Pindar, according to the Homeric scholia, told the story up to and including Herakles' wrestling contest with the river god Acheloios, B. ends with
Meleager mentioning his sister, Deianeira (175). Pindar makes Meleager
suggest to Herakles that he marry his sister, Deianeira, who is being pur-
sued by Acheloios; in B., by contrast, it is Herakles who addresses the fateful

question to Meleager, 'is there in Oineus' palace an unwedded daughter, resembling you in stature?' (165–8), thus expressing his admiration for (and erotic attraction to, see 168n.) the dead hero. Although Pindar's version is paraphrased by the scholia on *Il.* 24.194, it does not necessarily follow that Pindar invented it, for the story, or at least part of it, may have been told by Stesichoros in his *Kerberos*, or by some epic poet.

On the other hand, can we say whether Pindar's or B.'s version is the older one? In B., Herakles' question 'do you have a sister . . .' is motivated by his admiration for Meleager, whose account of the boar hunt and the ensuing battle had impressed him; B. thus offers a story that is coherent and logically motivated. Yet Pindar's story may have been the older one, and possibly quite different: e.g., Meleager's shade did not panic at the sight of Herakles because he recognized him and wanted to ask him to take care of his sister; he need not have told him of his own fate at all. If so – but all this is, of course, speculation – it may well have been B. who linked Herakles' encounter with Meleager in Hades to the Calydonian Boar Hunt by making Meleager's account of his own death prompt Herakles' fateful question. In his version, both heroes exemplify the statement that no mortal can be completely fortunate (53–5), so it seems logical that each should bring his own death upon himself: Meleager by killing his mother's brothers, Herakles by enquiring about Deianeira. As soon as her telling name ('man-destroyer') had been mentioned (173), B.'s account breaks off; there was no need to tell what she did: that story was well known, cf. [Hes.] fr. 25.20–5 and March, *The creative poet* 49–77.

The main story, that of the Calydonian boar and the fight over his hide, is first attested in poetry in Phoinix' speech in *Il.* 9.529–99, and in art on the François Vase (Florence, Museo Archeologico inv. 4209; see Simon, *Vasen* 69–77 and plates 51–7; Appendix no. 4). B.'s account agrees with Homer's in that (a) the fight between the Aitolians and the Kuretes is 'about the hide' (*Il.* 9.548 ἀμφὶ συὸς κεφαλῆι καὶ δέρματι λαχνήεντι, B. 5.124 περὶ δ᾽ αἴθωνος δορᾶς) and (b) Meleager kills one or more of his mother's brothers. The main difference is that in Homer his death is caused by his mother's curse; how he died remains unclear: τῆς δ᾽ . . . Ἐρινὺς ἔκλυε, *Il.* 9.571, while in the *Minyas* (Paus. 10.31.3 = fr. 5, *PEG* p.138 Bernabé) and in [Hes.] frs. 25.12 and 280.2 he is killed by Apollo. In B., however, it is the burning of the log by Althaia that ends his life. This version is also attested by Phrynichos' *Pleuroniai* (*TrGF* 3 F 6), but Pausanias adds that it was well known before

Phrynichos' time (10.31.4). This version was followed also by Aesch. *Cho.* 604–11, by Diodoros 4.34.6, and many later authors. March, *The creative poet* 44–6 has made a strong case for regarding Stesichoros as the poet who first introduced this motif; her main argument is that in his 'Boar Hunters' (Συοθῆραι, *PMG* 222), the Θεστιάδαι, Althaia's brothers, are mentioned: 'Their presence must mean that here they will be killed by Meleagros, and that in return he must be killed through his mother's anger – and this, surely, by the burning of the brand' (46).

3. Structure

The structure of this ode is symmetrical, the narrative section forming its centre-piece, preceded and followed by passages of praise for the victor, each followed by general statements ('*gnomai*'). The opening section ('*prooimion*') and the conclusion, linked by the same motifs, complete the 'frame' around this very clear structure which resembles that of Pindar's *O.*1 in its simplicity. Its sophistication lies in the correspondences between its parts and in their recurrent proportions.

The proem, rather unusually, begins with an address to Hieron and a flattering reference to his understanding of poetry. This leads to the motif of the poet's willingness to praise (9–16), which is echoed at the end (195–7), and of the vast potential for praise which Hieron's success is offering him. This is illustrated by the seemingly 'Homeric' simile of the eagle (16–36), which accounts for the unusual length of the proem (36 verses out of 200, = 18%).

The conclusion (191–200) resumes the 'willingness' motif introduced by the *gnome* (187–190), ending, as did the proem (36), with a prayer for god's favour and protection. The correspondences between the two sections are marked, as often in B., by verbal and thematic similarities: 10–12 ὕμνον . . . ξένος . . . πέμπει and 14–16 ἐθέλει . . . αἰνεῖν Ἱέρωνα → 195–7 πείθομαι . . . γλῶσσαν . . . πέμπειν Ἱέρωνι; 13–14 Οὐρανίας . . . θεράπων → 192–3 πρόπολος Μουσᾶν; 31 κέλευθος → 196 κελεύθου.

The proem is followed by the first praise passage (37–49), anticipated by ἕκατι Νίκας (33) and marked off by the names Pherenikos and Hieron. The link to the narrative section is provided by the statement which it illustrates (50–5). This statement, almost a *leitmotiv* of the Meleager story, serves as contrast, or 'dark foil', for the second praise passage (182–6) where the names

Pherenikos and Hieron are again closely linked: by saying that the stallion brought Hieron εὐδαιμονίας πέταλον, B. creates a very strong contrast to the sombre statement of 50–5. This statement, apart from introducing and interpreting the subsequent mythical section, also has a formal function in that it recalls, in μοῖράν τε καλῶν ἔπορεν (51), the opening word (εὔμοιρε), thus concluding the first part (proem and first praise) of the ode.

Like the ode as a whole, its mythical section (56–175) is also clearly structured. It begins with a relatively long introduction (56–77, i.e. 22 lines, or again 18%, of the total of 120 lines of the narrative section). The recurrence in this part of exactly the same proportion as that of the proem to the ode as a whole, 18% in either case, can hardly be a coincidence; it shows a remarkable degree of sophistication.

The main part of the mythical narrative is a sequence of five direct speeches, of which the third is Meleager's long monologue (93–154); it is preceded and followed by Herakles' questions (86–92 and 159–69) which are in turn preceded and followed by Meleager's address (78–84) and answer (170–5). The structure of the narrative section thus repeats that of the ode itself. It is also remarkable for the poet's choice of his literary models in elegiac and epic poetry, see 160–2n. and 162–4n.

1–16 The first part of the unusually long proem is a kind of dedication to the *laudandus*, marked off by the vocative at the beginning (Εὔμοιρε . . . στραταγέ, 1–2) and the name (Ἱέρωνα, 16). After the reference to Hieron's appreciation of poetry (3–6) it develops the 'willingness' motif (ἐθέλει . . . αἰνεῖν, 14–16) which recurs in the concluding section (187–97), rounding off the ode thematically.

1–2 Εὔμοιρε [Σ]υρακ[οσίω]ν . . . στρατα[γ]έ: εὔμοιρος is someone who has received a good portion or share; μοῖρα tends to be qualified, e.g. μοῖρα καλῶν Pindar, *I.* 5.15, similarly *N.* 10.20, B. 4.20. Hieron receives similar praise from Pindar, *P.* 3.84–6 τὶν δὲ μοῖρ' εὐδαιμονίας ἕπεται· λαγέταν γάρ τοι τύραννον δέρκεται, εἴ τιν' ἀνθρώπων, ὁ μέγας πότμος. The idea of Hieron's 'good share of blessings' is echoed at the end of the ode in πυθμένες . . . ἐσθλ[ῶν], ending on a similar note.

ἱπποδινήτων: only here and in the word-list *SH* 991 = *P.Hibeh* 172 col.ΙΙ 19, presumably from B. Adjectives in –τος can have active or passive meaning, according to circumstances; cf. Chantraine, *Morphologie* 284; E. Fraenkel on Aesch. *Ag.* 12 (νυκτίπλαγκτον . . . εὐνήν) with bibliography.

στρατα[γ]έ: this term is discussed by Jebb 465–7 who concludes 'that στραταγέ is merely a general designation, 'war-lord', and does not refer to a special office'. The two vocatives, εὔμοιρε and στραταγέ, anticipate the two themes of praise, Hieron's success at Olympia and his military power, which will be taken up by Νίκα and Ἄρης in 33–4.

3–6 γνώσηι... ὀρθῶς: after the references to Hieron's victory and, generally, his privileged position (εὔμοιρε) and his military record (στραταγέ), he is complimented on his connoisseurship of poetry. Pindar, in his ode for the same victory, pays him a very similar compliment, *O.* 1.103–5: πέποιθα δὲ ξένον | μή τιν' ἀμφότερα καλῶν τε ἴδριν †ἅμα† καὶ δύναμιν κυριώτερον | τῶν γε νῦν κλυταῖσι δαιδαλωσέμεν ὕμνων πτυχαῖς 'I am confident that there is no other host both more expert in noble pursuits and more lordly in power alive today to embellish in famous folds of hymns'. Both poets are unashamedly elitist in assuming that their poetry is not for the masses but for the few who have sophisticated understanding and taste, see 3.85n.

4 ἄγαλμα 'delight', aptly defined by Apoll.Soph. p.6.30 = Hsch. α 263 πᾶν ἐφ' ὧι τις ἀγάλλεται (cf. ἀγάλλειν 'to adorn' in Pindar. *O.* 1.86). B. uses the noun in the sense of 'monument' in 1.184 (εὐκλείας ἄ[γαλ]μα), in fr. 20B.5 metaphorically for 'song'; both meanings are implied in 10.11–14 ἀθάνατον Μουσᾶν ἄγαλμα ... τεὰν ἀρετὰν μανῦον ἐπιχθονίοισιν 'an undying ornament of the Muses ... informing mortals of your prowess'.

4–5 τῶν γε νῦν αἴ τις ἐπιχθονίων: cf. Pindar, *O.* 1.105 quoted above. Statements implying, or amounting to, a superlative are often qualified by τῶν νῦν, cf. E. Fraenkel on Aesch. *Ag.* 532 with further references.

αἴ = εἰ in Aeolic and West Greek ('Doric') dialects; cf. 17.64 where B. adopts the Homeric αἴ κε (*Il.* 4.249 ὄφρα ἴδητ' αἴ κ' ὕμμιν ὑπέρσχηι χεῖρα Κρονίων), but αἴ τις is not Homeric: it appears for the first time in Ibykos (if the lines are by Ibykos, *SLG* 221 = *P.Oxy.* 2637 fr. 1a.33). In B., however, αἴ τις ἐπιχθονίων is used for emphasis, as in Soph. *Trach.* 8, Ar. *Pl.* 655; for further examples see Thesleff, *Intensification* 190 § 381.

6–7 φρένα δ' εὐθύδικ[ο]ν: fair-mindedness is one of the compliments that tyrants often receive from poets: B. calls Hieron ἀστύθεμις 4.3, Pindar refers to his θεμιστεῖον ... σκᾶπτον *O.* 1.12, cf. *P.* 3.71 and *P.* 1.86; also *O.* 2.6 (Theron), *P.* 4.280 (Damophilos), *P.* 5.28–29 (Battiadai), *P.* 6.48 (Thrasyboulos).

εὐθύδικ[ο]ν: the compound occurs here for the first time, though as a name it is attested earlier, as E. Fraenkel pointed out (on Aesch. *Ag.* 761): Euthydikos dedicated a kore at Athens (Akropolis Museum inv. 686 + 609;

Boardman, *Sculpture* fig.160), dated *c.* 490 BCE; the inscription on the base is *IG* I² 589.

φρένα . . . ἀτρέμ' ἀμπαύσας μεριμνᾶν 'rest your mind in ease from its cares'. The idea that song provides a respite from cares and worries goes back to Hes. *Th.* 55: Mnemosyne bore the Muses to Zeus, λησμοσύνην τε κακῶν ἄμπαυμά τε μερμηράων, see West ad loc. with further references.

8 δεῦρ' <ἄγ'> ἄθρησον νόωι: the papyrus has δευραθρησον, but the responding lines (–◡ – ⨯– ◡ –) show that this line is one syllable short. The missing syllable might be restored (a) by adding a preposition to the verb, e.g. <ἐσ>- or <ἐπ>ἄθρησον, or (b) before νόωι, e.g. <σὺν> or <ἐν> νόωι, or (c) a particle after δεῦρ'.

(a) is unlikely because ἐσ– or ἐπαθρεῖν means 'to look at' and would require an object; moreover, when the verb is used in its extended meaning 'to see in the mind', it is used in the simple form (Soph. *OT* 1305, *OC* 1032, Eur. *Ba.* 1281). (b) <σὺν> νόωι violates 'Maas's Bridge' (see Maas, *Greek Metre* § 48: in dactyloepitrites, words or word-groups should not end before – ◡ – ‖ if the preceding *anceps* is long, i.e. . . . ⌒ ◡ – ‖), εὐνόως and εὐνοέων are prose words, and <ἐν> νόωι means 'in one's intention', as in ἐν νόωι ἔχειν, not 'intellectually'. B. is the first to use the verb in this sense: this is why he adds νόωι 'look here *with your mind!*' – only the simple instrumental dative will do, cf. Hdt. 3.41.1 νόωι λαβών, *AP* 7.234.3 ἔδρακε θυμῶι. I have therefore adopted (c): δεῦρ'<ἄγ'> ἄθρησον νόωι, cf. *Od.* 8.145 δεῦρ'ἄγε καὶ σύ . . . πείρησαι ἀέθλων, also [Hes.] fr. 302.2.

9–10 ἢ σὺν Χαρίτεσσι: for affirmative ἢ, see Denniston, *Particles* 280–2; cf. Pindar, *P.* 6.1 Ἀκούσατ' · ἢ γὰρ κτλ.

ὑφάνας ὕμνον   'having woven a song of praise'. The metaphor (also in Pindar, fr. 179) is inspired by an etymology which derived ὕμνος from ὑφαίνειν 'to weave', see 19.6–9n.

12 ἐς κλυτὰν πέμπει πόλιν: the transmitted text is πεμπει κλεενναν ες πολιν, which cannot be correct: (1) The responding lines are all (except 27, on which see below) one syllable shorter: –◡ – ⏞ – – ◡ – ‖; (2) it violates 'Maas's Bridge' (see above, 8n.); (3) the repetition κλεεννὰν → κλεινός (14) is awkward. The easiest correction is ἐς κλυτὰν πέμπει πόλιν (Maas). The first strophe is a kind of *propemptikon* for the ode; at its end, the 'sending' theme recurs once more in πείθομαι . . . πέμπειν Ἱέρωνι (195–7).

13–14 Οὐρανίας . . . θεράπων: in 192–3, Hesiod is referred to as πρόπολος Μουσᾶν whom B. follows (see on 195 πείθομαι). The idea that poets are 'servants' of the Muses was made popular by Hes. *Th.* 100, see West ad loc. with references.

14 ἐθέλει (εθελει δε pap.):   Walker 1897: 856 deleted δὲ here and μετ' in 30 (see below). The sentence beginning with ἐθέλει 'caps' the first strophe: 'Lord of Syracuse, look here! A poet is sending a song to your city: he wants to praise Hieron'. This 'capping' function of the 'willingness' theme would be obscured if it were connected by δέ – it has to be an *asyndeton explicativum*, which is essentially a rhetorical device designed to place emphasis on the last element of a sequence of sentences by omitting any connecting particle (on B.'s and Pindar's use of asyndeta, see Maehler, *Asyndeton* 421–30). Scribes, unaware of its function, often insert δέ, γε, or τε also in manuscripts of Pindar (*O.* 1.71; 6.72–4; 10.71; *P.* 3.105; 4.179; 8.43; *N.* 6.8; 8.37, etc.); cf. Barrett on Eur. *Hipp.* 40 and 1280.

16–30   The function of the beautiful simile of the eagle, inserted here between the 'willingness' theme (9–16) and the 'facility' theme (31–6), is to create high expectations of the way in which the poet will fulfil his promise to praise Hieron. It is also an impressive demonstration of the poet's self-confidence: 'I am willing to praise Hieron – I am like the eagle who flies unimpeded over mountains and the sea – thus, I have countless ways of praising the sons of Deinomenes.' A very similar image is employed by Dante, *Inferno* 4.94–6: 'Così vidi adunar la bella scola | Di quel signor dell'altissimo canto, | Che sovra li altri com'aquila vola', as Taccone, *Bacchilide* 47 has pointed out. The image of the eagle may be inspired by Homeric similes (*Il.* 22.308–11, cf. 21.251–2); here, as in Pindar (*N.* 3.80–2; 5.19–21; *O.* 2.86–8), it represents the poet. B. seems to have modelled his simile on the scene in the Homeric *Hymn to Demeter* (*h.Dem.* 375–83) where Kore on her chariot flies over sea, land and mountain peaks; B. substitutes the eagle for the divine horses but keeps the crucial element of the image, the ease of the flight. The limitless void of the sky indicates the vast potential for praise which Hieron offers the poet.

16–17 βαθὺν δ' αἰθέρα . . . τάμνων   'cleaving the deep heavens', cf. *h.Dem.* 383 ἠέρα τέμνον. Ibykos seems to have used this phrase, perhaps of Bellerophon (Lobel), in *SLG* 223(a) col.ιι 5–7 = *P.Oxy.*2637 fr. 5; it is parodied from Euripides' *Andromeda* (frs. 123–4) in Aristoph. *Thesm.* 1098–1102.

20 ἐρισφαράγου   'loud-thundering', cf. ἐσφαράγιζον· ἐδόνουν, μετὰ ψόφου ἤχουν Hesych. ε 6437, and West on Hes. *Th.*706 on the meaning of σφαραγίζειν.

23 λιγύφθογγοι   'clear-voiced', always said of heralds in Homer, here of small birds (like the nightingale in Ar. *Birds* 1380), in B. 10.10 of the poet referred to as a 'bee' (λιγύφθογγον μέλισσαν). The contrast between the eagle and the smaller birds may have become proverbial, as the close

parallel between 21–3 and [Hes.] fr. 33a.14–15, the Lesbian *inc.auct.* fr.10
L.-P., and Pind. *P.* 5.111–12 suggests. It also inspired Milton's image of the
Nation in his *Areopagitica*: 'Methinks I see in my mind a noble and puissant
nation rousing herself . . . methinks I see her as an eagle mewing her mighty
youth . . . while the whole noise of timorous and flocking birds . . . flutter
about' (John Milton, *Complete Prose Works* ii 558).

26–7 δυσπαίπαλα κύματα   'the rugged waves'; the epithet is first found
in Archil. 190 W., a variation on epic παιπαλόεις, said of mountains (*Il.*
13.17, *Od.* 10.97), rocky islands (*Il.* 13.33 etc.) and mountain paths (in similes,
Il. 12.168, 17.743, *Od.* 17.204), of waves only here. B. seems to have taken
it in the sense of 'difficult' (to traverse), as Leumann, *Hom.Wörter* 237 has
pointed out.

νωμᾶι   (νωμαι | ται **A**: νωμα | ται **A**¹: ται del. Walker): Antimachos
uses the middle with the meaning 'to distribute' (fr. 22 ἡγεμόνεσσιν . . .
κήρυκες . . . κύπελλα . . . νωμήσαντο), but in the sense required here ('to
move') the middle voice is not found before Quintus of Smyrna (3.439
σάκος . . . νωμήσασθαι); here it would be against the metre (see above
on 11–12), and parallels like Soph. fr. 941.11 (Kypris) νωμᾶι δ' ἐν οἰωνοῖσι
τοὐκείνης πτερόν and *AP* 9.339 πτερὸν αἰθέρι νωμῶν also suggest that the
active is required here. The fact that the scribe had originally written νωμαι
and then crossed out the iota may indicate that ται was a later addition in
his exemplar.

ἐν ἀτρύτωι χάει: as B. uses the epithet of time in the sense of 'lim-
itless' in 9.80 ([ἐς ἄτ]ρυτον χρόνον), he seems to have understood it as a
synonym of ἀτρύγετος, cf. αἰθέρος ἀτρυγέτοιο (*Il.* 17.425 etc.); he may
have been familiar with the etymology preserved by Herodian (*EM* 167.28
= Hdn.2.p.284 Lentz) which derived ἀτρύγετος from τρύεσθαι 'to be worn
out'; cf. Pind. *P.* 4.178 ἄτρυτον πόνον 'unceasing toil', also Soph. *Aias* 788
and Hdt. 9.52. The explanation ἀκαταπόνητος found in the scholia on
Homer (schol. D on *Il.* 1.316; schol. *Od.* 2.370), Apoll.Soph. 46.16, Hesych.
α 8167 etc. is based on the same etymology.

29–30 ἀρίγνωτος ἀνθρώποις ἰδεῖν   (μετ' ἀνθρώποις pap.): μετ' was
deleted by Walker (see 14n.), rightly, because μετά + dative always means
'amongst', 'in the company of' (*Od.* 9.369 etc.; cf. *h.Ven.*103 where Anchises
asks Aphrodite δός με μετὰ Τρώεσσιν ἀριπρεπέ' ἔμμεναι ἄνδρα). That cannot be said of the eagle who does not mingle with men but flies high in
the sky, 'a conspicuous sight for men'. The deletion of μετ' (and of δέ in 14)
normalizes the metre; there is no reason to assume metrical licences here.

31–6   This passage has a double function: (a) it makes clear the meaning
and relevance of the eagle simile (it illustrates the ease with which the poet
can find ways to praise Hieron's success), and (b) it provides an elegant
transition to the first praise passage (37–49), see above, p. 109.

31 τὼς νῦν . . . κέλευθος: see on 19.1–2. The image of 'countless paths
in all directions' is a variation on the theme of 'ease in praise' which recurs
in 195–7; for a discussion of Pindar's use of this theme, see Bundy 61–4.

33 κυανοπλοκάμου: see on 11.83.

ἕκατι Νίκας: see on 11.9 σέθεν δ' ἕκατι.

34 χαλκεοστέρνου τ' Ἄρηος: the compound, 'bronze-breasted', is found
only here and in Phlegon, *FGrHist* 257 F 36.3 χαλκόστερνοι δυνάμεις, after
Homer's χάλκεος Ἄρης (*Il.* 5.704 etc.). Hieron's success is praised 'by the
will of Victory (Νίκα) and Ares'; this takes up once more the twin themes
of Hieron's success in the games and in war, referred to by εὔμοιρε and
στραταγέ in the opening lines.

35–6 Δεινομένευς . . . παῖδες: the plural, following the reference to
'bronze-breasted Ares', implies a reference to Gelon's and his brothers'
victory over the Carthaginians at Himera on the north coast of Sicily in
480. Ten years later, Pindar also refers to their joint victory in *P.* 1.79
παρὰ . . . ἀκτὰν Ἰμέρα παίδεσσιν ὕμνον Δεινομένευς τελέσας, on which
see Hdt. 7.165–7; Diod. 11.20.22; Polyainos 1.28.1. For this victory, they
dedicated a golden tripod and a statue of Victory at Delphi, cf. Diod.11.26
and *AP* 6.214 = *Epigr. graeca* 203–6 Page; see ode 3.17–19n.

ἀγέρωχοι   'noble', οἱ ἄγαν ἔνδοξοι καὶ ἔντιμοι Hesych. α 462.

μὴ κάμοι θεός: the wish for divine favour recurs in 197–200 where it
specifically refers to peace and stability.

37–49   The description of the race, anticipated by ἕκατι Νίκας (33) and
concluded with νίκαν Ἱέρωνι . . . τιτύσκων (49), is the most vivid and
detailed account of a victory anywhere in epinician poetry. Apart from
a brief reference to the jockey, who remains anonymous (47), it focusses
entirely on the racehorse; ξανθός 'chestnut' is common as a name for horses
(*Il.* 19.400 etc.).

39 ἀελλοδρόμαν   'storm-paced', only here, a variation on epic ἀελ-
λόπος (*Il.* 8.409 and 24.77, of Iris; *h.Ven.* 217 of horses, also Sim. *PMG*
515 and Pind. *N.* 1.6). The notion of 'storm' to indicate the speed of
horses, taken up in 46, is also present in Homer's θείειν ἀνέμοισιν ὁμοῖοι,
Il. 10.437.

40 εἶδε . . . χρυσόπαχυς Ἀώς: horse races took place early in the morning, cf. Weniger 1904: 133–4 (on Paus. 5.9.3); Ebert, *Olympia* 43; cf. B.11.22 and the epigram on a boy's victory in the pankration *IG* xii 3.390 (1st cent. BCE) ἁ μία δ'ἀὼς δὶς Δωροκλείδαν εἶδεν ἀεθλοφόρον. Pindar uses a similar phrase for Xenokrates' chariot victory in *I.* 2.18 ἐν Κρίσαι δ' εὐρυσθενὴς εἶδ' Ἀπόλλων νιν πόρε τ' ἀγλαῖαν. For the idea that a god 'looks at' a man when he grants him a favour, see ode 11.15–17n.

42 γᾶι δ' ἐπισκήπτων πιφαύσκω   'resting my hand on the earth I proclaim'. The gesture means that the Earth, or some chthonic power, is called to witness a promise or an oath (*Il.* 14.271–6), or to help (*Il.* 9.568–9; *h.Ap.* 333; Hdt.4.172.3). Pindar, too, likes to support praising statements by an oath (*O.*2.92 and 6.20, *N.*11.24) or by an assurance to be a truthful witness (*O.*4.3–4 and 17–18, see Bundy, *Studia Pindarica* 60–1 n.66). In B., such strong statements tend to introduce superlatives (e.g., 1.159) or statements that amount to a superlative, see 11.24n.

43–5 οὔπω νιν . . . ὀρνύμενον   is a clever way of saying 'no other horse was in front of him', i.e. he was in front from start to finish. This has a close parallel in an epigram from Pergamon commemorating the victory of Attalos, the adoptive son of Philetairos, the founder of the Attalid dynasty, with the colt chariot at Olympia in the first half of the third century, Ebert no.59.8–9: ὁ δ' Ἀττάλου ἶσος ἀέλληι | δίφρος ἀεὶ προτέραν ποσ[σ]ὶν ἔφαινε κόνιν, = Moretti, *Iscrizioni agonistiche* 37; cf. also Kall. fr. 254.7–10 (*SH* p. 101).

προτέ[ρω]ν   'in front of him': the accent in the papyrus on ἐ shows that it had the masculine form, not προτε[ρᾶ]ν; besides, in choral lyric and in tragedy chariot horses are mares, single horses are stallions, see 3.3–4n.

46–8 ῥιπᾶι . . . ἵεται :   ῥιπή is a 'gust' of wind in Homer (*Il.* 15.171 ὑπὸ ῥιπῆς . . . Βορέαο) and Soph. *Ant.* 137 ῥιπαῖς ἐχθίστων ἀνέμων, cf. Pind. *P.* 9.48 and 4.195.

φυλάσσων   'means not merely "bearing his rider safe", but "attending to his guidance": the word κυβερνήταν brings this out' (Jebb).

48 νεόκροτον   'which brings new applause' (Campbell), 'greeted with fresh plaudits' (Jebb). In his victory odes, B. often highlights the reaction of others, e.g. spectators, to his *laudandus*' success, cf. 3.9 and 9.35.

49 Ἱέρωνι . . . τιτύσκων: taken up by Ἱέρωνι φέρων 185. These verbal repetitions signal to the audience that a section of the ode is being concluded as they create a kind of 'audible frame' around it, in this case framing the mythical narrative.

50–5   The gnomic statement serves a dual purpose: (1) it forms the transition from the first praise to the mythical section, while at the same time summing up the victor's praise (ὄλβιος κτλ.); (2) it provides, right from the outset, the poet's own interpretation of the myth which is about to be presented as an illustration of the *gnome*.

51 μοῖραν . . . καλῶν   'a portion of successes', not only victories in games but also, more generally, achievements and praise, cf. 4.18–20 and Pind. *I.* 5.12–15. The statement seems deliberately phrased in this general way, so as to apply not only to Hieron but also, by way of contrast, to Meleager and Herakles, neither of whom was 'fortunate in all things' (πάντα γ'εὐδαίμων), and whose fate did not allow them to 'pass their lives in affluence' (ἀφνεὸν βιοτὰν διάγειν).

52 ἐπιζήλωι: several compounds in –ζηλος are found in B. (πολύζηλος 11.63, πολυζήλωτος 10.48, 7.10, 1.184, 9.45), but none in Pindar (apart from ζαλωτός *O.* 7.6 in a comparison). It looks as if Pindar deliberately avoided any reference to ζῆλος, which to him may have had a strongly negative connotation, as it does to Agamemnon in Aesch. *Ag.* 939–40, see E. Fraenkel ad loc.

53–5 οὐ . . . πάντα γ' εὐδαίμων: no mortal can be 'fortunate in all things', he can only have 'a portion of successes' and not perfect happiness. This sombre statement sets the tone for the sad story that follows, which provides the dark background, 'vicissitude foil' in Bundy's terminology, for the victory celebration and the second praise passage, see on 186 εὐδ]αιμονίας πέταλον.

56 τ[ὸν γάρ π]οτ' ἐρειψιπύλαν: a tiny trace of the crossbar of τ is visible at the beginning of the line. The 'gate-wrecker' is Herakles; there was no need to name him, as everyone knew the story of Kerberos (see 60–2n.) which was one of the most popular topics on sixth-century black-figure vases. The compound is found only here, but cf. ἐρειψ[ι]πύ[ργοις 13.167, ἐρειψίτοιχοι Aesch. *Septem* 883.

58–9 Διὸς] ἀργικεραύνου   the compound, 'thunderbolt-flashing', is an epithet of Zeus in the *Iliad* (19.121, 20.16, 22.178), also Pind. *O.* 8.3 and in B. 29.2.

Φερσεφόνας τανισφύρου   Persephone has the same epithet, 'slender-ankled', in *h.Dem.*2 and 77. The spelling ταvι– for ταvυ– is by dissimilation from –σφυρος, cf. τανίφυλλος.

60–2   The Kerberos story is mentioned in *Il.* 8.368, but what B. had in mind seems to have been *Od.* 11.623–5 where Herakles' shade reports to Odysseus καί ποτέ μ' ἐνθάδ' ἔπεμψε κύν' ἄξοντ'· οὐ γὰρ ἔτ' ἄλλον | φράζετο (sc. Eurystheus) τοῦδέ τί μοι χαλεπώτερον εἶναι ἄεθλον. | τὸν μὲν ἐγὼν ἀνένεικα καὶ ἤγαγον ἐξ Ἀΐδαο, 'he once sent me hither to fetch the hound of Hades, for he could devise for me no other task mightier than this. The hound I carried off and led forth from the house of Hades.' B. embroiders by adding a graphic compound (epic καρχαρόδοντα), by clarifying (ἐς φάος), and by adding the monster's genealogy (62).

62 υἱὸν . . . Ἐχίδνας: in Hes. *Th.* 310–11, the offspring (τέκνα) of Echidna and Typhaon are the two dogs, Orthos and Kerberos, and Hydra. In early and classical Greek it is very unusual to refer to an animal, even a mythical one, as υἱός; Pegasos in Pind. *O.* 13.63 (υἱὸν . . . Γοργόνος) is a rare exception. In the Septuagint and New Testament it is not uncommon; examples include Ps. 28.1; Sir. 38.25; and Matth. 21.5. By calling Kerberos a 'son' of Echidna, B. may be trying to confer 'heroic' status on the monster; see also 104–5n.

65–7 οἷά τε φύλλ' ἄνεμος . . . δονεῖ: οἷά τε is used adverbially, as in Alkman 56.4 and perhaps Ibykos *SLG* 166.7. The passage in B. is modelled on Homer's famous lines *Il.* 6.146–9 οἵη περ φύλλων γενεή, τοίη δὲ καὶ ἀνδρῶν. | φύλλα τὰ μέν τ' ἄνεμος χαμάδις χέει, ἄλλα δέ θ' ὕλη | τηλεθόωσα φύει, ἔαρος δ' ἐπιγίγνεται ὥρη· | ὡς ἀνδρῶν γενεὴ ἡ μὲν φύει, ἡ δ'ἀπολήγει. Cf. *Il.* 21.464–6; Mimn. 2.1–5; Musaios B5 = Clem. *Strom.* 6.5; Sim. 19 West; Ar. *Birds* 685–7; Ap.Rhod. 4.214–19; Virg. *Aen.* 6.309–12 (which inspired Milton, *Paradise Lost* 1 302 'thick as autumnal leaves that strew the brooks . . .'). The passage in B. is not a fully-fledged 'Homeric' simile; its purpose is to evoke the idea of a scrambling crowd ('countless as leaves', Jebb), and also that of the precariousness of the human condition, in line with the pessimistic interpretation of this image in most writers after Homer.

ἀργηστάς   'bright, shining', = ἀργής (cf. Soph. *OC* 670 ἀργῆτα Κολωνόν), or perhaps 'clearly seen, distinct', as suggested by Braswell on Pind. *P.* 4.8 ἐν ἀργινόεντι μαστῶι.

69–70 θρασυμέμνονος . . . Πορθανίδα: Meleager, son of Oineus and grandson of Porthaon (the short form of the name, wrongly altered to

Πορθαονιδα by A³, is required by the metre; cf. Ἀλκμᾶν(α) for Ἀλκμάονα in Pind. *P.* 8.46, Ἀλκμανιδᾶν *P.* 7.2).

71 Ἀλκμήνιος: Herakles, Alkmena's son; the matronymic is formed like Τελαμώνιος, Νηλήιος, Καπανήιος etc.; cf. Wackernagel, *Kl.Schr.* 1358–9 and *Syntax* II 68–9.

73 νευρὰν . . . κορώνας ('he put) the string on his bow-hook'. The image is modelled on *Od.* 11.605–8.

λιγυκλαγγῆ 'clear-twanging', only here and 14.14 λι]γυκλαγγεῖς χοροί, perhaps coined by B. after the simile *Od.* 21.405–11 (cf. *Il.* 4.125).

74 χαλκεόκρανον 'bronze-headed', only here. In Homer, the arrow is χαλκήρης 'fitted to bronze' (Il. 13.650, Od. 1.262) or χαλκοβαρής 'top-heavy with bronze' (*Il.* 15.465, *Od.* 21.423).

75 εἵλετο ἰόν: B. seems to have believed, wrongly, that ἰός 'arrow' begins with ϝ, through confusion with (ϝ)ιός 'poison' and (ϝ)ιόν 'violet'; see also on 17.131. This is strange in view of *Il.* 4.116 (Pandaros) σύλα πῶμα φαρέτρης, ἐκ δ' ἕλετ' ἰόν.

78 νιν εὖ εἰδὼς προσεῖπεν 'knowing well, he addressed him', not 'spake unto him, for he knew him well' (Jebb, who took νιν as object of both εἰδώς and προσεῖπεν). In Homer εἰδώς never refers to a person as object; it seems likely therefore that here, too, the participle is used absolutely, as in *Il.* 1.384; 13.665; *Od.* 2.170 (in all three cases, of special or superior knowledge): Meleager knows that it is pointless to shoot at shadows of the dead. The scene may have inspired Virgil, *Aen.* 6.290–4 where Aeneas, suddenly frightened, draws his sword against the shadows, *et ni docta comes tenuis sine corpore vitas | admoneat volitare, cava sub imagine formae, | inruat et frustra ferro diverberet umbras.*

80 γελανώσας . . . θυμόν 'calm your heart'; the verb, found only here, means 'to make γελανής ('calm', Pind. *O.* 5.2; *P.* 4.181); see Braswell on Pind. *P.* 4.181(b): 'The adjective γελανής itself is ultimately related to γελάω (cf. Schwyzer I 513; Frisk, *Wörterbuch* and Chantraine, *Dict. s.v.* γελάω), the primary metaphorical meaning of which was 'shine'; see West on Hes. *Th.* 40 and Richardson on *h.Dem.*14. A secondary development is the sense "to rejoice at" anything pleasant.'

84 οὔ τοι δέος 'you have nothing to fear' (τοι = σοι), cf. *Il.*1.515 (Thetis to Zeus:) ἐπεὶ οὔ τοι ἔπι δέος, 12.246 (Hektor to Poulydamas) σοὶ δ' οὐ δέος ἔστ' ἀπολέσθαι. The irony is that Herakles, the mightiest of heroes, is scared (like Odysseus in *Od.* 11.43) and has to be reassured by the dead Meleager's shadow.

86–8 τίς . . . ἐν ποίαι χθονί: a variation on the epic τίς πόθεν εἶς ἀνδρῶν; (*Od.* 1.170 etc.). As Herakles' question arises out of amazement and admiration, so does Apollo's, who enquires about Kyrene, having seen her wrestling bare-handed with a lion: τίς νιν ἀνθρώπων τέκεν; ποίας δ ' ἀποσπασθεῖσα φύτλας | ὀρέων κευθμῶνας ἔχει σκιοέντων, | γεύεται δ' ἀλκᾶς ἀπειράντου; 'what mortal bore her? From what stock has she been severed that she lives in the glens of the shadowy mountains and puts to the test her unbounded valour?' (Pind. *P.* 9.33–5).

89–91   As Jebb has pointed out, Herakles naturally assumes that Meleager must have been killed by a great warrior whom Hera, Herakles' long-standing enemy, will now send forth against him (κεῖνον, 90); it is not until 136–44 that he learns that Meleager's own mother, Althaia, caused his death. 'The touch of poetical art given by κεῖνον is like that of Sophocles in the *Antigone* (v.248), when Creon, never dreaming that the breaker of his edict is a woman, asks τί φής; τίς ἀνδρῶν ἦν ὁ τολμήσας τάδε;' (Jebb).

90–1 ἐφ' ἁμετέραι . . . κεφαλᾶι   'against my life', cf. *Il.* 17.242 ὅσσον ἐμῆι κεφαλῆι περιδείδια, cf. *Od.* 2.237, Soph. *OC* 564.

91–2 τὰ δέ που . . . μέλει: cf. *Il.* 5.430 ταῦτα δ' Ἄρηϊ θοῶι καὶ Ἀθήνηι πάντα μελήσει (also *Il.* 17.515; 15.231; 22.11; 23.724; *Od.* 17.601). In Homer, που 'I suppose' is often added in statements that seem plausible in themselves, yet are impossible to verify, e.g. concerning the intentions of gods, cf. Wackernagel, *Kl.Schr.* 701.

94–6 χαλεπὸν . . . ἐπιχθονίοις: modelled on *Od.* 3.143–7 where Agamemnon prepares to offer sacrifices to appease Athena's wrath and the poet comments: νήπιος, οὐδὲ τὸ ἤιδη ὃ οὐ πείσεσθαι ἔμελλεν· | οὐ γάρ τ'αἶψα θεῶν τρέπεται νόος αἰὲν ἐόντων. B. reverses this by putting the gnomic statement at the beginning of Meleager's long account, which illustrates and confirms it. The view that the gods are implacable is most strongly stated in Aeschylus, cf. *Supp.* 385–6 μένει τοι Ζηνὸς ἱκταίου κότος, δυσπαράθελκτος παθόντος οἴκτοις and see E. Fraenkel on Aesch. *Ag.* 69–70 who saw in these passages a 'most decided conflict . . . with the convictions of popular belief and of the poet of the Λιταί (*Il.* 9.497ff.), whose lines are attacked on the same grounds by Plato's Adeimantos (*Rep.* 2.364d)'; Fraenkel also refers to *Prom.* 34 Διὸς γὰρ δυσπαραίτητοι φρένες and 184–5 ἀκίχητα γὰρ ἤθεα καὶ κέαρ | ἀπαράμυθον ἔχει Κρόνου παῖς.

97 καὶ γὰρ ἄν: examples are often linked to general statements by καὶ γάρ, cf. Pind. *O.* 7.27, *P.* 9.42 etc., see E. Fraenkel on Aesch. *Ag.* 1040. Here the phrase takes the form of the *apodosis* to an unfulfilled conditional clause: ['if it were otherwise,] Oineus would have . . .', cf. Pind. *O.* 9.29–31.

97–126   Meleager's account closely follows *Iliad* 9.533–49: there, too, the *exemplum* is introduced by καὶ γάρ, but otherwise literal repetition is carefully avoided. Listeners who were thoroughly familiar with Homer's account may have appreciated the choral poet's technique of variation and embroidery.

97 πλάξιππος Οἰνεύς: the compound is Homeric, though not given to Oineus, who is ἱππηλάτα (*Il.* 9.581) and ἱππότα (*Il.* 14.117).

98–9 καλυκοστεφάνου σεμνᾶς . . . λευκωλένου: Artemis, who is the dominant figure of this story, gets three epithets here instead of one as in Homer (χρυσόθρονος, *Il.* 9.533).

102 φοινικονώτων   'red-backed', only here; B. was fond of colour compounds, see 11.97–8n.

104–5 ἔσχεν χόλον   'she had conceived anger', for Homer's ἡ δὲ χολωσαμένη (*Il.* 9.538); Meleager does not say why, so that he can present his sad fate as totally undeserved and cruel, maximizing its potential for pathos. The audience may have remembered the reason given in Homer: Oineus had omitted to sacrifice to Artemis, *Il.* 9.534–7.

εὐρυβίαν . . . κάπρον: in epic and lyric poetry, this epithet is given to gods and heroes; in B. it gives the mighty boar heroic status. If some of the fragments of *P.Oxy.* LVII 3876 belong to Stesichoros' *Boar Hunters*, fr. 5.6 [εὐρυ]βίαν may refer to the boar.

ἀναιδομάχαν   'a ruthless fighter', only here, apparently coined by B. after Κυδοιμὸν ἀναιδέα δηιότητος *Il.* 5.593; see on 155 ἀδεισιβόαν.

107 πλημύρων σθένει   'in the floodtide of his might', for Homer's σθένεϊ βλεμεαίνων (of boars and lions: *Il.* 12.42, 17.20–2).

108 ὄρχους   'vine-rows'; in *Il.* 9.540, 'the boar devastates an orchard (ἀλωήν), for which B. substitutes a vineyard, apparently because he is thinking of the etymology (from οἶνος) of the name, Oineus (cf. Hekataios *FGrHist* 1 F 15), who had received the vines from Dionysos (Apollod. 1.8.1).

109 σφάζε τε μῆλα: in Homer, the boar destroys tall trees αὐτῆισιν ῥίζηισι καὶ αὐτοῖς ἄνθεσι μήλων 'with their roots and fruit-blossoms', *Il.* 9.542. In B., the Homeric 'apples' become 'sheep' because in this way they can form a powerful *tricolon*: the boar destroys vines – sheep – even humans, demonstrating its supernatural strength, see 104–5n. In this, B. was followed by Apollod. 1.8.2 and Ovid, *Met.* 8.296.

111 Ἑλλάνων ἄριστοι: in Stesichoros' *Boar-hunters* (*PMG* 222), the hunters include Lokrians, Achaians, Boiotians and Dryopes. Their names are listed in Apollod. 1.8.2, Ovid *Met.* 8.299–317 and Hyginus 173.

112–13 ἐνδυκέως . . . συνεχέως: the scholia BT on *Il.* 24.158 and on Nikand. *Ther.* 262 treat these words as synonymous, but in *Il.* 24.158 and 23.90 ἐνδυκέως seems to mean either 'kindly' or 'carefully' (the latter may be linked to the gloss δεύκει· φροντίζει in Hesych. δ 722). In *Od.* 14.109, however, it seems to mean 'eagerly' (Odysseus ἐνδυκέως κρέα τε ἦσθιε πῖνέ τε οἶνον | ἁρπαλέως); both B. and [Hes.] *Sc.* 427 seem to have adopted this meaning.

113–14 ἐπεὶ . . . κάρτος Αἰτωλοῖς ὄρεξεν: it was Meleager who killed the boar, after Atalante had first wounded it with an arrow; the hero modestly shares his triumph with the other Aitolians.

117 Ἄ[γκ]αῖον: he is Πλευρώνιος in *Il.* 23.635, but a son of Lykourgos from Arcadia in Apollod. 1.8.2 and, like several other 'boar hunters', one of the Argonauts, cf. Apollod. 1.9.16. On the François Vase, he is the dead man, inscribed ΑΝΤΑΙΟΣ, under the boar, whereas a fragment of a dinos in a Swiss private collection (Bollingen, R. Blatter coll.; Appendix no. 5) shows him in a very similar position with his name correctly spelled (ΑΝΚΑΙΟΣ).

Ἀγέλαον: he is a brother of Meleager only here and in Ant. Lib. 2.1 (Ἀγέλεως).

121–2 τοὺς δ' ὤ]λεσε . . . [πάντα]ς (Kenyon), or [τῶν δ'ὤ]λεσε . . . [πλεῦνα]ς 'more than these', if we accept Jebb's and Housman's supplements; but cf. Ant. Lib. 2.6 ἀπέθανον δὲ καὶ οἱ ἄλλοι παῖδες Οἰνέως μαχόμενοι 'the other sons of Oineus also died in the fight', which favours Kenyon's supplement.

οὐ γάρ πω: a reminder of the cause of the disaster, echoing 97–9 (cf. *Il.* 9.547).

δαΐφρων: explained as 'expert' and 'fierce, warlike' in Schol. BT on *Il.* 2.23 and in Hesych. δ 122, whereas Apoll. Soph. 56.18 and Schol. D on *Il.* 2.23 give only the second meaning, which B. follows here and in 137 (of Althaia).

123 ἀγροτέρα: 11.37n.

124 περὶ δ' αἴθωνος δορᾶς   'for the reddish-brown hide'. In Homer, the epithet describes the colour of a lion's skin; a boar is much darker: Homer calls its hide λαχνῆεν (*Il.* 9.548), which seems more appropriate. Did B. want to make the boar resemble a lion by giving it a 'leonine' epithet (cf. 107n. and 109n.)?

125 ἐνδυκέως: they fought 'hard', first with the boar (112–13n.), then against the Kouretes. In Meleager's pathetic and self-pitying account, the repetition emphasizes their hard struggle.

126   Schol. AB on *Il.* 9.529 explain that both Kalydonians and Kouretes were Aitolians, Oineus ruling over Kalydon, Thestias over Pleuron. μενεπτολέμοις   'staunch in battle'; they are μενεχάρμαι in *Il.* 9.529 and Stes. 222 col.ɪɪ 9.

129–135   In *Od.* 11.535–7, Odysseus concludes his dialogue with Achilles' shade with the statement that in war indiscriminate killing is common; cf. Soph. fr. 838 R. τυφλὸς γάρ, ὦ γυναῖκες, οὐδ' ὁρῶν Ἄρης | συὸς προσώπωι πάντα τυρβάζει κακά, 'Ares is blind, women, and cannot see, he who with his pig's face stirs up every kind of evil.' Despite the reference to a boar, this cannot come from Sophocles' *Meleagros* which had a chorus of priests, not women, according to Schol. A on *Il.* 9.575.

130 καρτερόθυμος Ἄρης: cf. Ἔριν . . . καρτερόθυμον Hes. *Th.* 225; in Homer, the epithet is given to heroes (*Il.* 13.350 Achilles, *Od.* 21.25 Herakles).

133 ψυχαῖς ἔπι δυσμενέων   'against the lives of the enemies', cf. ψυχά = 'life' in 151. Instead of simply saying δυσμενέσιν (as Homer would have done: cf. *Il.* 17.158 δυσμενέεσσι . . . δῆριν ἔθεντο), Meleager emphasizes the notion of 'life' because he was so cruelly deprived of his.

135 τοῖσιν ἂν δαίμων θέληι: a general conditional relative clause, cf. Goodwin, *Syntax* 204–5 § 532.

136 ταῦτ' οὐκ ἐπιλεξαμένα   'she gave no thought to this', i.e. that war is 'blind' and kills indiscriminately (for ἐπιλέγεσθαι in the sense of λογίζεσθαι cf. Hdt. 2.120.1; 3.41.1; 5.80.1 etc.). Meleager uses the statement 129–35 to present his (subjective) innocence: he did not intentionally kill his mother's brothers; he therefore feels that Althaia's revenge was doubly unjust and cruel, hence his triple condemnation of her as δαΐφρων (122n.), κακόποτμος (138), ἀτάρβακτος γυνά (139).

139 ἀτάρβακτος   'unflinching', only here and Pind. *P.* 4.84, either a variant form of ἀταρβής, ἀτάρβητος 'untrembling, fearless', or a verbal adjective from *ταρβάζειν or *ταρβάσσειν, cf. τάρβος 'fright'. Althaia, her son claims, did not tremble when she threw the log into the fire.

141 ὠκύμορον   'swift-dooming', like the arrows in Homer (*Il.* 15.441, *Od.*22.75). A fragment from Phrynichos' *Pleuroniai* also describes Meleager's death as swift: κρυερὸν γὰρ οὐκ | ἄλυξεν μόρον, ὠκεῖα δέ νιν φλὸξ κατεδαίσατο | δαλοῦ περθομένου ματρὸς ὑπ' αἰνᾶς κακομαχάνου (*TrGF* ɪ p.75), but it is not evident that B. borrowed anything from him. Meleager may well have been referred to as ὠκύμορος in some epic version of the story (like Achilles in *Il.* 1.417 etc.), which may have been the source for both Phrynichos and B. (and for the Boar Hunt scene on the François Vase ?).

ἐξαύσασα: the pap. has εγκλαυσασα, which cannot be right; after ἐκ λάρνακος, the sense requires something like 'taking out' (cf. *protulit hunc genitrix* in Ovid's account of the story, *Met.* 8.460), so the verb cannot be a compound of κλείειν 'to close' (ἐκκλάισασα, ἀγκλαύσασα), nor can it be a form of κλαίειν 'to weep': after 37–9, Althaia in tears would hardly be credible (even though in *Il.* 9.570 she weeps for her brothers); besides, καῖε . . . ἐκ λάρνακος would then be very elliptic ('she burnt it <having taken it> out of the chest'). The solution is offered by Hesych. ε 3617 ἐξαῦσαι· ἐξελεῖν and Pollux 6.88 καὶ τὸ ἐξελεῖν ἐξαῦσαι, which suggested ἐξαύσασα to Wackernagel 1905: 154.

143–4 μοῖρ᾽ ἐπέκλωσεν   might be a phrase adapted from epic poetry; it also occurs in Aesch. *Eum.* 334–5, cf. Kallinos 1.8 Μοῖραι ἐπικλώσωσ(ι) and Plato, *Epigr.* 6.2 Μοῖραι ἐπέκλωσαν.

  τότε ζωᾶς ὅρον . . . ἔμμεν: (fate had decreed that the log) 'then be the limit of my life', τότε = when Althaia burnt it. This is confirmed by Apollod. 1.8.2 τὰς Μοίρας φασὶν εἰπεῖν <ὅτι> τότε τελευτήσει Μελέαγρος, ὅταν ὁ . . . δαλὸς κατακῆι. Cf. Aesch. *Cho.* 607–11 (Althaia) καταίθουσα παιδὸς δαφοινὸν δαλὸν ἥλικ(α) 'the log that was contemporary with her son', . . . ξύμμετρόν τε διαὶ βίου μοιρόκραντον ἐς ἦμαρ 'its age tallying with his throughout his life to the day decreed by fate'. For ὅρος = 'time-limit' cf. Eur. *IT* 1219.

148 πύργων προπάροιθε κιχήσας   'having caught him in front of the towers' is explained by the following τοὶ δὲ . . . φεῦγον . . . Πλευρῶνα (149–51). As long as B. was following Homer's account, his narrative was moving in a linear fashion; now that Meleager is focussing on Althaia and his own miserable death, the narrative technique changes. Having put the crucial verb, καῖε, immediately after ἀτάρβακτος γυνά, B. then has to explain what had happened before – first the significance of the log (142–4), then the events that led Althaia to burn it (144–51).

151–4 μίνυθεν . . . ἥβαν προλείπων: the passage appears to be modelled on the description of Hektor's last moments in *Il.* 22.337–63: ὀλιγοσθενέων (only here) may be coined after ὀλιγοδρανέων *Il.* 22.337, and 153–4 seem to be a variation on *Il.* 22.362–3 ψυχὴ δ᾽ἐκ ῥεθέων πταμένη Ἀϊδόσδε βεβήκει | ὃν πότμον γοόωσα, λιποῦσ᾽ ἀνδρότητα καὶ ἥβην. All that B. adds is designed to create compassion with Meleager's sad fate by exploiting its emotional and tragic potential: his ψυχή is γλυκεῖα, his ἥβη is ἀγλαά, his last breath is a sob with tears, αἰαῖ . . . δάκρυσα τλά[μων.

155 ἀδεισιβόαν 'fearless of the battle-cry', also 11.61. B. has four more compounds of this type (α privative + 2 other elements): ἀναιδομάχας 5.105, ἀταρβομάχας 16.28, ἀκαμαντοράας 5.180, ἀμετρόδικος 11.68.

155–8 Weeping is out of character for Herakles: in the older (epic ?) versions of his myth, it is hard to imagine Herakles shedding tears. Here he weeps, for the first and only time – not out of pain or grief for himself, but out of compassion for young Meleager: B. exploits the potential for pathos to the full. The motif recurs in Aesch. *Prom.* 397–401 (the Okeanids weep out of pity for Prometheus) and in Eur. *HF* 1238 (Theseus for Herakles), cf. *HF* 1353–6 and Soph. *Trach.* 1070–5 (Herakles' self-pity). Later variations of this motif include the funerary epigram for Polystratos (790 Kaibel), the anecdote about the Aitolian Stichios killed by Herakles in his madness ('and for him alone, they say, the hero wept', Ptolemaios Chennos, Καινὴ ἱστορία 7.5), and the lamentation for a professor of Berytos for whom Constantinople mourns, ἡ πάρος αἰὲν ἄδακρυς ἐδάκρυσεν τότε Ῥώμη (Heitsch, *Dichterfragmente* no. 30.94).

160–2 The famous saying is quoted in two versions:
(a) hexameters (Alkidamas in Stob. 4.52.22 etc.)
    ἀρχὴν (v.l. πάντων) μὲν μὴ φῦναι ἐπιχθονίοισιν ἄριστον,
    φύντα δ' ὅπως ὤκιστα πύλας Ἀΐδαο περῆσαι
(b) elegiacs (Theognis 425–28 etc.)
    πάντων μὲν μὴ φῦναι ἐπιχθονίοισιν ἄριστον
      μήδ' ἐσιδεῖν αὐγὰς ὀξέος ἠελίου,
    φύντα δ' ὅπως ὤκιστα πύλας Ἀΐδαο περῆσαι
      καὶ κεῖσθαι πολλὴν γῆν ἐπαμησάμενον.
The original version is obviously (a) which was expanded to (b) when it was incorporated into a collection of elegiacs, such as the Theognidean corpus. Why B. adopted the elegiac version (b) is not clear – possibly because he found it more moving. At any rate, he was able to quote only the first half, because Meleager *did* die young, as he himself had just tearfully lamented, so naturally B. omits any reference to the second part of this *gnome*; the audience would surely have known it anyway.

162–3 ἀλλ' οὐ γάρ τις . . . μυρομένοις 'but there is nothing to be achieved by weeping . . .', almost = *Od.* 10.202 = 568 ἀλλ' οὐ γάρ τις πρῆξις ἐγίγνετο μυρομένοισιν, cf. Alkaios 335.2 προκόψομεν γὰρ οὐδὲν ἀσάμενοι, Stes. *PMG* 244 ἀτελέστατα (ἀτέλεστα τε Ahrens) καὶ ἀμάχανα τοὺς θανόντας κλαίειν. Achilles' consolatory address to Priam is in a similar vein: ἄνσχεο, μηδ' ἀλίαστον ὀδύρεο ... οὐ γάρ τι πρήξεις ἀκαχήμενος υἷος ἑῆος,| οὐδέ μιν ἀνστήσεις, πρὶν καὶ κακὸν ἄλλο πάθῃσθα, *Il.* 24.549. As the situation here is closely parallel to that in B. (direct speech, admonition to stop lamenting), it seems likely that B. had this scene in mind, rather than *Od.* 10.201–2 (past narrative). The odd statement in 164 ('one should speak rather of what one is likely to accomplish') could therefore be interpreted as a deliberate reference to the *Iliad* passage: while Achilles says something which cannot possibly be done, Herakles, by contrast, very pointedly suggests something (κεῖνο ὅ τι) practicable. The poet's choice of literary models is striking: they are all familiar passages; the Homeric *Hymn to Demeter* (see 16n.) must have been well-known in Sicily; the image of the leaves (*Il.* 6.146–9, see 65–7n.) was one of the best-known Homeric similes, as the adaptations suggest; Odysseus preparing for the slaughter of the suitors (see 73n.) is an impressive example of a hero stringing his bow; Prometheus in Hes. *Th.* 613–16 is the prototype of someone who, by challenging the gods, incurs their wrath and pays the penalty (see 94–6n.); Hektor's death is the most moving scene of a great hero dying (see 151–4n.); the most moving lamentation scene is the encounter of Priam with Achilles (see above). Educated listeners will have recognized these literary models and appreciated B.'s adaptations as 'highlights' of his narrative, which was probably what B. intended. If so, his address to Hieron 'you will rightly assess the sweet gift' etc. (3–6) will have prepared the addressee for this literary adventure.

164 ὅτι καὶ μέλλει τελεῖν: τελεῖν (future, see LSJ under μέλλω Ic) must be transitive, with the subject τις understood; for examples of 'omitted' τις cf. *Il.* 13.287; 22.199; Pind. *I.* 5.22; see Ed. Fraenkel on Aesch. *Ag.* 71 with bibliography.

167 ἀδμήτα   'unwedded', a virgin; Meleager refers to this in 174–175.

168 σοὶ φυὰν ἀλιγκία   'resembling you in stature' motivates Herakles' question; it is also a discreetly erotic compliment for Meleager (if the maiden resembles him, Herakles will be attracted to her). Dickens' *David Copperfield*, end of chapter 6 offers a striking parallel: 'Good night, young Copperfield', said Steerforth. 'I'll take care of you.' 'You're very kind', I gratefully returned. 'I am very much obliged to you.' 'You haven't got a sister, have you?', said Steerforth, yawning. 'No', I answered. 'That's a pity', said Steerforth. 'If you had had one, I should think she would have been a pretty, timid, little, brighteyed sort of girl. I should have liked to know her. Good night, young Copperfield.' – Pindar, fr. 249a (see above, p. 107) told the story differently: he made Meleager ask Herakles to marry his sister, presumably to protect her from Acheloios. By reversing this, B. can present Herakles, as well as Meleager, as an illustration of his introductory statement that no mortal can have complete happiness (50–5n.).

172 χλωραύχενα   'with pale neck': a pale complexion was considered attractive in women, hence compounds such as λευκώλενος and λευκοπάρειος, cf. πήχεε λευκώ *Od.* 23.240, λευκὴν δέρην Eur. *IA* 875. χλωραύχην is clearly a colour compound, as in Sim. *PMG* 586.2; it has nothing to do with 'freshness'; cf. χλωρηὶς ἀηδών *Od.* 19.518 and χλωρὸν δάκρυ Eur. *Med.* 906 (tears are warm and salty, not fresh: here too it must be a colour epithet, 'bright tears').

176–8 A formula of transition from the mythical narrative to the second praise passage. Similar formulas are frequent in Pindar, see Braswell on *P.* 4.247–8: 'The device is obviously a necessary part of a lyric poet's technique, since he can seldom develop a point with the fullness of epic.' Pindar also uses the image of the Muses' chariot as a metaphor for poetry, e.g. in *O.* 6.22–7 where the victor's mule chariot, led by the Muses, brings the poet to Syracuse. Parmenides' poem begins in strikingly similar fashion.

178–9 Δία . . . ἀρχαγὸν θεῶν: the concluding part of this ode begins and ends (200) with Zeus, as befits an Olympian victory ode. The second praise passage (178–86) is a brief summary of the first (37–49).

'Ολύμπιον: wrongly changed to 'Ολυμπίων by the corrector **A**³.

180 ἀκαμαντορόαν   'tireless stream', only here; see 155n.

181 Πέλοπός τε βίαν   'the might of Pelops'; the circumlocution with βία, common in Homer, is also found in Pindar (*O.* 1.88 of 'violent' Oinomaos; *P.* 11.61 of Kastor) and occasionally in tragedy (Aesch. *Sept.* 571 and 577; *Cho.* 893; Eur. *Phoen.* 56). For the worship of Pelops at Olympia cf. Paus. 5.13.1–2.

183 πο]σσὶ νικάσας δρόμωι: the first dative is instrumental, the second modal (or 'of circumstance'); Pindar uses the accusative instead: *O.* 4.22 ἐν ἔντεσι νικῶν δρόμον, also *O.* 13.30.

186 εὐδαιμονίας πέταλον   'the leaves of good fortune', i.e. the victor's olive wreath. The phrase refers back to the concluding sentence of the first praise passage, 46–9. Hieron's εὐδαιμονία stands in stark contrast to the sombre mood of the mythical narrative which exemplified the statement that no mortal can be entirely happy. Although this also applies to Hieron, he is certainly fortunate *now*.

187–9 χρή] δ᾽ . . . αἰνεῖν, φθόνον . . . ἀπωσάμενον   'one must praise, thrusting envy aside'. Bundy 57, commenting on the very similar passage in Pind. *I.* 1.41–6, claims that χρή 'issues a very much stronger imperative than do the other forms in which the χρέος motive is cast'. The passage in B. is a variation of the same χρέος ('obligation to praise') motive, on which see 3.67–71n. and 11.123n. It also echoes the 'willingness' motive in the proem (14–16) by the repetition of αἰνεῖν (16 and 188).

190 εἴ τις εὖ πράσσοι βροτῶ[ν   'any mortal who is successful'. Here the condition follows the vaunt (χρή . . . αἰνεῖν), whereas in Pindar's *I.* 1.41–6 the sequence is reversed. Cf. also *O.* 11.4–8 εἰ δὲ σὺν πόνωι τις εὖ πράσσοι, μελιγάρυες ὕμνοι | ὑστέρων ἀρχὰ λόγων | τέλλεται καὶ πιστὸν ὅρκιον μεγάλαις ἀρεταῖς· | ἀφθόνητος δ᾽ αἶνος Ὀλυμπιονίκαις | οὗτος ἄγκειται 'but if through toil someone should succeed, honey-sounding hymns are a beginning for later words of renown, and the faithful pledge of great achievements. Without stint is that praise dedicated to Olympic victors' (on ἀφθόνητος αἶνος 'ungrudging praise' see Bundy, *Studia Pindarica* 15).

191–3 Βοιωτὸς ἀνήρ . . . πρόπολος Μουσᾶν: Hesiod, the Μουσάων θεράπων (*Th.* 100), even though the exact quotation is not found in his extant works, unless it refers to *Th.* 81–97 (as suggested by Merkelbach and West on Hes. fr. 344) where Hesiod speaks of the Muses' gifts of persuasive speech and song to kings and poets respectively. If B. did have this passage in mind, his phrase [τούτωι] καὶ βροτῶν φήμαν ἔπ[εσθαι] (193–4) might echo Hesiod's οἵ δέ τε λαοὶ | πάντες ἐς αὐτὸν ὁρῶσι (*Th.* 84–5) and θεὸν ὣς ἱλάσκονται (*Th.* 91); it would, however, be a rather approximate 'quotation'. Theognis 169 ὃν δὲ θεοὶ τιμῶσιν, ὁ καὶ μωμεύμενος αἰνεῖ comes much closer to B.'s statement; it seems possible that both reflect a lost 'Hesiodic' statement, perhaps from the Χείρωνος ὑποθῆκαι, the 'instructions' given to the young Achilles by his tutor, Chiron, cf. [Hes.] frs. 283–5. Pindar also likes to highlight important statements by presenting them as quotations by famous wise men, cf. *P.* 9.93–6 (the old man in the sea), *I.* 6.67 (Hes. *Op.* 412), *P.* 6.20–7 (Chiron's teachings, [Hes.] fr. 283), *O.* 6.16–17 (Adrastos' saying, from the *Thebaid*), *I.* 2.9–12 (Aristodamos), fr. 35b (Chilon), also *N.* 3.29 and 9.6–7. Simonides, by contrast, modifies or rejects sayings of the 'seven Sages', *PMG* 542 and 581.

195–7 πείθομαι . . . πέμπειν Ἱέρωνι: πείθομαι refers to the preceding statement; B. 'obeys' or 'follows' Hesiod's saying by sending his ode to Hieron in order to spread his fame. Jebb's supplement οὐ[κ ἐκτὸς δίκας] (196) supplies the most suitable noun to qualify κελεύθου: 'without (straying from) the path (of justice)', cf. 11.26–7n.

εὐκλέα . . . γλῶσσαν 'speech that brings glory', cf. Pind. *O.* 2.90 ἐκ μαλθακᾶς . . . φρενὸς εὐκλέας ὀιστοὺς ἱέντες ('arrows' = words or songs of praise); *N.* 6.28–9 οὖρον ἐπέων εὐκλέα; Aesch. *Cho.* 321 γόος εὐκλεής 'lament that brings glory'.

πέμπειν Ἱέρωνι takes up the 'willingness' theme from the first praise passage, with echoing words: ξένος . . . πέμπει . . . κλεεννὰν ἐς πόλιν (11–12); see also 14–16n.

198 πυθμένες . . . ἐσθλ[ῶν]: πυθμήν is the 'stock' or 'root' of a tree, and even where the word is used metaphorically, the original meaning is felt (as here: indicated by the verb, θάλλουσιν); similarly in Aesch. *Cho.* 204 and 260, *Supp.* 106. From praising words (τόθεν) 'the tree-stocks of blessings flourish'. Pindar uses similar images in *N.* 8.40–2, *P.* 5.98–100, *I.* 6.19–21.

200 ἐν εἰρήν[αι φυλάσσοι: may Zeus secure peace, now that the Carthaginians have been defeated. The poet's concluding wish is not for further military successes, but for the preservation of peace. B. expresses his desire for peace either in person, as here and above all in his *Paean* (fr. 4), or through his characters, as in 11.69 and 15.45–6. His is a lone voice; similar views on peace and war are not found until the end of the fifth century, in Aristophanes and Euripides: see pp. 225–7.

ODE 6: FOR LACHON FROM KEOS

1. Lachon's victories

Odes 6 and 7 celebrate the victory of Lachon, son of Aristomenes, from Keos, in the sprint (στάδιον) of boys in the 82nd Olympiad (452 BCE). The date is given by the victory list *P.Oxy.* II 222 col.II 18 Λάκων Κε[ῖος παίδ(ων) στάδιον (the supplement follows from the position of this entry in the list). The spelling of the name is confirmed by the pun at the beginning of the ode (1–2n.), and by the victors' list from Iulis on Keos *IG* XII 5.608 lines 27–8, which record two Nemean victories by the same Lachon as a boy. The inscription from Keos has been reprinted with two improved readings and discussion by D. Schmidt 1999: 70.

Lachon's Olympic victory of 452 was celebrated προδόμοις ἀοιδαῖς (14–15). Does this refer to this ode being sung 'before *your* house', i.e. of the victor's father, Aristomenes, at Iulis, or 'before the *temple*' (of Zeus at Olympia) ? It is true that the beginning of ode 7, which addresses the sixteenth day of the month in which the games were held, i.e. either Parthenios or Apollonios, might suggest performance of this ode at Olympia because on that day the prizes were distributed (Schol. Pind. *O.* 5.13), but this is not conclusive as this address could just as well be the starting point of a more general victory ode performed in the victor's home town, for it is not impossible that ode 7 was triadic and originally much longer. If it was, it would have been composed for a performance at Iulis, while ode 6 was sung at Olympia; προδόμοις would then mean the front part of the temple, presumably the temple of Zeus which had been completed a few years earlier (before 456). The word is attested in Homer (*Il.* 9.473; 24.673; *Od.* 4.302) and Euphorion (*SH* 415 1 10 παρὰ πρόδομον θα[λάμοι]ǫ and perhaps 413.8 [π]ρǫδόμονδε), cf. ὀπισθόδομος 'the back chamber' (of the temple, where the treasure was kept), Ar. *Ploutos* 1193 etc.

2. *Structure of the ode*

Although this short ode consists of strophes of 8 lines each, its structure takes no notice of the strophic division. It falls into three sections of increasing length: (a) Announcement of the victory (1–3), (b) reference to previous victories of Kean athletes at Olympia (4–9), (c) Lachon's present victory (10–16). While part (a) serves as a kind of proem, parts (b) and (c) are closely interrelated: πάροιθεν (4) is taken up by νῦν (10), πύξ τε καὶ στά-διον κρατεῦ[σαν (7) is taken up by στάδιον κρατήσας (15) in verbal and metrical responsion, and ἄεισάν ποτ' Ὀλυμπίαι (6) is taken up by γεραίρει προδόμοις ἀοιδαῖς (14), also in responsion. The close verbal and metrical correspondences between parts (b) and (c) are indicative of the underlying idea that Lachon's victory should be seen as the latest in a long line of suc-cesses by Kean athletes, and that he proved himself to be worthy of them. Part (c), beginning with σὲ δὲ νῦν . . . (10), is also linked to the opening passage as it addresses Lachon directly, thus rounding off this short ode very neatly. Its structure is very similar to that of ode 2, as van Groningen, *Composition* 194 n.2 has observed.

1–2 Λάχων . . . λάχε: B. uses this type of pun only here, whereas Pindar has several examples: *O.* 6.55–7 Ἴαμος – ἴων, *P.* 4.27 μήδεσιν – Μήδεια, *I.* 6.53 αἰετός – Αἴας (cf. Apollod. 3.12.7, but linked to αἰαῖ in Soph. *Aias* 430), and fr. 105 (Ἱέρων) ζαθέων ἱερῶν ἐπώνυμε πάτερ, cf. also Likymnios *PMG* 770b Ἀχέρων ἄχεα πορθμεύει βροτοῖσιν. Simonides' pun on the name Κριός ('ram', *PMG* 507) is different in that it involves no word-play with etymologies, but a taunt on the man's name: 'the Ram was fleeced', cf. Page 1951: 140–2.

Διός = παρὰ Διός; verbs like λαγχάνειν, τυγχάνειν, δέχεσθαι, κομίζεσθαι can combine a direct object (acc.) with the genitive of a person, for which examples can be found in K-G I 394–5.

3–4 Ἀλφεοῦ προχοαῖσ[‿ – –] δι' ὅσσα: the choice of supplements will depend on whether ὅσσα is (a) relative, (b) exclamatory, or (c) interrogative. (a) seems the most likely: perhaps [ἀέθλων] (Housman), which would go with φέρτατον: 'Lachon won . . . the highest prestige (κῦδος) of the games'; but as λάχε . . . κῦδος is sufficient to indicate that he won his contest, ἀέθλων would not be strictly necessary, and one might instead think of an adjective or pronoun linked to κῦδος, such as (προχοαῖσ[ιν) ἶσον (Schwartz) or (–αισ[ι) τοῖον 'prestige equal <to that> for which . . .' or 'of the kind for which . . .', or perhaps even a verb: (-αῖσ[ι) ῥέξας 'having achieved <that> for which . . .'. Of the other two possibilities, (c) is unlikely (what could e.g. μαθόντος refer to?), and (b), though well attested in Pindar (see the passages listed by Radt on *Pae.* 6.87), is not found in B., and Jebb's objection (pp. 474–5) that it seems 'too jerky for our poet's style; his sentences are wont to flow on smoothly' seems valid, as it would indeed create a strangely unmotivated *asyndeton.*

4 πάροιθεν   'in earlier times'; the victories in the Olympic games won by previous Kean athletes put Lachon's present victory into perspective, as he has now (νῦν, 10) shown himself worthy of them. Previous Kean successes were in boxing and running (πύξ τε καὶ στάδιον, 7); unfortunately, the inscription from Iulis (*IG* XII 5.608) which lists Isthmian and Nemean victories does not allow us to verify whether the Keans were particularly successful in these disciplines, as it is damaged on the right and has lost nearly all the indications of contests.

5 ἀμπελοτρόφον Κέον: in his paean for the Keans (*Pae.* 4.21–6), Pindar makes the chorus praise the island for her excellence in games (ἀρεταῖς ἀέθλων), and her abundance of poetry (μοῖσαν παρέχων ἅλις); she also grows 'some' (τι) of Dionysos' 'lifegiving remedy for despair' (βιόδωρον ἀμαχανίας ἄκος, i.e. wine), but lacks horses and cattle.

6–7 ἄεισάν ποτ' Ὀλυμπίαι . . . κρατεῦ[σαν   is closely paralleled by the corresponding lines of the antistrophe (14–15 γεραίρει προδόμοις ἀοιδαῖς . . . κρατήσας). The parallel suggests that Ὀλυμπίαι (6) goes with ἄεισαν rather than with κρατεῦ[σαν: 'the youths sang at Olympia of vine-nurturing Keos as the winner in boxing and sprint'.

8–9 στεφάνοις . . . βρύοντες   'luxuriant with garlands'. B. is fond of the verb βρύειν 'to be exuberant' (3.15–16n.), whereas Pindar prefers θάλλειν, cf. *N.* 4.88 (the victor θάλησε Κορινθίοις σελίνοις 'flourished with Corinthian parsley') and *Parth.* 2.11 of the girls' choir στεφάνοις θάλλοισα. The later commentators of the *Iliad* treated the verbs as synonymous, cf. Schol. DBT on *Il.* 17.56 and Hesych. β 1249.

10 ἀναξιμόλπου   'song-ruling'; nearly all compounds in B. beginning with ἀναξι– (except ἀ[ναξιφόρ]μιγγος, 4.7) are *hapax legomena*, as is ὑμνοά-νασσα 12.1.

11 Οὐρανίας . . . Νίκ[ας: the song is Ourania's, the Muse's, and it honours the victor 'by the will of Victory'; the chorus speak as if the poet did not exist.

13 ποδάνεμον τέκος   'wind-footed son' of Aristomenes; the phrase refers back to πόδεσσι (2) and Lachon's sprint victory. In the *Iliad* (2.786 etc.), the epithet is always given to Iris (cf. *h.Ap.* 107); it may have occurred in Simonides, cf. the marginal note in *PMG* 519 fr. 118.6, possibly also in fr. 131.2]ει ποδα[νεμ– (Lobel).

14–15 προδόμοις ἀοιδαῖς   'with songs sung before the house'. The compound is here used as an adjective, like πρόναος in Aesch. *Supp.* 494 βωμοὺς προνάους. It seems that a masc. noun, ὁ πρόναος, did not exist (even though ὁ ὀπισθόδομος does, cf. Aristoph. *Pl.* 1193, Demosth. 13.14, 24.136 etc., of the Parthenon), but that a noun, τὸ πρόδομον 'that which is in front of the house', was derived from the adjective πρόδομος, –ον; Schwyzer II 508 n.1 discusses the evidence (add Euphorion *SH* 413.8 and 415 col. II 10). προδό-μοις ἀοι– responds with ποτ᾽ Ὀλυμπίαι (6); it seems to refer not to the victor's (or his father's) house on Keos, but to the house of Zeus, his large temple at Olympia; see the introduction to this ode, above pp. 129–30.

15 στάδιον κρατήσας → στάδιον κρατεῦ[σαν 7. The repetition empha-sizes the link between the previous Olympic successes of Kean athletes and Lachon's present victory, which 'brought fame to Keos' (16). The verb κρατεῖν with the contest as its direct object occurs in Pindar, *N.* 10.25–6 (in *zeugma*: ἐκράτησε . . . Ἕλλανα στρατὸν . . . καὶ τὸν Ἰσθμοῖ καὶ Νεμέαι στέφανον, 'he conquered the host of Hellenes . . . and the crown at both the Isthmos and Nemea') and in the Rhodian epigram for Hagesistratos, Moretti, *Iscrizioni* no. 47 = Ebert no. 72.1–3

    Τὰμ βαρύχειρα πάλαν, Ζεῦ Ὀλύμπιε, σὸν κατ᾽ ἀγῶνα
        ἀπτῶτ᾽ ἀγγέλλω παῖδα κρατεῖν Ῥόδιον
    Πολυκρέοντος υἱὸν Ἀγησίστρατον,

'I announce that at your festival, Olympian Zeus, a Rhodian, Hagesistratos the son of Polykreon, has won the heavy-handed wrestling contest without being thrown.' Cf. also the end of the epigram for Nikoladas from Corinth, attributed to Simonides (fr. 147 Diehl = *AP* xiii 19 = Ebert no. 26.11–12)

σταδίωι δὲ τὰ πάντα κρατήσας | εὔφρανεν μεγάλαν Κόρινθον.

ODE 11: FOR ALEXIDAMOS OF METAPONTION

1. Metapontion

Ode 11 celebrates the victory of Alexidamos, son of Phaïskos, from Metapontion in the wrestling in the age-group of boys. Its date is not known. Lines 10–14 make it clear that it was performed in the victor's home town.

In historical times, south Italian Metapontion was a colony of Achaians, situated on the east coast of Lucania, between the rivers Bradanos and Kasas (Casuentus, Basento). Its foundation was variously attributed to, among others, Nestor's Pylians on their return from the Trojan War (Strabo 6.1.15 C.264, also 5.2.5 C.222; cf. Solin. 2.10; Timaios *FGrHist* 566 F 51–2 = Athen. 12.523c–e, Lykophron 978–9 and *A.P.* 7.297), or to Epeios of Elis (Velleius 1.1), or to the Achaians who had been called to help defend Sybaris against Tarentum (Antiochos *FGrHist* 555 F 12; Livy 25.15.7). The latter foundation can be dated to the later seventh century BCE.

The foundation legend may have been the result of a desire to give this small and relatively insignificant country town in southern Italy a grand, heroic past. Pausanias, in his survey of the history of Achaia (7.6.3–4), expresses amazement at the fact that Achaia, so powerful at the time of the Trojan War (μεγίστη τοῦ Ἑλληνικοῦ μοῖρα), was so insignificant in the Persian Wars. The equation of the Homeric Achaians with the Peloponnesian Achaians who founded the town may have been B.'s invention, or he may have found it circulating among the Metapontians; in either case, it was more recent than the *Nostoi* (*PEG* p. 94), which told the story of Nestor's return in accordance with *Od.* 3.160–200, i.e. made him and Diomedes return straight home. See 126n.

Five temples have been located in the area of the town. The first three are dated to *c.* 580–570 BCE, the others to *c.* 530–470 BCE. Outside the town area, at S. Biagio della Venella, some 5 km to the west/north-west, is the important sanctuary of Artemis Hemera ('the gentle Artemis'), which, like many other sanctuaries in the region, shows a close connection with water-cults. The excavations directed by D. Adamesteanu have unearthed a large number of terracotta statuettes and busts of a goddess, as well as incense burners (θυμιατήρια) and other cult objects; some of those busts show the goddess holding a deer, i.e. she is Artemis as πότνια θηρῶν; see Adamesteanu, *La Basilicata antica* 55–65, with illustrations on pp.58–9. The attribution of this sanctuary is further confirmed by a black-figure lekythos found there (now in Naples, Nat. Mus., Collezione Santangelo 99; Appendix no. 6) with the dedication ΑΡΤΕΜΙΔΙ, and by Hyginus 186.6 (Melanippe) who says about the local king, Metapontus: *dies adven-erat ut Metapontus exiret ad Dianam Metapontinam ad sacrum faciendum*, which implies an Artemis sanctuary at some distance outside the town. Chrono-logically the finds from this sanctuary range from the later seventh to the fourth century BCE. On the basins and water conduits found at S. Biagio, cf. Carter, *Sanctuaries* 168–9: 'The cult focused on the spring which was channelled into a basin constructed of conglomerate stone. A number of structures decorated with polychrome terracotta revetments and ante-fixes rose on a level terrace above the spring in the sixth, fifth and fourth centuries BC'

2. The myth

The story of the madness and eventual healing of Proitos' daughters, as told by B., agrees so closely (apart from one essential detail, see below) with the version reported by B.'s contemporary, Pherekydes of Athens (*FGrHist* 3 F 114 = Schol. MV on *Od.* 15.225), that one must assume some connexion between them. Pherekydes says that the most glorious among the many miraculous exploits of the seer Melampous, son of Amythaon, was his cure of Lysippe and Iphianassa, daughters of Proitos, king of Argos: 'In their juvenile thoughtlessness they had offended Hera; for when they came to her temple, they disparaged it, saying that their father's house was richer. And when for this reason they had gone mad, Melampous came along and promised to cure them without fail, provided that he received a recompense proportionate to the cure. For the illness had lasted ten years already, causing distress not only to the girls but also to their parents. When Proitos offered to give Melampous a part of his kingdom and one of his daughters, whichever he wanted, Melampous cured their illness by propitiating Hera through prayers and sacrifices.' How does this relate to B.'s account?

Theoretically, there are three possibilities: (a) Pherekydes depends on B., (b) B. has used and modified Pherekydes, or (c) both depend on the same source. Before we can answer the question, we must examine the different versions of the myth. Essentially, two versions can be distinguished, a 'Dionysian' (I) and an 'Argive' version (II).

Version I: (a) The women of Argos (Apollod. 1.9.12; Hdt. 9.34; Diod. 4.68; Paus. 2.18.4) or (b) Proitos' daughters ([Hes.] fr.131 = Apollod. 2.2.2) are driven mad by Dionysos and cured by Melampous; in return, he and his brother, Bias, receive a part of the kingdom.

Version II: Proitos is king of either Argos or Tiryns; Hera punishes his daughters, Lysippe, Iphinoë and Iphianassa, (a) with a skin disease and hair loss for their lewdness (μαχλοσύνη, [Hes.] frs. 132–3), or (b) with madness because they had disdained her (Akusilaos *FGrHist* 2 F 28; Pherekydes *FGrHist* 3 F 114; Probus on Verg. *Ecl.* 6.48). They are cured (1) by Melampous (Pherekydes; Probus; *SEG* 15.195; without reference to the cause of their madness: Strabo 8.3.19; Steph.Byz. *s.v.* Λουσοί; Alexis fr. 117 = *PCG* II p.86), or (2) by Artemis (B. 11; Kallim. *h.* 3.236, probably based on Argive local legend; Paus. 2.25.3 links the sanctuary of Artemis Hemera at Lusoi to the cure by Melampous), or (3) by Asklepios (Polyarchos *FGrHist* 37 F 1).

Three of these versions (I.b, II.a, and II.b1) are attributed to 'Hesiod'; of these, only II.a is explicitly attested for the *Catalogue of Women* (frs. 132 and 133), while I.b may go back to the *Melampodeia*; II.b1 is attributed to 'Hesiod' by Probus, but attested as early as the fifth century by Pherekydes. Akusilaos and Pherekydes agree in that they both present the girls' madness as punishment for their arrogant behaviour towards the temple or the cult statue (Akusilaos) of Hera, although we cannot be quite sure whether Akusilaos attributed their cure to Melampous (II.b1) or to Artemis (II.b2). Be that as it may, the girls' contemptuous attitude towards the temple or statue, a wooden block (ξόανον), seems to reflect an age when large-format sculpture and temple architecture was beginning to replace the modest wooden temples and simple block statues of the older period, which were felt to be 'archaic' or 'primitive' – see below.

How does Pherekydes' version (II.b1) relate to that of B. (II.b2)? It seems unlikely that Pherekydes modified B. by replacing Artemis with Melampous, because (1) it would mean that he extended the girls' madness from one year (= 13 months, B. 11.92) to ten, and (2) B.11 was performed at Metapontion, a small town in Magna Graecia, from where knowledge of this ode would not easily have reached Athens and become known to

Pherekydes, given that in the first half of the fifth century the knowledge of
new poetry still depended, in the absence of a proper book-trade, on oral
performance and personal attendance or acquaintance.

Could B. have used and modified Pherekydes? This may be possible,
although neither the date of the ode nor the dates of Pherekydes' activity
(apart from his *agnoscitur* in 456/5 BCE, *FGrHist* 3 T 6) can be established.
But it seems equally possible that B. found the story in Akusilaos, whose
version would then have been the source of both Pherekydes and B., or
that they both go back to some local Argive source, such as the *Phoronis*, the
epic poem of the late seventh or early sixth century BCE about Phoroneus,
the mythical first king of Argos (*PEG* pp.118–21). There appears to be a
connexion between fr. 4 of the *Phoronis* (*PEG* pp.119–20) which says that
Kallithoë (= Io), priestess of Hera at Argos, was the first to adorn 'the goddess's tall column (κίονα μακρὸν ἀνάσσης) with garlands and tassels', and
Akusilaos' statement that the girls went mad because they had disparaged
the wooden image of Hera (διότι τὸ τῆς Ἥρας ξόανον ἐξηυτέλισαν). The
cult statue may have been referred to as a 'tall column', possibly because it
was replaced, at some point later in the poem, by a more advanced sculpture in the round. At any rate, the 'tall column' and the ξόανον may well
have been the same object, i.e. an archaic wooden image which was felt to
be primitive.

It seems likely, therefore, that the story of Proitos' daughters was told in
the *Phoronis* and hence summarized by Akusilaos, and that the 'Hesiodic'
account, lost after fr. 129.25, which Pherekydes followed, told essentially
the same story. If, as seems likely, both accounts had Melampous cure the
daughters (version 11.b1), B. may have replaced him with Artemis (version
11.b2) because he had a very good reason: he had to celebrate a young
athlete from Metapontion, about whose family or home town there was
nothing interesting to report, except that Artemis was worshipped there,
in a rural sanctuary outside the town, as protector goddess of Metapontion
and its people. In both main sections of the ode, the victor's praise (15–39)
and the mythical narrative (40–112), Artemis is the dominating figure on
which the unity of the ode depends.

3. *Structure*

The ode consists of three main parts: (a) the proem with the invocation
of Victory (1–14) and praise for the victor (15–39), (b) the myth (40–112),

and (c) the conclusion which links the address to Artemis to praise for the town and the 'Achaians' (113–26). Each section ends with a verbal echo of its beginning: (a) 1 Νίκα γλυκύδωρε → 39 νίκαν ἔδωκε, (b) 40–2 τᾶι . . . βωμὸν κατένασσε → 110 οἱ τέμενος βωμόν τε τεῦχον, (c) 113–14 ἀρηιφίλοις . . . Ἀχαιοῖς → 126 ἀλκὰς Ἀχαιῶν.

The first part falls into two sections: the proem (first strophe) in the shape of a prayer to Victory (Νίκα) in twice seven lines which form parallel structures (see 1–14n.) and the praise passage which first celebrates the present victory at Delphi (15–23), then mentions a possible Olympic victory that was denied (24–36), and eventually returns to the Delphic victory (37–9); of these passages, 15–23 and 24–36 correspond closely: 18–19 ἀνθέων . . . στέφανοι → 28–9 ἐλαίαι . . . στεφανωσάμενον, 19–20 ἐν πεδίωι . . . Κίρρας → 24–25 ἐν . . . Πέλοπος δαπέδοις, 23 πρὸς γαίαι πεσόντα → 31–3 [ποτὶ γᾶι (?)] . . . πέλασσεν. Particularly obvious is the contrasting correspondence between the denied victory (34–6) and the actual victory 'given' by Artemis (37–9). Proem and victor's praise are similarly linked, as ἵλεωι (15) refers back to ἔλλαθι (8). The end of the proem (13–14 Πυθιόνικον παῖδα . . . Φαῖσκου) forms a smooth transition to the next strophe; furthermore, the victor's home town is referred to in both sections (10 and 30).

The myth is narrated in a multiple ring composition, beginning with the end, the foundation of the sanctuary, followed by a first 'ring' which supplies the preceding stage on an a-b-a pattern (the sanctuary was founded because the girls had been cured from their madness sent by Hera, 43–6 and 53–8, the madness having been caused by their arrogance, 47–52). This is followed by a second 'ring' (59–84), the central part of which (64–76) explains why Proitos had left Argos and settled in Tiryns; here a motif appears which is equally relevant to the story of his daughters: disaster is averted, a dangerous situation is defused, the entreaties of the people secure a peaceful settlement. This central part is framed by two passages which correspond with each other symmetrically: 60 λιπόντες Ἄργος → 81 Ἄργος . . . λιπόντες, 61–2 ναῖον . . . ἡμίθεοι → 79–81 ἀντίθεοι ναῖον . . . ἥρωες, and the whole second 'ring' itself is framed by the 'flight' motif (φεῦγον 55 and 84) which rounds off the second triad by linking its last line (φεῦγον . . . θύγατρες 84) to its first (τὰς . . . ἐφόβησεν 43).

In the third triad, Proitos takes centre stage. The narrative culminates in two dramatic high points: Proitos' despair and wish to end his life (85–91), and his prayer to Artemis (97–105). Here, too, the 'flight' motif reappears (92–5). The first section (85–95) provides 'dark foil' for the happy conclusion of the scene (106–12). The foundation of the sanctuary (110–12) links the end of the narrative part to its starting point (40–42). This part thus becomes a hymn to Artemis, the helper and benefactor goddess, who also helped Alexidamos and found a remedy for his earlier misfortune: the connexion between the two main parts of the ode, or between myth and *laudandus*, is evident. Significantly, Artemis' cult name, Ἡμέρα, marks the transition from the first to the second (39n.).

The conclusion (113–26) forms the counterpart to the proem in that both coincide with self-contained metrical units (strophe and epode respectively) and in both the chorus addresses a goddess (Nika and Artemis). Artemis is said to have migrated from Arcadian Lusoi with the 'Achaians'; she now 'dwells' in Metapontion 'with happy fortune' or 'success' (115–16 σὺν δὲ τύχαι | ναίεις Μεταπόντιον) – 'success' here means Alexidamos' Pythian victory, which was the point of departure of this ode. Finally, the last sentence (123–6), by linking his victory with the great deeds of Homer's 'Achaians', gives it a mythical dimension (126n.).

In conclusion, it can be said that the ode is very carefully structured, with a vivid sense of ornamental symmetry and a perfect mastery of traditional forms of composition, offering clear thematic parallels between the victory praise and the mythical narrative, and also between the latter and the conclusion. Within the narrative part, the ring composition structures reveal a quite sophisticated narrative technique. Above all, it is the dominant figure of Artemis that gives the whole ode its poetic unity.

1–14 The first strophe is a prayer of thanks to Nika for Alexidamos' success at the Pythian games. It falls into two equal and corresponding halves: 1–7 Address to the goddess and predication (σοὶ . . .), 8–14 second address (ἔλλαθι) and predication (σέθεν δ᾽ ἕκατι . . .), leading on to the victor's praise. The first predication refers to Nika's function as a goddess (κρίνεις τέλος . . . ἀρετᾶς), the second to its effect on mortals, anticipated by καὶ θνατοῖς (7). As in Homer, there is a divine and a human level.

1–3 The supplements adopted here are based on the following considerations: (1) After the vocative, γάρ seems required because minor divinities are often provided with an explanation of their function or sphere of activity, cf. the beginnings of B. 10, Pind. *O.* 12, *O.* 14, *P.* 8, *I.* 5; also Virg. *Aen.* 1.65–6, etc. (2) After σοὶ πατήρ, a verb like ἔδωκε/δέδωκε or ὄπασσε seems likely, cf. B. 13.77–80. If that is right, (3) a suitable object needs to be found, bearing in mind that Nika 'determines the outcome for immortals and mortals' (6–7); σταθμάν or τεθμόν δέδωκεν seem possible, cf. Pind. *Pae.* 6.57 and *O.* 8.21–7, possibly also δῶκεν τάλαντον 'gave the scales', cf. *Il.* 19.223, Thgn. 157. Where this kind of predication is rather specific, it may be emphasized by μόνος/μόνα, 'a traditional element in Greek prayers and hymns' (Barrett on Eur. *Hipp.* 1280–2, with parallels), cf. Melinno's *Hymn to Rome, SH* 541.1–6 χαῖρέ μοι, Ῥώμα...σοὶ μόναι, πρέσβιστα, δέδωκε Μοῖρα κῦδος κτλ., and Kall. *h.* 5.132–3 Παλλάς, ἐπεὶ μώναι Ζεὺς τόγε θυγατέρων | δῶκεν Ἀθαναίαι πατρώϊα πάντα φέρεσθαι.

4 ἐν ... <τ'> Ὀλύμπωι: for τε connecting a main clause specifying or supplementing the preceding one, see K-G II 242 with examples; Schwyzer II 574; Ruijgh, *TE épique* §§ 20 and 27.

πολυχρύσωι: on Olympus, the gods live in golden houses (*Il.* 4.1–2; 13.21–2; Pind. *N.* 10.88; *I.* 3.78; Eur. *Hipp.* 69; *Heracl.* 915–16; *Ion* 459). As gold is a symbol of immortality, things belonging to gods are often golden, cf. Kirk on *Il.* 4.2.

5 Ζηνὶ παρισταμένα: Nika and the other children of Styx and Pallas 'have their seats always next to Zeus' (Hes. *Th.* 386–7), while Styx herself dwells far from the gods (*Th.* 777). In Pindar, this kind of association of divine powers is expressed by πάρεδρος (*O.* 2.76; *O.* 8.22; *N.* 7.1; *I.* 7.3; cf. Sim. *PMG* 519 fr. 120b.5). On B.'s interpretation of Hesiod's genealogy, see below, 9n.

6–7 κρίνεις τέλος ... ἀρετᾶς 'you judge the outcome of prowess', cf. 17.45–6 τὰ δ' ἐπιόντα δα[ίμω]ν κρινεῖ and Pind. *O.* 13.104 ἐν θεῶι γε μὰν τέλος (with reference to future successes).

ἀθανατοῖσίν τε καὶ θνατοῖς: the first half of the strophe refers to Nika's function among the immortals (which may imply a reference to the gods' victory over the Titans, cf. Hes. *Th.* 383–403), the second to her function among mortals. Lines 1–7 are a classic tricolon: (a) Invocation (Νίκα γλυκύδωρε), (b) first predication (?μόναι γάρ → Οὐρανίδας), (c) second predication (Nika as judge, ἐν πολ. Ὀλ. → ἀρετᾶς).

8 ἔλλαθι 'be gracious', an Aeolic form (perfect imperative) according to Choiroboskos, *An. Ox.* II 224.16. The α should be short, as in τέθνᾱθι and τέτλᾱθι, but is measured long here, apparently in analogy to Homeric ἴληθι (*Od.* 3.380).

9 κούρα Σ[τυγὸς ὀρ]θοδίκου: Styx is herself the 'great oath of the gods' (Hes. *Th.* 400); she punishes a god's perjury (*Th.* 793–5), which implies the notion of sanction against wrong-doing. B. develops this idea further by calling her 'right-judging' because he addresses his ode to her daughter

Nika who has taken the 'right' decision in awarding victory to Alexidamos, after he had earlier been denied an Olympic victory (see 24n.). B. adapts Hesiod's genealogy to the system of 'epinician' values.

σέθεν δ' ἕκατι   'thanks to you'. ἕκητι after a god's name in the genitive (= 'by N's will') is first found in the *Odyssey* (15.319; 19.86; 20;42) and in early lyric poetry; the later meaning 'for the sake of', 'because of' is not found before Pindar and tragedy; the earliest instance is *P.* 10.58 of 498 BCE: ἕκατι στεφάνων (equivalent to Νίκας ἕκατι), then *N.* 8.47 ἕκατι ποδῶν 'on account of <the speed of> his feet' and *Pae.* 9.45–6 (Apollo entrusted the people of Thebes to Teneros) ἀνορέας . . . ἕκατι σαόφρονος 'because of his sagacious courage'; the three passages illustrate the shift in the use of ἕκατι + gen.; cf. Leumann, *Hom.Wörter* 251–8.

10–11 εὐγυίων . . . νέων: the compound is unparalleled, as are nearly all compounds with γυι(ο)– or –γυιος. While Pindar applies them to human limbs only in *O.* 9.111 (δεξιόγυιος) and *N.* 9.24 (νεογυίους φῶτας) and elsewhere uses them in phrases like ἀγλαόγυιον Ἥβαν (*N.* 7.4) or νίκαν θρασύγυιον (*P.* 8.37), B. applies them in vivid descriptions of physical beauty (Briseis is ἱμερόγυιος 13.137; the Nereids' limbs shine like fire, 17.103–5) or physical strength (γυια[λκέα σώ]ματα 9.38).

12 εὐφροσύναι   'festivities', see 3.85–92n.

θεότιμον ἄστυ: praise for the victor's home town was a standard element in victory odes. In three of his odes, B. refers to it briefly first, using it as a cue for the myth, but then treats it more fully in the final part, as he does here in 115–26; cf. 9.4 → 98–104 and 13.71 → 182–9. In all three odes, the myth is conceived as praise for the victor's homeland or home town. In Pindar, too, references to the home town in the early part of the ode tend to be brief, while in the central part they are often quite detailed; a good example is *O.* 13 where the first reference (3–23) is just a list of the assets of Corinth, whereas the second celebrates the town in a mythical narrative (49–92), and *N.* 1 where praise for Ortygia (1–4) is followed by a much longer praise for Sicily (13–18); see Thummer I 65.

13–14 ὑμνεῦσι δὲ . . . Φαΐσκου: the end of the prayer of thanks to Nika furnishes two essential items of information, the name of the games and the patronymic which gives the cue for the description of the wrestling contest that follows, providing a smooth transition to the victor's praise (15–39).

15–17 ἵλεωι . . . βλεφά[ρω]ι   'with gracious eye'; Pindar uses similar expressions in *I.* 2.18 (εἶδ' Ἀπόλλων νιν πόρε τ' ἀγλαΐαν), *P.* 8.18–20 (Apollo

εὐμενεῖ νόωι ... ἔδεκτο ... ἐστεφανωμένον υἱόν); in *O.* 14.15–16 and *P.* 12.4–
5, other goddesses 'receive' the victor, or (in *Paean* 5.44–8) the chorus. ἵλεωι
takes up ἔλλαθι (8), providing a link between the first two strophes. For
βλέφαρον in the sense of 'gaze' cf. Sim. *PMG* 579.4 (Ἀρετά is not visible
πάντων βλεφάροισι θνατῶν). The idea that a god controls a mortal by
'gazing' at him is first found in *Il.* 1.200; cf. Hes. *Th.* 82 (hence Kall. fr. 1.37
and Horace, *Carm.* 4.3.2), Ibykos *PMG* 287, Aesch. *Septem* 667, Pind. *P.* 3.85,
O. 7.11, *P.* 8.68, Ap. Rhod. 4.475–6; further parallels have been collected
by Headlam on Herodas 4.73.

17–20 πολέες ... στέφανοι ... ἔπεσον: the spectators showered the
victor with garlands, cf. Pind. *P.* 9.123 and Paus. 6.7.1; the custom was
known as φυλλοβολία, cf. Eratosthenes, *FGrHist* 241 F 14. Pindar and B.
use the image metaphorically, cf. *P.* 8.57 and B. 4.10n.

  ἐν πεδίωι ... Κίρρας: 4.14n.

21 ἦρα ... πάλας: ἦρα + gen. 'on account of' (= χάριν + gen.) is first
found here, unparalleled before the Hellenistic age (Kall. fr. 231
etc.); its origin may have been the explanation of Homeric ἦρα
'gratification' (*Il.* 1.572 etc.) as χάριν: Schol. A on *Il.* 1.572 explains that
'more recent authors (οἱ νεώτεροι) use the word as a conjunction in the
accusative, in the sense of χάριν, ἕνεκα' (= Suda ε 2316).

22–3 οὐκ ε [ῖ]δέ νιν ἀέλιος ... πεσόντα: an explanatory *asyndeton* which
'caps' the preceding praise passage. B. uses the same phrase in a positive
sense in 5.40 εἶδε νικάσαντα ... Ἀώς; negative phrases expressing 'victory'
are used occasionally, perhaps for the sake of variation, by Pindar (*P.* 5.34;
I. 2.20–1; *N.* 3.15–16; *N.* 6.14; *N.* 7.72 αὐχένα ... ἀδίαντον) and B. 5.43–5;
cf. *AP* 9.588; 16.24 and 25; Quint. Smyrn. 4.296 and 319.

  κείνωι γε σὺν ἄματι   'throughout that day' (on this rare meaning of
σύν see 125n.). On that day, at any rate (γε), Alexidamos was successful (even
though on a previous occasion he had been disappointed); see Denniston
122–3 on this usage of γε.

24 φάσω δέ: phrases of this type are sometimes used to introduce
superlatives or statements equivalent to superlatives (5.42n.). Compared
to 5.42–5 ('no horse was in front of Pherenikos'), 8.19–25 ('nobody won
more victories than Liparion'), Pind. *O.* 2.90–5 ('there was no benefactor greater than Theron'), the statement announced in 11.24 is indeed
a bold one: he would have won at Olympia, had not a god, or human
error, deprived him of victory (34–6). The motif of the 'lost victory' occurs
first in Homer, *Il.* 23.382–97, and in B. 4.11–13, Pind. *N.* 6.61–3 and

N. 11.22–9; B. 11.24–36 is more radical in that it amounts to an allegation of corruption, or at least bias, on the part of the judges (= τις in 27).
Examples of unfair decisions by judges in the Olympic games are reported
by Plut. *Mor.* 1000a (the people of Elis favour Eleian competitors), Paus.
6.3.7 (two judges were fined by the Olympic Council for voting in favour
of an Eleian), and Diod. 1.95.2 (Bokchoris tells the Eleians that they can
conduct the Games most fairly if no Eleian takes part, cf. Hdt. 2.160). In
B. 11.24–36, the motif of the 'lost victory' serves a dual purpose: (1) it is
an additional element of praise for the victor (he ought to have won, he
deserved victory), (2) it is 'foil' for the actual victory. As the passage is framed
by references to the actual victory in 23 (κείνωι γε σὺν ἄματι . . .) and 37
(νῦν δὲ κτλ.), the second function is strongly emphasized. References to
earlier misfortunes in Pind. *O.* 12.10–19 and *I.* 1.36–8 serve an analogous
purpose.

26–7 δίκας κέλευθον εἰ μή τις ἀπέτραπεν ὀρθᾶς   'had not someone
twisted the course of upright justice'. The phrase implies the idea of Justice
walking on a straight path; humans can deviate from it (παρεκβαίνουσι
δικαίου, Hes. *Op.* 226), but Justice is herself 'the course (path) of justice',
i.e. the procedure of finding and administering justice. This course can be
diverted or deflected, so that it is no longer 'straight' (cf. Pind. *O.* 7.46–7 'the
cloud of forgetfulness παρέλκει πραγμάτων ὀρθὰν ὁδὸν ἔξω φρενῶν). This
idea, too, goes back to Hesiod (*Op.* 262 βασιλῆες . . . ἄλληι παρκλίνωσι
δίκας σκολιῶς ἐνέποντες). By combining Hesiod's images of Justice walking
on her path and of the 'crooked judgements', B. mixes the notions of
Δίκη 'Justice' and δίκαι 'judgements', as does Pindar when he says of the
victor, Diagoras, in *O.* 7.90–1 that he 'travels straight on a path hostile to
arrogance', ὕβριος ἐχθρὰν ὁδὸν (= δίκας ὁδόν) εὐθυπορεῖ.

   τις: one of the judges of the games (ἀγωνοθέται).

27–30 εἰ μή τις . . . ἱκέσθαι: if Platt's supplements in 30 Ἰταλ]ί[αν
πάτ]ραν θ' be accepted, the unfulfilled conditional clause would lack the
particle ἄν in the *apodosis*. For examples in both poetry and prose, see K-G
I 216 (§ 393.2 and 3) and Schwyzer II 353.

28 παγξένωι . . . ἐλαίᾶι   'the olive that is there for all comers'; cf. Pind.
O. 3.18 (the olive at Olympia is φύτευμα ξυνὸν ἀνθρώποις).

30 πορτιτρόφῳ [Ἰταλ]ί[αν   'calf-breeding Italy'; the Sicilian historian
Timaios claimed that the name 'Italia' was derived from the Greek word
for cattle, ἰταλοί (= *vituli*), which were plentiful in Italy; cf. *FGrHist* 566 F
42a = Gellius, *NA* 11.1.1.

31–3 − ⌣ ⌣ − ⌣ ⌣ −] παῖδ᾽ . . . ποικίλαις τέχναις πέλασσεν: παῖδ(α)
must be the object of πέλασσεν; the dative, τέχναις, could be indirect
object in the sense of (a) 'he entangled him in his tricks' or 'skill' (cf. [Hes.]
fr. 33a.21–2 Periklymenos πολέας δὲ μελαίνηι κῆρι πέλασσε | κτείνων), or
(b) 'he provided him with tricks' (cf. Pind. *O.* 1.78 κράτει δὲ πέλασον sc. ἐμέ
'give me strength'), or (c) an instrumental dative, with something like 'to the
ground' (οὐδεῖ ?, ποτὶ γᾶι?) to be supplied in 30 (cf. B. 9.37–8 ὑπερθ]υμῶι
σ[θένε]ι . . . [σώ]ματα [πρὸς γ]αίᾳ πελάσσα[ς 'with bold strength . . .
throwing bodies to the ground', cf. *Il.* 23.719 οὔτ᾽ Ὀδυσεὺς δύνατο σφῆλαι
οὔδει τε πελάσσαι, sc. Aias in wrestling). I have adopted (c) because in the
context of wrestling, ποικίλαις τέχναις is most likely to be an instrumental
dative, as in B. 13.49 (cf. Pind. *P.* 4.249), and because B. 9.37–9 provides
a close parallel for a vivid description of the wrestling match. This would
point to something like '(he would have come home victorious), *for* he had
his opponent on the ground': [οὔδεῖ γ᾽ ἀντίπαλον] or better [ἤ τινα γὰρ
ποτὶ γᾶι] (30) παῖδ(α) . . . πέλασσεν (33) 'for he brought many a boy to
the ground by his cunning skills' (for τινα = 'many', cf. Pind. *N.* 1.64 καί
τινα . . . ἀνδρῶν).

34–6 ἀ]λλ᾽ ἢ θεὸς αἴτιος, ἢ [γ]νῶμαι . . . βροτῶν κτλ.:   in Homer, to
make a god responsible is always presented as an antithesis, e.g. when Priam
says to Helen (*Il.* 3.164–5) 'for me, you are not guilty: the gods are guilty who
have stirred up war against me', or when Telemachos excuses Phemios (*Od.*
1.347–8) 'not the singers are guilty, ἀλλά ποθι Ζεὺς αἴτιος', while Homer's
heroes excuse themselves by shifting the blame onto the gods (Agamemnon
in *Il.* 19.86–7, Odysseus in *Od.* 11.558–60), even Achilles' horse, Xanthos,
apologizes for having predicted his master's death, *Il.* 19.409–10 οὐδέ τοι
ἡμεῖς αἴτιοι, ἀλλὰ θεός τε μέγας καὶ Μοῖρα κραταιή); cf. Thgn. 133–4 and
Eur. *Suppl.* 734–6. B., however, presents this motif as an alternative, adapting
it to the overriding requirement of the victory ode, i.e. to turn everything
that could be said about the victor or the circumstances of his victory to his
advantage – even a *lost* victory! The first part of the alternative (θεὸς αἴτιος)
is conventional and merely prepares the ground for the second (γνῶμαι . . .
βροτῶν): Alexidamos was powerless against either. The purpose here is not,
as in Homer, to present an excuse but to turn even failure or disappointment
into praise: he did defeat his opponent(s) (31–3n.), only a superior power –
god, or human envy – was able to wrest victory from his hands.

γ]νῶμαι πολύπλαγκτοι βροτῶν 'the judgements of mortals which
often go astray'. For the compound in passive sense, cf. *Od.* 17.425

144   COMMENTARY: Ode 11.36–39

(ληιστῆρες), Aesch. *Supp.* 572 (Io), also Eur. *Hipp.* 240 παρεπλάγχθην γνώμας ἀγαθᾶς, and the late epigram *IG* 14.1424 (4th cent. CE ?) βροτῶν πολυ-
πλάγκτοισιν πραπίδεσσιν; in active sense B. 13.181 of the sea which drives
ships off course, as does the wind in *Il.* 11.308 (in Soph. *Ant.* 615 πολ. ἐλπίς
could be either).

36 ἄ]μερσαν: usually with gen., but in *h.Dem.* 312 and here with acc. in
analogy to ἀφελεῖν, cf. *Il.* 16.53–4 ὁππότε δὴ τὸν ὁμοῖον ἀνὴρ ἐθέλῃσιν
ἀμέρσαι | καὶ γέρας ἂψ ἀφελέσθαι.

37–9 νῦν δ' . . . ἔδωκε takes up 10–14 καὶ νῦν κτλ.; the verbal echo
audibly marks the end of the first praise passage. In addition, Artemis is
introduced here: it is to her that Alexidamos owes his victory, and she is
also the central figure of the myth for which her mention in 37 provides
the cue.

Ἄρτεμις ἀγροτέρα: cf. *Il.* 21.470–1 πότνια θηρῶν, | Ἄρτεμις
ἀγροτέρη. The epithet (whether it be derived from ἀγρός or from ἄγρα)
points to the open countryside. B. may have understood this cult title in
the sense of 'huntress', as τοξόκλυτος (39) suggests; cf. the scholion *PMG*
886.3–4 ἐλαφηβόλον τ' ἀγροτέραν Ἄρτεμιν. Likewise, Pindar describes
the huntress, Kyrene, as ἀγροτέρα (*P.* 9.6).

χρυσαλάκατος: in Homer and in the Homeric hymns, it is always
said of Artemis (*Il.* 16.183 etc.). Pindar and B. give this epithet to other
goddesses, too: Pind. *O.* 6.104 (Amphitrite), *N.* 6.36 and *Thren.* 3.1 (Leto),
N. 5.36 (Nereids), *Hymn* 1.1 (Melia); B. 9.1 (Charites). None of these goddesses have anything to do with arrows, which makes the derivation offered
by the scholia on *Il.* 16.183, 20.70 and 6.491 (καλλίτοξος, ἠλακάτη = βέλος
'arrow', or κάλαμος, δόναξ 'reed') unlikely, even though it seems to have
been known in the fifth century, as Aesch. fr. 8 R. called river-banks πολυη-
λάκατα. Alternatively, the compound could mean 'of the golden shuttle',
which would make it a typically female epithet suggesting brightness and
divine splendour. The four epithets given to Artemis here go in pairs, the
first and the last describing the huntress (ἀγροτέρα – τοξόκλυτος), the
other two the 'soother' (χρυσαλάκατος – ἡμέρα).

Ἡμ]έρα,   the 'Gentle', was Artemis' cult name at Lousoi (*IG* v 2.403;
Paus. 8.18.8; Kall., *h.Dian.* 236). The contrast to Artemis the huntress and
πότνια θηρῶν is clearly deliberate, as in Anakreon *PMG* 348 (ἀγρίων
δέσποιν' Ἄρτεμι θηρῶν . . . οὐ γὰρ ἀνημέρους ποιμαίνεις πολιήτας 'mistress of beasts of the wild, Artemis, . . . they are no wild and untamed

people that you have for your flock', and Kall. *h.Dian.* 236 (where ἄγριον
refers to the Proitids' madness healed by Artemis Ἡμέρα); cf. *IG* xii 1.698.7
(Rhodes, 3rd cent. BCE: Ἡμέριος son of Ἄγριος). The 'cluster' of four epithets at the point where Artemis makes her first appearance illustrates her
importance. She is the dominating figure of the ode, who links the myth of
Proitos' daughters to Metapontion and Alexidamos.

40–112   B. begins with the end of the story, then goes back in stages to its
beginning, and eventually moves forward again to its conclusion (110–12).
The narrative is punctuated by the recurrence of the 'flight' motif between
each section: 43 → 55 φεῦγον → 82–4 ἀπεσσύμεναι . . . φεῦγον →93–4
ἠλύκταζον . . . φεῦγόν τε. Into this 'rondo' structure are inserted two
digressions, the first of which (47–54) names the cause of the girls' madness
and flight, the second (59–81) explains why they lived with Proitos at Tiryns,
having left Argos ten years before. The point farthest back in time is the
quarrel between Proitos and Akrisios (64–6). Then, two further scenes,
Proitos' despair (85–91) and his prayer at the river Lousos (95–105), lead
to the girls' deliverance by Artemis and their dedication of the sanctuary
(106–12) with which the narrative had begun. It is a 'classic' example of
ring composition.

40 Ἀβαντιάδας: Abas, son of Lynkeus and Hypermestra, was Proitos'
and Akrisios' father, Apollod. 2.2.1; cf. Paus. 2.16.1–2 for the list of the
mythical kings of Argos.

41 κατένασσε: the compound is usually said of 'settling' people, only
here in the sense of 'he established' a sanctuary and altar (= ἱδρύσατο).

     πολύλλ[ι]στον: said proleptically, 'at which many prayers would be
made'. On the proleptic use of adjectives, see 16.26n.

43–5 ἐξ ἐρατῶν . . . μελάθρων Προίτου: ἐρατός is a favourite word
in lyric poetry, cf. B. 17.110 (Amphitrite's palace) and fr. 4.79 (symposia
in peacetime). The contrast between their father's 'lovely' house and 'all-
powerful' (παγκρατής) Hera who chases them from it highlights the daughters' misery. As so often, B. focusses on the emotional aspect of his story; his
choice of the epithets is designed to create compassion for the girls, whose
cruel fate is described before its cause is mentioned (47–8n.).

45–6 παραπλῆγι . . . ἀνάγκαι: παραπλήξ is first found in *Od.*
5.418, said of the beach on which the waves break obliquely; of mental derangement first here and in Hdt. 5.92.7; cf. Ar. *Lys.* 831 ἄνδρα

παραπεπληγμένον (of sexual passion), *Plutos* 242 παραπλῆγ'ἄνθρωπον. The word is used with active meaning ('hitting the mind sideways', παρα–) only here in B.; cf. Io's φρενοπληγεῖς μανίαι Aesch. *Prom.* 878.

ζεύξασ': the image of the yoke (Hes. *Op.* 581 and 815 ἐπὶ ζυγὸν αὐχένι θεῖναι) is used metaphorically in *h.Dem.* 216–7 ἀλλὰ θεῶν μὲν δῶρα καὶ ἀχνύμενοι περ ἀνάγκηι τέτλαμεν ἄνθρωποι· ἐπὶ γὰρ ζυγὸς αὐχένι κεῖται ('we humans suffer the gods' gifts groaning, through necessity, for on the neck there is a yoke', after *Il.* 6.458). Cf. Thgn. 1023–4; 1357–8; 847–8 and Barrett on Eur. *Hipp.* 1389–90. Madness, in particular, is often seen, as here in B. and also in tragedy, as a yoke, cf. Soph. *Ai.* 123 (Aias) ἄτηι συγκατέζευκται κακῆι and Aesch. *Prom.* 577–8 where Io says to Zeus τίποτε ταῖσδ'ἐνέζευξας . . . ἐν πημοναῖσιν;

47–8 παρθενίαι . . . ψυχᾶι 'with childish soul': B. presents their youth as extenuating circumstance (surely not as 'aggravating their presumption', as Jebb thought); cf. Soph. *Ai.* 558–9 (Aias to his son:) τέως δὲ κούφοις πνεύμασιν βόσκου, νέαν ψυχὴν ἀτάλλων [Eur. *Hipp.* 1006 is different: παρθένον ψυχὴν ἔχων refers to chastity]. ψυχή meaning 'soul' (of a living person) is not found before Herakleitos (B 45, see Snell, *Discovery* 17) and the lyric poets (see H. Fränkel, *Early Greek poetry* 298 on Anakreon *PMG* 360).

τέμενος: Hera's sanctuary near Argos. Although Proitos and his family had moved from Argos to Tiryns (57 and 71), the Heraion remained part of his kingdom, cf. Paus. 2.16.2.

49 πορφυροζώνοιο 'purple-belted', only here and (as a gloss on ἰόζωνος in Kallim. fr. 110.54) in Hesych. 1737. Hera's belt, which she obtained from Aphrodite in *Il.* 14.214–7, is there described as ποικίλος; for the erotic connotations of the colour 'purple' in lyric poetry cf. Sappho fr. 54; Anakreon *PMG* 357 and 358.

50–2 φάσκον . . . εὐρυβίᾱ: in the sanctuary, the girls claim that their father was much richer than Hera; their arrogance evidently refers to the modest temple and/or its cult image. The same motive for their punishment is reflected by both Pherekydes (*FGrHist* 3 F 114 παραγενόμεναι γὰρ εἰς τὸν τῆς θεοῦ νεὼν ἔσκωπτον αὐτὸν λέγουσαι πλουσιώτερον μᾶλλον εἶναι τὸν τοῦ πατρὸς οἶκον 'when they entered the goddess's temple they ridiculed it, saying that their father's house was much richer'), whose account agrees closely with the wording in B. (see above, pp. 134–6), and Akusilaos (*FGrHist* 2 F 28 τὸ τῆς Ἥρας ξόανον ἐξηυτέλισαν), which suggests that they both summarized the story from an epic source, such as the *Phoronis*, or the

'Hesiodic' *Catalogue*, (see above, p. 135). The story of Niobe's punishment is similarly motivated.

51 προφέρειν 'was superior'; the intransitive use is not attested before the fifth century, e.g. in Hdt. 6.127.4 (Hippokleides πλούτωι καὶ εἴδεϊ προφέρων Ἀθηναίων) and Thuc. 1.123.1 (εἰ ἄρα πλούτωι . . . καὶ ἐξουσίαι ὀλίγον προφέρετε); for further parallels, see LSJ *s.v.* προφέρω ιν.2.

παρέδρου 'consort' ('not elsewhere used of a wife', Kenyon) for the conventional epic παράκοιτις.

52 σεμνοῦ Διὸς εὐρυβία: Kenyon's correction (ευρυβϊαι pap.) is likely to be correct in view of 5.99 σεμνᾶς χόλον Ἀρτέμιδος λευκωλένου and 5.174–5 χρυσέας Κύπριδος θελξιμβρότου: the phrase here may well follow the same pattern (simple adjective + name of divinity + compound epithet).

54 παλίντροπον ἔμβαλεν νόημα   (ομμα pap.; the scribe misread H for M in his exemplar): Hera 'put into their hearts (στήθεσσι) deranged thinking' (not 'an impulse that turned them to flight', Jebb and LSJ); πάλιν means either 'again' or 'back', so παλίντροπον νόημα might be a thought that turned the girls 'back' (home), not away from home. What the compound means here is illustrated by other phrases describing mental derangement: Io speaks of her φρένες διάστροφοι (Aesch. *Prom.* 673), and Aias uses the same phrase (Soph. *Ai.* 447); cf. Soph. *Phil.* 815 τί παραφρονεῖς αὖ; Aesch. *Sept.* 806 παραφρονῶ φόβωι λόγου. Normal, healthy thinking travels towards its target in a straight line; if it is disturbed, it is hit off course, or led astray, so that it cannot reach its target but is turned 'aside' or 'sideways' (παρα-) or 'back' (παλιν-); see Griffith on Aesch. *Prom.* 133–4; O'Brian-Moore, *Madness* 58.

The girls' madness is referred to again at the end of their story when Proitos prays to Artemis, asking her 'to deliver his children from the wretched frenzy that deranged them' (τέκνα δυστάνοιο λύσσας | πάρφρονος ἐξαγαγεῖν, 102–3): the close correspondence of beginning and end of the mythical narrative section confirms that παλίντροπον νόημα is παραφρονεῖν, παράνοια.

55–6 φεῦγον . . . φωνὰν ἱεῖσαι: in their frenzied flight in the wooded hills, the girls resemble maenads, cf. *h.Dem.* 386 ἤϋτε μαινὰς ὄρος κατὰ δάσκιον ὕληις and Eur. *Ba.* 217–20, as do their terrible shrieks, cf. Eur. *Ba.* 155–9. This may be a reminiscence of the original 'Dionysiac' version of the myth, in which the madness was sent by Dionysos and cured by Melampous (Diod. 4.68 and Apollod. 1.9.12, see above p. 135).

ὄρος ἐς τανίφυλλον: Tiryns is in the Argive plain which consists mainly of pastures, the ἱππόβοτον Ἄργος; wooded hills are quite a distance away. Kall., *h.Dian.* 235 makes them roam οὔρεα . . . Ἀζήνια, the hills of northern Arcadia.

57 Τιρύνθιον ἄστυ λιποῦσαι: cf. Phrynichos' *Phoinissai, TrGF* 1 3 F 9 Σιδώνιον ἄστυ λιποῦσαι – both phrases possibly borrowed from epic.

58 θεοδμάτους   'god-built', i.e. by the Cyclopes at the order of Zeus, cf. Apollod. 2.2.1; Schol. Eur. *Or.* 965; Strabo 8.6.2 (C 368); Paus. 2.16.5 and 25.8.

ἀγυιάς: here, B. seems to distinguish between ἄστυ 'city' and ἀγυιαί 'streets' or 'town quarters' (cf. 3.16 and fr. 4.79), as does Homer (*Il.* 5.642 Herakles Ἰλίου ἐξαλάπαξε πόλιν, χήρωσε δ' ἀγυιάς); in 9.17 and 52, and in 14B.4, ἀγυιαί seems to be an 'augmentative' plural (like μέγαρα, δόμοι etc., see Schwyzer II 43 with examples and bibliography) in the sense of 'city', as in Pindar, *P.* 2.58; 8.55; 9.83. This usage, not found before the fifth century BCE, seems to be peculiar to choral lyric.

59 ἤδη γάρ   is the beginning of a digression which explains why Proitos and his daughters live at Tiryns, not at Argos where their ancestors Danaos, Lynkeus and Abas had lived. This digression ends with 81, returning to its point of departure: 60 λιπόντες Ἄργος → 81 Ἄργος λιπόντες, 61 ναῖον → 80 ναῖον, 62 ἡμίθεοι → 79 ἀντίθεοι (ἥρωες).

61 ἀδεισιβόαι   'fearless of the battle-cry' (5.155n.).

62 χαλκάσπιδες   may be a reference to the battle between Proitos and his brother Akrisios, when (wooden!) shields were used for the first time, according to schol. Eur. *Or.* 965; cf. Paus. 2.25.7 and Apollod. 2.2.1.

63 πολυζήλωι   'much envied' (= πολυζηλώτωι), see Barrett on Eur. *Hipp.* 168. Ten years of peaceful rule over Tiryns are the 'foil' to Proitos' misery and despair, 85–95.

64–76 νεῖκος γάρ . . . ἀχέων: exactly in the middle of the first digression (59–81), B. inserts a second digression to explain why Proitos had left Argos – a further step back in time, preceded and followed by passages of five lines each. The formal symmetry of the central passage is shown by verbal and thematic correspondences: 64–5 νεῖκος γάρ ἀμαιμάκετον . . . ἀνέπαλτο → 76 παῦσαι στυγερῶν ἀχέων (noun-adjective-verb ↔ verb-adjective-noun) and 68 ἤρειπον . . . μάχαις τε λυγραῖς → 72 ἐς ἀργαλέαν πεσεῖν ἀνάγκαν. It was probably not for the sake of completeness that B. inserted a passage with such an elaborate 'ring' structure – he could have given the reason for Proitos' move in a few words – but because this part of the story was important to him and/or to his audience. It is, in fact, the *leitmotiv* of this ode, on which its thematic and formal unity rests: god (Zeus) grants the prayers of supplicants in distress and delivers them from their anguish – Artemis 'cured' Alexidamos' disappointment at Olympia by granting him victory at Delphi – Artemis will also heal Proitos' misery and grief by delivering his daughters from madness. The thematic parallel is emphasized by the verbal echo: 76 παῦσαι στυγερῶν ἀχέων ↔ 108–9 παῦσεν . . . μανιᾶν ἀθέων.

64 ἀμαιμάκετον   'overmastering' (not 'stubborn', Jebb and LSJ) because it contrasts with βληχρᾶς . . . ἀπ' ἀρχᾶς (65). B. may have derived the word either from α + μαιμάω/μαίομαι ('against which one cannot strive' → 'irresistible', 'unconquerable'), or from α + μάχομαι; either etymology would be compatible also with Pindar's use of the word (*P.* 3.33 μένει θυιοῖσαν ἀμαιμακέτωι, of Artemis; *P.* 4.208 κινηθμόν, of the Symplegades; *I.* 8.35 of Poseidon's trident; *P.* 1.14 πόντον κατ'ἀμ.); cf. Braswell on Pind. *P.*4.208(b). It seems likely, therefore, that the explanations offered by the scholia, e.g. on Pind. *P.* 4.208 (368) ἀκαταμάχητον, schol. T on *Il.* 6.179 (Χίμαιραν ἀμαιμακέτην] τὴν ἄγαν μαιμῶσαν ἢ τὴν ἀκαταμάχητον) were already familiar in the fifth century BCE.

65 βληχρᾶς . . . ἀπ' ἀρχᾶς   'from a feeble beginning' – B. does not say what this was. Pindar apparently claimed that the quarrel was sparked off by Proitos' seduction of his niece, Danae (fr. 284 = schol. ABD on *Il.* 14.319, and Apollod. 2.4.1). As no other reason is mentioned anywhere else, it seems that B. knew this story but did not wish to mention it; by calling it a 'feeble beginning', he plays it down because it would have discredited Proitos, whom he portrays as a positive character in 85–105. In addition, he thus creates an example of an insignificant cause that threatens to throw entire populations into conflict and ruin (68), illustrating the absurdity of war; see below, 69n.

ἀνέπαλτο   'had sprung up', from ἀναπάλλεσθαι 'to leap up', cf. *Il.* 23.692; Leumann, *Hom.Wörter* 60 suspects that the original form may have been ἔπ–αλτο (from ἄλλομαι, as an early case of *psilosis*), interpreted as ἔ–παλτο in epic sources.

67–8 διχοστασίαις ἤρειπον ἀμετροδίκοις   'they were about to wreck their people with their unrighteous quarrels'. ἐρείπειν 'to tear down' is first used metaphorically in Sim. *PMG* 543.5 of Danae: ἄνεμός τε . . . κινηθεῖσά τε λίμνα δείματι ἔρειπεν 'the wind blowing and the sea stirring shattered her with fear'; cf. Soph. *Ant.* 596–7 ἀλλ' ἐρείπει θεῶν τις, sc. the Labdakids' house. For the imperfect 'of attempted action' (ἤρειπον 'they were about to wreck') cf. Eur. *IT* 27 ἐκαινόμην ξίφει and K-G 1 141–2 with more examples, also Goodwin, *Syntax* 12 § 36.

ἀμετροδίκοις: only here; 'compounds with ἀμετρο– usually mean 'unmeasured' in respect to that which is denoted by the subst.' Jebb, who quotes ἀμετροεπής (*Il.* 2.212, of Thersites who is ἄμετρος ἐν τῶι λέγειν, schol. D ad loc.). B. seems to have interpreted this as 'he who ignores the measure of speech' and coined ἀμετρόδικος as an analogy.

69 λίσσοντο: the subject is λαοί (67). In 15.45–6, it is the *people* of Troy who pray to the gods to end the misery of war. B. strongly emphasizes that war, caused by the greed or arrogance of the leaders, brings nothing but suffering to their people, and so, if Proitos and Akrisios had gone to war against each other, this would have been the predictable result. The horror of war is brought into prominence three times, always at the end of a sentence and with strongly 'loaded' epithets: 68 μάχαις τε λυγραῖς – 72 ἀργαλέαν . . . ἀνάγκαν – 76 στυγερῶν ἀχέων. Pindar has a similar but much shorter scene in *P.* 4.154, where he makes Jason ask Pelias τὰ μὲν ἄνευ ξυνᾶς ἀνίας λῦσον, but he does not elaborate. B. appears to have felt more strongly about the issue of war and peace; see Introd. to his *Paean* for Asine (fr. 4, pp. 225–7).

70 πολύκριθον   'barley-rich'; the compound, elsewhere attested only in Euphorion (51.14) and Suda *s.v.* κρίμνον, may have been coined as a variation on Homer's πολυλήϊος (*Il.* 5.613).

λαχόντας   'having received' the rich land, inherited from their father, Abas. The implication is that the plain around Argos is so fertile that it can support both brothers if the younger one settles in nearby Tiryns, so there is no need to fight. This is an interesting 'correction' of the (apparently older) version of the story, according to which the brothers, after their father's death, went to war against each other; it was only after Akrisios' victory that they agreed that Proitos should leave and settle in Tiryns (Schol. Eur. *Or.* 965 and, with slight variations, Apollod. 2.2.1 and Paus. 2.25.7). In B., however, the people (λαοί) appeal to their leaders to avoid the horrors of war and to find a peaceful solution; see 74n.

71 τὸν ὁπλότερον: only in Apollod. 2.2.1 are the brothers twins who fight already in their mother's womb, as did Esau and Jacob in Genesis 25.22. Is it conceivable that Apollodoros' account originated from a mis-understanding of line 65 βληχρᾶς . . . ἀπ' ἀρχᾶς 'from a tender age', as Christ 1898: 142 suspected?

74 τιμῶν Δαναοῦ γενεάν: Zeus was willing to 'honour the race of Danaos', not by granting it supremacy or victories in war, but on the contrary, by sparing it the distress of war. Abas, father of Akrisios and Proitos, was a son of Lynkeus, the nephew and son-in-law of Danaos.

76 στυγερῶν ἀχέων   'from their hateful distress', after Homer's στυγεροῦ πολέμοιο, Il. 4.240; 6.330, cf. B. 5.111 στυγερὰν δῆριν.

77–8 Κύκλωπες . . . ὑπερφίαλοι: the same epithet is given to the Homeric Cyclopes (Od. 9.106), which the scholia refer to their physical height (μεγαλοφυῶν τῶι σώματι), whereas Apoll.Soph. and the D-scholia on Il. 15.94 take it to mean 'overweening, arrogant' (= ὑπερήφανος), as do Hes. Th. 139 and B. 15.62–3 (of the Giants, after [Hes.] fr. 43a.65). This meaning may suit the present passage too, since it would add to the prestige of Proitos and his heroes if even the mighty Cyclopes 'who have an overbearing heart' (ὑπέρβιον ἦτορ ἔχοντες, Hes. Th. 129) were at his service. For the Cyclopes as builders of the walls of Tiryns cf. Apollod. 2.2.1 and Schol. Eur. Or. 965 (of the walls of Mycene as well: Paus. 2.16.5), also Strabo 8.6.11 (C.373). They had come either from Thrace (Schol. Eur.) or from Lycia (Apollod. and Strabo); at any rate, it was believed that walls of such magnitude could not have been built by indigenous Greeks.

79–81 ἀντίθεοι ναῖον . . . Ἄργος . . . λιπόντες   summarizes the beginning of this digression, in reverse order (60–2 λιπόντες Ἄργος ναῖον . . . ἡμίθεοι), signalling to the audience the end of the digression; see above, 64–76n.

83 κυανοπλόκαμοι   'dark-haired', as are Nika (5.33) and Theba (9.53); Thetis is κυανόπλοκος in Pindar (Pae. 6.83). On κυάνεος 'dark' cf. Irwin, *Colour terms* 79–110.

84 ἄδματοι θύγατρες   'virgin daughters'. B. portrays the girls as very young (see on 47–8 παρθενίαι . . . ψυχᾶι) in order to create compassion both for the girls and for their wretched father (85–91), so he had to remove any notion of μαχλοσύνη 'lewdness' that was attributed to them in an earlier version, cf. [Hes.] frs. 132–3.

85 τὸν δ᾽ εἷλεν ἄχος κραδίαν   'grief seized him, i.e. his heart', the 'whole and part' construction (σχῆμα καθ᾽ ὅλον καὶ μέρος) common in Homer, cf. Il. 23.46–7 (Achilles' reaction to Patroklos' death) οὔ μ᾽ ἔτι δεύτερον ὧδε | ἵξετ᾽ ἄχος κραδίην and h.Dem. 40 (of Demeter) ὀξὺ δέ μιν κραδίην ἄχος ἔλλαβεν, cf. K-G I 289.9 with more examples, also Schwyzer II 81.

85–6 ξεῖνα . . . μέριμνα   'a strange thought'. ξένος as adjective is first found here and in Pind. P. 4.118; for the meaning 'unfamiliar', Kenyon

refers to Aesch. *Prom.* 688–9 where the chorus say οὔποθ᾽<ὧδ᾽> οὔποτ᾽
ηὔχουνξ ἔνους | μολεῖσθαι λόγους ἐς ἀκοὰν ἐμάν 'I never expected that
such strange words would ever come to my hearing'.

μέριμνα: is this (a) the thought of suicide, or (b) concern for his daughters? In either case, the implication is that Proitos had never before suffered
such grief and/or thought of suicide. In favour of (a) is the fact that both B.
and Pindar use the noun in the sense of βουλή 'deliberation, plan, ambition'
(B. 3.57, fr. 20B.10, Pind. *P.* 8.92 etc.) because they seem to have derived
it from μερμηρίζειν (glossed as βουλεύεσθαι in schol. bT on *Il.* 1.189, cf.
schol. Eur. *Or.* 633 διπλῆς μερίμνης] ὡς . . . διστακτικῶς ἀναλογιζομένου).
B. may have been thinking of *Il.* 1.189 (see below, 87–88n.).

87–8 δοίαξε δὲ . . . πᾶξαι: the verb is found only here and in Ap. Rhod.
who uses δοιάζεσκεν in the sense of Homeric δοάσσατο (3.819–20, 3.770
and 3.954–5, 4.575–6, cf. Hesych. δ 2086), while Ammonios (p. 147 Nickau)
makes a clear distinction: δοάσσατο = ἔδοξεν 'he decided', δοιάσσατο =
ἐδίστασε 'he was in two minds'. The same etymological combination
seems to have been familiar to B. who construes δοιάζειν + infinitive,
like βουλεύεσθαι, = 'to resolve'. He may have been thinking of *Il.* 1.188–
9 Πηλείωνι δ᾽ ἄχος γένετ᾽, ἐν δέ οἱ ἦτορ | στήθεσσιν λασίοισι διάνδιχα
μερμήριξεν and in particular of *Od.* 10.438–42 μερμήριξα | σπασσάμενος
τανύηκες ἄορ . . . ἀλλά μ᾽ ἑταῖροι | μειλιχίοις ἐπέεσσιν ἐρήτυον. However,
while in both these scenes it is anger that inspires the hero's violent reaction,
in B. it is grief and despair that find dramatic expression in Proitos' pathetic
resolve to kill himself. As no other source mentions this, it may well be B.'s
own invention. Cf. 3.29–49 where, however, Kroisos' decision is motivated
more by his pride and desire to die with dignity than by despair.

92–3 τρισκαίδεκα . . . μῆνας᾽:   i.e., one year. According to Pherekydes,
(above, p. 134), perhaps reflecting an epic source, their madness lasted ten
years; B. may have found this excessive.

93 ἠλύκταζον   'they roamed'. This form occurs only here and in
Hdt. 9.70.4; it is derived from ἀλυκτεῖν, found once, as perf. passive, in
Il. 10.94 where Agamemnon says ἀλαλύκτημαι, κραδίη δέ μοι ἔξω |
στηθέων ἐκθρώισκει 'I am beside myself, my heart leaps out of my breast'
(explained as τεθορύβημαι, πλανῶμαι, ἀπὸ τοῦ ἀλᾶσθαι τῆι διανοίαι in
Apoll. Soph.). B. 'has used ἠλύκταζον in a way which blends the notions
of mental and physical unrest' (Jebb).

95–6 ἀλλ᾽ ὅτε δὴ . . . ἵκανεν: Homer, too, uses the phrase after
statements of time, cf. *Il.* 6.174–5, 9.470–4, 24.784–5, *Od.* 12.397–9, also

h.Dem. 47–51. B., however, abruptly changes both subject and scene in order to speed up the narrative, as does Pindar in *P.* 4.224.

Λοῦσον: the river of Lousoi in Northern Arkadia, between Kleitor and Kynaitha, near the modern village of Χαμάκου, about 1000 metres above sea-level. The town was destroyed in hellenistic times; Pausanias (8.18.7–8) saw it in ruins, but a substantial amount of cultic material from the sanctuary of Artemis survives from the eighth century BCE onwards. Cf. Reichel and Wilhelm 1901; Jost, *Sanctuaires* 46–51; Tausend 1993: 13–26; Mitsopoulos-Leon 1993: 33–9; Sinn 1992: 177–87.

97–8 φοινικοκ[ραδέμνο]ιο   'of the crimson headdress'. B. is remarkably fond of colour compounds, especially those denoting 'red', most of which are not found in any other author; so φοινικοκράδεμνος (here and 13.222), φοινικόθριξ 11.105, φοινικόνωτος 5.102, φοινίκασπις 9.10, πορφυροδίνας 9.39, πυρσόχαιτος 18.51; also πορφυρόζωνος (only 11.49 and Hesych. ι 737: perhaps coined by B.); φοινικοστερόπας (only 12.40 and Pind. *O.* 9.6).

99 βοῶπιν   'ox-eyed', of Artemis only here; the epithet is often given to goddesses and heroines: Amphitrite (B. 17.110), Harmonia (Pind. *P.* 3.91), Klytaimestra ([Hes.] fr. 23a.9), Stheneboia ([Hes.] fr. 129.20), various nymphs and heroines in Homer (*Il.* 18.40; 3.144; 7.10). It can hardly be interpreted as a hidden allusion to a metamorphosis into cows, or as 'bestial imagery', as Stern 1965: 280 suggested.

101 ἱππώκεος ἀελίου: the compound, found only here, is formed like ποδώκης. In Homer, Dawn (Ἠώς) drives a two-horse chariot across the sky (*Od.* 23.244–6); the Sun himself does so in post-Homeric poetry: *h.Dem.* 63 and 88–9; Mimn. 12; Stesich. *PMG* 185 with Pherekydes *FGrHist* 3 F 18a.

102–3 λύσσας πάρφρονος: see on 54 παλίντροπον... νόημα. Throughout the mythical narrative, the notions of 'madness' and 'flight' alternate: madness in 45–6, 54, 102–3; flight in 43, 55–6, 82–4, 92–4.

103 ἐξαγαγεῖν: the infinitive depends on κίκλη[ισκε in 99; Proitos 'called on' Artemis 'to deliver' his daughters from their frenzy (only 103–4 are direct speech). For κικλήισκειν with infinitive in Homer, cf. *Il.* 9.567–71 (Althaia) ἠρᾶτο . . . κικλήισκουσ' Ἀΐδην καὶ . . . Περσεφόνειαν . . . παιδὶ δόμεν θάνατον. The construction is common in both poetry and prose; see the examples in Schwyzer ιι 374–5.

105 ἄζυγας   'not yet yoked', = ἀδμήτας and ἠκέστας in Homer (*Il.* 10.292–4 = *Od.* 3.382–4; *Il.* 6.94 etc.) who says that young heifers which had not yet been under the yoke were used for sacrifice.

φοινικότριχας: red cows were preferred as sacrificial animals, cf. 5.102 βοῶν φοινικονώτων and *Il.* 13.703, 16.487–8, *Od.* 13.32, 18.371–2, Pind. *P.* 4.149 and 205, Theokr. 25.128, whereas black bulls are sacrificed to Poseidon in *Od.* 3.6.

106 ἀριστοπάτρα   'daughter of the noblest father'; the epithet may imply that Artemis feels sympathetic towards a father who cares so much for his daughters. The word, found only here as an epithet, occurs as a personal name in Strabo (15.702); cf. Ἀριστοπάτειρα, daughter of the famous boxer Diagoras of Rhodes (hypothesis to Pind. *O.* 7), and Antipatros, son of Kleinopatros, a boxer for whom Polykleitos made a statue. Lykophron 838 coined the compound χρυσόπατρος for Perseus.

108 καλυκοστεφάνους   'bud-garlanded', as is Artemis herself in 5.98. Here the compound may be used proleptically: Artemis stopped their frenzy, so that they could garland themselves; cf. 11.41n. (βωμὸν . . . πολύλλιστον), and on the proleptic use of epithets, 16.26n.

109 μανιᾶν ἀθέων   'god-forsaken frenzies'. ἄθεος, like its stronger equivalent μισόθεος (Aesch. *Ag.* 1090, see E. Fraenkel ad loc.), is the criminal who ignores god, but also someone who is ignored, or abandoned, by god; cf. *Od.* 18.353 οὐκ ἀθεεί (= οὐκ ἄνευ θεοῦ, schol.) and especially Soph. *OT* 661 (chorus) ἄθεος ἄφιλος . . . ὀλοίμαν, 254 γῆς ὧδ᾽ἀκάρπως κἀθέως ἐφθαρμένης, *El.* 1181 ὦ σῶμ᾽ἀτίμως κἀθέως ἐφθαρμένον. It is in this sense that B. uses the word: by their madness, the girls have been reduced to a state where they had been abandoned by the gods, until Artemis rescued them. Here, too, B. tries to create compassion.

110–12   The narrative moves to a very swift conclusion, yet even this short section, despite its rapid pace, shows the poet's desire for careful composition and variation: each of the three short sentences has a verb in the imperfect, the first at the end (τεῦχον), the second at the beginning (χραῖνον), the third in the middle (ἵσταν).

111 μήλων: Proitos had promised to sacrifice red cows (104). As Simonides called the bull who abducted Europa not only ταῦρος but also μῆλον and πρόβατον (*PMG* 562), one might suspect that B., too, could have used the word in the general sense of 'cattle'. On balance, however, it seems more likely that Proitos' sacrifice of cows is taken for granted, and that the sheep are an additional sacrifice by the girls themselves.

112 χορούς ἵσταν γυναικῶν   'they instituted choruses of women', evidently an *aition* explaining the origin of female choruses in the cult of Artemis

Hemera at Lousoi. Choruses of dancing girls are very often associated with cults of Artemis: see introduction to ode 20 (p. 225); Calame, *Les chœurs de jeunes filles* 1 174–90; Burkert, *Greek religion* 103; 150–2.

113 ἀρηϊφίλοις: the people of Metapontion were peaceful and usually remained neutral in wars, as did the people of Achaia in the Peloponnese, at least until the fifth century BCE. By calling them 'war-loving', B. anticipates their equation with the Homeric Achaians, see below, 126n.

115 σὺν δὲ τύχᾱι 'with happy fortune' is a very approximate rendering which does not take the etymology into account. Parallels like B. 5.52, 9.51, Pind. *N.* 5.48, *N.* 10.25, *I.* 8.67, *N.* 6.24 (σὺν θεοῦ δὲ τύχᾱι), *O.* 8.67 (τύχᾱι δαίμονος), *N.* 4.7 (σὺν Χαρίτων τύχᾱι), *P.* 2.56 (σὺν τύχᾱι πότμου) suggest that the notion of τυγχάνειν 'to achieve', 'to gain one's request', 'to hit one's target' was associated with the noun. Even though σὺν τύχᾱι is a general phrase, in epinician odes it implies victories in games, so here the Pythian victory which Alexidamos had been granted by Artemis.

119–20 Κάσαν: the river which flows south of Metapontion and into the gulf of Taranto; Pliny, *NH* 3.15.3 calls it Casuentus, its modern name is Basento.

προγο | νοιεσσάμενοι (pap.) must be corrupt, as the metre indicates: 119 must end in ⏑ – | (or even ⏑ – ‖, with period end). πρόγονοι could well be a gloss (like ποταμῶι in 16.34), which may have been added to clarify who the subject of this sentence was (if it was not stated, it had to be inferred from Ἀχαιοῖς in 114), or it replaced the word it was meant to explain. In any case, a finite verb is required, either at the end of 119, or it is hidden in εσσάμενοι. The latter approach is implied in the emendation Κάσα (gen.) παρ᾽ εὔυδρον πόρον (ῥόον Maas) | ἔσσαν πρόγονοι, suggested by Carey 1980: 238; the former would produce an alternative solution: Κάσαν παρ᾽ εὔυδρον κτίσαν (Turyn 1924: 112) | σταθμασάμενοι κτλ., 'they founded a delightful grove, measuring it out by the fair waters of the Kasas', cf. Pind. *O.* 10.45 (Herakles) ἐν Πίσαι . . . σταθμᾶτο ζάθεον ἄλσος.

123–4 δικαίας . . . φρένας: cf. 3.67–8 ὅσ[τις μ]ὴ φθόνωι πιαίνεται and Pind. *N.* 8.40–2 ἀΐσσει δ᾽ ἀρετὰ . . . ἐν σοφοῖς ἀνδρῶν ἀερθεῖσ᾽ ἐν δικαίοις τε πρὸς ὑγρὸν αἰθέρα 'excellence grows like a tree that springs up to fresh dew, when lifted among wise and just men to liquid heaven.' These are variations of the motive, well attested in Pindar, of the 'matching praise', which is often linked to the condition 'if someone is fair-minded', cf. Pind. *I.* 1.41–5 and the discussion of the variations of this motive by Bundy, *Studia*

Pindarica 53–61. While Pindar often speaks of 'envy' (φθόνος) and 'blame' (μῶμος), B. appears confident that great achievements will meet with due recognition; cf. 5.187–9n. and 190n.

εὑρήσει: cf. Pind. *O.* 13.112–13 πᾶσαν κάτα | Ἑλλάδ᾽ εὑρήσεις ἐρευνῶν μάσσον᾽ ἢ ὡς ἰδέμεν 'one may scour the whole of Greece and find more cities than the eye can encompass' . . . 'a speedy and graceful exit' (Bundy, *Studia Pindarica* 72).

126 μυρίας ἀλκὰς Ἀχαιῶν   'countless deeds of valour of Achaians'; for this meaning of ἀλκά cf. Pind. *N.* 7.12. The 'Achaians' are, of course, the Homeric heroes of the Trojan War, whose heroic exploits B. claims for the Peloponnesian Achaians who founded Metapontion. On Metapontion itself, or on Alexidamos' family, B. seems to have found nothing particularly praiseworthy to say, so he was probably grateful for the opportunity to link her founders to the Homeric Achaians. This equation produced the legend, originally confined, it seems, to the area of Metapontion and Sybaris, that the town had been founded by Nestor's Pylians on their way home from the Trojan War, as Strabo says (see above, p. 133). Unless it was his own invention, B. may have known, perhaps through Alexidamos' family, a local legend about the foundation of Metapontion by Pylians returning from Troy, which he then told so as to link the present to the heroic past. This is why the last two lines are so general: σὺν ἅπαντι χρόνωι means both the present and the mythical and historical past, and ἀλκὰς Ἀχαιῶν includes Alexidamos' Pythian victory as well as the exploits on the battlefield at Troy. The victory which B. celebrates in this ode is thus presented as proof that the Metapontians, protected and favoured by Artemis, are the legitimate descendants of Homer's Achaians.

DITHYRAMBS

ODE 15 = DITHYRAMB 1

1. Performance

The first ode in the book of Dithyrambs had a double title which is partly preserved in the top margin of pap. **A**, above the first line: [Αν]τηνοριδαι [η Ελενη]ς απαιτησις, 'Antenor's Sons, or the demanding of Helen'. This title was also written on a *sillybos*, a parchment tag attached to pap. **O**, but then washed out and replaced by Βακχυλιδου Διθυραμβοι, which confirms that this ode was, in fact, the first in Bacchylides' book of Dithyrambs. The sons of Antenor and Theano must have had a role to play in the part which is now lost. There seem to have been fifty of them: Schol.T on *Iliad* 24.496 says that whereas Hekabe's nineteen sons are credible, the fifty sons attributed to Theano by B. are not. This suggests that the fifty singers who formed the chorus that performed this dithyramb somehow represented the fifty 'Sons of Antenor'; dithyrambic choirs consisted of fifty singers, see Pickard-Cambridge, *Dramatic festivals* 75 n.4; *Dithyramb* 32.

Athens seems the most likely performance context in view of Menelaos' speech which clearly and repeatedly echoes Solon and ends with a warning against *Hybris* that destroyed the Giants (59–63). Ever since the reorganization of the Panathenaic festival in 566/5 BCE, the battle between the Olympian gods and the Giants had been the dominant theme of this festival. It could be seen in the west pediment of the Peisistratids' temple of Athena on the Acropolis and later on the metopes on the east side of the Parthenon, and on the inside of the shield of the Athena Parthenos. Most significantly, it was also the theme represented on the *peplos* that was carried in the Panathenaic procession and offered to the statue of Athena Polias; see Vian, *La guerre des géants* 251–3; *LIMC* IV 210.

If this dithyramb was indeed composed to be performed at the Panathenaia, the appearance of Theano, priestess of Athena, and her speech in the first triad may have evoked a poignant parallel to the Panathenaic procession and the *peplos*, for in *Iliad* 6.297–311 the same Theano leads the Trojan women up to the acropolis of Troy, puts the *peplos* on the knees of Athena's statue in her temple and prays for the salvation of her city. In this way, both the beginning and the conclusion of this dithyramb seem to be linked to the Panathenaia. One might speculate that the chorus, or the singer who recited Menelaos' speech (50–63), may even have pointed to the Gigantomachy embroidered on or woven into the *peplos* which was carried in the procession for all to see.

2. The myth of Antenor and Theano

According to Proklos' summary of the Trojan Cycle (*PEG* 42), the *Kypria* told how the Greeks landed and the fighting began; it then mentions an embassy that was sent to Troy to demand the return of Helen and the 'possessions' (τὰ κτήματα, obviously the treasure that was taken by Paris when he abducted Helen). Apollodoros' *Epitome* is slightly more explicit: the embassy was led by Odysseus and Menelaos, but when the Trojans called an assembly to discuss their proposals, they not only refused to give Helen back but even threatened to kill the Greek ambassadors; these were, however, saved by Antenor (Apollod. *Epit.* 3.28). In the *Iliad* (3.205–24), Antenor himself gives a (decorous) account of that assembly, describing Menelaos' and Odysseus' appearance and manner of speaking, though not the content of their speeches.

B.'s version seems to be based on this passage as well as on the account in the *Kypria*, which apparently also inspired a beautiful late Corinthian crater, now in the Vatican, datable to *c.*560 BCE (Appendix no. 7). Its significance was first recognized by Beazley 1957: 233–44 and plates 11–16; new photograph (after cleaning) in Davies 1977: 73–85 and pl.17; Amyx, *Corinthian vase-painting* I 264, II 576, III plates 116 & 117; Schefold, *Myth and legend* 86 pl.72. It shows first the herald, Talthybios, and behind him Odysseus and Menelaos sitting on the steps of an altar and being greeted by Theano who is followed by three women; behind them are fourteen warriors on horseback and two on foot. Six of the riders are identified by name, two of whom are attested as sons of Antenor (Glaukos and Eurymachos, see Paus. 10.27.3); it therefore seems likely that all of them are meant to be Antenor's sons.

Of the first column of this dithyramb only the ends of the first 14 lines survive in the papyrus. They do, nevertheless, provide some clues as to the probable content of the lost portion. Theano, Odysseus and Menelaos are introduced in the first stanza. Menelaos plays an active role in the last part, from line 47 onwards; Theano seems to have addressed the Greek ambassadors from line 10, and her speech may have ended at line 24. It seems very likely that Odysseus, too, played an active part in this poem (cf. line 5), which corresponded to his presence on the Vatican crater and in the *Kypria* version of the story. The subject of ἄγον in 37 must be Antenor's sons, who escorted the ambassadors into the city and, presumably, to the temple, where they would be protected by Athena's priestess, Theano, and her husband, Antenor. πάντα . . . μῦθον Ἀχαιῶν (38–9) must refer to Antenor's role in explaining to Priam and his children 'the whole speech of the Achaians'. When the Trojans have been summoned to an assembly, Menelaos speaks in very general terms, and it seems to have been Odysseus' task to explain the embassy's proposal to the Trojans. His speech, which set out the terms under which the Greeks were prepared to end the fighting and sail home again, must have been placed somewhere in the lost portion between lines 25 and 36; the poem's alternative title, Ἑλένης ἀπαίτησις, may well reflect Odysseus' speech.

2 [κεδνὰ πα]ρᾴκριτις: cf. B.3.33 σὺ[ν ἀλόχωι] τε κεδ[νᾶι] and *Il.* 24.730 ἔχες δ'ἀλόχους κεδνάς.

3 Παλλάδος ὀρσιμάχου   'battle-rousing Pallas'; the compound, like ἀερσιμάχ[ους] in B.13.100, ὀρσίαλος (Poseidon) 16.19, ὀρσιβάκχας, (Dionysos) 19.49, ὀρσίκτυπος (Zeus) in Pindar, *O.* 10.81, ὀρσινεφής (Zeus) *N.* 5.34, is found nowhere else; all of these seem to have been coined in choral lyric poetry. Of those compounds formed of verb + noun ('verbale Rektionskomposita', cf. Schwyzer I 441–5) which are unique to B., the majority are of this type (like, e.g., δεξίστρατος 15.43, θελξιεπής 15.48, ἐρειψιπύλας 5.56 etc.), whereas tragic poets seem to have coined relatively more compounds made up of noun + verb; on these, see Williger, *Komposita*.

3–7   For a reconstruction of this passage, the following points are relevant: (a) as Theano appears in the nominative in 2 and 7, she is likely to be the subject of the whole sentence and possibly also of προσήνεπεν (9); (b) a finite verb that governs the datives in lines 5 and 6 must have stood at the beginning of one of lines 3–5; (c) [χ]ρυσέας (4), which must be acc. plur. rather than gen. sing. ('golden Athena' would hardly be credible), requires a suitable noun. Points (b) and (c) are offered by *Il.* 6.297–8 where Theano opens the temple doors to Hekabe and the Trojan women: αἱ δ'ὅτε νηὸν ἵκανον Ἀθήνης ἐν πόλει ἄκρηι, | τῆισι θύρας ὤϊξε Θεανὼ καλλιπάρηιος, hence Crusius' proposal (3) [ὤϊξεν ἁγνὸν] Παλλάδος ὀρσιμάχου (4) [ναὸν πύλας τε χ]ρυσέας (5) [ἀγγέλοις ἵκουσι]ν Ἀργείων (Crusius 1898: 163). [ἀγγέλοις . . .] Ἀργείων implies that Menelaos and Odysseus have come to announce the Argives' peace terms, cf. *Il.* 11.138–41 (in the Trojans' assembly, Antimachos had suggested killing Μενέλαον . . . ἀγγελίην ἐλθόντα σὺν ἀντιθέωι Ὀδυσῆϊ, 139–40), also 3.206 (ἀγγελίης, see Kirk ad loc.).

9 [‒‒◡◡‒◡◡‒]ν προσήνεπεν: 'she addressed'; it is usually the host who addresses the stranger(s), not the other way round. The following passage was probably Theano's speech with which she welcomed the ambassadors (see below on 23–4).

10 [‒‒◡‒‒‒‒◡ ἐ]ΰκτιμέναν   probably refers to Troy. Theano may have said something like 'Strangers, having come to well-built Troy' etc.

12 [‒◡‒‒‒‒◡‒]δων (or]λων) τυχόντες: possibly a reference to the ambassadors' encounter with her fifty sons, e.g. [τῶν δὲ πεντήκοντ' ἐμῶν παί]δων τυχόντες, since the statement in schol.T on *Il.* 24.496 Βακχυλίδης πεντήκοντα τῆς Θεανοῦς ὑπογράφει παῖδας must be based on a line in the early part of this ode.

13 [‒◡◡‒◡◡‒‒‒◡◡]. σὺν θεοῖς: the line should end in ‒◡◡‒; to restore the metre, one might insert <δὲ>, <τε> or <γε> after σύν, which would be possible only if the letter preceding could be read as]ε (e.g. ἔλθετ]ε), which is, however, very uncertain.

23–4 ‒‒‒◡‒ οὐ γὰρ ὑπόκλοπον φορεῖ | βροτοῖσι φωνάεντα λόγον σοφία (= fr.26 Sn.):   quoted by Clement, *Paedag.* 3.100.2, apparently from an anthology. There is no gap in any other of B.'s poems in dactyloepitrites that would accommodate this quotation, except the second strophe or antistrophe of this dithyramb (23–4 or as Blass suggested, 30–1). Who is likely to have made this statement? Jebb thought of Odysseus 'deprecating the suspicion that his plea for a peaceful settlement veiled some insidious design'. But then σοφία could hardly mean 'our reasonable proposal', and why should he have said 'to mortals' (βροτοῖς) if he meant 'to you, the Trojans'? The alternative would be to give these words to Theano, who may have concluded her speech by saying 'wisdom (= if you are wise) conveys your message clearly, for everyone to hear, without guile'. If this is correct, the quotation probably belongs in lines 23–4, giving Theano a speech of 15 lines and still leaving room for a speech of some ten lines by Odysseus. The point of ὑπόκλοπον would be to warn Odysseus that she is aware of his reputation for lies and deceit.

37 ἆγον: the subject of ἆγον must be the sons of Antenor and Theano who escorted the ambassadors to the assembly place while their father informed Priam. Antenor is called 'wise-counselling' (εὔβουλος) because when the Trojans assembled after the duel between Hektor and Aias (*Il.* 7.345–54), he advised peace, urging them to give Helen back as well as the treasures taken by Paris. He may have acted likewise in the earlier assembly which the *Kypria* described (*PEG* p.42.55–6 διαπρεσβεύονται πρὸς τοὺς Τρῶας, τὴν Ἑλένην καὶ τὰ κτήματα ἀπαιτοῦντες) and which B. refers to in lines 40–3.

40–1 δι᾿ εὐρείαν πόλιν: B. creates 'epic flavour' by adapting a common Homeric formula, cf. *Il.* 2.141 Τροίην . . . εὐρυάγυιαν.

43 δεξίστρατον: formed like ὀρσίμαχος (above, 3n.).

44 αὐδάεις λόγος: a 'clear message', not 'the loud rumour' (Jebb) or the herald's 'loud summons' (Campbell); λόγος is more than 'summons', and αὐδάεις, like φωνήεις (24), means 'voiced, articulate', as in *Il.* 19.407 where Hera makes Achilles' horse αὐδήεντα so that it can tell its master of his impending death; in the scholia the word is explained as 'using articulate speech' (schol. D: φωνῆι ἐνάρθρωι χρώμενον). Here αὐδάεις λόγος seems to take up φωνάεντα λόγον, meaning 'a message that speaks clearly' while it passed by word of mouth through the city, the message (λόγος) being the terms of the embassy's peace proposals (μῦθον Ἀχαιῶν 39).

45–6 ἀνίσχοντες χέρας . . . παύσασθαι δυᾶν 'raising their hands to the immortal gods they prayed to be released from their sufferings'; cf. *Il.* 3.318 where Greeks and Trojans alike pray that war might be averted (λαοὶ δ᾿ ἡρήσαντο, θεοῖσι δὲ χεῖρας ἀνέσχον). Similarly, in B. 11.69–72 the peoples of Proitos and Akrisios beseech their masters to avoid war. On Bacchylides' views on peace, see on his *Paean* for Asine (pp. 225–7).

47 Μοῦσα, τίς πρῶτος . . . : modelled on the poet's short invocations of the Muses in the *Iliad* (11.218–19, 14.508–9, 16.112–13) which all ask 'who was the first . . .' or 'how for the first time . . .' Here πρῶτος seems to imply that Menelaos' speech before the Trojan assembly was followed by others', perhaps by a lively debate, as suggested by the *Kypria* and Apollodoros' *Epit.* 3.28. Here, too, B. is creating 'epic flavour' by adapting a Homeric narrative device.

   λόγων δικαίων: the Greeks' just demands.

48 Πλεισθενίδας: in line 6, in the same position in the strophe, Menelaos is called Ἀτρείδας. In Homer, Agamemnon and Menelaos are the sons of Atreus and grandsons of Pelops (*Il.* 2.104). Later genealogies make them sons of Pleisthenes and grandsons of Atreus (Hes. frs.104 and 105; Hellanikos *FGrHist* 4 F 157; Apollod.3.2.2), sometimes combining the Homeric and the 'Hesiodic' genealogies by making Atreus adopt his grandsons after the early death of his son Pleisthenes (schol. AD on *Il.* 2.249 and schol. Eur. *Or.* 4). Although B. uses the Homeric patronymic in line 6, here he calls him 'descendant of Pleisthenes' in order to avoid any association or reminiscence of the horrendous crimes of Atreus, so that he can present him as the advocate of righteousness. Cf. Ibykos *SLG* 151.21–2 Πλεισθενίδας βασιλεὺς ἄγος ἀνδρῶν, Ἀτρέος ἐσ[θλὸς] πάϊς ἔκγ[ο]νος.

49 κοινώσας Χάρισσιν: sc. λόγον or γᾶρυν. The active forms of the verb mean 'to impart information' or 'to share with', see Pfeijffer, *Three Aeginetan odes of Pindar* 266–8 for a full discussion of this verb. Menelaos 'makes <his speech> common to the Graces', makes them share it, rather as Jason's parents save their child νυκτὶ κοινώσαντες ὁδόν 'letting the night share the road', Pindar, *P.* 4.114–15. B.'s phrase implies that the Graces take a hand in making Menelaos' speech 'spell-binding' (θελξιεπής). The function of the Graces (Χάριτες) is not to inspire the poet (this is the Muses' prerogative), but to give 'grace' (χάρις) to a poem, to make it pleasing and elegant. The phrase σὺν Χάρισ(σ)ιν/Χαρίτεσσιν (B. 5.9; Pind. *I.* 5.21; *N.* 5.54; *N.* 9.54) indicates that they help the poet elaborate his poem, see 19.5–7n. The spelling Χάρισσιν is an artificial lengthening to suit the metre, on the analogy of Homeric ἔπεσσι, νέκυσσι, γένυσσι, πίτυσσι, cf. Chantraine, *GH* I 222.

50 ὦ Τρῶες ἀρηΐφιλοι: in Homer, the Trojans are never called 'war-loving'; nineteen of 26 occurrences in the *Iliad* and one in the *Odyssey* refer to Menelaos. In applying the epithet to the Trojans, Menelaos seems to address a warning to them.

52 οὐκ αἴτιος: an obvious reference to, almost a quotation of, the famous speech in the first assembly of the gods in *Od.* 1.32ff. where Zeus states that mortals should not blame the gods for their misfortunes but are themselves responsible, quoting Aigisthos as a warning example. Solon also refers to Zeus's speech in 15.1–3 and in his *Eunomia* elegy (4.5–8), which Menelaos' speech recalls. The function of intertextual references like these is probably to remind the audience that the idea in question has been voiced before by a poet whose prestige and authority will give it added weight.

53–4 ἐν [μέσ]ωι: in *Iliad* 18.507 it is a prize which 'lies in the middle' between the contestants, as in Demosthenes' *First Philippic* (4.5) ἄθλα τοῦ πολέμου κείμενα ἐν μέσωι, although in B. the emphasis is less on contest or competition.

κεῖται . . . πᾶσιν ἀνθρώποις: Menelaos means that a just solution is available 'to all men', Trojans and Greeks. But in the trial scene on the Shield of Achilles (*Iliad* 18.497–508), the δίκη which the judges are expected to find seems to be the appropriate amount of blood-money or compensation that would be acceptable to both sides, and this is what δίκη appears to mean generally in early poetry, e.g. in Hesiod, *Op.* 238 ('atonement', M. L. West), rather than 'justice'. B., too, was thinking of the personified Δίκη along similar lines.

54–5 Δίκαν ἰθεῖαν ... ἀκόλουθον   'unswerving Justice, who follows . . .' The implication is that 'good government' (Eunomia) is the prerequisite for 'straight' justice (the opposite of Hesiod's δίκαι σκολιαί 'crooked judgements', *Op.* 219, 221, 250, 264). Dike is the 'companion' (ἀκόλουθος) of Eunomia and Themis, which means that in a city governed by good laws and fairness, appropriate settlement is warranted. This is in accordance with Hesiod's genealogy which made Themis the mother of Eunomia, Dike, and Eirene; cf. Pindar, *O.* 13.6–8. Unlike Hesiod and Pindar, B. does not name Eirene here because in this situation 'peace', i.e. a peaceful end to the dispute, would appear as the next step, the result of Dike, the settlement on the terms proposed by the ambassadors.

56 ὀλβίων ... σύνοικον   'blessed are they whose sons choose her to share their home' (also quoted in *BKT* IX 187). The sense is: where good laws and enlightened justice rule, a fair settlement can be achieved: those who opt for this will enjoy wealth. The *asyndeton* shows that this line caps the preceding statements. In epic and early lyric poetry, a climax to an argument, or a capping statement, is often added without a connecting particle (ἀσυνδέτως). On Pindar's uses of *asyndeton*, see Race, *Style and rhetoric* 41–57 and Maehler, *Asyndeton*.

57–9 ἁ δ' ...Ὕβρις: the opposite of Dike, as in Hesiod, *Op.* 213ff. and throughout Solon's *Eunomia* elegy (4 W.); cf. also Archil. fr.177 W.; Xenophanes 1.15–17; Theognis 291–2 and 378–9. Hybris 'blooms' (θάλλουσα) in slippery profiteering (αἰόλοις κέρδεσσι, a reference to Paris' deceit and greed in taking Menelaos' treasures) and outrageous follies (his abduction of Helen). Hesiod, too, and in particular Solon had emphasized the link between greed or profiteering (κέρδος) and transgression (ὕβρις), cf. Solon 4.5ff., 6.3–4, Theognis 39–52; 833–6.

ἐξαισίοις   'beyond fate', i.e. ὑπὲρ αἶσαν, cf. *Iliad* 15.598 ἐξαίσιον ἀρήν, where Thetis' prayer/request to Zeus is called 'outrageous', for the first and only time in the *Iliad*, at the very moment when its consequences are reaching their climax, see Janko ad loc.

59–61 ἁ ... φθόρον: '(But she who blossoms in shifty tricks and outrageous follies, Insolence,) she swiftly gives <a man> another's wealth and power, but again throws <him> into deep ruin.' Kenyon and Jurenka took this ἅ as a demonstrative pronoun which picks up the first ἅ (57), whereas Jebb wanted the second ἅ to be a relative pronoun. In favour of Kenyon's reading is the punctuation in the papyrus after φθόρον and the fact that αὖτις δ(ὲ) marks a strong contrast (πλοῦτον/ δύναμιν – φθόρον): the last two lines then come as an *asyndeton*, a capping statement, which corresponds as a warning (negative) to the *asyndeton* encouragement in 56 (positive); cf. 56n. above. The two halves of Menelaos' speech are closely parallel, and the warning reference to the Gigantomachy thus becomes the climax of the whole ode.

60 ἀλλότριον: 'what belongs to someone else'; although this clearly refers to Helen, Menelaos speaks in general terms. This gives his speech greater authority than if he had said 'Hybris gave Paris *my* wealth and *my* power' (sc. over my wife). Paris, who should be the indirect object of ὤπασεν and the direct object of πέμπει, is not named: his fate, however, will be similar to that of the Giants.

63 Γᾶς] παῖδας: Kenyon's supplement is certain, cf. Hesiod, *Th.* 183ff. and 954–5. According to Apollod. 1.6.1–2, the Giants hurled rocks and burning oak trees against the sky. In art, the Gigantomachy becomes extremely popular from the middle of the sixth century; see Vian, *Répertoire des Gigantomachies*, and *LIMC* IV 191–270.

ODE 16 = DITHYRAMB 2

1. Performance

Despite the address to Pythian Apollo and the reference to paeans and choirs of Delphians, this ode is certainly not a paean since its main part (13–35) has nothing to do with Apollo. The only hint that it may have been composed to be performed at Delphi is the statement in 11–12 that 'so much' (τόσα) was sung 'by your much-praised temple'; but this τόσα refers to songs performed during Apollo's absence from Delphi during the winter months which the god spends with the Hyperboreans. These songs seem to have been 'cletic' hymns recalling the god to Delphi; one such hymn had been composed by Alkaios, of which some details survive in the paraphrase by the rhetorician Himerios (fourth century CE; Alkaios fr.307 = Himerios, *Or.* 48.11 Colonna), see below. The first stanza of this ode may have been modelled on this hymn, which may be echoed also in Euripides' *Ion* 82–183.

The main narrative section which fills the antistrophe and epode is introduced by 'until then' (πρίν γε, i.e. before Apollo returns), 'we sing' (κλέομεν 13). According to Plutarch (*Mor.* 389c), the Delphians performed paeans with their sacrifices during most of the year, but from the beginning of winter they replaced the paean by the dithyramb for three months, calling on Dionysos instead of Apollo. If, as seems likely, this statement reflects fifth-century practice, B.'s ode could well be such a dithyramb, performed at Delphi during the winter months before Apollo's return. But it seems equally possible that it was performed at Athens (Kamerbeek, *Plays* II 6). See also on line 18 below.

2. *The myths*

(a) *Apollo and the Hyperboreans* The story was told in Alkaios' hymn to Apollo, which began ὦναξ Ἄπολλον παῖ μεγάλω Διός. Himerios' paraphrase gives a general idea of its content: 'Zeus gave the new-born Apollo a golden *mitra* and lyre, and a chariot harnessed to swans. He sent him to Delphi and the streams of Castalia, to speak as a prophet of justice and right to Hellas. Apollo mounted the chariot, and set its course not for Delphi but for the land of the Hyperboreans. When the Delphians heard of this, they composed a paian and song, and founded dances of youths around the Tripod, summoning the god to return. He remained among the Hyperboreans a whole year, delivering the law; and when he thought it high time for the Delphic tripods to make music in their turn, he ordered his swans to fly back from the Hyperboreans. Now it was summer, and . . . because summer was aglow, and Apollo was in the land, the lyre puts on a sort of summer dress in honour of the god: the nightingales sing him the kind of song that you expect of birds in Alcaeus; swallows and cicadas forget the tale of their own sufferings, and devote their songs wholly to Apollo, Castalia flows with streams of silver, Cephisus heaves like Homer's Enipeus – even the waters are aware that a divinity is in the land' (Page, *Sappho and Alcaeus* 244–5).

In B., too, the god is presented as absent, in the north: 'by flowering Hebros he takes pleasure (from dance?) or the long-necked swan, gladdening his heart (by its honey-)sweet voice' (see on 7). He seems, however, to be expected back soon (see on 8). Although there is no chariot here and only one swan, the situation appears to be very similar.

(b) Herakles, Deianeira, and Nessos   In B., the events leading to Herakles' death are presented in reverse order, in three stages: (1) Having destroyed Oichalia, Herakles is about to sacrifice to Zeus on the Kenaion promontory (13–22); (2) Fate inspired Deianeira's plan when she learned that he was about to send Iole into her house as his 'wife' (ἄλοχον) (23–9); (3) it was on the bank of the river Lykormas where she received the fateful gift from Nessos.

Sophokles presents essentially the same version in his *Women of Trachis*. Although the poisoned robe that killed Herakles is mentioned in [Hes.] fr. 25.20–5, there is no evidence in either poetry or art before Sophokles and B. to suggest that the poison was a deceptive gift from the dying centaur, Nessos, who offered the blood from his wound to Deianeira to use as a lovecharm. As very little survives of the epic versions, such as the Οἰχαλίας ἅλωσις by Kreophylos, the Ἡράκλεια of Peisandros of Rhodes or the Ἡρακλειάς in 14 books by Panyassis of Halikarnassos (*PEG* 157–87), our chief evidence is Attic vases, listed in Brommer, *Vasenlisten* 153–8.

While the earlier versions of the Nessos-Deianeira story have Herakles threaten Nessos with his club and/or sword, occasionally with bow and club, only two show the centaur actually wounded or attacked with an arrow: (1) On a fragment of an early Attic dinos of the seventh century (Appendix no. 8), a centaur with an arrow stuck in his side turns round towards his attacker who threatens him with his sword; in this situation, he would obviously have no chance at all to collect his poisoned blood and hand it to Deianeira; (2) a Caeretan hydria (Appendix no. 9) places the scene on either side of a palmette below the handle: on the right, the centaur and the woman moving away from him, and on the left, Herakles threatening him with an arrow. The same painter has, however, painted the same scene on two other hydrias where the figures are not divided by the handle (Appendix nos. 10 and 11); here Herakles attacks with bow and club, while Deianeira comes running from the right and has almost reached him. All three vases obviously show essentially the same scene; on all three, Deianeira is running away from Nessos towards Herakles before the arrow is actually shot off, so that 'there can have been no thought in the artist's mind of Nessos offering Deianeira a lovecharm' (March 54).

The argument in favour of the lovecharm being an innovation by a fifth-century poet rests not only on a negative consideration (the lack of evidence before Sophokles and B.), but also on a positive one. The arrow is crucial to the lovecharm version because it links Nessos' death with Herakles' own death through the poisoned blood, and it is this link which gives this version its tragic character, in that (a) Herakles' victory over Nessos carries the seed of his own doom, his own deed will in the end destroy him, and (b) Deianeira becomes the innocent/guilty victim of a cruel deception. In order to turn the old story into a tragic plot, the innovator had to introduce some odd elements which must have stretched the audience's credulity to the limit: how would the mortally wounded centaur have been able, in the middle of the river, to collect his blood? With his hands? Or in a vessel? Where could that have come from? Whoever invented the 'lovecharm' version must have expected the audience to accept it without asking how it could have happened.

It cannot be ruled out that there may have been an earlier source for the 'lovecharm' version, such as Panyassis' *Herakleia* (*PEG* 174–84) or some early tragedy. There is, however, no evidence that any poet before Sophokles and B. connected Herakles' death with Nessos' poisoned blood; it therefore seems very unlikely that there was an earlier source that could have inspired them both. The implication must be that one depends on the other – but which way round? Kenyon was convinced that Sophokles 'had Bacchylides in his mind' (Kenyon p. 148) but, as most scholars now agree, B.'s version would simply not have been intelligible to an audience who were unfamiliar with the version which connected the death of Nessos by Herakles' arrow with Herakles' own death by the poisoned robe: how could they have guessed what 'plan' (μῆτις) it was, which Deianeira wove (ὕφανε, 24–5), or Nessos' δαιμόνιον τέρας (35)? It therefore seems likely that the version which B.'s 'allusive manner in 16, which presupposes familiarity with the story of the robe' (Easterling, *Soph.Trach.* 22), takes for granted, was indeed Sophokles' *Trachiniai*. Chronologically there would be no problem since *Trachiniai* is an early play, as most scholars believe; if so, the two poets' poetic activity overlapped for many years (see Schwinge, *Trachinierinnen* 130–2; Hoey 1979: 210–32 with bibliography; March, *Creative poet* 62–3).

1 . . .]ιου . ι ϙ . . . ἐπεί: no plausible reading of the traces has yet been proposed. Before ἐπεί, some form of exhortation seems likely, i.e. an imperative or optative, addressed perhaps to Delphi, or to the audience, possibly an invitation to pay attention to the ode which is about to be performed.

2 ὀλκ]άδ(α):   a ὀλκάς was a heavy freight vessel, so the metaphor implies that the Muse has sent a heavy load of song to the Delphians' choir (ἐμοί). Pindar wants his victory ode to sail from Aigina 'on every freight-ship and boat' (ἐπὶ πάσας ὀλκάδος ἔν τ' ἀκάτωι, *N.* 5.2): but his are real ships, not metaphors as in Simonides (*PMG* 535) and perhaps Alkman (*PMG* 142 = 199 Calame).

5 – ⌣ ⌣]ν (or ᾳι), then ειτις would fit the traces; however, if one supplies ἐς θεὸ]ν (Jebb) or ἢ καλὸ]ν (Handley), τις would have to refer to Apollo, which would be odd: why would the god not be named?

6 . . . . . ἀ]γάλλεται 'he takes pleasure', see above, p. 165; a dative seems likely in the gap, perhaps (if six letters can be fitted in the gap) μούσαι or μολπᾶι.

7 . . . . .]δεϊᾶι: the last letter had apparently been changed to N but then crossed out and replaced by a small superscript *iota*. As diaeresis in this papyrus is fairly frequent over initial ι and υ, the letter ϊ may well be the initial letter of a word: ἰᾶι ('voice', long ago suggested by Kuiper), preceded perhaps by μελια]δε<ῖ>, 'honey-sweet'. The idea that swans sing sweetly, however unrealistic it may seem, was widespread, cf. Eur. *Phaethon* fr.773.34 μελιβόας κύκνος, *IT* 1104 κύκνος μελωιδὸς Μούσας θεραπεύει, etc. Plutarch says of Pythian Apollo that he μουσικῆι ἥδεται καὶ κύκνων φωναῖς καὶ κιθάρας ψόφοις (*Mor.* 387c). Kallimachos calls the swans 'birds of the Muses, most tuneful of winged creatures' (Μουσάων ὄρνιθες, ἀοιδότατοι πετεηνῶν) and makes them circle Delos during Leto's labour, *h.* 4.249–54.

8 . . . . . . (.)]δ̓ ἵκηι: this verse should respond with 20, which would mean accommodating five syllables (⌞ ⌣ – – ⌣ ⌣) into the space of six or, at most, seven letters. This seems impossible: either this line, or 20, appears to be corrupt. If, as Paul Maas suspected (*Resp.* ii 23 n.2), the problem is in line 20, the gap in line 8 would require only two syllables (– ⌣); ἵκηι must, in any case, be a 2nd person sing. of the aorist subjunctive (= Homeric ἵκηαι), which might suggest something like πρὶν τό]δ̓ ἵκηι 'until you come here': examples of πρίν + subjunctive (without ἄν) in the sense of 'until, before' in situations either repeated or expected to happen, can be found in K-G ii 454–6 and in Schwyzer ii 313.

9 πεδοιχνεῖν: = μετοίχεσθαι, or μετέρχεσθαι 'to go after', the flowers of paeans; the flower metaphor for song is very common in choral lyric poetry, see on fr.4.63.

11–12 τόσα χοροὶ Δελφῶν . . . κελάδησαν: τόσα could be a relative or a demonstrative pronoun. While relative τόσος tends to correlate to a demonstrative τόσος (as in Pindar, *N.* 4.4–5, or Kall., *Ap.* 94), demonstrative τόσον or τόσα ('so much', or 'these things/words') often follow brief direct speeches, as in *h.Merc.* 90–4; Pindar, *O.* 13.67–72; see the examples collected by Führer, *Reden* 40. This strongly suggests taking τόσα as a demonstrative pronoun, 'these things' (or 'this much') the Delphian choirs sang . . .', which would make the preceding lines a quotation, or direct speech. The whole passage, lines 1–10, may be a cletic hymn sung by the Delphians to recall Dionysos from the Hyperboreans, rather similar to Alkaios' hymn (see above, p. 165).

13 πρίν γε κλέομεν   'beforehand, we tell'. It is best to take κλέομεν as a genuine present (with strong punctuation after ναόν 12), to make clear what the chorus are doing *now*, in which case πρίν will have to be an adverb: 'before/until (the Delphians sing,) we tell . . .'. The alternative, taking πρίν as a conjunction = '(the Delphians sang) before we tell/told . . .' (γ᾽ἐκλέομεν Maas, *Resp.* II 23 n.2) would not make sense in the context, because it would leave unclear what the chorus are singing *now*.

13–15 λιπεῖν . . . Ἀμφιτρυωνιάδαν: acc. + inf., governed by κλέομεν.

Οἰχαλίαν: a mythical town in central Euboia, home of Eurytos and his daughter Iole, cf. Soph. *Trach.* 74–5 and 750; Kreophylos fr.2 (*PEG* p.162); Hekataios in Pausanias 4.2.3 (*FGrHist* I F 28). It was supposed to have been at or near Eretria.

πυρὶ δαπτομέναν: 'devoured by fire'; the verb may have been chosen to signal Herakles' own death which was to follow his destruction of Oichalia, as Simonini suggested (1977: 490). Cf. *Iliad* 23.182–3 where Achilles promises Ἕκτορα δ᾽ οὔ τι | δώσω Πριαμίδην πυρὶ δαπτέμεν, ἀλλὰ κύνεσσιν.

16 ἀμφικύμον᾽ ἀκτάν: the cape (now Cape Λιχάδα) is 'washed by waves on either side'; it is the promontory at the north-western end of Euboia. Cf. Soph. *Trach.* 752–3 ἀκτή τις ἀμφίκλυστος Εὐβοίας ἄκρον | Κήναιόν ἐστι. Similar epithets are given to islands: Ithaka is ἀμφίαλος (*Od.* 1.386 and 395), Rhodes is ἀμφιθαλάσσιος (Pindar, *O.* 7.33), Salamis is περικύμων (Eur. *Troad.* 800).

18 θύεν: Doric infinitive, like ἐρύκεν (17.41), ἴσχεν (17.88), φυλάσσεν (19.25). The last three cases, unlike 16.18, are guaranteed by the metre.

ἐννέα ταύρους: in Soph. *Trach.* 760–1, Herakles sacrifices twelve bulls to Zeus; why B. makes him split the same number of victims between three gods (nine for Zeus, two for Poseidon, and one heifer for Athena) is not evident. The suggestion (March, *Creative poet* 63 n.65) that the inclusion of Athena and Poseidon, 'divinities particularly important to Athens', may reflect an Athenian setting for this dithyramb, is attractive.

20–1   Line 20 presents three problems: (a) It must respond with line 8 which is obviously much shorter; (b) the apparent 'correption' (shortening of the final diphthong by the next syllable beginning with vowel) in ὀβριμοδ-ερκεῖ ἄζυγα is awkward, the more so as it would respond to an 'internal correption' in 8 (παῖηόνων) which is rare (though not unparalleled, see on 17.92); (c) παρθένωι seems strangely redundant as an apposition to κόραι. All three difficulties disappear if one deletes κόραι τ' (as an intrusive gloss) and inserts <δ'> after ὀβριμοδερκεῖ, as suggested by Maas, *Resp.* II 23 n.2.

23 τότ' ἄμαχος δαίμων: 'irresistible Destiny' (Jebb); only here does the noun have this meaning which is common in tragedy, while in all other instances in B. (3.37; 5.113 and 135; 9.26; 14.1; 17.46; fr.13; fr.25.1) it means 'god', or 'a god', as it does in Homer. Of course, δαίμων is still personified here to the extent of 'weaving' a plan.

24–5 Δαϊανείραι: like Nessos in 35, she does not get an epithet, while Iole, her rival, is 'white-armed' (27); as Charles Segal observed, 'her fame by itself, breaking into a stretch of highly ornate noun-epithet combinations, conveys an effect of lonely pathos which is exactly appropriate for her situation' (1976: 104).

πολύδακρυν . . . μῆτιν: a 'plan' that was to cause her many tears; on the 'proleptic' use of epithets, see below on 26 ταλαπενθέα.

ἐπίφρον(α):   in Sophokles, the chorus, ignorant of the consequences, can say to her δοκεῖς παρ' ἡμῖν οὐ βεβουλεῦσθαι κακῶς, *Trach.* 589. By contrast, B., and his audience, knew the terrible outcome of Deianeira's 'plan' which πολύδακρυν anticipates; to call it ἐπίφρονα sounds sarcastic: it may have seemed 'shrewd' to her because she could not foresee the result. The discrepancy between the audience's superior knowledge and Deianeira's ill-fated 'plan' heightens the tragic *pathos* of her situation.

26 ἀγγελίαν ταλαπενθέα   'a message that was to cause suffering'; cf. ὑσμίνας ταλαπενθέας in Panyassis' fr.16.5 (*PEG* p.180), δυσπενθής in Pindar, *P.* 11.18 and 12.10, μόρον . . . πολυπενθῆ in Aesch. *Pers.* 547. Other examples of 'proleptic' use of epithets in B. are ταῦσιον 5.81, ἀπορθήτων ἀγυιᾶν 9.52, ε [ὑναῖς] . . . ἀριγνώτοις 9.64, βωμὸν . . . πολύλλ[ι]στον 11.41, καλυκοστεφάνους κούρας 11.108, πολύστονον 17.40; other examples from epic and tragedy can be found in K-G I 276 and Schwyzer II 181e.

27–8 λευκώλενον . . . ἀταρβομάχας: the irony implied in the contrast
between the two epithets is also present in Soph. *Trach.* 354–5 Ἔρως δέ νιν |
μόνος θεῶν θέλξειεν αἰχμάσαι τάδε, the 'fearless fighter' is defeated by Iole's
tender beauty.

29 ἄλοχον: the crucial noun is placed in the middle of the ὅτι–clause,
without an epithet: Herakles is sending the captured Iole 'as his bedfellow'
into her 'rich' (λιπαρόν) house, which she will soon have to share with her
rival. ἄλοχος < ἁ *copulativum* (ἀθροιστικόν) + λέχος, cf. ἄκοιτις, ἀδελφός
etc., see Chantraine, *Dict.* II 634; more examples in Schwyzer I 433.

30 ἆ δύσμορος, ἆ τάλαιν(α):   this double apostrophe seems to reflect
Deianeira's reaction to the messenger's revelation in Soph. *Trach.* 375–7
οἴμοι τάλαινα . . . τίν' εἰσδέδεγμαι πημονὴν | ὑπόστεγον λαθραῖον ὦ
δύστηνος. While ὦ + vocative of a proper name or adjective is fairly common in B., ἆ is found only here and at 3.10, where it expresses admiration
(ἆ τρισευδαίμων ἀνήρ, cf. Thgn. 1013 ἆ μάκαρ). It often expresses compassion or pity, as here; cf. Sem. 7.76 ἆ τάλας ἀνήρ. Not surprisingly, the
interjection ἆ is particularly common in tragedy; B. may have chosen it to
give the passage a 'tragic' flavour.

    οἷον ἐμήσατ[ο]:   her 'plan' (μῆτις) was Deianeira's only active involve-
ment; in reality, however, this had also been 'woven' for her by Destiny (δαίμων . . . ὕφα[νε, 23–4), and the other two finite verbs referring to her show her in a passive role, reacting rather than acting
(πύθετο 26, δέξατο 35); in this respect, too, she resembles Sophocles'
Deianeira.

31 φθόνος εὐρυβίας νιν ἀπώλεσεν: 'it was jealousy . . .'; φθόνος is not
an aspect of Destiny, or the gods, or any superhuman power, but rather a
power within Deianeira herself, on the same level as her ignorance of the
consequences, or lack of forethought. The superior power is δαίμων, 'Fate',
which uses her jealousy and ignorance to destroy her as well as Herakles.
For φθονεῖν with an erotic connotation, 'to be jealous', cf. Eur. *HF* 1309–10
(Hera) ἣ γυναικὸς οὕνεκα | λεκτρῶν φθονοῦσα Ζηνὶ κτλ.

34 ἐπὶ {ποταμῶ[ι]}:   an interlinear gloss which has crept into the text.
This happens not infrequently in texts of poetry; examples in Pindar and
Aeschylus include Pind. fr. 70.2 Μέλ[α]ν[ό]ς τε {ποταμοῦ} ῥοαί (where
the gloss is betrayed by the metre), fr. 75.12 {Σεμέλην}, fr. 107a.7 {ἕτερον},
O. 7.49 {Ζεύς}, *P.* 1.92 (πετάσαις gloss on ἐξίει), *P.* 6.46 {ἔδειξεν}, *I.* 3.76
{Διί}, Aesch.*Pers.* 6 Δαρειογενὴς {Δαρείου υἱός} codd. ΜΦ, Aesch. *Supp.*
634 {πόλιν}.

ῥοδόεντι: on flowers, and in particular roses, in erotic situations see on 19.39–40.

Λυκόρμᾱι: the river – later called Euenos (cf. on ode 20) – flows through Aetolia into the gulf of Patra.

35 δαιμόνιον τέρ[ας: 'a portent sent by gods' (Jebb), or by fate. To Deianeira, the dying centaur's gift may have seemed a 'godsend', from which she expected a miracle. At the same time, δαιμόνιον suggests that ultimately it was the ἄμαχος δαίμων, or Fate, which handed it to her. What this τέρας was, the poet does not say, and there is no way the audience could have guessed – unless they knew the new version which Sophokles had presented in his *Trachiniai,* perhaps a short while earlier, as Schwinge, *Trachinierinnen* 131, March, *Creative poet* 63 and others have argued; see above, pp. 166–7.

ODE 17 = DITHYRAMB 3

1. Performance and date.

The last three lines of this ode show that it was addressed to Delian Apollo and performed by a chorus from Keos. One might wonder, therefore, whether this ode was not, in fact, a paean rather than a dithyramb, even though dithyrambs seem to have been performed at the great Delian festival which the locals called τὰ Ἀπολλώνια, while to the other Greeks it was known as τὰ Δήλια or Δηλιακά. The Homeric hymn to Apollo describes it as an Ionian family festival, 'where the long-robed Ionians gather with their children and respected wives' and hold competitions 'in boxing, dance, and song' (*h.Ap.* 147–50). The most memorable part of it (μέγα θαῦμα, 156) is the chorus of Delian maidens who praise Apollo, Leto, and Artemis:

μνησάμεναι ἀνδρῶν τε παλαιῶν ἠδὲ γυναικῶν
ὕμνον ἀείδουσιν, θέλγουσι δὲ φῦλ' ἀνθρώπων.
πάντων δ' ἀνθρώπων φωνὰς καὶ βαμβαλιαστὺν
μιμεῖσθ' ἴσασιν· φαίη δέ κεν αὐτὸς ἕκαστος
φθέγγεσθ'· οὕτω σφιν καλὴ συνάρηρεν ἀοιδή (160–4),

'commemorating men and women of old, they sing a hymn, spell-binding the tribes of humans. They know how to represent the voices of all men and the sound of castanets; each one might think it's his own voice: in such a way were they gifted with beautiful song.' In other words, it was a mimetic performance of a story from mythology.

This is, of course, also true of Bacchylides' ode. Though included in the book of dithyrambs, it seems to have been a paean, not only because it is addressed to Apollo at the end but also in view of the preceding lines (124–9); they describe how the Athenian boys and girls greet Theseus when he re-emerges from the depth of the sea: the girls with shrieks (ὀλολυγή), the boys with a *paian*, i.e. with the female and male versions of ritualized cries of joy (on the close link between *ololygē* and *paian* see Calame, *Les chœurs de jeunes filles* 1 149–52). This is *mimesis*: Bacchylides' chorus recreates that scene; at the end of their performance, they almost take on the *persona* of the young Athenians.

If the ode was, in fact, a paean (cf. Jebb p. 223), why was it classified as a dithyramb and included in this book? A fragment of an ancient commentary, or *hypomnema*, on another ode of Bacchylides (ode 23) tells us that Kallimachos defined it as a paean, whereas Aristarchos regarded it as a dithyramb 'because it contained the story of Kassandra' (διὰ τὸ παρειλῆ[φθαι ἐν α]ὐτῆι τὰ περὶ Κασ[σάνδρας]), 'and so he gave it the title *Kassandra*' (ἐπιγράφει δ'αὐτὴν [καὶ Κασσ]άνδραν) (*P.Oxy.* 2368 col.i 9–13). The author (Didymos ?) seems to agree with Aristarchos and his classification criterion; he criticizes Kallimachos for failing to understand that the characteristic feature of the dithyramb (κοινόν, what dithyrambs have 'in common') was mythological narrative (οὐ συνέντα ὅτι [μύθου σύσ]τημα κοινόν ἐ[στι τοῦ δ]ιθυράμβου, lines 17–19). The disagreement implies that paeans and dithyrambs (those of Bacchylides, at any rate) were so similar in character that doubts could arise over their classification. Since ode 17, apart from its last three lines, consists exclusively of mythical narrative, Kallimachos (or whoever classified this ode), in accordance with this criterion, placed it with the *Dithyrambs*.

The date of this ode can be established with some degree of confidence. It tells of the confrontation between the young prince Theseus who accompanies the seven boys and seven girls, the Athenians' tribute to Crete, and King Minos who had come to collect them in his own ship. The confrontation culminates in Theseus' leap into the sea, his descent to the palace of Amphitrite, and his unexpected re-emergence, adorned with the goddess's gifts. The voyage to Crete, Theseus' encounter with Ariadne, his fight with the Minotaur and the rescue of the fourteen young Athenians was known to poetry and art from Homer's time onwards (*Od.* 11.321–5; in art, the earliest representation is a large relief pithos in Basel, dated 670–660 BCE; Appendix no. 12). It is most splendidly shown in the top register of the François vase in Florence (Appendix no. 4) which shows Theseus leading the fourteen young Athenians towards Ariadne. She greets him holding up a black ball – the roll of thread which will be vital in leading him out of the Labyrinth when he has killed the Minotaur. Ariadne's gesture thus anticipates the outcome of the adventure. The nurse, the traditional match-maker who stands between her and Theseus, also points to events that are still to come. On the other hand, the ship, with its bow turned to the left, i.e. to the open sea, and the man who is swimming towards the shore, both indicate what happened immediately *before* their landing on Crete: here it is an Athenian ship which did not pull ashore (perhaps because Crete was then hostile territory?), so that Theseus and the fourteen boys and girls had to swim ashore; in case they survive, the ship stays near the coast, ready to sail away with them. This is the vase-painter's way of incorporating, or at least of hinting at, events that are chronologically outside the scene he is painting – a beautiful illustration of what A. M. Snodgrass has called the vase-painters' 'synoptic method' which allows them to include elements of the story that either precede or follow the main episode shown (see Snodgrass, *Narration*). The top register of the François vase seems to reflect a crucial episode in the story as it was known in the sixth century BCE.

Of the episode narrated in ode 17, however, no trace is found in either art or poetry before the fifth century. It therefore seems very likely that it is Bacchylides' own invention. The earliest, and most impressive, representation in art is a large cup in the Louvre by the potter Euphronios, painted (according to Beazley, *ARV*² 318.1) by Onesimos, dated to between 500 and 490 BCE (Louvre G 104; Appendix no. 13). On the outside it shows four of Theseus' opponents in his early exploits: Skiron, Prokroustes, Kerkyon, the Bull; the inside shows a very young Theseus, supported on a Triton's hands, being greeted by Amphitrite; seated on a richly decorated throne, she is holding a large wreath of white (now faded) and red blobs in her left hand. Between them stands a tall Athena, apparently in the background and invisible since none of the other figures look at her; she holds her spear in her left hand while her right hand supports a small owl, the symbol of the city she protects, aptly interpreted by Dugas and Flacelière, *Thésée* 63 as representing, invisible and yet dominating events, the spirit of Athens, which is a combination of her courage (indicated by the spear) and her wisdom (see the owl) which will help Theseus overcome all the difficulties. The vase-painter's ingenious addition of the tall figure of Athena indicates her continued protection of the young hero, just as Amphitrite's wreath (her wedding gift) anticipates his encounter with Ariadne: a highly sophisticated development of the early vase-painters' 'synoptic method' (see above on the François vase, p. 174). All the figures are identified by inscriptions.

This picture encapsulates the essential elements of Bacchylides' episode, beginning with Athena who speeds the ship on her voyage by sending the north wind (lines 5–8), to the wreath which Amphitrite hands to Theseus: it is 'dark with roses' (ῥόδοις ἐρεμνόν, 116), hence the red blobs on the cup; the Triton's gesture means that Theseus is under the protection of the marine gods. It is impossible not to 'read' it as an illustration of Ode 17, bearing in mind that the vase-painters do not, as a rule, themselves create new versions of myths but respond to customer demand created, in the sixth and fifth centuries, by public performances of poetry. The Louvre cup thus gives us a precious *terminus ante quem*, making this ode one of the earliest extant poems of Bacchylides, together with fr. 20B, the drinking song for the young Macedonian prince Alexander which can also be dated to the early 490s (see below, pp. 244–5). There is no reason to link Ode 17 to the foundation of the Delian League in 478/7, as Severyns suggested. Theseus becomes very prominent, rather suddenly, in Attic art in the last quarter of the sixth century, see Brommer, *Theseus* 75; Neils, *Theseus (passim)*, and *LIMC* vii 926–34. Around 500 BCE he appears on the metopes of the south side of the Athenian treasury at Delphi, as the more visible counterpart to Herakles whose deeds are shown on the metopes of its north side; see Brommer, *Theseus* 68ff. with bibliography; Boardman, *Greek Sculpture* 190 and fig.213; Neils, *Theseus* pl. v figs. 19–24.

2. The myth

Ode 17, like 15, bears a double title: ἠΐθεοι ἢ Θησεύς. The youths (ἠΐθεοι) are the fourteen young Athenians, seven girls and seven boys, whom the Athenians had to send as a periodic tribute to Crete, where they would be eaten by the Minotaur in the Labyrinth. According to Hellanikos (*FGrHist* 4 F 164), Minos came himself to Athens to select them. When the tribute was due for the third time, Theseus, the young son of Aigeus, the king of Athens, sailed with them. On Crete, he encountered Ariadne, king Minos' daughter, who gave him the ball of thread that would, once he had slain the Minotaur, help him find his way out of the Labyrinth; their encounter is illustrated on the François vase, see above, p. 174. This part of the story is already referred to in the *Odyssey* (11.321–5), the Labyrinth in *Iliad* 18.590–4 (according to the scholiast's interpretation of χορὸν . . . οἷόν ποτ' ἐνὶ Κνωσῶι εὐρείηι | Δαίδαλος ἤσκησεν καλλιπλοκάμωι Ἀριάδνηι, see Leaf II 610), and it was told, according to Proklos' summary (*PEG* p. 40), in the *Kypria* in one of Nestor's digressions.

This is the framework into which the episode narrated in Ode 17 has been fitted, with great dramatic effect, as tension builds up right from the beginning. Minos, stirred by Aphrodite, cannot keep his hands off the 'white cheeks' of one of the maidens, Eriboia (Επιβοια on the François vase) who cries for help; Theseus rebukes Minos in a bold speech, emphasizing that while Minos may be the son of Zeus and Europa, he too has a divine father, Poseidon, to whom Pittheus' daughter, Aithra, has borne him. 'Therefore', he challenges Minos, 'curb your insolence!' (39–41). He is ready to fight, should Minos violate any of the fourteen young people.

Minos, angered by the young prince's boldness and perhaps 'still more by the implied doubt of his divine parentage' (Jebb p. 224), prays to Zeus for its confirmation by a thunderbolt, which promptly comes, and then challenges Theseus to retrieve a golden ring which he throws into the sea. Theseus leaps from the sterndeck and is carried by dolphins to the bottom of the sea, where he sees the Nereïds and Poseidon's wife, Amphitrite, who gives him a cloak and a wreath. With these gifts, Theseus emerges at the stern of the ship, to Minos' dismay but the Athenians' delight, 'a miracle for all' (θαῦμα πάντεσσι, 123).

As mentioned above (pp. 174–5), this episode was in all likelihood Bacchylides' own invention, and its earliest representation in art, the Euphronios/Onesimos cup in the Louvre, almost certainly reflects a performance of this ode. There are other reflections: two slightly later Attic vases illustrate the encounter between Theseus and Amphitrite (Appendix nos. 14 and 15), two more (Appendix nos. 16 and 17) place Poseidon in the centre (which is how one might have imagined this scene without direct knowledge of Bacchylides' poem), and one more has Theseus seated between Amphitrite and Poseidon (Appendix no. 18). All five vases are dated to 480–470 BCE. The episode was also the subject of a wall-painting by Mikon in the temple of Theseus in Athens, mentioned by Pausanias (1.17.3); unfortunately, his description is not very helpful: the painting, he says, is 'not clear' (οὐ σαφής) unless one knew the story, partly because of its age (when he saw it, it would have been more than six hundred years old), partly because the painter 'had not painted the whole story' (οὐ τὸν πάντα ἔγραψε λόγον). Then he tells the story according to the mythological handbooks which he used, which differed from Ode 17 in one interesting detail: they *said* (λέγουσιν – this is no longer his description of Mikon's painting!) that Theseus brought back from the sea that ring and a golden wreath, and a very similar version was used by Hyginus in his *Poet. astron.* 2.5. The detail of the retrieved ring is probably due to the mythographers' tendency to tidy up loose strands of a story; Bacchylides himself does not mention the ring again, because to return it, obeying Minos' order, would have been an anticlimax, humiliation rather than triumph. Amphitrite's gifts, on the other hand, the purple cloak and the wreath of roses, once her own wedding present from Aphrodite, are the visible signs of the gods' favour which 'shone on his limbs' (λάμπε δ'ἀμφὶ γυίοις θεῶν δῶρα, 123–4), while Minos' ring, presumably a signet ring and therefore a symbol of power, is lost in the sea. The very visible nature of the divine gifts also explains why Theseus does not meet Poseidon who did not have anything so spectacular to give him (the three wishes which Poseidon grants Theseus in Euripides' *Hippolytos,* 887–98 and 1315–19, were not *visible* proof of his paternity and favour, and may have been a later innovation anyway); instead, he meets Amphitrite whose wreath of roses is an omen for Theseus' impending encounter with Ariadne and whose purple cloak protects him in the sea, as Ino's 'shawl' (κρήδεμνον) protects Odysseus when his raft has been shattered (*Od.* 5.333–462).

1 κυανόπρωιρα 'with dark prow'; this form also appears in the poetic word list *SH* 991.32 (= *P.Hibeh* II 172; 3rd century BCE), cf. Simonides *PMG* 625; in Homer, the compound adjective has two terminations (feminine in -ρος, *Il.* 15.693, *Od.* 3.299).

μέν: for 'inceptive' μέν (without a following δέ) see the examples, mostly from tragedy and Aristophanes, in Denniston 382–4.

2 δὶς ἑπτ[ά]: later authors (Euripides *HF* 1326–7, Plato *Phd.* 58a, Diodoros 4.61.3), refer to the fourteen young Athenians with the same phrase, which may have been coined by an epic source (the *Kypria* ?, see above, p. 176). Theseus is not included in this number; the oldest evidence for Theseus plus the 'twice seven' youths is a 7th century Boiotian skyphos (Appendix no. 20). Pherekydes, however, counts Theseus as one of the Fourteen, *FGrHist* 3 F 148.

3 Ἰαόνων: see on 18.2.

5–6 τηλαυγέï . . . πίτνο[ν] αὖραι: 'northerly breezes fell on the far-shining sail'. πίπτειν, said of wind, means 'to die down', as in *Od.* 14.475, 19.202, Hes. *Op.* 547, but with ἐς or ἐν + object 'to fall upon', cf. Hes. *Th.* 873 αὖραι . . . πίπτουσαι ἐς . . . πόντον, *Op.* 510–11 (Boreas) χθονὶ . . . ἐμπίπτων.

φάρεï: φᾶρος is 'cloth', e.g. the white cloth which covers Patroklos' corpse in *Il.* 18.353. Its extended meaning, 'cloth' > 'sail', is based on *Od.* 5.258–9 where Kalypso φάρε' ἔνεικε . . . ἱστία ποιήσασθαι, cf. Eur. *Hec.* 1082. It is 'shining afar', so presumably white, in contrast to the dark prow. The version followed by Plutarch (*Thes.* 17.4) has Theseus sail with a black sail, but with instructions to set a white one in case he were saved – or a red one, according to Simonides, from whose poem (a dithyramb ?) Plutarch quotes four lines (*PMG* 550). Both Plutarch and Simonides imply an Athenian ship, as does the François vase, not Minos' own, as Bacchylides seems to do.

7 ἕκατι τρ[ε]λεμαίγιδος Ἀθάν[ας: for Athena 'shaking' (πελεμίζειν) her aegis, see [Hes.] *Sc.* 344–5 αἰγίδ' ἀνασσείσασα and Eur. *Ion* 210 γοργ-ωπὸν πάλλουσαν ἴτον. By the will (ἕκατι, cf. Leumann, *Hom. Wörter* 251–8) of Athena, the north wind will drive the ship southward towards Crete. The implication of this phrase is, as Ruth Scodel has pointed out (1984: 137), that the goddess will help Theseus and his protégés and pro-tect them on their dangerous journey. This is also the message of her picture which Onesimos has so ingeniously 'translated' into art on the Euphronios cup in the Louvre by giving her the little owl as a symbol of her city.

8 κνίσεν τε Μίνω<ï> κέαρ: for κνίζειν in an erotic sense ('stir, arouse') cf. Pindar, *P.* 10.60, Hdt. 6.62, Eur. *Med.* 568, Theokritos 4.59. As the responsion in line 31 shows, the name has to be trisyllabic here ($-- \smile$, as in [Hes.] fr. 145.10), but $- \smile -$ in line 68; whether short or long, the final iota was certainly pronounced.

10 [ἀ]γγνὰ δῶρα: the distance between the first two letters after the gap excludes [α]ἰνά. For the meaning of ἁγνός ('sacred, belonging to a god or gods'), see Gerber 1965: 212–13.

12–13 θίγεν δὲ λευκᾶν παρηΐδων: for θιγγάνειν in an erotic sense cf. Archil. 118 W. χεῖρα Νεοβούλης θιγεῖν. The girl's cheeks are white, not because she panics (this might be the implication in Eur. *Med.* 923 and *El.* 1023), but because white skin was traditionally an essential element of female beauty, cf. *Od.* 18.192–6 (Athena makes Penelope 'whiter than ivory') and the evidence collected by Irwin, *Colour Terms* 112–14.

14–15 βόαϛέ τ' Ἐρίβοια: a pun on the girl's name ('far-shouting') derived from βοᾶν rather than βοῦς (both etymologies are attested in scholia); so also in 13.102–4 Ἐριβοίας παῖδ' ὑπέρθυμον βοά[σω] Αἴαντα.

χαλκοθώρα[κα: in 47 he is ἀρέταιχμος, but neither epithet necessarily means that Theseus was actually wearing a corselet and carrying a spear on board Minos' ship – the point is rather that for reasons of poetic symmetry, he needs a warlike epithet to give him a heroic stature like that of his opponent, the 'warlord' of Knossos (39); cf. μενέκτυ[πον] Θησέα (1–2) ≈ μενεπτόλεμος ἥρως (= Minos, 73).

16–20 ἴδεν . . . δίνα[σ]εν . . . ἄμυξεν . . . εἶρεν: four finite verbs at short intervals suggest excitement; reactions to Theseus' bold speech are similarly expressed in 47–52: εἶπεν . . . τάφον . . . χόλωσεν . . . ὔφαινε . . . εἶπέν τε.

17–18 μέλαν . . . ὄμμα: μέλαν may be predicative, expressing pain (cf. *Il.* 4.117 μελαινέων . . . ὀδυνάων, also 4.191, 17.83, 499, 573) or rage (as in the English phrase 'giving someone a black look'), cf. *Il.* 1.103–4 μένεος δὲ μέγα φρένες ἀμφὶ μέλαιναι | πίμπλαντ', see Kirk ad loc. and S. West on *Od.*4.661–2; Combellack 1975: 81–7.

21–3 ὅσιον . . . θυμ[όν]: ὅσιον (predicative) is 'righteous, morally appropriate', cf. 3.83 ὅσια δρῶν.

μεγάλαυχον . . . βίαν: Kenyon's correction is necessary, as the papyrus' reading μεγάλουχον ('holding big things' ?) would not make sense in this context. Cf. Philikos' hymn to Demeter, *SH* 680.28 [μεγ]άλαυχόν τε βίαν ἔτικτεν, also Pindar, *P.* 8.15 βία δὲ καὶ μεγάλαυχον ἔσφαλεν ἐν χρόνωι ('violence makes even a good man fall over time'). The verb, αὐχεῖν, does not mean 'to vaunt' but 'to feel strong, be proud', see Fraenkel on Aesch. *Ag.* 1497 and Barrett on Eur. *Hipp.* 952.

24–5 ἐκ θεῶν μοῖρα παγκρατὴς . . . κατένευσε: while in the *Iliad* it is Zeus who signals his decisions by 'nodding assent' (2.112, 8.175, etc.), B. makes 'all-powerful fate' the subject; he clearly sees Moira as superior to the gods who administer her decisions to mortals, so ἐκ θεῶν goes with κατένευσε rather than with μοῖρα, cf. Aesch. *Pers.* 100–1 θεόθεν γὰρ κατὰ Μοῖρ' ἐκράτησεν | τὸ παλαιόν.

25–6 καὶ Δίκας ῥέπει τάλαντον: unless this is a kind of parenthesis (' – and the scales incline –', i.e. confirm), one needs to supply ὅποι 'wherever, whichever way', because ῥέπειν ('incline') is always intransitive (only the compound, ἐπιρρέπειν, can have an accusative object). For the image of the 'scales of Justice', see on 4.11–13.

28–9 βαρεῖαν . . . μῆτιν: 'hard to bear' (cf. 96 βαρεῖαν . . . ἀνάγκαν), rather than 'grievous' or 'disastrous'. Theseus would find it 'unbearable' if Minos raped any of his protégés: he would rather risk his life and fight him, lines 41–6.

29–33 εἰ καί σε . . . ἀλλὰ κἀμέ: after *Il.* 1.280–1, where Nestor says to Achilles 'you are, admittedly, stronger, having a goddess as your mother, yet he (Agamemnon) is superior . . .' (εἰ δέ σὺ καρτερός ἐσσι, θεὰ δέ σὲ γείνατο μήτηρ, | ἀλλ' ὅ γε φέρτερός ἐστιν . . .); see the examples of εἰ καί + indicative collected by Denniston, *Particles* 300; on ἀλλά following a conditional clause, see Denniston 11.

31 μιγεῖσα: sc. Διί, understood from Διός (30). In Crete, Europa became mother of Minos and Rhadamanthys, *Il.* 14.321–2, [Hes.] fr. 140–1.

34 Πιτθέος θυγάτηρ: Aithra, daughter of Pittheus, king of Troizen, and granddaughter of Pelops, see *LIMC* I 420–31. In his reply, Minos accepts Theseus' claim of divine parentage, i.e. of equal status with himself, as a hypothesis (εἰ δὲ καί σε . . . , 57–63), daring him to prove it.

35 πλαθεῖσα: corresponds to μιγεῖσα 31, as Theseus is careful to balance his claim against his opponent's.

36–8 χρύσεον . . . κάλυμμα: what kind of object could this be? In Homer, 'golden' refers either to gods and things belonging to them, or to metal objects such as a belt (*Il.* 4.132–3, *Od.* 5.232 = 10.545) or a necklace (*h.Ven.* 88f.) but not to a piece of fabric, such as a veil. Besides, line 38 appears to be one long syllable short. Maas (*Resp.* II 19) suspected κάλυμμα to be a gloss that had supplanted the original word. If this is what happened, we should be looking for a four-syllable word (⌣ – – ⌣) for a golden object, such as a piece of jewellery, or a belt; περίζωμα and περίβλημα are prose words, and περίπτυγμα (in Eur. *Ion* 1391 the 'wrapping' of a baby basket) may be a long shot.

40 πολύστονον: see on 16.24 πολύδακρυν. The compound, used proleptically, amounts to a warning before the open threat in which the speech culminates (41–6).

41 ἐρύκεν: Doric infinitive, see 16.18n. Here the short ending is required by the metre.

43–4 τιν' ἠϊθέ[ων] . . . ἀέκοντα: including the women; the ἠΐθεοι are the fourteen, or 'twice seven', young Athenians.

46 δα[ίμω]ν κρινεῖ: see on 5.91–2. Homer's fighters usually refer to δαίμων, as Hektor does in *Il.* 7.291–2 (μαχησόμεθ', εἰς ὅ κε δαίμων | ἄμμε διακρίνηι), while the poet himself names individual gods. This difference was first observed by Jörgensen 1904: 357–82.

49–50 ὑπεράφανον [θ]άρσος 'proud boldness', in a positive sense, as in Ibykos, *PMG* 282.16–17 ἡρώων ἀρετὰν ὑπεράφανον. The audience's reaction to significant events is an important element in Bacchylidean narrative: see 86 (τάφεν, sc. Minos), 92–6 (the young Athenians), 120–9 (Minos and the Athenians), and on 3.9 for further examples.

50 Ἁλίου τε γαμβρῶι: Pasiphaë, Minos' wife, was a daughter of Helios (Ap. Rhod. 3.999, Paus.5.25.9).

50–1 χόλωσεν ἦτορ, ὕφαινέ τε: the subject of χόλωσεν is Theseus (to be inferred from ἥρως 47), the subject of ὕφαινε is Minos; cf. Hes. *Th.* 568–9 for a similarly abrupt change of subject: (Prometheus angers Zeus,) ἐχόλωσε δέ μιν φίλον ἦτορ, ὡς ἴδ'(sc. Zeus!) ἐν ἀνθρώποισι πυρὸς . . . αὐγήν.

ποταινίαν: Minos is 'weaving' a 'novel' plan by forcing Theseus to accept his challenge and to leap into the sea; having himself challenged Minos and claimed divine parentage, Theseus had no other option.

53–8 εἴ πέρ με . . . εἰ δὲ καί σε . . . : Minos takes up Theseus' challenge (29–38), referring to his parentage in the same way as Theseus had referred to his own (29–32) – he is getting his own back. The two speeches show the opponents on equal terms, thus heightening the dramatic tension: the odds appear to be against Theseus, but the outcome of the confrontation remains open until Theseus surfaces again with Amphitrite's gifts.

53–4 νύμ[φ]α Φοίνισσα: Europa, see 17.31n.

56 πυριέθειραν ἀστραπάν 'a fire-tressed lightning flash'. Pindar invented a similarly bold compound: πυρπάλαμον βέλος . . . Διός, *O.* 10.80: Pindar calls lightning 'fire-handed' because it sets on fire what it hits, cf. πυρφόρον . . . κεραυνόν *N.* 10.71.

60–2 χρύσεον χειρὸς . . . κόσμον: a ring, perhaps a signet-ring, as Pausanias calls it σφραγῖδα (1.17.3), see above p. 177.

63 δικών 'throwing'; the verb occurs only in the aorist (ἔδικον, δικεῖν).

πατρὸς ἐς δόμους: 'Minos hints a doubt as to whether Theseus is Poseidon's son; that is the sting' (Jebb); see also on 79–80.

66 ἀναξιβρέντας: the 'Lord of thunder' will send the lightning flash. There is no need to change the papyrus reading (-βρόντας Kenyon), cf. Pindar, *Paean* 12.9 ἀργιβρέντας . . . Ζῆνα, and see Schwyzer I 499–500 (with *addenda* 839).

68 Μίνωϊ: pap. **A** has ΜΙΝΩΙ, the metre requires shortening ('correption') of the ω by the following vowel which must be long, like the iota in dative singular endings in Homer (*Il.* 14.459 Αἴαντῖ δὲ μάλιστα, 22.314 κόρυθῖ δ' ἐπένευε – these and many other examples from Homer can be found in K-B 1 310.11; see also Chantraine, *GH* 1 217). In 8, however, Μίνω<ῐ> must be – –˘.

70 πανδερκέα: it seems that B. used πανδερκέα, which nearly always has active meaning ('seeing all'), in a passive sense, 'seen by everybody'; he may have been thinking of phrases like φάος πολυδερκέος 'Ηοῦς in Hes. *Th.* 451, where the scholion explains the compound as ὑπὸ πολλῶν ὁρώμενον. Pap. **O** has a variant reading, πάνταρκέα, which would have to be neuter plural, = πάντα τὰ ἀρκοῦντα 'all the necessary things' (cf. Eur. *Phoen.* 554), and would hardly make sense here.

72 χεῖρα πέτασε (– ˘–̈): pap. **A** has ΧΕΙΡΑΣ ΠΕΤΑΣΣΕ, **O** ΧΕΙΡΑ〚Σ〛 ΠΕΤ[; as the corrector of **O** realized, the singular is required here: raising both hands is a gesture typical of prayers, whereas here Minos is emphatically urging Theseus to do as he has been told, and emphatic or excited exhortations tend to be accompanied by a deictic gesture, i.e. the stretching out of the right hand, as illustrated by the spectators of the chariot race on the dinos fragment by Sophilos in Athens: Nat. Mus.15499; *ABV* 39.16 (Appendix no. 21).

73 μενεπτόλεμος ἥρως: Minos is 'staunch in battle', a 'warlord' (πολέμαρχος 39), an 'army leader' (στραταγέτας 121); the audience is consistently led to expect a fight, a violent clash – instead, the conflict is resolved on a different level; see Scodel 1984: 142.

75 †βλέπεις† cannot be right: (a) the metre requires – ˘ – and a word beginning with vowel (so that the preceding μέν can be measured short), (b) the tense is wrong: the lightning comes in a split second, so nothing but an aorist will do. Perhaps B. wrote ἔδρακες, which was replaced by a supra-linear gloss (δρακεῖν and δέρκειν are glossed by forms of βλέπειν in Hesychios δ 673 and 2307).

75–6 σαφῆ Διὸς δῶρα: σαφῆ is predicative, 'you saw clearly Zeus' gifts'; the emphasis is always on *visible* confirmation: 57 σᾶμ'ἀρίγνωτον, 69–70 τιμὰν . . . πανδερκέα. B. puts the plural here because the Διὸς δῶρα for Minos will be matched by the θεῶν δῶρα brought back by Theseus (124).

77–9 Κρονί[δας] . . . Ποσειδάν: Κρονίων or Κρονίδας alone refers to Zeus; 'when Κρονίδας or Κρόνιος is said of Poseidon, he is always named (as here and in Korinna fr.1 [= *PMG* 658], Pind. *O.* 6.29) or indicated, as in 18.21 by Λυταίου | σεισίχθονος' (Jebb).

79–80 ὑπέρτατον κλέος χθόνα κατ' ἠΰδενδρον: Minos, reassured by the thunderbolt sent by Zeus and now openly triumphant, ends his speech with cruel mockery – he expects his opponent to meet not with 'supreme fame throughout the well-wooded earth', but with a miserable death by drowning in the sea.

81–4   Theseus jumps – the only possible answer to Minos' scornful challenge – from the ἴκρια, a half-deck at the stern of the ship (cf. *Od.* 13.74–5), also called ἐδώλια, as in Hdt. 1.24.4–6 who makes Arion sing, στάντα ἐν τοῖσι ἐδωλίοισι, before jumping into the sea where he is carried by a dolphin. Did B. know this story, and did it inspire lines 97–100?

85 θελημὸν ἄλσος: the sea is Poseidon's 'sacred precinct', which is 'willing' to receive his son, Theseus. The adjective, (ἐ)θελημός, is first found in Hes. *Op.* 118, where it is said of the people of the golden age, who ἐθελη- μοὶ | ἥσυχοι ἔργ᾽ ἐνέμοντο 'unforcedly, lived quietly off their fields', see West ad loc. The scholia on Hes. *Op.* 118–19 claim, wrongly, that ἐθελημοὶ καὶ ἥσυχοι ταὐτόν ἐστιν, ἡσύχως καὶ ἑκουσίαι γνώμηι, and this explanation recurs in Hesych. θ 213 θελημόν· ἥσυχον. Ap.Rhod. uses the word in this sense, 2.557–8 θελήμονα . . . εἰρεσίην 'quiet rowing', whereas Emp. fr. 35.5–6 and later Kallimachos, *h.Dian.* 31 appear to have understood the word in the sense of 'willing, friendly', which is also found in Hesychios (ε 641 ἐθελημοί· πρόθυμοι).

86–7 τάφεν δὲ . . . ἔνδοθεν κέαρ: why is Minos taken aback? After all, Theseus did what he had dared him to do. Perhaps he did not expect that Theseus would accept the challenge, or he may sense 'deep down in his heart' (ἔνδοθεν κέαρ) that things are not going as planned, and so gives order to sail on, 'close to the wind' (κατ᾽ οὖρον), to make quite sure that Theseus will drown.

88 ἴσχεν: infinitive, see 16.18n. In line 23, this form of the aorist means 'hold down, control', but it is often used as a metrically convenient substitute for ἔχειν, e.g. in Pindar, fr. 61.2 σοφίαν . . . ὀλίγον τοι ἀνὴρ ὑπὲρ ἀνδρὸς ἴσχει, *P.* 11.29 ἴσχει τε γὰρ ὄλβος οὐ μείονα φθόνον. Besides, ἔχειν (ἴσχειν) νῆα means 'to steer a ship' (*Od.* 9.279, 10.91, 11.70, also in prose: Thuc. 7.35.2 ἴσχοντες πρὸς ταῖς πόλεσι), like προσίσχειν in Hdt. 4.156.3. There is therefore no reason to suppose that ἴσχεν . . . νᾶα here means 'he ordered to *stop* the ship'; that the opposite is meant is confirmed by 90–1.

89 μοῖρα . . . ὁδόν: the 'path' of the ship has become the 'path' of events, which are about to take a turn not foreseen by Minos; cf. Eur. *Hel.* 1318 (Zeus) ἄλλαν μοῖραν ἔκραινε.

90 δόρυ   'ship', after Homer's δόρυ νήϊον; 'in Homer, however, δόρυ in this sense is applied specifically to the ship's beam, not to the ship as

a whole', Braswell on Pind. *P.* 4.27(a). Cf. Sim. *PMG* 543.10 ἐν ἀτερπέϊ
δούρατι (of Danae's and Perseus' chest) and Aesch. *Pers.* 411.

σόει: imperfect of σοέω, cf. σεύω/σεύομαι. In Homer, all forms of
σεύω/σεύομαι are treated as if they began with σσ– (e.g., *Il.* 17.463 ὅτε
σεύαιτο, 23.198 τε σεύατο, also λαόσσοος 13.128); a noun derived from this
stem, *σσόϜος, reflected in Hesychios' lemma σοῦς· ἡ πόρευσις, generated
a *verbum denominativum* σοέω (cf. Wackernagel, *Kl.Schr.* 1 220–1), the active of
which is attested only here.

91 βορεάς . . . ἀήτα: a reminder of the opening section, esp. 6
βορήϊαι . . . αὖραι. The papyrus has ΒΟΡΕΟΥΣ corrected to ΒΟΡΕΑΣ,
i.e. βορεάς (adjective), as in Aesch. fr.195.2 βορεάδας ἥξεις πρὸς πνοάς.

93 ἠϊθέων <—> γένος: however the first word is measured (– ◡ –, i.e.
ᾱϊθέων or ἠϊθέων), it appears to be one long syllable short, but no suitable
monosyllable has been suggested; besides, ἠϊθέων seems oddly redundant
next to Ἀθηναίων: perhaps it was added above the line as an explanation,
but was then misunderstood as a 'correction', of the word below which may
have been an epithet of γένος: ἀβροπενθές ? (cf. Aesch. *Pers.* 135 where the
Persian women, bereft of their husbands, are ἀβροπενθεῖς). In B., ἀβρός
seems to have no negative connotation, cf. 18.2n.

95 λειρίων . . . ὀμμάτων: they shed tears from their 'tender eyes', cf.
Suda λ 396, where it is glossed as 'with soft/gentle (προσηνεῖς) eyes'. B.
may have been thinking of Homer's χρόα λειριόεντα (*Il.* 13.830) which
the scholia explain as 'tender as a flower' (εὐανθής, ἀνθηρόν, or ἀπαλόν,
Apoll. Soph.); this meaning is also evident in Pindar's wonderful metaphor
describing the coral as λείριον ἄνθεμον ποντίας ἕέρσας (*N.* 7.79).

97–8 δελφῖνες {εν} ἁλιναιέται: pap. **A** has ΕΝΑΛΙ | ΝΑΙΕΤΑΙ (the
grave accent indicates that the syllable is unaccentuated, i.e. the syllables
so marked are part of a longer word), but εν is against the metre. In an
older text without accents, it would have been easy to mistake ΑΛΙ for a
separate noun (ἁλί) which would then require the preposition ἐν, 'dwelling
in the sea' (ἐν ἁλὶ ναιέται) rather than 'sea-dwelling' (ἁλιναιέται). Plutarch
has collected stories of dolphins saving human lives in *De sollertia animalium*
36 (*Mor.* 984a–985c); on Arion's story and the hymn attributed to him (=
PMG 939, quoted by Aelian, *Hist. animalium* 12.45), see Bowra, *On Greek
margins* 164–81 and Hooker 1989: 141–6.

99–100 πατρὸς ἱππίου δόμον   recalls *Il.* 13.17–38, where Poseidon in his
marine palace yokes his horses before driving across the sea in his 'unwet-
ted' chariot (οὐδ' ὑπένερθε διαίνετο, 30); see below on 122. On Poseidon

Hippios and his connection with horses, especially in cults in Arcadia, see Jost, *Sanctuaires* 284–92.

102–3 ἔδεισ' ὀλβίοιο Νηρέος κόρας: pap. **A** has ΈΔΕΙΣΕ ΝΗΡΕΟΣ ΟΛΒΙΟΥ ΚΟΡΑΣ, which can be made to correspond to ‿ – – ⏓ – ‿ – ‿ – ‿ – either by transposing two words and slight modification, giving ἔδεισ' ὀλβίοιο Νηρέος κόρας, as Ludwich suggested, also Richards (1898: 77), or by Kenyon's ἔδεισε<ν> Νηρῆος, which has been accepted by most editors; in favour of the former proposal is the close correspondence of sound, i.e. vowels, of (Νη)ρέος κόρας with 37 τέ οἱ δόσαν and 80 κλέος χθόνα in the metrically corresponding verses.

103–4 ἀπὸ γὰρ ἀγλαῶν . . . γυίων   'from their shining limbs'. Mortals often perceive gods in a supranatural sheen, see *h.Ven.* 86–90; *h.Dem.* 189 and 280; Soph. *OC* 1650–2; in *Od.* 19.40, Telemachos infers from the light in the hall that 'indeed, there is a god inside' (ἦ μάλα τις θεὸς ἔνδον).

108 ὑγροῖσι ποσσίν: the Nereids are dancing 'with supple feet', not 'on sea-wet toes' (Burnett, Art 22). For this meaning of ὑγρός cf. Pindar, *P.*1.9 (the eagle of Zeus) κνώσσων ὑγρὸν νῶτον αἰωρεῖ. Jebb cites Xenoph. *Eq.* 1.6 (horses should ὑγρὰ ἔχειν τὰ σκέλη) and Pollux 4.96 ὑγρὸς ὀρχηστής. B. may, however, have chosen the epithet because of its ambiguity, implying a kind of 'pun'.

   In poetry and art, Nereids, daughters of Nereus and Doris (Hes. *Th.* 240–64), accompany marine gods. As here in B., they are said to dance also in Euripides (*Ion* 1078–86; *IT* 427–9): while the Muses sing in praise of Zeus and the Olympian gods (Hes. *Th.* 36–53; Pind. fr. 31), the Nereids' dance pays homage to Amphitrite and Poseidon, in silence but to great visual effect, as Theseus' reaction indicates. Strangely, dancing Nereids seem to be unknown to archaic and classical Greek art, whereas 'tableaux' showing Poseidon's or Amphitrite's marine cortège (and occasionally also Aphrodite's, cf. Apul., *Met.* 4.31) were popular; cf. Soph. *OC* 716–19; Plato, *Kritias* 116e; many illustrations can be found in *LIMC* VII *s.v.* Nereiden; see also Barringer, *Divine escorts* 162–5.

109–10 ἄλοχον φίλαν σεμνὰν βοῶπιν: B. accumulates epithets in order to give a higher profile to a prominent figure at a crucial juncture of his story. Here it is Amphitrite who suddenly appears before the young hero's eyes, as if this were a fairy tale; in 5.98–9 and in 11.37–9 it is Artemis who makes her entry, see on 11.39.

112 ἀμφέβαλεν ἀϊόνα πορφυρέαν: in Homer, ἀμφιβάλλειν is often construed with the double accusative, as here, of the person and the object, 'to throw over' someone a garment or the like, e.g. *Il.* 24.588 ≈ *Od.* 3.467 ἀμφὶ δέ μιν φᾶρος καλὸν βάλον ἠδὲ χιτῶνα. The verb strongly suggests a piece of cloth, a shawl or cloak; the noun is attested in Hesych. ε 2225 ἔλυμα . . . καὶ τὸ ἱμάτιον. καὶ ἡ ἀιών, and Latte has drawn attention to ασνσς in *P. Amherst* 1 3a col.2.20 (= Wilcken, *Chrestomathie* 126) which he regarded as a non-Greek word used for a linen garment or cloak (Latte 1932: 272 and 1955: 192). It may well be an Egyptian noun for 'cloth' or 'cloak': demotic *ʾȝjw* (Erichsen, *Demotisches Glossar* 55) and Coptic ΕΙΑΑΥ, ΕΙⲰ, ΙⲰ (Crum, *Coptic Dictionary* 88a). Words for fashion items are often imported from another country, together with the fashion item itself (e.g., brassière, chiffon, décolleté, mohair, cashmere, shawl).

The painter of the crater from Ruvo, now in Harvard (Appendix no. 17) gave Theseus a fringed shawl.

114–16 ἀμεμφέα πλόκον . . . ῥόδοις ἐρεμνόν: Aphrodite's wedding gift for Amphitrite was 'dark with roses'; B. may have been thinking of a twisted gold wreath with inserted roses. For the erotic symbolism of roses cf. Stesichoros, *PMG* 187 (wreaths of roses are thrown to Helen and Menelaos at their wedding), and Eur. *Med.* 841 εὐώδη ῥοδέων πλόκον ἀνθέων. The mythological handbooks seem to have described Amphitrite's wreath as 'golden' (Paus. 1.17.3) and studded with gem stones rather than real roses (Hyginus, *Poet. astron.* 2.5 *coronam . . . compluribus lucentem gemmis*).

δόλιος Ἀφροδίτα: in lyric poetry, Aphrodite is often called 'crafty', first in Sappho 1.2 (δολόπλοκε, an epithet borrowed by Theognis 1386, cf. *PMG* adesp. 949; Sim. *PMG* 541.9–10 and perhaps *PMG* adesp. 919.7), also Sim. *PMG* 575.1 (δολομήδης). δόλιος fem. is first found here, then in Eur. *Hel.* 238 (ἁ δὲ δόλιος . . . Κύπρις). The thread, which Ariadne gives Theseus to help him find his way out of the Labyrinth, was a crafty gift inspired by love, cf. Apollod. *Epit.* 1.8.

117–18 ἄπιστον . . . οὐδέν: a double *asyndeton* (not connected to either the preceding or the following sentence by particles) with a double function: it caps the description of Theseus' reception by Amphitrite, and it marks the transition to the next stage of his story, his reappearance. On B.'s use of *asyndeta* see ode 19.8n. and Maehler 2000; on the functions of general statements or *gnomai*, see the Introduction, p. 24.

θέωσιν: the papyrus has θελωσιν, which cannot be right: (a) the corresponding verse 52 begins with – ⏑ , and (b) in all the variations of this *topos* (see on 3.57–8) B. and Pindar say 'whatever the gods *do* or *accomplish*', not 'what they wish for', which would be rather pointless. θέωσιν (aorist

subj. of τιθέναι, 'they may bring to pass', cf. *Od.* 8.465 οὕτω νῦν Ζεὺς
θείη) resolves both difficulties; for the confusion, cf. *Il.* 18.601, where the
MSS are divided between θέῃσιν (from θέειν 'to run') and the nonsensical
θέλησιν.

φρενοαραῖς βροτοῖς: the compound means 'fitted together in his
mind' (cf. *Od.* 10.553 φρεσὶν ἧισιν ἀρηρώς), or 'having his head screwed on' –
nobody in his right mind would doubt the overwhelming power of the gods:
for them, nothing is impossible; to accept this shows common sense.

119 ναᾶ πάρα . . . φάνη: Theseus' re-emergence 'next to the ship' is
the dramatic climax of the whole story, emphasized by *asyndeton*. As often in
B., its impact is illustrated by the audience's reactions (see on 49–50 above,
and on 3.9): on Minos (120–1), on the maidens (125), and on the youths (128).

119–21 φεῦ, οἵαισιν ἐν φροντίσι . . . ἔσχασεν: the interjection φεῦ is
very common in tragedy and in Aristophanes, rare in prose (Xenophon,
Plato), not found in lyric poetry except here; cf. Schwyzer II 600–1 on the
different types of interjections. Sophokles, like B. here, sometimes uses φεῦ
with exclamations (*OT* 316, *El.* 920, *Ai.* 1266), as does Aristophanes (*Frogs*
141, *Ploutos* 362); B. may well have borrowed it from tragedy.

ἔσχασεν: Theseus 'deflates' his opponent in his φροντίδες, or, as
Kenyon aptly put it, 'the reappearance of Theseus pricked the bubble of
Minos' self-gratulation'. In medical writers, and also in Xen., *Hell.* 5.4.58,
the verb means 'to slit' (a vein), which seems far removed from its meaning
in the maritime metaphors in Pindar, *P.* 10.51 (κώπαν σχάσον), Eur. *Tro.*
811 (πλάταν ἔσχασε ποντοπόρον) and Kall. fr. 11.3 (σχάσσαντες ἐρετμά).
Both meanings may ultimately go back to something like 'to loosen' (a grip),
'to release' (tension), hence in medicine 'to release' (blood pressure etc.) by
cutting a vein. A close parallel to B.'s phrase is σχάσας τὴν φροντίδα in Ar.,
Clouds 740: in both passages the idea seems to be that 'thinking', like rowing,
is a concentrated effort that implies tension and comes to a halt when that
tension peters out. This might also be the clue to the other passage where
Pindar uses the verb, *N.* 4.64: Peleus, wrestling with Thetis who changes
into fire, then into a lioness, λεόντων ὄνυχας . . . ἀκμὰν καὶ δεινοτάτων
σχάσαις ὀδόντων 'made the lions' claws and teeth lose their force', 'made
them limp'.

122 ἀδίαντος: Theseus returns fom the bottom of the sea 'unwet'; this
word, perhaps inspired by *Il.* 13.30 (Poseidon's chariot, see on 99–100), is
evidently chosen to emphasize the miraculous nature of his reappearance
(θαῦμα πάντεσσι, 123) which had been announced in 117–18.

124–5 θεῶν δῶρα: the plural seems to indicate that the 'gifts' (the cloak and the wreath, 112–16) come from both Amphitrite and Poseidon. The ring is not brought back: the symbol of Minos' power is lost in the sea; see above, p. 177.

ἀγλαόθρονοι . . . κοῦραι: the seven Athenian maidens on board the ship, not the Nereids; the only reason for believing that these might be Nereids, their epithet ἀγλαόθρονοι, is inconclusive, since Pindar also calls Danaos' daughters ἀγλαόθρονοι, *N.* 10.1, Kadmos' daughters εὔθρονοι, *O.* 2.22, whether these compounds be derived from 'throne' (θρόνος) or 'ornaments' (θρόνα), see Risch 1972: 17–25; Merkelbach 1973: 160. The Nereids stay with Amphitrite; there is not a word about their accompanying Theseus back to the surface. The *gnome* 117–18 marks the transition from the marine world back to the human world. Theseus' reappearance is reflected in the onlookers' reactions: their 'new-founded joy' (σὺν εὐθυμίαι νεοκτίτωι 125–6) can only be that of the Athenian maidens; see Gerber 1982: 3–5.

127–9 ὠλόλυξαν . . . παιάνιξαν: the two verbs express the female and male forms of ritual invocation, *ololyge* and *paian*; cf. Sappho, fr. 44.31–3 γύναικες δ᾽ ἐλέλυσδον . . . πάντες δ᾽ ἄνδρες . . . ἴαχον ὄρθιον Πάον᾽ ὀνκαλέοντες, Xen. *Anab.* 4.3.19 ἐπαιάνιζον πάντες οἱ στρατιῶται καὶ ἀνηλάλαζον, συνωλόλυζον δὲ καὶ αἱ γυναῖκες ἅπασαι, cf. also Soph. *Tr.* 205–11. On the close link between *paian* and *ololyge* see Calame, *Les chœurs de jeunes filles* I 149–52, who concludes (151) that *ololyge* tends to appear in ritual contexts which require the invocation of a god, either to ask for his protection, or to thank him for his support. Here, the maidens and youths sing in separate groups, but close (ἐγγύθεν, 128) to each other, in accordance with the formula which first introduced them (δὶς ἑπτά).

130 Δάλιε: on the Delian festival, the 'Apollonia', see Introduction, pp. 172–3. B. uses the prayer for success here, in the festival competition, to merge, as it were, the song which concludes the mythical narrative (the *ololyge* and *paian* of the young Athenians) with the Keian choir's paean to Apollo. Although prayers for future successes, or for divine help and protection generally, conclude several of Pindar's victory odes (*O.*1, 6, 8, 13, *P.* 5, 8, *N.* 9, *I.* 7, see Bundy 77; see also B. 5.197–200), they are, more generally, 'in essence a concluding motive belonging to the hymnal form' (Bundy 78). The hymn is an offering presented to the god by the choir; this is, of course, also true of Pindar's paeans; cf. *Pae.* 5.43–8 ἰήϊε Δάλι᾽ Ἄπολλον· | Λατόος ἔνθα με παῖδες | εὐμενεῖ δέξασθε νόωι θεράποντα | ὑμέτερον κελαδεννᾶι | σὺν μελιγάρυϊ παιᾶνος ἀγακλέος ὀμφᾶι, 'ῑεῖε Delian

Apollo – there may you children of Leto with a glad mind welcome me as your attendant with the ringing honey-voiced sound of a far-famed paean'; cf. also *Pae.* 1.9–10; 2.102–8; 6.177–83, and the end of Aristonoos' paean for Delphi, lines 44–8 ἰήϊε Παιάν, χαρεὶς ὕμνοις ἡμετέροις, ὄλβον ἐξ ὁσίων διδοὺς ἀεὶ καὶ σώιζων ἐφέποις ἡμᾶς, ὦ ἰὲ Παιάν, 'O Paean, if you were pleased by our hymns, visit us, giving prosperity always by lawful means, and protecting us' (*Coll. Alex.* 162–4 = Käppel, *Paian* 384–6 = Furley and Bremer II 45–52).

131 φρένα ἰανθείς: B. could have avoided the hiatus by writing φρένας, but he may have thought that ἰαίνεσθαι begins with digamma (for a similar mistake, see on 5.75 ἰόν). ἰανθείς 'warmed' (= 'cheered') corresponds to χαρείς in Aristonoos' paean (quoted in the previous note); similarly Pindar says of Zeus, *O.* 2.13: ἰανθεὶς ἀοιδαῖς εὔφρων ἄρουραν ἔτι πατρίαν σφίσιν κόμισον λοιπῶν γένει, 'cheered by my songs, graciously preserve their ancestral land for their children still to come'. The idea that the god may, if he or she is pleased by the song or the prayer, be willing to respond favourably appears to be the origin of the χαῖρε formula which concludes many of the shorter Homeric hymns; cf. also Pindar, *I.* 1.32.

ODE 18 = DITHYRAMB 4

1. Performance and date

Although there can be no doubt that this dithyramb was composed for the Athenians, it is less clear at which festival it was performed. The Great Dionysia, Thargelia, Hephaistia, Theseia, and the Great Panathenaia have been suggested. In view of the way in which Theseus is described in the last stanza, where he is given the typical attire and weapons of an Athenian ephebe, one might think of a festival at which ephebes played a prominent part. Merkelbach thought of the following scenario (see Merkelbach, *Theseus* 56–62, followed by Ieranò 1987: 87–103): On the day of the festival, a trumpet signal summoned the public to the theatre; when the Athenians had gathered there, they were presented with a dramatic performance, a mini-drama consisting entirely of dialogue. The chorus leader asked the king, Aigeus, why he had called an assembly, and the king then reported what a messenger had just told him about a young hero and his exploits, ending with 'and he is said to be heading for splendour-loving Athens' (δίζησθαι δὲ φιλαγλάους Ἀθάνας, 60). Shortly afterwards the 'hero' may have appeared in a group of second-year ephebes who, coming back from the Isthmos where they had been stationed, now entered the theatre from the Eleusinian road. These ephebes now performed a military display (ἀρήϊον ἄθυρμα, 57), showing off what they had learnt during the preceding months.

Speculative, of course, but perhaps not unlikely: according to Aristotle, *Ath. Pol.* 42.4, in their second year the ephebes showed their military skills to the people who gathered in the theatre. The young hero who is approaching Athens and whose identity is still unknown to the king and the chorus but not to the audience, is described as παῖς πρώθηβος (56–7), he carries two spears and a sword and wears a Thessalian cloak (χλαμύδα 54); *Ath. Pol.* 42.5 also says that ephebes wear cloaks during their two-year military service (φρουροῦσι δὲ τὰ δύο ἔτη χλαμύδας ἔχοντες).

If Theseus is indeed portrayed as a typical Athenian ephebe here, the ode may date to the time when the Athenians kept garrisons, manned by ephebes, along the Isthmos, i.e. from 460 to 444 when Athens controlled the region of Megara. Thukydides repeatedly refers to νεώτατοι (1.105.4; 2.13.7); in addition, Siewert (1977) draws attention to some fifth-century allusions to the ephebic oath which had remained unnoticed: Thuc. 1.144.1; 2.37.3; Soph. *Ant.* 663–71; Aesch. *Pers.* 956–62, so that the Attic *ephebeia* can be traced back to the middle of the fifth century, cf. Gercke 1997:1072.

At this point, a bold conjecture by J. P. Barron may become relevant (Barron 1980: 1–8), who suspects that Theseus' attributes (κυνέαν Λάκαιναν 50, οὔλιον Θεσσαλὰν χλαμύδα 53) may refer to the names of Kimon's three sons Lakedaimonios, Oulios and Thessalos; on these, see Davies, *Athenian propertied families* 304–7 and Kirchner, *Prosopographia attica* 10212 (under Miltiades II). According to Plutarch (*Kimon* 16.1), Lakedaimonios and Oulios were twins; their parents, Kimon and Isodike, married *c.*480, and if their sons were born *c.*478–475 they would have been ephebes *c.*460–55. Could it be, then, that all three of them were among the ephebes (νεώτατοι) who in 458, together with the veterans (πρεσβύτατοι) and under Myronides' command, defeated the Corinthians at Geraneia, the mountain ridge between the Isthmos and Megara, while the main part of the Athenian army was fighting the Aiginetans? Their victory was famous, cf. Thuc. 1.103; Diod. 11.79; [Lysias], *Epitaphios* 48–53; Andokides 3.6; Aristides' *Panathenaikos* (*or.* 1) 214–17 Lenz-Behr; see Gomme on Thuc. 1.105.4 and Pelekidis, *Histoire de l'éphébie attique* 47–9.

Supposing that Ode 18 was performed at the Panathenaia of 458, in late August, the young hero's attributes may well have been understood by the audience as tributes to Kimon's sons if these were among the victorious ephebes who returned to Athens that summer. If, moreover, they had inherited the Thracians' red hair from their grandmother, Hegesipyle (who was the daughter of a Thracian chieftain), even the colour of Theseus' hair (κρατὸς . . . πυρσοχαίτου, 51) may provide a clue, see Barron 1980: 2 with n.19. This may, of course, be nothing more than a string of strange coincidences; but as there are so many, they may not be coincidences after all; the idea is certainly attractive.

2. The myth

There is dramatic irony in the fact that the young hero's identity is not revealed in the ode and remains unknown both to king Aigeus, his human father, and to the chorus who represent the people of Athens, but will have been clear to the 'real' people of Athens, the audience of Bacchylides' dithyramb, from the herald's account of his five great deeds (19–30): as so often in tragedy, they know more than protagonist or chorus or both.

How can they know about them? The five deeds of Theseus which B. describes all appear for the first time on Attic vases of the last quarter of the sixth century, often combined to a 'cycle'. Of the 23 'cycle' vases listed in Brommer (*Theseus* 67–8 and *Vasenlisten* 211–12), only two are black-figured, 21 are early Attic red-figured, 18 of these are cups; see *LIMC* VII 922–34 nos. 33–53. At the turn of the century, the Treasury of the Athenians at Delphi deploys Theseus' early deeds in its nine metopes on the south side (this is the side which a visitor, coming up the sacred way through the sanctuary, would see first). On the metopes, see Brommer, *Theseus* 68–9 and plates 1–4a; Boardman, *Greek sculpture* 190 and fig. 213; Neils, *Theseus* pl.5 figs. 19–24.

Theseus' rather sudden rise to prominence in Attic vase painting in the decade 520–510 BCE cannot be coincidence. Its aim was evidently to put Theseus, the Attic/Ionian hero, of whom not much had been seen or heard in earlier art or poetry, on a par with the Dorian Herakles, an initiative which probably reflects the growing power of Athens in the time of Peisistratos and his sons. It is highly unlikely that it was generated by the vase-painters themselves; the vases almost certainly reflect poetry, perhaps an authoritative poem commissioned either by Peisistratos or by one of his sons, or possibly by their rivals, the Alkmeonids. If it was a poem, could it have been the *Theseid* mentioned by Plutarch, *Thes.* 28.1 (= *PEG* pp. 135–6)? Was it an epic poem? There may have been an older epic *Theseid* which told of Theseus' Cretan adventure, the killing of the Minotaur, and his encounter with Ariadne, even though not a single hexameter has survived. These old stories, and especially Theseus' fight with the Minotaur, appear on Corinthian vases (and through them, on Etruscan vases) and in Boiotia before they appear in Attica.

Theseus' exploits on the Isthmos, by contrast, which all appear first in Attic art in the last quarter of the sixth century, are probably inspired by an influential poem composed and/or performed in Athens around 520 BCE. According to Plutarch (*Thes.* 20.1–2), Peisistratos had been keen to promote Theseus as the national hero of Athens and to enhance his reputation by removing from Hesiod's works a line which presented Theseus as a womanizer (Plutarch quotes as his source Hereas of Megara, *FGrHist* 486 F 1), and by inserting a line describing Theseus and Peirithoos as sons of gods into the *Odyssey* (*Od.* 11.631) 'as a favour to the Athenians' (χαριζόμενον Ἀθηναίοις). Such cosmetic surgery would not have been necessary if there had been an authoritative *Theseid* in the time of Peisistratos, and the vase paintings do indeed suggest a later date, not long before 520. The most prominent poet who lived at Athens, at the invitation of Peisistratos' son Hipparchos ([Plato], *Hipparchos* 228c), was Simonides. Plutarch quotes four lines from a lyric poem (*Thes.* 17.5 = *PMG* 550) which told of Theseus' departure from Athens and his agreement with his father who gave him a 'purple sail' (φοινίκεον ἱστίον) to substitute for the black one in case he were saved. This seems to imply that the poem also told of Theseus' tragic mistake: on the journey back from Crete, both he and his steersman whom Simonides named as Phereklos, son of Amarsyas, forgot to change the sails, and Aigeus, seeing the ship approaching with a black sail, 'threw himself from the rock [= the Akropolis] in despair' (ἀπογνόντα ῥῖψαι κατὰ τῆς πέτρας ἑαυτὸν καὶ διαφθαρῆναι, Plut. *Thes.* 22.1). It seems possible, although it cannot be proved, that Simonides' poem also told of Theseus' exploits on his way from Troizen to Athens, since nearly all the 'cycle' vases, and in particular the early ones, show those exploits combined with Theseus' fight with the Minotaur, as do the metopes on the south side of the Athenian Treasury at Delphi. Simonides also mentioned Theseus' rape of the leader of the Amazons, whom he named as Hippolyte, not Antiope, as she is called in most other sources (Apollod.

Epit. 1.16; cf. Lorenzoni 1980–82: 51), but whether he did so in the same poem we cannot say. Plutarch (*Thes.* 27.5) derived this information not from Simonides but from Kleidemos (*FGrHist* 323 F 18). On Attic vases, where the Amazon is named she is always Antiope or Antiopeia, see Bothmer, *Amazons* 124–5.

3. Structure

The structure of ode 18 is unique among the extant dithyrambs of B. and Pindar in that (a) it consists of four strophes (not triads) alternating between speakers, and (b) it consists entirely of dialogue; there is no narrative. The first strophe is addressed to the 'King of Athens', who is identified as Aigeus, son of Pandion, in line 15. The speakers' identity is not explicitly stated; they must be Athenian citizens, since they speak of 'our land' (5). They have been summoned, presumably to the agora, by a trumpet signal (3–4) and are now waiting for their king to explain why. The second strophe is the king's explanation; strophe 3 continues the citizens' questions, which in strophe 4 the king answers with the physical description of the unnamed young hero who is about to arrive at Athens.

The setting of this strophic dialogue resembles the assembly of the Ithakians at the beginning of the second book of the *Odyssey* (see 3n.) and the opening of Soph. *OT* (where, however, the roles are reversed: it is the king who asks the assembled suppliants); particularly close is Aesch. *Ag.* 82–103 where the chorus of old Thebans ask Klytaimestra what news she has received.

It is conceivable that the unusual form of ode 18 was suggested to B. by the parodos of Aeschylus' *Agamemnon*; if the date tentatively suggested for ode 18 (August 458) is correct, B. may have witnessed the performance of the *Oresteia* at Athens in the spring of that same year.

1 Βασιλεῦ: Aigeus, see on 15.

2 ἁβροβίων . . .Ἰώνων: cf. 17.3 κούρους Ἰαόνω[ν]. The Athenians always regarded themselves as Ionians; Theseus was said to have marked the boundary, after the annexation of the region of Megara, at the Isthmos by a stela which defined the land on its eastern side as Ἰωνία (Plutarch, *Thes.* 25.4). The luxurious lifestyle of the 'old' Ionians = Athenians is often referred to in comedy (Kratinos' *Ploutoi*, fr. 257 = *PCG* IV 252, Telekleides fr. 25 = *PCG* VII 677), by Thuc. 1.6.3, and by Herakleides Pontikos (in Athen.

12.512bc) who points out that luxury had not made them decadent because they were the ones who 'defeated the might of all Asia' at Marathon, and those who are most famous for their 'wisdom' (σοφία) consider 'pleasure' (ἡδονή) the greatest good, for which he quotes Simonides (*PMG* 584). In Herakleides' view, the age of pleasure and luxury at Athens lasted until the Persian wars.

3 τί νέον ἔκλαγε: the series of questions which begins here recalls a scene at the beginning of Book 2 of the *Odyssey* where, in an assembly of the people of Ithaka, old Aigyptios opens the debate by asking 'And now who has called us together? On whom has such need come either of the young men or of those who are older? Has he heard some tidings of an invading host, which he might tell us plainly, seeing that he has first learned of it himself? Or is there some other public matter on which he is to speak and address us? A good man he seems in my eyes, a blessed man. May Zeus fulfil unto him himself some good, even whatsoever he desires in his heart' (νῦν δὲ τίς ὧδ' ἤγειρε;τίνα χρειὼ τόσον ἵκει | ἠὲ νέων ἀνδρῶν, ἢ οἳ προγενέστεροί εἰσιν;| ἠὲ τίν' ἀγγελίην στρατοῦ ἔκλυεν ἐρχομένοιο, | ἥν χ' ἡμῖν σάφα εἴποι, ὅτε πρότερός γε πύθοιτο;| ἠέ τι δήμιον ἄλλο πιφαύσκεται ἠδ'ἀγορεύει;| ἐσθλός μοι δοκεῖ εἶναι, ὀνήμενος· εἴθε οἱ αὐτῶι | Ζεὺς ἀγαθὸν τελέσειεν, ὅ τι φρεσὶν ᾗσι μενοινᾶι, *Od.* 2.28–34). The situation which B. evokes in the first stanza is very similar to (and may have been inspired by) Aesch. *Ag.* 82–103, esp. 82–7 σὺ δέ, Τυνδάρεω | θύγατερ, βασίλεια Κλυταιμήστρα, | τί χρέος; τί νέον; τί δ' ἐπαισθομένη, | τίνος ἀγγελίας | πειθοῖ περίπεμπτα θυοσκεῖς; 'But you, daughter of Tyndareos, Queen Klytaimestra, what is it now? what news? what did you notice, what message has persuaded you to supervise sacrifices sent around?' Like the old men of Thebes in *Ag.*, the citizens of Athens in this ode have assembled to question their sovereign about a message they know has just arrived.

3–4 χαλκοκώδων σάλπιγξ: 'in peacetime', B. says (fr. 4.75), 'there is no din of bronze trumpets'. The trumpet was the obvious instrument for giving signals in war and in military training, but was also used in competitions to announce the entry of the contestants: Pollux 4.87 says that 'the trumpet entered the contests from military training; it is sounded each time the contestants are called up'; cf. Pickard-Cambridge, *Dramatic festivals* 67; West, *Ancient Greek music* 118–21. It therefore seems plausible that a trumpet signal could actually have been given to announce the performance of this dithyramb. The shape of the instrument is illustrated by a well-preserved specimen in Boston, see Sachs, *History of musical* *instruments* 145–8; Caskey 1937: 525–7. An ivory mouthpiece was fitted into a bronze tube which ended in a bell-shaped opening (the κώδων), as described in Schol. Soph. *Aias* 17 κώδων καλεῖται τὸ πλατὺ τῆς σάλπιγγος. Passages like *Il.* 18.219 and 21.388 suggest that it produced a very loud sound.

6 ἀμφιβάλλει implies something like a 'hunting-net' as its object, as in Soph. *Ant.* 342–3 κουφονόων τε φῦλον ὀρνίθων ἀμφιβαλὼν ἄγρει and in *trag. adesp.* 127.6–10 ὁ δ᾽ ἀμφιβάλλεται ταχύπους . . . ἄφνω δ᾽ ἄφαντος προσέβα . . . πολύμοχθος Ἅιδας. Demosthenes also uses the metaphor of casting-nets and stake-nets to describe Philip's tactics (4.9 προσπεριβάλλεται and περιστοιχίζεται, cf. 6.27).

8 ληισταὶ κακομάχανοι 'evil-planning robbers' who drive sheep away. Cattle- and sheep-rustling was the most common cause of armed conflicts in Greek mythology, cf. *Il.* 11.670–705, Hes. *Op.* 163 μήλων ἕνεκ᾽ Οἰδιπόδαο, *Od.* 9.405, Pindar, *P.* 4.148–50 (Pelias and Jason), Ap.Rhod. 1.1340–1.

11 κραδίαν ἀμύσσει 'rends your heart'; the original meaning of the verb seems to be 'to scratch', cf. *Il.* 19.284–5 (Briseïs mourns Patroklos' death), χερσὶ δ᾽ ἄμυσσεν | στήθεά τ᾽ ἠδ᾽ ἁπαλὴν δείρην ἰδὲ καλὰ πρόσωπα. B. uses it, here and in 17.18–19, in the same sense as Aesch. *Pers.*161 καί με καρδίαν ἀμύσσει φροντίς.

The chorus ask three questions in descending order of urgency: (1) Is an enemy army approaching our city?, (2) are some robbers stealing sheep?, or (3) what else worries you? If they were really alarmed, they would put them in reverse order, because in a *tricolon* the important point would normally come last. Their relative detachment gradually changes into optimism during their second speech (31–45) which creates an ironic contrast to their king's growing alarm in 46–60.

12 εἴ τινι βροτῶν: 'you, if any mortal . . .' amounts to a superlative, as in 5.4–5 and Pindar, *P.* 3.85–6 λαγέταν γάρ τοι τύραννον δέρκεται, εἴ τιν᾽ ἀνθρώπων, ὁ μέγας πότμος, both times with reference to Hieron. Here, the chorus' confident assertion that Aigeus, 'if any mortal', has the support of valiant young men (ἀλκίμων ἐπικουρίαν . . . νέων), is ignored by the king but highlights the military value of the Athenian ephebes; see Introduction, pp. 189–91.

15 Πανδίονος υἱὲ καὶ Κρεούσας finally establishes the addressee's identity: he is king Aigeus, son of Pandion and father of Theseus. Pandion was one of the ten eponymous heroes of the Attic 'tribes' (φυλαί), see Kearns, *The heroes of Attica* 87–91, 115–17, 191–2 and Kron, *Phylenheroen* 104–19. Kreusa appears as his wife, and mother of Aigeus, only here; in Eur. *Ion* 57–8 and 1589–1600 (and hence in Apollod. 3.15.1) she is the wife of Xuthos and mother (by Apollo) of Ion.

16–17 Νέον ἦλθε<ν>   answers the first question (τί νέον ἔκλαγε, 3): a messenger has 'just' arrived, the king has summoned his people without delay.

δολιχὰν ἀμείψας . . . κέλευθον   'having completed the long journey' (about 70 km). Transitive ἀμείβειν = 'to exchange'; if its accusative object is a place, it means 'to cover' or 'to cross', as in Aesch. *Pers.* 69 πορθμὸν ἀμείψας (also middle, cf. Simonides' epigram *AP* 7.677.2 = Page, *Epigr.* 99–102, quoted in Hdt. 7.228: ποταμὸν . . . ἀμειψάμενοι), Eur. *Or.* 1295 κέλευθον, *Iph.Aul.* 144 πόρον.

18 ἄφατα δ' ἔργα   'indescribable deeds'; B. seems to use the compound in the sense of 'terrifying', cf. Pindar, *N.* 1.47 where μελέων ἀφάτων refers to the bodies of the snakes strangled by Herakles. This phrase, which prefaces the account of the five 'Isthmian' exploits, epitomizes the king's alarm.

19–20 τὸν ὑπέρβιον . . . Σίνιν: the epithet vaguely hints at Sinis' violence, but B. does not specify what Sinis did. The audience will have known him as the 'pine-bender', πιτυοκάμπτης, who tied strangers to a bent pine-tree which he then released, catapulting them into the air; Theseus killed him in the same way, see Apollod. 3.16, Plut. *Thes.* 8.3, Paus. 2.1.4, Hygin. *fab.* 38. He appears on several of the early 'cycle' vases, e.g. Brommer plates 9b, 11b, 12, 13 = Neils, *Theseus* nos. 55, 3, 94, 111 respectively. Diodoros 4.59.3 and the *hypothesis* b to Pindar's *Isthmians* (III p.192 Drachmann) make Sinis tie his victims' arms to *two* bent pines which, when released suddenly and simultaneously, tore the bodies apart.

21–2 Κρονίδα Λυταίου σεισίχθονος τέκος: Poseidon's cult name Λύταιος is attested only here. It refers to Lytai in the Tempe valley in Thessaly, so called because Poseidon 'loosened' the rocks to let the water of the Peneios through to the sea (Steph. Byz. *s.v.* Λυταί, cf. Hdt. 7.129.4). Sinis is a son of Poseidon only here and in *hypothesis* b to Pindar's *Isthmians*; in schol. Eur. *Hipp.* 977 he is the son of Polypemon.

23 σῦν δ' ἀνδροκτόνον: on many 'cycle' vases, the 'man-killing sow' is shown together with an old woman who begs Theseus to have mercy on the animal. On one cup (Madrid 11265; *ARV²* 1174.1; Appendix no. 22) she is named Κρομμυω, so she is the nymph of the village of that name, half-way between Corinth and Megara.

24 Κρεμ<μ>υῶνος: ancient sources are split between Κρεμμ– and Κρομμ–. The papyrus shares the spelling with -ε- with Steph. Byz. who refers to Eudoxos, with Pliny, *HN* 4.7.11 (*Cremmyon*), and Hyginus, *Fab.* 38.

25 Σκίρωνα: a robber who forced passers-by to wash his feet and then kicked them over the 'Skironian cliffs' (Eur. *Hipp.* 979; Paus.1.44.8; Diod. 4.59.4; Hyginus, *Fab.* 38.4). B. does not specify Skiron's misdeeds but simply calls him 'wicked' (ἀτάσθαλος). He appears already on Attic black-figured vases (Appendix nos. 23, 24, 25). On the vases, he is often identified either by the washbasin or by the tortoise which ate his victims, according to Apollod. *Epit.* 1.2 who adds that his father was Pelops or, according to others, Poseidon. In contrast to this negative Attic version, the Megarians promoted a very different image; Plutarch (*Thes.* 10.2) says that they presented him as righteous and as avenger of robbers, and as father-in-law of Aiakos, the most righteous of men, 'struggling "against the long time"', as Simonides put it' (τῶι πολλῶι χρόνωι πολεμοῦντες, *PMG* 643), implying that their writers (συγγραφεῖς, *FGrHist* 487 F 1) were trying to counter a long-established negative tradition about Skiron. Against the background of the old hostility between Megara and Athens, mythology turned into a political propaganda war.

26 τάν τε Κερκυόνος παλαίστραν: Pausanias (1.39.3) mentions a place near Eleusis that was known as 'Kerkyon's wrestling school'. Kerkyon, son of Branchos and Argiope (Apollod. *Epit.* 1.3), forced passers-by to wrestle with him and killed them all, before Theseus defeated him through his wrestling skill (τέχνη), as Pausanias says, or by lifting him up and crashing him to the ground, according to Apollodoros and some of the vases (e.g. Appendix nos. 26 and 27).

27–8 ἔσχεν: 'he stopped', as in 41. Pindar uses the verb in the same sense when he tells the story of Herakles and Antaios, which looks remarkably similar to that of Theseus and Kerkyon: *I.* 3/4.72 (Herakles came to Libya,) κρανίοις ὄφρα ξένων ναὸν Ποσειδάωνος ἐρέφοντα (sc. Antaios) σχέθοι, 'to stop him from roofing Poseidon's temple with the skulls of strangers'. On Antaios, see Apollod. 2.5.11; Diod. 4.17.4; Pherekydes, *FGrHist* 3 F 76.

Πολυπήμονος . . . σφῦραν: Prokoptas (the 'cutter') had to drop the mighty 'hammer of Polypemon'. This implies that Polypemon was his predecessor, perhaps his father (cf. Ovid, *Ibis* 407 *Sinis et Sciron et cum Polypemone natus*); only Pausanias identifies the two as one person (1.38.5). In Apollod. *Epit.* 1.4 he is called Damastes, ὃν ἔνιοι Πολυπήμονα λέγουσιν, also in Plutarch (*Thes.* 11.1), cf. Hesych. δ 183. In most other sources he is simply called Prokroustes (Diod. 4.59.5; Hygin. *Fab.* 38; Ovid, *Met.* 7.438 and *Her.* 2.69), and this name appears also on some vases (Appendix nos. 22 and 28; also on the outside of the kylix in Paris, Louvre G 104 – Appendix no. 13). According to Apollod. *Epit.* 1.4 and Plut. *Thes.* 11.1, he had two beds, one long and one short; he fitted his tall victims to the short bed by lopping off their extremities, and forced the short ones onto the long bed where he hammered them to length; Diod. 4.59.5 and schol. Eur. *Hipp.* 977 mention only one bed. On the vases he is identified by the hammer with which Theseus kills him; about half of them, the early ones in particular, omit the bed, as do the metopes of the Athenian Treasury at Delphi and the Hephaisteion in Athens.

30 ταῦτα δέδοιχ᾽ ὅπᾶι τελεῖται: both here and in 45, τελεῖται is future, as in Aesch. *Ag.* 67–8 ἔστι δ᾽ ὅπηι νῦν ἐστι· τελεῖται δ᾽ ἐς τὸ πεπρωμένον. Aigeus is worried how this will end, i.e. whether the young hero is approaching with friendly or with hostile intentions. While the audience will have recognized Theseus from the king's description of his deeds, neither the king himself nor the chorus know who the anonymous hero is, but their reactions are very different, see on 45.

32 τίνα … στολάν: στολή can mean 'equipment' or 'clothing' ('equipment': Aesch. *Supp.* 764, *Pers.* 1018; 'clothing': Aesch. *Pers.* 192, Soph. *Phil.* 224, Ar. *Eccl.* 846 στολὴ ἱππική, cf. Hdt. 1.80.2). The chorus' questions concerning στολή, weapons (33–4) and companions (35–7), will be answered in reverse order by the king: companions (46), weapons (47–9), clothes (50–4), so στολάν in 32 is likely to refer to his *chiton* and *chlamys*.

33–4 σὺν πολεμηΐοις ὅπλοισι στρατιὰν ἄγοντα: similar questions are asked in similar situations; at Ithaka, one of the elders asks 'who has summoned us to the assembly? Has he had news of an army approaching?' (ἦέ τιν᾽ ἀγγελίην στρατοῦ ἔκλυεν ἐρχομένοιο; *Od.* 2.30, see above on line 3). In Soph. *OT* 750–1, Oedipus asks Iokaste about Laios: πότερον ἐχώρει βαιός, ἢ πολλοὺς ἔχων | ἄνδρας λοχίτας, οἷ᾽ ἀνὴρ ἀρχηγέτης; and in Aesch. *Cho.* 766–8, the chorus ask whether Aigisthos is to come alone or with his bodyguard, to which the nurse replies ἄγειν κελεύει (sc. Klytaimestra) δορυφόρους ὀπάονας.

35 μοῦνον σὺν ὀπάοσιν: the papyrus has ΟΠΛΟΙΣΙΝ, a visual error caused by ὅπλοισι in the preceding line. On his 'companions' see below on 46.

36–7 ἀλάταν ἐπ᾽ ἀλλοδαμίαν 'a wanderer in foreign lands', cf. Eur. *Hipp.* 897–8 ἀλώμενος | ξένην ἐπ᾽ αἶαν, Aesch. *Ag.* 1282 φυγὰς δ᾽

ἀλήτης, τῆσδε γῆς ἀπόξενος. Everyone was a 'foreigner' outside his own city, unprotected and therefore dependent on a network of guest-friendship (ξενία); it was not advisable to travel alone: on vases, Theseus is often shown with armed companions (see on 46).

38 ἰσχυρόν τε καὶ ἄλκιμον   'strong and valiant'; ἰσχυρός means 'physically strong', cf. Eur. fr. 290 N² ἄνδρα σκαιὸν ἰσχυρὸν φύσει | ἧσσον δέδοικα τἀσθενοῦς τε καὶ σοφοῦ, whereas ἄλκιμος also implies courage. The chorus express admiration rather than fear or concern.

41 ἔσχεν   'halted', see on line 27.

ἦ θεὸς αὐτὸν ὁρμᾶι: in the mouth of the Athenians' chorus, this phrase expresses admiration: whoever this unknown hero may be, if he can accomplish such amazing deeds, surely a god must be driving him on. Homeric heroes are sometimes driven by a god; in *Iliad* 9.702–3 Diomedes says about Achilles that he may come back to fight, ὅππότε κέν μιν | θυμὸς . . . ἀνώγηι καὶ θεὸς ὄρσηι: here, both his heart and a divine agent seem to pull in the same direction, whereas in the *Odyssey* these same agents are often seen as alternatives, as in *Od.* 4.712–13 where Medon replies to Penelope's question why her son has gone to Pylos: 'I do not know whether some god drove him, or whether his own heart (θυμός) felt the urge to go to Pylos', cf. *Od.* 16.356–7 (the suitors have realized that Telemachos has evaded their ambush): 'either one of the gods told them, or they themselves saw the ship pass'. Amazing inspiration or energy is also explained as 'driven by a god': so Demodokos ὁρμηθεὶς θεοῦ ἤρχετο, *Od.* 8.499, Orestes in Eur. *El.* 70 is πρὸς θεῶν ὁρμώμενος, as is Ankaios in Ap. Rhod. 2.895: δὴ γὰρ θεοῦ ἔτραπεθ' ὁρμῆι.

The affirmative ἦ is required here (see the examples in Denniston 280), not the disjunctive ἤ, as suggested by Slings (1990: 9–10) on the grounds that the chorus' questions in this stanza should match those in the first (5–11). The syntax in the third stanza is different from that in the first, as the first question, τίνα . . . τίνα τε (31–2) is a double question, not an alternative one like ἦ τις . . . στραταγέτας ἀνήρ; ἢ ληισταί (5–8), but then an alternative question follows, πότερα . . . ἢ μοῦνον (33–5), and there is no reason to assume that it should be followed by another alternative question. The chorus' comment 'Truly a god must be driving him' is their conclusion from the account of the unknown hero's incredible exploits which they have just heard of. Similarly, Pindar concludes (or rather, makes his chorus conclude) from the account of Pelops' ivory shoulder that 'indeed, there are many wonders' (ἦ θαύματα πολλά, *O.* 1.27); cf. also Aesch. *Ag.* 1481.

42 δίκας: in the plural, the usual meaning in early epic is 'decisions' about conflicting claims, hence 'judgements', as in *Od.* 11.570 on Minos, the judge of the dead: οἱ δέ μιν ἀμφὶ δίκας εἴροντο ἄνακτα, cf. Hes. *Op.* 225, 262, *Th.* 85–6. 'Punishments' is a natural extension of this meaning. In Euripides' *Skiron*, Theseus sees himself in the role of avenger: ἔστι τοι καλὸν κακοὺς κολάζειν (fr. 678 N²).

43–4 οὐ γὰρ ῥάιδιον . . . κακῶι   'for it is not easy to perform deed after deed without meeting disaster'. Platt 1898: 63 took this to mean 'it is not easy for one who is always doing evil (ἔρδοντα sc. κακά) to escape evil', similarly Fagles in his translation: 'Outrage mounting on outrage | always meets its retribution' (*Bacchylides* 59). This cannot be right because, linked by γάρ to the preceding sentence, it explains not that the wrongdoers are punished but that the hero is 'driven' by a god: 'the unbroken series of his victories argues that Theseus is under divine protection' (Jebb).

45 πάντ(α) . . . τελεῖται: future, see on 30. The similarity in wording is surely intentional: the chorus' concluding line echoes Aigeus' worried statement, but in a quite different sense: coming after 41–4, 'in the long run, everything will be accomplished' can only mean that 'sooner or later it will turn out that he was indeed, as we suspected, under divine protection'. Aigeus' and the chorus' contrasting expectations seem designed to create ironical suspense for the audience: they know who the hero is, but how are they to imagine him? Will his physical appearance justify Aigeus' concern or the chorus' optimistic anticipation? This is rather like the suspense experienced by the spectators of a tragedy: although they know the basic elements of the myth, they want to *see* how it is staged, what it will *look like* on stage – the very terms *theatron* and *spectaculum* emphasize the visual aspect of drama. Aigeus' description of the hero's appearance is like a messenger's speech in tragedy: it invites the audience to create a picture in their imagination of something they will not physically see on stage – unless, as Merkelbach speculated (see Introduction, pp. 189–90), it paves the way for the entry of the Athenian ephebes into the theatre.

46 Δύο οἱ φῶτε: Aigeus answers the chorus' questions in reverse order, beginning with the last one (35–6). Theseus' two companions appear on some vases, e.g. on a kantharos in Munich (inv. 2565; *ARV²* 889.169; Appendix no. 29) and on a bell-crater in Sydney which may illustrate Theseus' arrival in Attica, published by Pryce 1936: 77–8 and pl.5 (Appendix no. 30; not in Neils). In some later sources they are named as Peirithoos and Phorbas, cf. Kearns, *Heroes of Attica* 193–4.

φῶτε μόνους: for the combination of dual with plural forms, cf. Plato, *Euthyd.* 273d ἐγελασάτην . . . ἄμφω βλέψαντες εἰς ἀλλήλους. Other examples can be found in K-G I 70–3.

47 φαιδίμοισι δ' ὤμοις: Homer often speaks of 'gleaming limbs' (φαίδιμα γυῖα), only in *Od.* 11.127–8 (≈ 23.275) of Odysseus' 'gleaming shoulders' (hence Soph. frs.453 and 454). Homer's fighters wear a sword-band (ἀορτήρ or τελαμών) over their shoulder; see Foltiny 1980: E 239. A good illustration is the Corinthian *pinax* in Newhall 1931: 22, showing Herakles fighting the Hydra (first half of 6th cent. BCE).

48 ξίφος ἔχειν <◡ ◡–◡– – >:   the scribe left the second half of this line blank, presumably because he could not decipher it in his exemplar. He also left the first half (after the initial Δ) of 60 blank, perhaps for the same reason; it was subsequently filled in by the corrector, **A²**. Desrousseaux's supplement <ἐλεφαντόκωπον> has been universally accepted; a sword with an ivory handle was not only a precious weapon and an indication of wealth (cf. Alkaios fr. 350.1–2 ἦλθες ἐκ περάτων γᾶς ἐλεφαντίναν | λάβαν τὼ ξίφεος χρυσοδέταν ἔχων), but, more importantly, it was the key element of the *gnorismata* which Aigeus had left with Aithra on his departure from Troizen, sword and sandals, by which his son could later be recognized by his father on his arrival at Athens. It had to be a distinctive sword: *cum pater in capulo gladii cognouit eburno | signa sui generis* (Ovid, *Met.* 7.422–3) and *regale patriis asperum signis ebur* (Seneca, *Phaedra* 899). Particularly relevant is Longos, *Daphnis and Chloe* 1.2 and 4.21 where the *gnorismata* of Daphnis are described; they are a purple cloak (χλαμύδιον ἁλουργές), a brooch of beaten gold (πόρπη χρυσήλατος), and a small sword with ivory handle (ξιφίδιον ἐλεφαντόκωπον) – these attributes, none of which suit their rustic environment in Longos, may have been borrowed from a description of Theseus on his way to Athens.

49 δύ(ο) . . . ἄκοντας: Homer's fighters usually carry two spears (*Il.* 3.18, 10.76, 11.43, 16.139 etc., also Jason in Pindar, *P.* 4.79). In many tombs from Mycenaean times to the seventh century, two spears of equal size, sometimes three, have been found, cf. Snodgrass, *Early Greek armour and weapons* 136–9 and *Arms and armour of the Greeks* 57–8.

50 κηΰτυκτον κυνέαν: in *Il.* 3.336, Paris puts on κυνέην εὔτυκτον, also Patroklos (16.137) and Teukros (15.480). In Homer, the κυνέη, 'properly a dog-skin cap, became a common term for the helmet, including metal ones, in general. It can be made of other skins (10.257f., 335) or of bronze', Kirk on *Il.* 3.336. Theseus, however, is never shown wearing a helmet; on some vases he is wearing a traveller's hat, a πέτασος, which is sometimes called a κυνέη; in Soph., *OC* 313–14, Ismene is wearing a broad-brimmed sun-hat which is referred to as κυνῆ Θεσσαλίς, and the scholion on Ar. *Birds* 1203 says that in the Peloponnese a πέτασος was called κυνέα, quoting a line from Soph. *Inachos*, fr. 272. So it seems that in some parts of Greece, at least, a κυνῆ was, if specified by Θεσσαλίς, or, as here, Λάκαινα, a traveller's hat, although a 'Laconian' hat is not otherwise attested (B. may have chosen this epithet not to designate a particular type of hat, but as an allusion to Kimon's son Lakedaimonios, see Introduction, pp. 190–1).

51 κρατὸς πέρι: the papyrus has ὙΠΕΡ, against the metre, which may have been a gloss that replaced ΠΕΡΙ. While Demosthenes uses περί and ὑπέρ indiscriminately (see the examples collected in K-G 1 548 § 450), in hellenistic Greek ὑπέρ increasingly replaced περί in a local sense (see Schwyzer 11 503), so that someone may have felt the need to clarify this unfamiliar use of περί.

πυρσοχαίτου: no other source gives Theseus auburn hair. Although Pasiphae, in Euripides' *Cretans* (fr.7.14–15 Cozzoli), includes red hair in her description of an attractive man, many writers express a strong prejudice against it, cf. [Arist.] *Phgn.* 812a16 οἱ ξανθοὶ εὔψυχοι· ἀναφέρεται ἐπὶ τοὺς λέοντας· οἱ πυρροὶ ἄγαν πανοῦργοι· ἀναφέρεται ἐπὶ τὰς ἀλώπεκας, also Aelian, *NA.* 15.14.12. Foreigners are often described as red-haired, especially those who live in cold and damp climates, such as Illyrians, Dalmatians, Germans, Sauromatai and Skythians, says Galen, *De temperam.* 2.5 (1618 K.), cf. [Arist.] *Problemata* 38.2 (966b32), and Xenophanes says the same of the Thracians, fr. 18 G.-P. If Barron is right in suspecting that Theseus' physical description in this stanza alludes to the three sons of Kimon (see above, p. 190), this feature may also be part of it, as their paternal grandmother, Hegesipyle, was the daughter of a Thracian chieftain, but we do not know whether her son or her three grandsons had red hair. Plutarch says only that Kimon had plenty of 'woolly' hair, οὔλῃ καὶ πολλῇ τριχὶ κομῶν τὴν κεφαλήν (*Kim.* 5.3).

52–3 χιτῶνα πορφύρεον: purple was the royal colour *par excellence*; moreover, a purple garment (χλαῖνα) revealed Telemachos as Odysseus' son to Menelaos (*Od.* 4.115 and 154), as it indicated Odysseus' rank (*Od.* 19.225, 250). The *gnorismata* left with the young shepherd, Daphnis, include a purple cloak (χλαμύδιον ἁλουργές), which Longos may have borrowed from a description of Theseus, see on 48 (πορφύρεον may, however, be suspect, see the next note).

χιτῶνα πορφύρεον στέρνοις τ' ἀμφί: τε in fourth position is unparalleled. To remove this anomaly, Platt (1898: 63) suggested στέρνοις τε πορφύρεον | χιτῶν' ἀμφί, but (a) that transposition would make 53 begin with a short syllable (the three corresponding lines 8, 23, and 38, all begin with a long syllable), and (b) it would remove ἀμφί much too far away from στέρνοις. A different solution was suggested by W. S. Barrett (in an unpublished note, see Maehler, *Lieder* II 236) who suspects that B. wrote τ' ἀργύφεον, which was then corrupted to τ' ἀργυρέον, and that 'someone faced with the absurdity of a silver χιτών was moved (not thinking of the rare ἀργύφεον) to make a deliberate change of ταργυρεον to πορφυρεον, and to transfer the τε that was thus abolished to the one place where metre would now admit it'. ἀργύφεος 'white-shining' is said of clothing (*Od.* 5.230 = 10.543, the φᾶρος of Kalypso and Kirke; Hes. *Th.* 574, Pandora's dress), or more generally 'white': a sheepskin (*h.Dem.* 196, cf. Aphrodite's στήθεα ἀργύφεα in *h. Hom.* 6.10), or 'bright', of the Nereids' marine cave (*Il.* 18.50).

53–4 οὔλιον Θεσσαλὰν χλαμύδ(α):   οὔλιος usually means 'destructive' (= οὐλόμενος), but here it must be 'woollen' (= οὐλάν), like Odysseus' purple cloak (*Od.* 19.225). The word also occurs as a cult name of Apollo and Artemis: Theseus was said to have prayed to Ἀπόλλωνι Οὐλίωι and Ἀρτέμιδι Οὐλίαι before his departure for Crete (Pherekydes, *FGrHist* 3 F 149). Οὔλιος is attested as a personal name of one of the ancestors of the elder Miltiades (Pherekydes, *FGrHist* 3 F 2) and of one of the three sons of Kimon, see p. 190.

χλαμύδ(α): a Thessalian χλαμύς was a horseman's short cloak (Pollux 10.164 and 7.46), and as such became the hallmark of an ephebe in military training, cf. Arist., *Ath. Pol.* 42.4 (quoted on p. 190); Philemon fr.34 (*PCG* VII p.245) ἐγὼ γὰρ ἐς τὴν χλαμύδα κατεθέμην ποτέ | καὶ τὸν πέτασον, Antidotos fr.2 (*PCG* II p.309) πρὶν ἐγγραφῆναι καὶ λαβεῖν τὸ χλαμύδιον. Theseus, the young hero on his way to Athens, is thus portrayed as the quintessential Athenian ephebe. In Heliodoros' *Aithiopika* (1.10.1), the Athenian Knemon tells of Demainete's passionate outburst when she saw him dressed as ephebe, with χλαμύς and garland: embracing him, she cried out ὁ νέος Ἱππόλυτος, ὁ Θησεὺς ὁ ἐμός!

55–6 Λαμνίαν . . . φλόγα: 'Lemnian fire' appears in writers from the fifth century onwards, cf. Soph. *Phil.* 986–7 ὦ Λημνία χθὼν καὶ τὸ παγκρατὲς σέλας | ἡφαιστότευκτον and 800–1 τῶι Λημνίωι τῶιδ' ἀνακαλουμένωι πυρὶ | ἔμπρησον, also Ar. *Lys.* 299 and Lykophron, *Alex.* 227, where the scholion, quoting Hellanikos (*FGrHist* 4 F 71b), explains that it was Lemnos where Hephaistos had his workshop and arms manufacture (II p.104 Scheer), and Antimachos (fr. 46 Wyss) places the 'fire of Hephaistos' on the summit of Mount Mosychlos on Lemnos, which he may have thought of as a volcano. Although ever since Homer's time Lemnos had been linked with Hephaistos (*Il.* 1.593–4, *Od.* 8.283–4, see Nilsson, *Griech. Religion* I 497; Farnell, *Cults* v 374–95; Burkert, *Greek religion* 167), the island never had a volcano; on the origins of the fire ritual on Lemnos, see Burkert 1970: 1–16. B.'s phrase ὀμμάτων . . . στίλβειν ἄπο . . . φλόγα reflects the proverbial Λήμνιον βλέπειν 'with fierce look', cf. Hesych. λ 873; *CPG* II 122 and 505; βλέπειν πῦρ Menander, *Misoum.* 321.

57 πρώθηβον: Homer has πρωθήβης (*Il.* 8.518, *Od.* 8.263, *h.Ap.* 450), fem. πρωθήβη (*Od.* 1.431). Theseus was only sixteen when he set out from Troizen, according to Pausanias (1.27.8); on the early red-figure 'cycle' vases he always appears unbearded. As well as being consistent with his description as an Athenian ephebe, it also makes his exploits all the more remarkable.

ἀρηΐων δ' ἀθυρμάτων   'war-like pastimes', like 'war and the brazen din of battle' (58–9). Heroes have their aggressive ambitions in their genes, which manifest themselves in their early youth; Achilles, from the age of six, παῖς ἐὼν ἄθυρε μεγάλα ἔργα with his spear, hunting lions and boars (Pindar, *N.* 3.43–8), and his keen interest in weapons gave him away among the daughters of Lykomedes (*Kypria* fr.19, *PEG* p. 56).

60 φιλαγλάους Ἀθάνας: the last line echoes the first. It has a triple function: (1) It rounds the ode off by returning to its point of departure; Athens is splendour-loving (B. uses this epithet also in 13.229 and 24.13; Pindar gives it to Akragas in *P.*12.1, and also speaks of Athens' 'splendid market-place' in his dithyramb, fr.75) as the Athenians live in luxury (see on 2 ἀβροβίων Ἰώνων). The 'bronze-din of battle' (59) matches the 'bronze-belled trumpet' (3–4), μεμνᾶσθαι πολέμου recalls πολεμηΐαν ἀοιδάν (4). These thematic correspondences, in reverse order, create a kind of symmetrical frame. (2) It finally reveals *why* the king is so alarmed: after 57–9, 'he is aiming for splendour-loving Athens' must mean 'he is coming to sack the city'; this is the culmination of the ironic divergence between the king's worried ignorance and the audience's knowledge that the anonymous hero is Aigeus' own son who will be happily reunited with his father moments later, vindicating the chorus' optimism. (3) It caps the hero's description in the last stanza, which moves from 'external' features (his two companions, the sword, two spears, his hat and dress) to 'internal' ones (his fierce determination, as revealed by his eyes; his thoughts of war-games, and his intention to head for Athens). This could have been the perfect moment for a group of Athenian ephebes, dressed and equipped like Theseus, to appear in the theatre – Merkelbach's scenario (see above, pp. 189–90) may not be altogether fanciful.

ODE 19 = DITHYRAMB 5

1. Performance

The title in the papyrus, Ιω Αθηναιοις, indicates that this dithyramb was composed for an Athenian festival (ὀλβίαις Ἀθάναις 10), and as its narrative culminates in the birth of Dionysos, there can be little doubt that this festival was that of Dionysos, i.e. the Great Dionysia. Among the extant dithyrambs of Bacchylides, this is the only one that tells a story directly linked to Dionysos. About its date, nothing can be said with certainty; there are, however, indications in the way the myth is presented that suggest a date of composition not later than about 460 BCE, see below, 2 (a) on Io.

2. The myth

(a) Io, Hermes and Argos   Hermes' commonest epithet in Homer is ἀργεϊφόντης, which some ancient commentators explained as 'the one who slew Argos' (ὥς τινες κατ᾽ ἐπωνυμίαν, schol. A on *Il.* 2.103), while others rejected this etymology and explained the epithet as ἀεργοφόντης in the sense of 'one who does not carry out murders' because they thought of Hermes as a peaceful god (ὁ ἀργὸς φόνου καὶ καθαρός . . . ἢ καταργοῦντα τοὺς φόνους· εἰρηνικὸς γὰρ ὁ θεός, Apoll. Soph. 42.10–11; cf. schol. bT and D on *Il.* 2.103). Homer, they argue, did not know the story of Io, as the episode of Argos was invented by later poets (τὸν γὰρ Ἰοῦς ἔρωτα οὐκ οἶδεν ὁ ποιητής· πέπλασται δὲ παρὰ τοῖς νεωτέροις τὰ περὶ τὸν Ἄργον). The first of the 'later' poets was supposed to be 'Hesiod', i.e. the *Catalogue of Women* (fr.124), where Io is a daughter of Peiren (on her genealogy, see West, *The Hesiodic Catalogue* 76–7), while according to Apollodoros (2.1.3) many of the tragedians made her a daughter of the Argive river-god Inachos. Apollodoros adds that she was a priestess of Hera at Argos and that Zeus, having seduced her, tried to protect her from Hera's jealousy by turning her into a white cow and swearing an oath that he had not touched her.

The claim that this kind of oath, a ὅρκος ἀφροδίσιος, does not attract the anger of the gods (or, as Plato says, ἀφροδίσιον γὰρ ὅρκον οὔ φασιν εἶναι, *Symp.* 183b), is here attributed to 'Hesiod' and linked to the story of Zeus and Io; given that Apollod. 2.1.3 refers to Hesiod and Akusilaos, it seems likely that this section of his account is based on Akusilaos (*FGrHist* 2 F 26) and, through him, on the *Catalogue of Women*.

Hera demanded the cow from Zeus and appointed Argos 'the all-seer' (πανόπτην) as her guardian; he tied the cow to an olive-tree in the sacred grove of Mycene. Zeus then sent Hermes to steal the cow, but in vain, as his intention was revealed (this motif recalls *Il.* 24.24 where the gods urge Hermes to steal Hektor's body from Achilles, a suggestion which is rejected by Zeus as impossible because Thetis is with her son day and night, *Il.* 24.71–3). Unable to act secretly, Hermes confronts Argos and kills him with a stone, whereupon Hera sends the gadfly which chases and tortures the bovine Io all the way from Argos through Asia and Phoenicia to Egypt.

The moment before the killing of Argos is illustrated on a beautiful black-figured north-Ionian amphora from Vulci, dated around 530 BCE (Munich 585; Appendix no. 31). In the centre, a palm tree suggests a grove, in front of which a cow stands facing left. Behind her sits the ugly giant Argos; on his chest, close to his left shoulder, a third eye is visible, and so we may assume a fourth one on the righthand side as well, see Steinhart, *Das Motiv des Auges* 121 and pl.46. In his right hand he is holding the rope which is tied around the cow's horns; one end of it is wound around his body, while Hermes who is approaching from the left (running, or on tip-toes?) with winged boots and a *pilos* but unarmed, grabs the other end with his left hand. In front of him stands a dog, with its head turned back towards him. The bearded giant's mouth is wide open, he is shouting something, perhaps he has just noticed Hermes. The painter has chosen the moment of the most intense tension: Argos is just about to jump to his feet, and Hermes will grab the stone (his right hand is already reaching out) that will kill the giant.

A slightly different scene appears on an amphora in London which is stylistically close to Exekias and may be roughly contemporary with the first one (Brit. Mus. 1848.6–19.4; Appendix no. 32). Argos, with two faces like Janus, is crouching on the ground, supporting himself with his right hand, raising his left hand as if in defence or begging for mercy. Hermes, attacking him from the right, has grabbed his elbow with his right hand and is about to strike him with the sword in his raised left hand. The right-hand half of the scene is taken up by the large cow facing right; behind her is Hera moving to the left and raising both arms as if begging for Argos' life.

Here, Argos' two faces, back and front, seem to be the painter's interpretation of his description in the *Aigimios*, [Hes.] fr. 294 = schol. Eur. *Phoen.* 1116:

> καί οἱ ἐπὶ σκοπὸν Ἄργον ἵει (sc. Hera) κρατερόν τε μέγαν τε,
> τέτρασιν ὀφθαλμοῖσιν ὁρώμενον ἔνθα καὶ ἔνθα,
> ἀκάματον δέ οἱ ὦρσε θεὰ μένος, οὐδέ οἱ ὕπνος
> πῖπτεν ἐπὶ βλεφάροις, φυλακὴν δ' ἔχεν ἔμπεδον αἰεί·

how else could he have rendered the phrase 'watching with four eyes here and there'? Other sources give him a third eye on his neck and make him sleepless (Pherekydes, *FGrHist* 3 F 66), others imagine him as having eyes all over his body in accordance with his epithet πανόπτης 'all-seeing'. The earliest evidence for this is a *pelike* (jug) in Paris (Louvre G 229, *ARV²* 289.3; Appendix no. 33, with inscription ΠΑΝΟΠ[); its date is 470–460, about contemporary with the earliest literary reference, Aesch. *Supp.* 304; so also Eur. *Phoen.* 1115 and Ar. *Eccl.* 80. The story continues to be popular with Attic vase painters throughout the fifth century; most of them can be found in Yalouris, *Le mythe d'Io* 3–23 and in *LIMC* v 665–9. They all show Hermes attacking the giant with a sword.

The representation of Io, however, undergoes a very interesting change. On the early vases, such as the black-figured amphora in Munich (above p. 206), she appears as a cow, sometimes even as a bull, e.g. on a red-figured *stamnos* in Vienna (Kunsthist. Museum IV 3729; *ARV²* 288.1; Appendix no. 34). Pausanias saw her on the 'Throne of Amyklai': 'Hera is looking towards Io who is already a cow' (3.18.13); this was a work of Bathykles of Magnesia, dated to the second half of the sixth century.

However, at some point between 460 and 450 her appearance changed from bovine to human: first, it seems, on an Attic *pelike* in Naples (Mus. Naz., ex Spinelli 2041; *ARV²* 1122; Appendix no. 35) and on a *skyphos* in Palermo (Fondazione Mormino 178; *ARV²* 1689; Appendix no. 36); on both these vases, which are dated *c.* 460–450, she appears in human form but with cow's ears and horns, and this is how she is consistently rendered by vase painters from the middle of the fifth century onwards. The only exception seems to be a Lucanian jug in Boston of *c.* 440–430 (MFA 1901.562; Appendix no. 37): a cow with a girl's head and a cow's horns, a belated south-Italian variation.

This sudden change in her iconography is likely to have been inspired by poetry, more precisely by a public performance at Athens of a dithyramb or a drama. As far as we can see, Io appears on stage for the first time (in human shape but with bovine horns) in Aeschylus' *Prometheus Bound*, where she is addressed by the chorus as 'cow-horned maiden' (βουκέρως παρθένος 588), and Prometheus refers to her as κόρη (589 and 739) and νεᾶνις (704); she herself refers to her cow's horns (κεραστὶς δ᾽, ὡς ὁρᾶτ᾽, 674). This innovation is all the more remarkable, as Aeschylus' *Suppliants*, performed in 463, presented the traditional version (291–315), where Io is thought of as a cow, having been transformed by Hera (299); but here Io is merely described, and does not appear on stage. The crucial innovation in the *Prometheus Bound* is reflected in the Attic vases from at least the middle of the fifth century onwards. It therefore seems likely that this play was performed after 463, the date of the *Suppliants*, but not long after 460. As B. clearly sees Io as a cow, his dithyramb almost certainly antedates the *Prometheus* and the Attic vases where Io appears in human form. It is not possible to establish a more precise date for Ode 19.

There is, however, an interesting detail in this ode which also appears in the *Prometheus*. In lines 35–6, the Muses are mentioned, apparently in connection with Argos' death. What they did may be inferred from Ovid (*Met.* 1.682–8) and Valerius Flaccus (4.381–90) who both say that Hermes tried to send Argos to sleep by playing a flute or pan-pipes (pan-pipes also played a role in Sophocles' *Inachos*, fr. 269c), and this feature seems to be implied also in Io's frenzied vision in Aesch. *Prom.* 566–75: she sees the dead giant coming towards her and driving her along the sea-shore, and she hears 'a wax-made reed(-pipe) drone its soporific melody' (ὑπὸ δὲ κηρόπλαστος ὀτοβεῖ δόναξ | ἀχέτας ὑπνοδόταν νόμον, 574–5). This must be Hermes' pan-pipe (*syrinx*) 'with which he put Argos to sleep before killing him' (Griffith on Aesch. *Prom.* 574; this had already been suggested by Galiart, *Beiträge zur Mythologie* 142 n.2). In both B. and Aeschylus the allusion to 'music' is so brief that the audience could hardly have gathered what it referred to, unless they knew this part of the story already.

(b) Epaphos   In this ode, B. gives in a very summary form the genealogy of Dionysos, covering four generations in as many lines. Io was pregnant when she arrived in Egypt. Her son Epaphos became king of Egypt, his daughter Libye (who was apparently not mentioned by B.) became the mother of

Agenor and Belos, Agenor was the father of Kadmos and grandfather of Semele, the mother of Dionysos. Belos' son Danaos returned to Argos with his fifty daughters who will be, as Prometheus announces to Io, 'the fifth generation from him' (ἀπ' αὐτοῦ = Epaphos, counting inclusively, Aesch. *Prom.* 853).

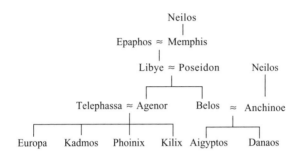

This genealogy agrees with that in Aesch. *Suppl.* 291–324, and with Apollodoros (2.1.4 and 3.1.1).

3. Metre

Although the strophe is essentially dactyloepitritic, i.e. a combination of *hemiepes* (– ⏑ ⏑ – ⏑ ⏑ –) and *creticus* (– ⏑ –), usually in pairs connected by a short 'link'-syllable (– ⏑ – ⏑ – ⏑ –), these verses have three unusual features: (a) all their 'link'-syllables are short (*brevia*, not the usual *ancipitia*), and (b) the paired cretic appears four times in a shortened form, leaving out the last *breve*, so that the rhythm slows down at the end, giving the verse the character of a *clausula* (verses 4, 7, 10, and 16); moreover (c), in the last part of the strophe the rhythm seems to assume an 'aeolic' character, as verses 15, 17 and 18 all start like *glyconics*: (⏓)⏓– ⏑ ⏑ – ⏑ – . . .

Verses of an 'aeolic' character can also be seen in the epode: 2, 10, 11, 12 (?), 14 (?), 15, where, however, the loss of nearly all the verse-ends makes detailed analysis impossible. At any rate, the subtle change in the rhythm

towards the end of the strophe seems to continue into the epode in a kind
of 'sliding transition'.

The metrical, or rather rhythmical, innovations may have corresponded
to musical innovations. Unfortunately, very little is known about the musical
aspect of fifth-century lyric poetry, so that further speculation would be fruit-
less. It does, however, seem plausible that B. was fully aware of moving into
uncharted territory, as far as metre and music were concerned; the opening
lines of the ode, as well as the exhortation ὕφαινε νῦν . . . τι καινόν (8–9)
strongly suggest this, as Snell (*Bacchylides* pp. XXXI–XXXII) has pointed out.

1–2 Πάρεστι . . . μελέων: 'there are countless paths of immortal songs'
for him who has received the 'gifts of the Muses' (3–4), i.e. a talent for creating poetry. This is different from the seemingly quite similar phrases used by
Pindar in his victory odes, e.g. in *I.* 3/4.19 ἔστι μοι θεῶν ἕκατι μυρία παντᾶι
κέλευθος . . . ὕμνωι διώκειν, *I.* 6.22–3 μυρίαι δ᾽ ἔργων καλῶν . . . κέλευθοι, *N.*
6.45–6 πλατεῖαι πάντοθεν λογίοισιν ἐντὶ πρόσοδοι νᾶσον εὐκλέα τάνδε
κοσμεῖν, *I.* 2.33–4 οὐ γὰρ πάγος, οὐδὲ προσάντης ἁ κέλευθος γίνεται, εἴ
τις εὐδόξων ἐς ἀνδρῶν ἄγοι τιμὰς Ἑλικωνιάδων and by Bacchylides himself in 5.31–3 and 195–7: these, as Bundy has seen (II 61–4), are all variations
on the theme of 'ease in praise' where it is the victory which makes it 'easy'
for the poet to praise the victor (see on 5.31). In 19.1–4, by contrast, it is
not an event that opens up the paths of song but an innate ability which
poets have traditionally felt to be beyond their own rational control and
therefore due to a divine agent, the Muses, and the paths of song which
it opens for them are paths of narrative imagination, or different ways of
telling a myth. Both the 'path' metaphor (κέλευθος 1 ≈ ὁδόν 13), the verb
λαχεῖν (3–4 ≈ 13–14), and the 'gift' metaphor (δῶρα 4 ≈ γέρας 14) recur at
the end of the introductory section, thus rounding it off neatly. In between
comes the invitation to the poet to invent ('weave', ὕφαινε 8) 'something
new' (τι καινόν) for 'much-loved, blessed Athens' (9–10).

    ἀμβροσίων μελέων: Hesiod speaks of the Muses' 'immortal song'
(they go to Mount Olympos ἀμβροσίηι μολπῆι, *Th.* 69), Theognis 18 of
their 'immortal mouth'; the idea that the song itself, the poet's creation, can
achieve immortality does not seem to occur before Pindar (*P.* 4.299 παγὰν
ἀμβροσίων ἐπέων, cf. *I.* 3/4.58 τοῦτο γὰρ ἀθάνατον φωνᾶεν ἕρπει, εἴ τις
εὖ εἴπηι τι 'if someone praises something') and B. who calls his victory ode
'an undying ornament of the Muses' (ἀθάνατον Μουσᾶν ἄγαλμα 10.11)
and their 'sweet gift' (γλυκύδωρον ἄγαλμα 5.4).

3–4 ὃς ἂν . . . λάχησι: the papyrus has λαχηισι, but the correct Doric ending of the aorist subjunctive is –ησι, see Schwyzer 1 661c. The verb implies that a poet may be 'awarded' the Muses' or the Graces' gift, cf. B.1.151 εὖ δὲ λαχὼν Χαρίτων and *PMG* 1001 κεῖνον . . . ἰοπλοκάμων Μοισᾶν εὖ λαχεῖν. Hesiod was the first Greek poet who defined the relationship between the poet and the Muses as one of beneficiary and benefactors, and poetic talent as their 'holy gift for men' (ἱερὴ δόσις ἀνθρώποισιν, *Th.* 93) whom they 'honour' and 'love' (*Th.* 81 and 97), and this idea was repeated in many variations by later poets from Archilochos (fr. 1.2) and Alkman (*PMG* 59b = 149 Calame) onwards.

5–7 ἰοβλέφαροι . . . βάλωσιν: 'the violet-eyed maidens, the garland-bearing Graces' etc. is still part of the conditional relative clause beginning with ὃς ἂν (3), from which one has to supply 'for whom' (ὧι ἂν). Examples of sentences with different subjects, joined by τε, are not uncommon in Homer, e.g. *Il.* 15.680–3, cf. Ruijgh, *TE épique* § 637; K-G II 242; Schwyzer II 574; Pindaric examples have been collected by Braswell on *P.* 4.222c who rightly observes that 'a single τε is used to join a clause or sentence which explains or indicates a consequence of what has just been mentioned'. His observation applies here, too: 'whoever has been awarded the Muses' gifts, and <so> the Graces bestow honour on his songs'. As their name suggests, they give 'grace' (χάρις), the pleasing form which delights the audience. This is why they 'bring garlands' (φερεστέφανοι 6): the formal beauty of the ode, the elegance of its diction, style, and structure, will win a prize in the competition of dithyrambs. But they do not *inspire* the song – that is the Muses' prerogative. The distinction is kept up fairly consistently in early poetry and in Pindar, see Verdenius, *Commentaries* I 103–6. Pindar, *O.*1.30–1 clearly relates Χάρις to the formal aspect of poetry, not to its content: Χάρις δ', ἅπερ ἅπαντα τεύχει τὰ μείλιχα θνατοῖς, ἐπιφέροισα τιμὰν (sc. to the words, μύθοις) καὶ ἄπιστον ἐμήσατο πιστὸν ἔμμεναι – even what is unlikely or unbelievable (like Pindar's version of the Pelops myth which he is about to tell) can convince people through the elegance of its form.

8 ὕφαινέ νυν: the enclitic νυν is found only here in B., but frequently in Pindar. On the etymology which links ὕμνος with ὑφαίνειν see on 5.9–10. The *asyndeton* makes it clear that the imperative, addressed by the chorus to the poet (see below on 11), results from the preceding sentence: 'The gifted poet has many ways of telling a story – *so* weave now something new . . .' It also serves a formal purpose in that it links the two halves of the introductory section together, of which 1–8 is a general statement, which is then (from the asyndetic ὕφαινε 8 to 14) applied to the present celebration.

8–10 ἐν ταῖς πολυηράτοις . . . ὀλβίαις Ἀθάναις: both epithets seem to have been regular components in praises of Athens, cf. Solon 4.21; Ar. *Clouds* 299–301; Pindar, fr.76. The tragedians, in particular, flatter their audiences with praise of Athens' wealth and splendour: Eur. *Med.* 824–32, *Tro.* 803, *IT* 1130–1, *Alc.* 452 λιπαραῖσί τ' ἐν ὀλβίαις Ἀθάναις, Soph. *OC* 707–19; see also on 18.2.

καινόν: this was the original reading of the papyrus, which the corrector, **A**³, changed to κλεινον. This is surely wrong, because τι κλεινόν 'something famous' could only mean, proleptically, 'something that is to become famous', which would hardly make sense here, whereas τι καινόν 'something novel' would appear to have been announced in the opening line. What B. means by this is likely to relate to some formal aspect of this ode, perhaps its metre, see above, pp. 209–10;. Like B. here, Pindar often emphasizes that he is offering something new, see *N.* 8.20–1; *O.* 3.4–6; *O.* 9.49; *I.* 5.62–3; cf. the parody in the *parabasis* of Aristophanes' *Wasps* 1051–6.

11 εὐαίνετε Κηΐα μέριμνα 'renowned Kean mind'. As Kuiper (1928: 57) has pointed out, the audience must have understood this as an address to the poet by the chorus, who pay him a nice compliment: he is 'well-praised' (on εὐαίνετος, see Braswell on Pind. *P.* 4.177(a) εὐαίνητος Ὀρφεύς). Ultimately it is, of course, a self-address by the poet, the 'nightingale of Keos' (3.97–8n.). In B. and Pindar, μέριμνα is a thought which is focussed on an objective, or 'purposeful planning', see 11.85–6n.

12–14 πρέπει σε . . . γέρας: *asyndeton* again (see on 8), this time capping the whole introductory section and echoing its opening lines. The general statement 'whoever has received the Muses' gifts' in the conditional relative clause (3–8) is here applied to specific persons: Μουσᾶν (4) is answered by Καλλιόπας (13), ὅς ἂν . . . λάχῃσι (3) by Κηΐα μέριμνα (11), the poet himself. The point at which the focus switches from the general to the specific is the mention of Athens (9–10). The city where this dithyramb is being performed thus becomes the recipient of praise, rather like the victor in a victory ode. The superlative φερτάταν . . . ὁδόν, as well as ἔξοχον γέρας, suggests that the poet (Κηΐα μέριμνα), having been granted (λαχοῖσαν, cf. Alkaios 309) an 'outstanding gift' by the Muse, is about to produce a superb poem.

14 γέρας: not 'the glorious theme (Io)', as Jebb thought, but the gift of poetry (δῶρα Μουσᾶν 4).

15 †τιην†:   ΤΙΗΝ in the papyrus could be interpreted as (a) τί ἦν … ὅθ(ε) 'how was it when …', or (b) 'what was Io when she …', or (c) τί; ἦν … ὅθ(ε) 'what? It happened that …' Both (a) and (b) would be a question extending to κόρα (18), answered from 19 onwards; (c) is unlikely because isolated interrogative τί, while not uncommon in prose, is not found in poetry, and ἦν ὅτε 'once upon a time' is not separated, except sometimes by a particle (ἦν δὲ ὅτε Xen. *Hell.* 4.7.6). (b) is unlikely because the interrogative τί and its subject (βοῦς 16 and κόρα 18) would be too far apart, and the question 'what was she …?' would already have been answered by βοῦς. With (a), 15–18 would become another question addressed by the chorus to the poet, like τίς πρῶτος … in 15.47; this is possible, although it would be colloquial and prosaic: cf. Herodas 5.10 τί ἐστι; *Mime* fr. 7.28 and 66 τί γέγονεν; (pp.49–51 Cunningham); Kall. *Epigr.* 13.3 ὦ Χαρίδα, τί τὰ νέρθε; "πολὺς σκότος." αἱ δ’ ἄνοδοι τί; Plato, *Phd.* 58a τί οὖν ἦν τοῦτο; *Symp.* 213b τουτὶ τί ἦν; The main objection is the metre, which requires – ◡ , responding to Ἄργον 33 (this is the only case in this ode where strophe and antistrophe do not correspond). Conjecture, therefore, seems to be required to restore metre and sense, taking into account that the papyrus punctuates after γέρας (14). Kenyon's ἦν ποτ’ (with <τ>ότ’ in 19) deserves consideration: ' "there was a time when …", an abrupt beginning of which B. is quite capable' (Kenyon 187), which would be paralleled by Pindar, fr. 83 ἦν ὅτε σύας Βοιώτιον ἔθνος ἔνεπον, although ἦν χρόνος is more common in poetry: ἦν χρόνος ὅτ’ ἦν ἄτακτος ἀνθρώπων βίος Kritias, *TrGF* 1 43 F 19.1, ἦν χρόνος ἅνικ’ ἐγώ … Theokr. 7.1. Alternatively, one could think of the affirmative ἦ, which often begins a sentence in B. (5.9; 9.36; 13.54 ἦ ποτέ φαμι κτλ., referring to the future; 18.41) and Pindar (*O*.1.28; *P*.1.47; *N*.8.24): 'Indeed, once, when the golden heifer …', see below on 16.

15–16 λιποῦσα φεῦγε: 'having left Argos, she was in flight' – from whom? In Aesch. *Prom.* 663–72, Io reports how her father Inachos had received oracles telling him to push her out of his house and the land (ἔξω δόμων τε καὶ πάτρας ὠθεῖν ἐμέ 665), against his will, forced by Zeus (ἐπη- νάγκαζέ νιν | Διὸς χαλῖνος πρὸς βίαν πράσσειν τάδε, 671–2). She then runs to the meadows of Lerna, where her encounter with Zeus takes place (this is suggested by lines 649–54: Io's dreams, and the oracle given to her father, send her to a place where Zeus can meet her), even though the watchful giant Argos was guarding her πυκνοῖς ὄσσοις δεδορκώς (678–9) – he is here imagined as he appears on many fifth-century vases, with eyes all over his body (see p. 207). She then alludes very briefly to his death (ἀπροσδόκητως δ'αἰφνίδιος αὐτὸν μόρος | τοῦ ζῆν ἀπεστέρησεν, 690–1), as if she had not witnessed the killing, or as if she were too distraught to tell the details.

This sequence of events is assumed also in B. who adds that it was Hera who instructed Argos to watch Io (19–25); he also gives a more detailed account of how Argos was killed (see below on 29–36).

χρυσέα βοῦς: the cow is white on some of the vases and in Apollod. 2.1.3. In poetry, 'golden' is sometimes said of gods (Nika in Pindar, *I.* 2.26; Kypris in B. 5.174; Artemis in B. 11.117), more often of what belongs to gods, such as Poseidon's horses in Pindar, *O.* 1.41, or comes from the gods, such as the 'cargo-ship of songs' in B.16.2. Gold neither rusts nor rots, hence its significance as a symbol of eternity. This explains phrases like B.10.40 (the wise man) ἐλπίδι χρυσέαι τέθαλεν 'blossoms in golden hope' because he hopes to win immortal fame, and Pindar, *O.*11.13 ἐπὶ στεφάνωι χρυσέας ἐλαίας 'on account of the golden olive wreath' which was the victor's prize at Olympia, which will immortalize his victory (see Verdenius, *Commentaries* II 135 on *I.* 2.26). Here, the 'golden' cow may mean that she has become a divine possession, as Zeus had to hand her over to Hera (Apollod. 2.1.3).

17 εὐρυσθενέος . . . Διός: in Homer, this is Poseidon's epithet (*Il.* 7.455; *Od.* 20.140). B. uses several compounds beginning with εὐρυ–, cf. 3.6n. See also on 18 below.

φραδαῖσι 'instructions', cf. φράζειν 'to show the way', 'to advise'. These are the dreams and oracles through which Zeus forced Inachos to drive his daughter out of Argos, for as long as she was a priestess in the precinct of Hera, Zeus could not have approached her without being noticed by Hera. In Ovid, *Met.* 1.597, Jupiter plunges the region into darkness to stop Io's flight (*caligine terras | occuluit tenuitque fugam rapuitque pudorem*, 599–600).

18 ῥοδοδάκτυλος κόρα: with cruel irony, B. gives this epithet to the unfortunate girl whose 'rosy fingers' have just been turned into hard hooves. The sharp contrast between 'wide-powered Zeus' and the 'rose-fingered' girl maximizes the emotional potential of this scene.

19–20 <τ>ότ':   with Kenyon's correction of OT in the papyrus, the structure is clear: while Io was 'in flight' (φεῦγε), Hera 'instructed' (κέλευσεν) Argos to guard her; this means that 15–25 are one long sentence which the two correlative temporal adverbs divide into two unequal halves. Maas (*Resp.* II 30) explains the difficulty with the text as transmitted: ὅτ(ε) . . .

κέλευσεν could not possibly pick up the first ὅτε (15 ὅθ' . . . φεῦγε) because of the difference in the tenses of the verbs.

ὄμμασι . . . ἀκαμάτοις: as πάντοθεν suggests, B. imagines Argos as having eyes all over his body, as he is shown on many vases, in accordance also with Aeschylus, *Supp.* 304 (πανόπτης) and *Prom.* 568 (μυριωπός) and 678–9 (πυκνοῖς ὄσσοις δεδορκώς).

23 ἄκοιτον ἄϋπνον: asyndetic pairs of epithets, usually with alliteration, are found in poetry from Homer onwards, cf. *Il.* 1.99 ἀπριάτην ἀνάποινον, *Od.* 15.406 εὔβοτος εὔμηλος, Soph. *Ant.* 339 Γᾶν ἄφθιτον ἀκαμάταν, also in triplets: *Il.* 9.63 ἀφρήτωρ ἀθέμιστος ἀνέστιος, and without alliteration: Ibykos, *PMG* 287.1 ἐρεμνὸς ἀθαμβής, although the combination of asyndeton with alliteration was apparently felt to be particularly powerful. This is essentially a rhetorical device (a means to focus the audience's attention), even though it was not used particularly frequently in Attic oratory; examples include Dem. 4.36 ἐν δὲ τοῖς περὶ τοῦ πολέμου καὶ τῆι τούτου παρασκευῆι ἄτακτα ἀδιόρθωτα ἀόρισθ' ἅπαντα, also 25.52 ἄσπειστος ἀνίδρυτος ἄμεικτος, Xen. *Cyr.* 7.5.53 ἄσιτος καὶ ἄποτος, see also Richardson on *h.Dem.* 200. Pindar and B. use this device much more sparingly than Homer and the tragedians do; Pindar calls Hektor Τροίας ἄμαχον ἀστραβῆ κίονα *O.* 2.82, B. (?) has ἀκρίτοις ἀλ[άστοις] ὑπὸ πένθεσιν fr. 60.10–11.

24 καλλικέραν δάμαλιν: the 'lovely-horned heifer'; B. imagines her as a cow, as does Aesch. *Supp.* 299–314. It was her appearance on stage in *Prom.* 561–886 that changed her iconography; see pp. 207–8.

25–7 οὐδὲ Μαίας υἱὸς δύνατ' . . . λαθεῖν νιν: this implies that Hermes had been commissioned by Zeus to steal the cow; it was only when he discovered that this was impossible that he killed Argos (Apollod. 2.1.3 and schol. *A* on *Il.* 2.103). B. seems to imply that all his eyes were always awake; the idea that half of them sleep while the other half stay awake is first found in Eur. *Phoen.* 1116–17, where a figure of Argos ('Panoptes') on the shield of Hippomedon is described.

29–36 εἴτ' οὖν . . . ἤ . . . :   for this kind of disjunctive 'whether . . . or . . .' (εἴτε . . . ἤ) cf. Eur. *IT* 272–3 εἴτ' οὖν' ἐπ' ἀκταῖς θάσσετον Διοσκόρω | ἢ Νηρέως ἀγάλμαθ'. By offering alternative speculative explanations of Argos' death, the dithyrambic chorus in B. seems to adopt the attitude of ignorance often displayed by choruses in tragedy: cf. Eur. *Hipp.* 141–60 (speculation about the possible causes of Phaidra's suffering), Soph. *Aias*

172–81 (about the possible causes of Aias' madness), *OT* 1098–1109 (about who Oedipus' parents might be).

29–31 εἴτ' οὖν γένετ' . . . ἀγγελο[ν Διὸς] κτανεῖν 'whether it came about that . . . Zeus' messenger killed'; this construction, impersonal γίνεται with acc. + inf., is rare in poetry; cf. Archil. 118; Aesch. *Ag.* 34–5 γένοιτο . . . χέρα . . . βαστάσαι and the anonymous trimeter, possibly from Euripides' *Meleagros*, *TrGF* II 188 ὦ Ζεῦ, γένοιτο καταβαλεῖν τὸν σῦν ἐμέ. It is quite common in hellenistic and later prose, e.g. in the New Testament (Luke 3.21 ἐγένετο ἀνεωιχθῆναι τὸν οὐρανόν, also 6.1 and 16.22; Mark 2.33; Acts 4.5, etc.).

ἐ[⏑–⏑–⏑: Jebb assumed a contrast between 'by an open attack' and 'by assault on the sleeping Argos', and accordingly suggested ἐ[ν μάχας ἀγῶνι or ἐ[ς χέρας μολόντα (but the latter, at least, would hardly be compatible with λ[ίθωι 32). Equally possible might be an indication of the locality: ἐ[ν βοῶν νομαῖσι ? It happened 'on the grassy meadows of Lerna' where Inachos kept his herds and where the dream had ordered Io to go: ἔξελθε πρὸς Λέρνης βαθὺν | λειμῶνα, ποίμνας βουστάσεις τε πρὸς πατρός, Aesch. *Prom.* 652–3.

31–2 [Γᾶς . . .] ὀβριμοσπόρου 'Earth of mighty offspring' (the compound is found only here). Aeschylus calls Argos παῖδα Γῆς (*Supp.* 305) and γηγενῆ (*Prom.* 677), following Akusilaos (*FGrHist* II F 27, quoted in Apollod. 2.1.3).

λ[ίθωι: the question is not whether Hermes killed him but *how* he killed him, therefore κτανεῖν (31) needs to be specified; λ[ίθωι is supported not only by Apollod. 2.1.3 (= schol. A on *Il.* 2.103) λίθωι βαλὼν ἀπέκτεινε τὸν ᾿Αργον, but also by the black-figure amphora in Munich (above, p. 206) which shows Hermes approaching unarmed, trying to steal the cow and reaching out (for a stone) in case the giant discovers him.

33–4 ἤ ῥα καὶ ϙ[: Jebb preferred ἤ ῥα because he took this to be another alternative, 'or whether Argos was exhausted by his anxieties'. This cannot be right because (a) μέριμναι are here not 'anxieties' (see below on 34–5), and (b) the papyrus has ΗΡΑ: the circumflex makes it clear that the affirmative ἦ is meant, which often begins a phrase or a sentence in B. and Pindar (see above on 15); ἦ + ῥα (= ἄρα) is very frequent in Homer (*Il.* 3.183; 4.82, etc.).

ἦ ῥα . . . μέριμγ[αι: with ἦ ῥα, this must be an emphatic statement, the subject of which is μέριμναι. μέριμνα is 'planning', or 'thought directed towards a purpose', see on 11.85–6. This meaning is illustrated, e.g., by

Empedokles 11.1 νήπιοι, οὐ γάρ σφιν δολιχόφρονές εἰσι μέριμναι 'fools: their thoughts do not go far', and Aristophanes' *Clouds* 1404 where Pheidippides says 'Having been trained by Socrates', γνώμαις δὲ λεπταῖς καὶ λόγοις ξύνειμι καὶ μερίμναις 'I am familiar with subtle ideas and arguments and thoughts', cf. also B. 5.7. It follows that μέριμναι here cannot be those of Argos, for he had κάδεα (36), he had to 'care' (κήδεσθαι) for the cow; they must be the 'thoughts' or 'plans' of Hermes, or the gods in general, whose 'designs' are 'inscrutable'. Along these lines, one could try something like ἦ ῥα καὶ ϙ[ἰκτρὰ θεῶν τελοῦσιν] ἄσπετοι μέριμν[αι, 'indeed, pitiable things the gods' inscrutable designs achieve', a comment on the preceding sentence.

35–6 ἢ Πιερίδες . . . ἀνάπαυσ[ιν – ◡ ⏓ :   the alternative to εἴτ' οὖν (29). Ovid, *Met.* 1.682–721 tells how Hermes eventually succeeded, by playing his pan-pipes and telling a long-winded story, to put all of Argos' eyes to sleep (cf. also Valerius Flaccus 4.381–90). This may be based on Soph. *Inachos*, fr. 269c.4, where Hermes' pan-pipes (σύριγγες) seem to have played a role. The Muses (Πιερίδες) provide music, or a story, or both, which sends Argos to sleep (as Ovid says); see above, p. 208. If this is meant by κάδεων ἀνάπαυσ[ιν, Argos' 'rest' was deadly, and something like αἰμύλωι μέλει is needed in 35 to indicate how the Muses achieved (φύτευ[σαν 'planted', 'engendered') his fatal repose: ἀνάπαυ[σιν ἐσχάταν would bring out the grim irony.

37–8 ἐμοὶ . . . ἀσφαλέστατον ἀπρϙ [(or ἀπρε[):   ἀσφαλέστατον makes it almost inevitable to supply an infinitive at the end of the verse. Then ἁ in ἀπρε[might be neut.pl., i.e. the object of that infinitive: ἃ πρέ[πει λέγειν would refer back to the end of the introductory section. There the chorus told the poet to take the right route (12–13 πρέπει σε φερτάταν ἴμεν ὁδόν), here the poet says 'whatever the way in which Argos was killed, for me, at any rate (μὲν οὖν), it is safest to say the appropriate things', thus paving the way for the rapid account of Io's descendants from Epaphos to Dionysos. It could certainly be said to be 'appropriate': B.19 is, in fact, the only one of B.'s extant dithyrambs to show a direct connection with Dionysos.

39–40 παρ' ἀνθεμώ[δεα] Νεῖλον: Io, pregnant and tormented by the gadfly sent by Hera after the killing of Argos, gives birth to Epaphos on the 'flowery' bank of the Nile. On the significance of flowers in erotic contexts see on 16.34.

40–1 ο[ἰστροπλάξ: cf. Aesch. *Prom.* 681 οἰστροπλὴξ δ' ἐγὼ μάστιγι θείαι, 589 τῆς οἰστροδινήτου κόρης, *Supp.* 17 τῆς οἰστροδόνου βοός and

573 οἰστροδόνητον ’Ιώ. In 41 Jebb supplied γαστρὶ τὸν Διός because (a) φέρουσα παῖδ[α alone would not make it clear that the child was still unborn when she arrived in Egypt, and (b) it had to be said that Zeus was the father. For γαστρί, Jebb quoted Il. 6.58–9 μηδ’ ὅντινα γαστέρι μήτηρ . . . φέροι and Plato, Laws 792e τὰς φερούσας ἐν γαστρί. Another possibility would be παῖδ’[ὑποκόλπιον Διός], cf. Kall. H. 4.86.

42–4 As the metre of the epode cannot be established, there is no point in proposing exact supplements; something like ἔνθα νι[ν τέκ’ Ἀἰγυπτίων . . . πρύτ[ανιν will not be too far from what B. wrote.

43 λινοστόλων 'linen-robed'; from at least the time of Herodotos (2.37 and 81), Greek authors saw linen clothing as a typical feature of Egyptian life. The hellenistic Isis hymn of Andros (IG xii 5.739, republished with commentary by Peek, Isis-Hymnus) calls Isis Αἰγύπτου βασίλεια λινόστολε, cf. AP 6.231 λινόπεπλε δαῖμον, and Plutarch (De Iside 4 = Mor. 352c–e) explains that Egyptian priests shave all their body hair off because they consider all hair an impure excretion of the body, so they refuse to wear woollen clothes, accepting only linen ones because linen, i.e. flax, grows from the 'immortal earth' and makes light and pure garments. Cf. Pliny, HN. 19.14 Aegyptio lino minimum firmitatis, plurimum lucri . . . uestes inde sacerdotibus Aegypti gratissimae and Juvenal 6.533 grege linigero.

44 ὑπερόχωι βρύοντ[α τιμᾶι 'basking in outstanding honour'. βρύειν is frequent in B. (3.15–16; 6.9; 13.179; 29g.1); it also occurs in Simonides (PMG 519 fr. 77.5) and Likymnios (PMG 770a) but not in Pindar.

45 μεγίσταν τε θνατ[. . . : Jebb's supplement θνατ[ῶν ἔφανεν γενέθλαν would refer to the offspring of Epaphos' daughter Libye, i.e. Belos and Agenor, cf. Aesch. Supp. 317–9 and Apollod. 2.1.4. Bacchylides seems to have disregarded Libye; Agenor appears only in the patronymic to Kadmos (46), which takes him very rapidly to Semele and the birth of Dionysos.

49 ὀρσιβάκχα[ν: found nowhere else, as are other compounds of this type (ὀρσίμαχος 15.3, ὀρσίαλος 16.19). Jebb quotes the anonymous verses εὔιον ὀρσιγύναικα μαινομέναις Διόνυσον ἀνθέοντα τιμαῖς PMG 1003, which Plutarch quotes three times (Mor. 389b, 607bc, 671c).

50–1 Dionysos is 'Lord of splendid festivals' (or 'competitions') 'and garland-wearing choirs', with supplements by Jurenka (ἀγλαῶν τε κώμων) and Wilamowitz (στεφαν[αφόρων ἄνακτα); West (1993: 237) suggested ἀγλαῶν ἀγώνων. At the end of this dithyramb the narrative converges with the reality of the performance, the Dionysiac festival.

ODE 20 = DITHYRAMB 6

1. Performance

The title Ἴδας Λακεδαιμονίοις, preserved in the papyrus, implies that this ode must have contained some clear indication that it was performed at Sparta, or at any rate in Laconia. As it begins with a reference to 'such a song' (τοιόνδε μέλος 3) as was 'once' (ποτε) sung by Spartan maidens at the wedding of Idas and Marpessa, it seems likely that it was performed by a girls' chorus; cf. Theokr. 18 (with Hunter, *Theocritus* 151). Choirs of girls are associated with festivals of Artemis, e.g. of Orthia at Sparta (on which see Calame, *Les chœurs de jeunes filles* 1 276–97) which was connected with the story of the abduction of Helen, either by Theseus and Peirithoos when she was dancing (χορεύουσαν) at the sanctuary of Artemis, or by Idas and Lynkeus, as Plutarch (*Thes.* 31) reports, quoting Hellanikos (*FGrHist* 323a F 18; the abduction of Helen by Theseus and Peirithoos was also represented on the 'Throne of Amyklai' which Pausanias describes, 3.18.15). There were other sanctuaries and festivals of Artemis in Spartan territory where choruses of Spartan girls played a part. On the border between Laconia and Messenia, on the west side of the Taygetos mountain ridge, was a sanctuary of Artemis Limnatis where Spartan girls were said to have been abducted by the Messenians (Paus. 4.4.2). Pausanias tells two versions of this story, a Spartan one which has the girls raped by the Messenians (which led to the first Messenian war, according to Strabo 8.4.9), and a Messenian one which claimed that the 'girls' were in fact young (beardless) Spartans disguised as girls and armed with daggers; they had been smuggled into a reunion of Messenian nobles whom they were to murder, but they were discovered and killed (see also Calame, *Les chœurs* 1 253–64).

A similar abduction story was connected with the annual festival of Artemis Karyatis at Karyai in the mountains north of Sparta which divide Laconia from Arcadia, where Spartan girls danced and performed choral songs (Paus. 3.10.7). During one of these festivals Aristomenes, the Messenian freedom fighter during the decade 500–490 BCE, ambushed the Spartan girls who had been dancing there, and took away the daughters of the wealthiest and most respected Spartans (Paus. 4.16.9). As the myth of Idas, Euenos and Marpessa which B. tells in this ode was a similar abduction story, it may well have been composed to be performed by a Spartan girls' chorus at one of these festivals of Artemis. The evidence for Spartan cult dances has been collected and discussed by Constantinidou 1998.

2. The myth.

(a) Idas, Euenos and Marpessa Marpessa, daughter of Euenos and
Demonike or Demodike (Apollod. 1.7.7–8), or Euenos and Alkippe, daughter of Oinomaos, according to [Plut.] *Parallela minora* 40a (*Mor.* 315e), was
guarded by her father at Ortygia near Chalkis in Aetolia (on the gulf of
Kalydon, opposite Patras); he challenged her suitors to a chariot race,
defeated them all and nailed their skulls to the front of his house (schol.B^b
on *Il.* 9.557). This motif, an obvious parallel to the story of Oinomaos, his
daughter Hippodameia and Pelops, is explicitly attested for B. by schol.
Pind. *I.*4.92a Βακχυλίδης δὲ Εὔηνον ἐπὶ τῶν Μαρπήσσης μνηστήρων (sc.
τοῦτο ποιεῖν ἱστορεῖ) – presumably in this ode, not in fr. 20A. The scholia
to Pindar seem to have had no older evidence for this story.

Idas, however, a son of Aphareus, came on a chariot with extremely
swift horses, which he had received from his divine father Poseidon,
and – without taking part in the murderous race against Euenos – abducted
Marpessa when she was dancing at a festival celebrating Artemis (χορεύουσαν ἐν Ἀρτέμιδος schol. B^b on *Il.* 9.557; ἐκ χοροῦ [Plut.] *Mor.*315e). From
Chalkis he drove west towards Pleuron, crossing the river Lykormas with
his winged horses (Apollod. 1.7.8 speaks of his ἅρμα ὑπόπτερον). The pur-
suing Euenos, unable to cross, slaughtered his horses and threw himself
into the river, which was then named after him.

(b) Idas and Apollo After driving westwards to Pleuron, Idas and Marpessa
must have somehow turned east or south-east again and crossed the gulf of
Kalydon, because they then reached Arene in Triphylia or Messenia. This
strange detour seems to suggest that at this point two different versions
may have been linked together which originally had nothing to do with
each other, i.e. an Aetolian one (the Euenos story, with the abduction of
Marpessa), and a Messenian one (Idas and Lynkeus) which was later trans-
ferred to Sparta (Ἴδας . . . Λακεδαιμόνιος δὲ τὸ γένος, schol. BT on *Il.*9.557).
In Messenia, Apollo confronts Idas and tries to take Marpessa from him;
when Idas boldly raises his bow against the god, Zeus intervenes: he sends
Hermes with the instruction to let the girl herself choose; she chose Idas,
for fear that Apollo would abandon her once she had grown old.

This part of the Idas-Marpessa story was told by Simonides (*PMG* 563).
It seems likely that its most dramatic episode, the confrontation between
Idas and Apollo, was also told by B.: it was told by Homer, *Il.* 9.558–60,

and it was depicted on the 'Chest of Kypselos', according to Pausanias, who quotes two hexameters, 5.18.2; it appears on several Attic red-figure vases, such as a *psykter* in Munich dated *c*.480–470 (Munich 2417, Appendix no. 38), on a *stamnos* divided between Paris and Florence dated *c*.470–450 (Appendix no. 39), and an amphora in London of c. 450 BCE (BM 95.10–31.1; Appendix no. 40). These vases may reflect an Athenian performance of Simonides' poem.

1 Σπάρται . . . ἐν ἐ[ὐρυχόρωι: the supplement is based on *Od.* 13.414; 15.1; Pindar, *N.* 10.52; *AP* 7.301.2 (Simonides); Hdt. 7.120.4 etc.

2–3 ξανθαὶ Λακεδα[ιμονίων] | τοιόνδε μέλος κ[ελάδησαν παρθένοι] ?
Alternatively, one could try ξανθαὶ Λακεδα[ιμονίων κλεινῶν θύγατρες] | τοιόνδε μέλος κ[ελάδησαν, but if lines 1–3 respond, as seems likely, with 9–11, the first option may be preferable. For Spartan girls, blonde hair seems to have been particularly desirable, as Alkman refers to it three times (*PMG* 1.101; 3.9; 59b.3); they 'once sang such a song at Sparta', when Idas brought (ἄγετο) Marpessa as his bride. This would have been a wedding song, and B. seems to follow here a pattern established for wedding songs or *hymenaioi*, as the similarity with the wedding song of Basileia and Peise-tairos in Aristophanes' *Birds* 1731–42 and with the beginning of Theokritos' Ἑλένης ἐπιθαλάμιος (18) indicates. This does not necessarily mean that B.20 is itself a wedding song; rather, it may be a case like B.16, which begins with a reference to paeans sung by a Delphic chorus, although the ode as a whole seems to be a dithyramb.

6 Μάρπησσαν ἰότ[ριχα νύμφαν?   The compound, 'violet-haired', ought to begin with digamma (ϝ), but B. apparently ignored it here since the last syllable of Μάρπησσαν is not lengthened. ϝ is also disregarded in δόσαν ἰόπλοκοι 17.37 (˘ ˘ ˘ – ˘ –), but wrongly assumed in εἵλετο ἰόν (= ϝιόν) in 5.75: B. was evidently unsure about its etymologically correct use.

7–8 φυγὼν . . . Ποσ⟨ε⟩ι[δάν: with Poseidon as a new subject we would have two subjects and therefore either (a) two main clauses, e.g. τέλος· τῶι γὰρ ὄπασσεν (or πόρεν), or τὸν γὰρ φύλαξεν, or (b) a conjunction like εὖτε, ὅτε, ἐπεί: after the almost inevitable τ[έλος, any word beginning with vowel and a long syllable would fit easily into a dactylo-epitritic verse, so one could try, *exempli gratia*:

φυγὼν θανάτου τ[έλος εὖθ᾽ ὑπόπτερον
ἀναξίαλος Ποσ⟨ε⟩ι[δὰν ἅρμ᾽ ὄπασσεν κτλ.

There is, however, a difficulty in the restoration Ποσ<ε>ι[δάν. The sequence ⏑ – ⏑ ⏑ – ⏑ – – cannot easily be fitted into dactylo-epitrites, which would normally require ⏑ ⏑ – after ⏑ – ⏑ ⏑ –. Although ποσι[as transmitted in the papyrus, seems to be the start of the god's name, it is always Ποσει-δάων, Attic Ποσειδῶν, Doric Ποσειδάν, Ποτειδάν, Ποhοιδᾶν etc., never Ποσῖδάν. A possible solution is that line 8 could be the last verse of the strophe: it might be a kind of 'clausula' ending in ⏑ – – (instead of ⏑ ⏑ –), like the last line of the strophe in Ibykos, *PMG* 282 (⏑ – ⏑ ⏑ – ⏑ – –). On this assumption one could perhaps suggest

> φυγὼν θανάτου τ[έλος, ἄρμ' ἐπεὶ πόρεν   ⏑ – ⏑ ⏑ – ⏑ ⏑ – ⏑ – ⏑ – |
> ἀναξίαλος Ποσ<ε>ι[δάν.   ⏑ – ⏑ ⏑ – ⏑ – – |||

9–10 ἵππους . . . ἐΰκτ[ιμέναν, perhaps followed by σεύοντι· τὸν δέ 'and wind-swift horses, as he was speeding towards Pleuron, the well-built city. But him . . .'

11 χρυσάσπιδος υἰὸ[ν Ἄρηος: the 'one with golden shield' can, in this context, only be Ares, the father of Euenos. What followed was probably, if Euenos was in the accusative, something like 'frustration [or rage] seized [Euenos] when he saw . . .' etc.

FRAGMENTS

FRAGMENTS 22 + 4 = PAIAN FOR ASINE

1. Text and performance

Parts of this paean are quoted in anthologies: Athen. 5.5 p.178b (= fr. 22), Plut. *Numa* 20.6 and Stob. 4.14.3 Βακχυλίδου παιάνων (= fr. 4); the first ten lines of the passage in Stobaios overlap the last ten lines of P. Oxy. 426 (pap. **T**), as Snell (1932) saw. The lines quoted by Athenaios were identified as the first five lines of an epode by Barrett (1954) who established the metrical pattern as a triad of ten + ten + ten lines. His interpretation has greatly enhanced the understanding of this interesting ode, the only one of Bacchylides' paeans of which substantial parts survive. Barrett saw that the ninth line of the papyrus (]φαcινειc) must be]φ' Ἀcινεῖς (= now line 47), and that these 'people of Asine' in the Argolid must be the mythical Dryopes who had been settled there by Herakles at Apollo's request, as Pausanias tells us (4.34.9); see Strid, *Dryoper*.

The sanctuary at Asine, *c.*8 km south-east of Nauplia, was that of Apollo Pythaieus, of which Pausanias saw the ruins (2.36.4–5); he mentions that the town of Asine had been destroyed and its population resettled in Messenia on the gulf of Kalamata by the Argives in the eighth century, but that the temple had been spared. Archaeological evidence (see Frödin & Persson, *Asine*) 'suggests that after the destruction of Asine the sanctuary of Apollo Pythaieus continued in use as a centre of Apolline worship in the neighbourhood, embracing at any rate the towns of Argos and Epidauros. If therefore our ode appears on internal evidence to have been performed there in the first half of the fifth century BCE, we have no reason to doubt that in fact it was; and the ode will in fact become a further piece of evidence for the continuance of the cult' (Barrett 1954: 429).

Papyrus **T** preserves, on the back of a documentary text, 32 lines with part of the upper margin. If, as seems likely, it contained only this paean (not the whole book of paeans), the first line of the verso, which is the ninth verse of a strophe, may have been preceded either by one column of 38 lines, or by two columns of 34 lines each. On the first assumption, 13 lines would be lost between fr. 22 (= lines 21–5) and the first line of the papyrus text (= line 39); alternatively, the gap would be 43 lines long. The assumption of a shorter gap seems more probable because it would not take more than 13 lines to tell how Herakles was received by Keyx, then defeated the Dryopes and brought them to Delphi as an 'offering' (ἀνάθημα) to Apollo, as Paus. 4.34.9 says (see below).

2. The myth

The Asinaians, Pausanias informs us (4.34.9), originally dwelt in the Parnassos region where they were known as Dryopes. Herakles defeated them in battle and took them to Delphi, but Apollo's oracle instructed him to lead them to the Peloponnese, where they settled at Asine in the Argolid, as well as at Hermione, Halieis and other places; 'it is a reasonable assumption that the whole coast from Asine to Hermione was Dryopian' (Barrett 1954: 427).

Different reasons are given for their fight with Herakles. Diodoros (4.37.1) makes Herakles punish them for an offence against the Delphic sanctuary, whereas both Apollod. 2.7.7 and the scholiast on Ap. Rhod. 1.1213 say that Herakles took from a Dryopian, Theiodamas, one of his two bulls and slaughtered it because he (or his little son, Hyllos) was hungry and could find nothing else to eat, whereupon Theiodamas led the Dryopes into battle against him (according to Apollodoros, Herakles does not fight the Dryopes immediately after his encounter with Theiodamas, but continues his journey to Trachis where he is received by Keyx). The Dryopes seem to have had a bad reputation as bandits, because Herakles was said to have removed the whole tribe 'because of their banditry' (διὰ τὴν λῃστείαν, schol. Ap. Rhod. 1.1213, cf. Pherekydes, FGrHist 3 F 19), and given that this instruction came from Apollo, one may suspect that their main occupation had been to rob travellers approaching Delphi by land, rather like the Krisaians did to those coming by sea in the Sacred War of c.590 BCE; see Barrett 1954: 440, who quotes the hypotheses a and b to Pindar's Pythians (schol. Pind. II pp.2–3 Drachm.).

This charge is likely to be an Argive fabrication (Barrett 1954: 440), which may have exploited the 'etymology' of their name, Ἀσινεῖς (= 'the innocuous ones'), which implies that prior to their transplantation, the Dryopes had caused much damage. B. may have referred to this interpretation of their name (see on 47). On the Dryopes in general and the historical and archaeological evidence, see Strid, Dryoper.

3. The praise of peace

The pacification of the aggressive Dryopes and their transformation into 'harmless' Ἀσινεῖς leads to one of the most remarkable passages in B., his wonderful hymn to Peace, which – as far as we can see – had no parallel in his time. It was not until the later fifth century that Euripides and Aristophanes praised the benefits of peace, no doubt as a reaction to the devastation and loss of life caused by the Peloponnesian War. Euripides praises Peace as βαθύπλουτος and καλλίστα μακάρων θεῶν in the *Kresphontes* (fr. 453.2, cf. *Or*.1682–3), an idea echoed in Aristophanes' *Georgoi* fr.111 (*PCG* III 2 p. 82); she 'enjoys wealth' (Eur. *Supp.* 491) and helps farmers to earn a living (Aristophanes frs. 111 and 402; Philemon fr. 74 = *PCG* VII p.264; Menander fr. 719 K. = 556 Koerte). Euripides also calls her ὀλβοδότειρα and κουροτρόφος (*Bacchae* 419–20: 'neither epithet needs explanation in our time', Dodds ad loc.). Peace is associated with song and festivity (Eur. *Kresphontes*, fr. 453.7–8), with the Muses (Μούσαισι προσφιλεστάτη, *Supp.* 489), and Opora ('Harvest') and Theoria ('Holiday') are her companions (Ar. *Peace* 520–6). Representations of Eirene in art do not appear before the end of the fifth century: see Shapiro, *Personifications* 45–50.

In early Greek poetry, peace is always seen as unity within the community or the *polis*; Demokritos says it succinctly: domestic discord is disastrous for both sides, winners and losers (στάσις ἐμφύλιος ἐς ἑκάτερα κακόν· καὶ γὰρ νικέουσι καὶ ἡσσωμένοις ὁμοίη φθορή, B 249; cf. Plato, *Laws* 628c, quoted below), but unity enables cities to carry out great things, including wars (ἀπὸ ὁμονοίης τὰ μεγάλα ἔργα καὶ ταῖς πόλεσι τοὺς πολέμους δυνατὸν κατεργάζεσθαι, ἄλλως δ'οὔ, B 250). Moreover, if peace reigns within, there will also be prosperity. At the end of the *Odyssey*, Zeus tells Athena (24.485–6) that the people of Ithaka should love one another, as before the killing of the suitors: 'there must be plenty of wealth and peace' (πλοῦτος δὲ καὶ εἰρήνη ἅλις ἔστω). Hesiod's Horai are born by Themis to Zeus: Eunomia, Dike, and 'blossoming Eirene' (Εἰρήνην τεθαλυῖαν, *Th.* 902) – Peace makes everything blossom, and in *Op.* 227–9 Hesiod says that where justice is respected, τοῖσι τέθηλε πόλις, λαοὶ δ' ἀνθεῦσιν ἐν αὐτῆι· | εἰρήνη δ' ἀνὰ γῆν κουροτρόφος, οὐδέ ποτ' αὐτοῖς | ἀργαλέον πόλεμον τεκμαίρεται εὐρύοπα Ζεύς, 'their city blossoms, and in it the people flourish; peace that nourishes young men is on the land, and far-seeing Zeus never assigns them woeful war', an idea which Pindar takes over from Hesiod: in Corinth dwell Eunomia, Dike and Eirene, τάμι' ἀνδράσι πλούτου

(*O.* 13.7). Theognis, too, stresses the link between peace and wealth: Εἰρήνη καὶ πλοῦτος ἔχοι πόλιν, ὄφρα μετ᾽ ἄλλων | κωμάζοιμι· κακοῦ δ᾽ οὐκ ἔραμαι πολέμου, 'may peace and plenty rule the town, so we can all | make merry. I've no love of cruel war' (885–6). Hesiod, Pindar, and Theognis explicitly refer to peace *in cities*, not to peace between city-states, or to peace in general.

Bacchylides, too, sees wealth and festivity as fruits of peace. What is so new and remarkable in his concept is his portrayal of peace as a universal blessing. For him, peace is not internal concord and unity in the city (which, as Demokritos B 250 says, does not exclude wars with other cities), but a desirable state of bliss, a boon for all. In addition to prosperity and festivity he mentions γυμνάσια, αὐλοί and κῶμοι as things that young people care for (67–8) while their weapons are rusting, covered in spiders' webs; they are allowed to enjoy their sleep in the mornings without being woken by the sound of trumpets, and the town is filled with feasting and love-songs.

What motivated B. to include this vision of the blessings of peace in his paean? We cannot tell whether this was in response to the audience's expectations and/or whether it had a special relevance to the situation in the Argolid at the time. Whatever prompted the poet to express this view here, it is consistent with other passages where peace is opposed to the horrors of war; cf., in particular, his wish that Hieron may continue to rule 'in peace' (5.200) and his account of the confrontation between Proitos and Akrisios (11.64–76) where the people (λαοί) beseech their leaders to avoid war, which is closely paralleled by the Trojans' reaction to the embassy of Odysseus and Menelaos (15.45–6 θεοῖς δ᾽ ἀνίσχοντες χέρας . . . εὔχοντο παύσασθαι δυᾶν). It therefore seems likely that these passages reflect the poet's personal conviction which overrides the needs of different genres of odes (victory odes, dithyrambs, paean).

In Bacchylides' time, this concept of universal peace has neither precedent nor parallel in contemporary literature. The Danaids' passionate prayer for peace in Aesch. *Supp.* 625–709 is different in that they pray for peace only for *their* city, Argos: 'and let no murderous havoc come upon this city to ravage it' (μηδέ τις ἀνδροκμὴς λοιγὸς ἐπελθέτω τάνδε πόλιν δαΐζων, 678–80). Herodotos, however, seems to echo B. in his account of the Kroisos story (1.87): rescued from the pyre, Kroisos blames the Delphic oracle for his misfortune, 'for nobody is so unreasonable as to prefer war to peace' (οὐδεὶς γὰρ οὕτω ἀνόητός ἐστι ὅστις πόλεμον πρὸ εἰρήνης αἱρέεται), for in peace the sons bury their fathers, but in war the fathers bury their sons. So for Herodotos, too, as for B., a state of peace between cities was a desirable ideal, and war its perversion (cf. Hdt. 8.3.1). This is a far cry from the traditional Greek view on war and peace, summed up in Plato's *Laws* in order to justify the need for 'guardians': πόλεμος ἀεὶ πᾶσιν διὰ βίου συνεχής ἐστι πρὸς ἀπάσας τὰς πόλεις (625e), so even in peace-time guardians are indispensable: 'for, as we would say, "peace", as the term is commonly employed, is nothing more than a name, the truth being that every state is, by a law of nature, engaged perpetually in an informal war with every other state' (ἣν γὰρ καλοῦσιν οἱ πλεῖστοι τῶν ἀνθρώπων εἰρήνην, τοῦτ᾽ εἶναι μόνον ὄνομα, τῶι δ᾽ ἔργωι πάσαις πρὸς πάσας τὰς πόλεις ἀεὶ πόλεμον ἀκήρυκτον κατὰ φύσιν εἶναι, 626a). The 'Athenian' does, however, conclude that war always harms both the victors and the vanquished, so one should pray for peace and restraint instead: 'the highest good, however, is neither war nor civil strife – which things we should pray rather to be saved from – but peace with one another and friendly feeling' (τό γε μὴν ἄριστον οὔτε ὁ πόλεμος οὔτε ἡ στάσις, ἀπευκτὸν δὲ τὸ δεηθῆναι τούτων, εἰρήνη δὲ πρὸς ἀλλήλους ἅμα καὶ φιλοφροσύνη (628c), so the law-giver should legislate on matters of war for the sake of peace, not the other way round: 'nor will he make a finished lawgiver unless he designs his war legislation for peace rather than his peace legislation for war' (γένοιτο . . . οὔτ᾽ ἂν νομοθέτης ἀκριβὴς εἰ μὴ χάριν εἰρήνης νομοθετοῖ μᾶλλον ἢ τῶν πολεμικῶν ἕνεκα τὰ τῆς εἰρήνης, 628d).

The view expressed here by Plato that the 'natural' state of the world is war remained almost unchallenged throughout the hellenistic age – praises of peace, like that in Apollodoros of Karystos (fr. 5, *PCG* II p.489), are lone voices. It is not until the time of Augustus that the ideal of universal peace reappears, as a powerful element of Augustus' political programme, the pacification of the Empire in the *pax Romana* which the Senate honoured in 13 BCE with the commission of the *Ara Pacis*. On war and peace in general, see Zampaglione, *The idea of peace in antiquity*; Sordi (ed.), *La pace nel mondo antico*.

21–5 These lines (= fr.22) are quoted in Athenaios (5.5.178b), who says that in B. they refer to Herakles ὡς ἦλθεν ἐπὶ τὸν τοῦ Κήυκος οἶκον. Apollod. 2.7.7 also mentions Herakles' visit to Keyx at Trachis; Herakles, he says, on his way through the land of the Dryopes met Theiodamas, and as he was in need of food, he slaughtered one of Theiodamas' two

bulls and ate it. But when he reached Trachis, he was entertained there
by Keyx and then defeated the Dryopes (ὑποδεχθεὶς ὑπ' αὐτοῦ Δρύοπας
κατεπολέμησεν), cf. also Diod. 4.36.5–37.1. This episode must precede the
events narrated in lines 39–60; it need not have taken up more than 13
lines, which is the minimum length of the gap indicated by the metre (i.e.,
lines 6–10 of an epode and lines 1–8 of the following strophe).

22 θοίνας 'meal', 'dinner party', often – as here – in the plural: Alkman
PMG 98 (= 129 Calame); Thgn. 239; Aesch. *Prom.* 530; in sing.: [Hes.] *Sc.*
114; Pind. fr. 70a.11; Aesch. fr. 350.7 (of Thetis' wedding). Homer uses only
the verb: θοινηθῆναι *Od.* 4.36.

ἔντυον: Homer has both ἐντυ- (*Il.* 5.720 ἔντυον ἵππους, *Od.* 23.289
ἔντυον εὐνήν) and ἐντῦν– (*Il.* 9.203 δέπας, *Od.* 3.33 ≈ 17.182 δαῖτ'ἐντυνό-
μεναι, 15.500 δεῖπνον, 16.2 ἄριστον). The original meaning seems to be 'to
provide with tools' (ἔντεα) = 'to equip', hence 'to prepare'; see Braswell on
Pind. *P.* 4.181d and van Groningen on Thgn. 196.

23–5 ‘'αὐτόματοι . . . φῶτες'': the proverb (Zenobius, *Cent.* 2.19 = *CPG* i
p.37) is quoted by Plato (*Symp.* 174b) who jokingly refers to *Il.* 2.404–8 (where
Agamemnon invites all the Achaean leaders to a meal, except for Menelaos
who comes uninvited, αὐτόματος), with a pun on the name of Agathon
to whose house Socrates and his friends are going uninvited. The motif of
'gate-crashing' guests or uninvited strangers is found already in Archilochos
(fr. 124) and Asios (*PEG* i p.129); it is also implied in Hermes' grim warning
to Prometheus (Aesch. *Prom.* 1021–5) that the eagle will lacerate his liver,
ἄκλητος ἕρπων δαιταλεύς (1024). It later becomes popular in comedy:
Kratinos fr. 182 (*PCG* iv p.214), Eupolis fr. 315 (*PCG* v p.480), Alexis fr. 241
(*PCG* ii p.156).

δαῖτας εὐόχθους 'plentiful meals'; the epithet is first found here, then
in Eur. *Ion* 1169, but εὐοχθεῖν occurs in Hes. *Op.* 477. The etymology is
unclear; there may be a connection with ὀχθεῖν 'to be laden', perhaps of
banquet-tables, cf. Chantraine, *Dictionnaire* i 386.

40 – ◡ – –]ει τελευτ[– : if]ει is the correct reading of the traces (see
Barrett 1954: 443), it is likely to be a verb-ending, perhaps a future rather
than a present, if it was part of a god's announcement or prophecy: e.g.
ὕβριος δείξ]ει τελευτ[άν (sc. Herakles).

41 – –]κ έλευσεν Φοῖβος: 6–7 letters are lost at the beginning. If the
preceding lines form part of a speech, possibly a prophecy by Apollo,
κέλευσεν preceded by a demonstrative pronoun as object may have served
as a *verbum dicendi* to indicate the end of a direct speech, analogous to the

epic ὡς φάτο etc.: ὡς τούς] κέλευσεν ? That would make it similar to Pind. *Pae.* 2.73–9 where a prophecy in direct speech (73–5) is followed by ἄγγελλε δὲ λόγον . . . Ἑκάτα (see Führer, *Reden* 63–5).

41–43 [Ἀλκμήνας] . . . ͘υ[ἰὸν στέλλεν] ἐκ ναοῦ: Barrett's supplements imply that Apollo's instruction, given in direct speech in the preceding stanza, is here summed up.

παρ[– ᵕ –: Παρ[νασσίδος or Παρ[νασσίας (sc. χώρας) 'the region of Parnassos' Barrett (1954: 430), who, however, doubts whether B. would have used either of these forms.

44–46 Herakles settles the Dryopes at Asine and marks their boundary by a twisted olive tree, as Pausanias 2.28.2 reports: 'Going up the road to Mount Koryphon [between Epidauros and Asine], there is on the way a tree of the so-called "twisted olive": it was Herakles who had turned it into this shape with his hand.' 'Pausanias gives no indication whether Herakles marked the frontier with an olive at one place or at more . . . ; ἐλαίας therefore may be either gen. sing. or acc. plur.', Barrett 1954: 430.

44 ἀλλ' ὃ γε τᾶ]ιδ' ἐνὶ χώρα<ι>? a pronoun in the nominative, referring to Herakles, is called for, because there can be little doubt that Herakles is the subject of στ]ρέψας in 46. τᾶ]ιδ' ἐνὶ χώρα<ι> 'here in this region' refers to Asine where this paean was being performed.

45 – ᵕ – – –]χῖσεν ταν φυλλο̇.[– : only eight, or at most nine, letters are lost at the beginning, which can hardly have accommodated five syllables; some corruption may have occurred here.]χισεν can only be (ἐ)τεί]χισεν or (ἐ)σ]χισεν: the former would not make sense here, as 'a series of twisted olives round a frontier is not a τεῖχος' Barrett 1954: 431; the latter may refer to 'splitting' the earth, i.e. digging up the ground (in order to plant an olive tree), as Aietes does in Pindar, *P.* 4.228, cf. also fr. 128f (of Kaineus); *N.* 9.24–5 (Zeus) σχίσσεν . . . χθόνα.

47–48 – ᵕ ᵕ –]φ' Ἀσινεῖς [– – ᵕ]λεͅσͅφ̇ ' (or]λε[ι]τ̇'): Herakles resettled 'the plundering Dryopes . . . so that, due to the large population, they might be prevented from committing crimes' (*Et. Gen.* s.v. Ἀσινεῖς; similarly schol. Ap. Rhod. 1.1212–19a), so that they became ἀσινεῖς 'harmless'. If B. here referred to the same etymology, one might try, e.g., ἠδ' ἐτέως σ]φ' Ἀσινεῖς [εὔντας κά]λεͅσͅφ̇ 'he (= Herakles) called them truly Ἀσινεῖς.' The only difficulty is that the accusative should be Ἀσινέας (or Ἀσινῆς), not Ἀσινεῖς which would be the normal acc. plur. in hellenistic and later Greek; it may have replaced an original Ἀσινέας (see Barrett 1954: 433).

49 –˘]ες ἐξ ἁλικων τε.[–˘––:   Ἁλικῶν, i.e. the people of Halieis (on the south coast of the Argolid), or ἁλίκων, i.e. 'groats of rice-wheat', of which some kind of sacrificial cake was made (Athen. 14.647d) ? The difficulty about Halieis is that it is about 30 km south-east of Asine, so how can Melampous come from there, if he set out ἐξ Ἄργευς (50) ?

50–3   The seer Melampous, son of Amythaon, comes from Argos and founds an altar and sanctuary of Apollo Pythaieus. This passage is the only evidence for his connection with Asine. On Melampous see *Od.* 15.225–42; [Hes.] fr. 37; Apollod. 1.9.11–12; Löffler, *Die Melampodie*; E. Simon, *LIMC* VI 405–10.

52 βω]μόν τε Πυθα<ι>εῖ κτίσε[–˘˘–:   for the spelling Πυθαιεύς see Barrett 1954: 434. At the end, perhaps μηλοθύταν (cf. B. 8.17), or κτίσε[ν ἀκρότατον, as the site of the sanctuary is on the top of a hill called Varvouna.

54–6 'From that root sprang this precinct, and Apollo gave it honour passing great' Barrett 1954: 435. For the metaphor 'root' ≈ 'foundation' cf. Pind. *P.* 4.14–16. Apollo honoured Melampous' foundation, making it grow into the sanctuary where this paean is now being performed, τόδε χρ[ησμωιδὸν αὔξων] . . . [ἄλσο]ς.

58–60   The metre of the last three verses of the epode cannot be completely established. For 58–9 Barrett suggested τᾶν αἴμ]ονες, ὦ ἄνα, Τρο[ζηνίων σε κοῦροι κλείζον]τι, 'expert in these (sc. songs, μολπᾶν), o Lord, the youths of Troizen praise you', but other supplements can be thought of (νῦν εὔφρ]ονες . . . τέ[ρπονται πολῖται ?).

60 (.) . . . . . .].ϙιοισιν[may be – ˘ –]. αι οιcῐν[– . . . or (–) – ˘ –]. αι οι σῐν[˘ – , see Barrett 1954: 438. One would expect this line to have formed a transition from Apollo the giver of wealth to the blessings of peace. The transition from 60 (epode B) to 61 (strophe Γ) appears to be abrupt; Maas (1932: 471 = *Kl.Schr.* 35) compares Pindar's *Paean* 6, where the transition from the end of the second triad with the mythical narrative about Neoptolemos (108–20) to the beginning of the third (address to Aegina, 123) is similarly abrupt. But, as lines 58–60 cannot be confidently restored, the transition may have been less abrupt than it seems.

61–70   Snell's combination of the last ten lines of pap. **T** with the first nine lines of fr. 4, preserved in Stob. 4.14.3, has helped to correct the latter in a number of places and has confirmed several conjectures (see the app. crit.). Above all, the papyrus shows the ancient colometry, which enabled Maas to establish the responsion (Maas 1932).

61 τίκτει 'creates'; for the metaphor cf. 10.46 τὸ μέλλον δ' ἀκρίτους τίκτει τελευτάς, Solon 6.3 τίκτει γὰρ κόρος ὕβριν (cf. Thgn. 153); Thgn. 392 (poverty) τίκτει ἀμηχανίην. The use of genealogical metaphors, such as Pindar's ὕβριν, κόρου ματέρα (*O.* 13.10) or χρόνος ὁ πάντων πατήρ (*O.* 2.17, cf. πλούτου μητέρα . . . Δήμητρα *PMG* 885, πειθαρχία . . . εὐπραξίας μήτηρ Aesch. *Sept.* 224–5) is as old as Homer's μητέρα μήλων ('producing sheep', *Il.* 2.696; 11.222 etc.). On genealogies of abstractions see West, *Hesiod: Theogony* pp. 33–4.

62 μεγαλάνορα πλοῦτον: the idea that wealth 'makes a man great' is shared by Pindar, cf. *O.* 1.2 μεγάνορος . . . πλούτου and *P.* 5.1–4 Ὁ πλοῦτος εὐρυσθενής, | ὅταν τις . . . | βροτήσιος ἀνὴρ πότμου παραδόντος αὐτὸν ἀνάγηι | πολύφιλον ἐπέταν, 'wealth has wide strength, when . . . a mortal man receives it from destiny and takes it as a companion which brings many friends'. Conversely, Pindar says that discord (στάσις) is 'a giver of poverty, a hostile nurse' (πενίας δότειραν, ἐχθρὰν κουροτρόφον, fr. 109) and that 'war is something sweet for the inexperienced, but the one who is experienced dreads it exceedingly in his heart when it comes' (γλυκὺ δὲ πόλεμος ἀπείροισιν, ἐμπείρων δέ τις ταρβεῖ προσιόντα νιν καρδίαι περισσῶς, fr. 110 from the same dancing song). The link between peace and wealth is often emphasized in poetry, cf. *Od.* 24.486 (quoted above, p. 231), *PMG* 1021 ὦ γλυκεῖ Εἰράνα, πλουτοδότειρα βροτοῖς, and Eur. fr. 453.1 Εἰρήνα βαθύπλουτε.

63 ἀοιδᾶν ἄνθεα: for the metaphor, see on 16.8–9. The link between peace and poetry or song is also emphasized by Euripides, cf. *Supp.* 491 Εἰρήνη . . . Μούσαισι προσφιλεστάτη and fr. 453 (from the *Kresphontes*) where the chorus praise Peace as offering καλλιχόρους ἀοιδὰς φιλοστεφά-νους τε κώμους, 'songs with lovely choirs and garland-loving revels'.

64–8 The main verb, τίκτει (61), governs not only the direct objects (πλοῦτον and ἄνθεα) but also the consecutive infinitives αἴθεσθαι and μέλειν, 'Peace achieves . . . wealth and the bloom of songs, and that offerings burn on altars and that the young care for sport, music and revels.' This kind of 'zeugma' (which 'yokes' together nouns or adjectives and infini-tives) has many parallels in Homer, e.g. *Il.* 7.203 δὸς νίκην Αἴαντι . . . εὖχος ἀρέσθαι, *Od.* 3.370 ἵππους, οἵ τοι ἐλαφρότατοι θείειν καὶ κάρτος ἄρισ-τοι, also in tragedy: Soph. *OC* 607–8 μόνοις οὐ γίγνεται | θεοῖσι γῆρας οὐδὲ κατθανεῖν ποτε. Examples illustrating the various uses of consecutive infinitives (after transitive and intransitive verbs, after nouns, after adjectives etc.) can be found in Schwyzer II 362–6 and in K–G II 2–17; for Homer see Chantraine, *GH* II 301–4 who distinguishes consecutive, determinative, and complementary infinitives.

65 ξανθᾶι φλογί   'in yellow flame', as in 3.56 ξανθὰ[ν φλόγα], a bold usage, not paralleled in poetry.

66 εὐμάλλων τε μήλων: the papyrus has]λωντε[, Stobaios transmits μηρίταν εὐτρίχων in SM (μηρῦταν εὐτρόχων A). It seems that in the text of Stobaios' anthology, the original εὐμάλλων had been replaced by a gloss, εὐτρίχων. The metre favours μηρί' εὐμάλλων (– ⏑ – – –), as B. tends to avoid | – ⏑ – ⏑ – . . . in dactyloepitrites; see Barrett 1956: 250. This compound is found only here and in Pindar, *I.* 5.62 (εὔμαλλον μίτραν); similar compounds are the Homeric πηγεσίμαλλος (*Il.* 3.197) and δασύμαλλος (*Od.* 9.425, both said of a ram, 'thick-fleeced'), and βαθύμαλλος (Pindar, *P.* 4.161, of Phrixos' ram).

67–8 γυμνασίων τε . . . μέλειν: both athletics and music are integral elements of Greek festivals from Homer's Phaiacians onwards; the Ionians celebrate Apollo's festival on Delos πυγμαχίηι τε καὶ ὀρχηθμῶι καὶ ἀοιδῆι (*h.Ap.* 149), and for Plato the best education (παιδεία) is still the time-honoured and traditional one, ἡ μὲν ἐπὶ σώμασι γυμναστική, ἡ δ' ἐπὶ ψυχῆι μουσική (*Rep.* 376e). Significantly, it was with athletic and musical contests that Alexander celebrated his conquest of Egypt in Memphis, twice (ἀγῶνα ἐποίησε γυμνικόν τε καὶ μουσικόν, Arrian 3.1.4 and again 3.5.2), obviously because he saw these as the key elements of Greek civilization which he wanted to display in the newly conquered foreign land.

69–70   The image of the discarded weapons covered in cobwebs recurs in Eur. *Erechtheus* where the chorus of old men wish 'may my spear rest, so that with spiders thread twines round it, while I live in my old age with tranquillity' (κείσθω δόρυ μοι μίτον ἀμφιπλέκειν ἀράχναις, μετὰ δ'ἡσυχίας πολιῶι γήραι συνοικοίην, fr. 369.1–2 N²), and in Theokritos' prayer for Syracuse, 16.96–7: 'may spiders spin their delicate nets over armour, and the cry of onset be no more even named' (ἀράχνια δ'εἰς ὅπλ'ἀράχναι | λεπτὰ διαστήσαιντο, βοᾶς δ' ἔτι μηδ' ὄνομ' εἴη); cf. Nonnos 38.13–14 'and the shield which Bakchos had borne for six years lay far from the battle covered with spiders' webs' (ἔκειτο δὲ τηλόθι χάρμης | Βακχιὰς ἑξαέτηρος ἀραχνιόωσα βοείη).

69 πόρπαξιν: the πόρπαξ is the bronze handle of a hoplite's shield or a *pelta*, see Snodgrass, *Arms and armour* 53–5 and 95.

70 ἀραχνᾶν,   responding to παιδικοί (80) and, very probably, to [μάντι]ς
ἐξ (50), must be – ⌣ –. While initial ῥ– is often 'prolonged', lengthening
the preceding syllable (cf. West, *Metre* 15–16) as in line 54 above (ἀπὸ
ῥίζας) and 13.96 τε ῥοδό[παχυν], 16.34 ἐπὶ ῥοδόεντι, also in compounds
(e.g. ἀρρήτων, B. fr. 5.3), it is rare for single –ρ– within a word to have
this effect, except occasionally in names (e.g. Ἀρραβίας Theokr. 17.86,
see Gow ad loc.). B. may have treated the word on the analogy of compounds like ἄρρητος, ἄρρηκτος or καλλίρροος, (where –ρ– stands for –Ϝρ–);
this seems preferable to the alternative assumption (considered by West,
Metre 74) that ⌣ ⌣ – at the beginning of a verse or period might respond
with | – ⌣ –.

71–2 ἔγχεα . . . εὔρως: the idea that in times of peace, the weapons
are covered by rust, recurs in Tibullus 1.10.49–50 *pace bidens vomerque nitent,
at tristia duri | militis in tenebris occupat arma situs*, who may well have been
inspired by this passage in B.; cf. Ovid, *Fasti* 4.927–30, and the parallels
from English literature quoted by K. F. Smith on Tib.1.10.49–50. The motif
of the discarded weapons is used in two epigrams by Mnasalkas (*AP* 6.125
and 128, = Page, *Epigr.* 2590–9) and one by Anyte (*AP* 6.123 = Page, *Epigr.*
676–9), which is characteristically different in tone: whereas in Mnasalkas'
epigrams the shield is presented as a symbol of military prowess and pride,
Anyte gives voice to her horror of bloodshed: 'stay here, man-killing spear,
spill no longer dreadful enemy blood round your brazen claw, but resting in Athena's lofty marble hall announce the prowess of Echekratidas
the Cretan' (κράνεια βροτόκτονε, μηδ' ἔτι λυγρὸν | χάλκεον ἀμφ' ὄνυχα
στάζε φόνον δαΐων).

75 χαλκεᾶν . . . σαλπίγγων: on trumpets, see on 18.3–4. In hellenistic
epigrams trumpets, like shields and spears, are dedicated in temples after
they have outlived their usefulness, cf. *AP* 6.46 (= Page, *Epigr.* 3336–9) and
its counterpart 159 (= Page, *Epigr.* 3340–3) by Antipatros of Sidon (late 2nd
cent. BCE).

76–7 μελίφρων ὕπνος   'mind-sweetening sleep'; the phrase occurs once
in Homer (*Il.* 2.34, more often μελιηδής, νήδυμος), where this compound
is often connected with wine. The idea seems to be that a good, long sleep
has a relaxing effect on the mind, rather like that of wine; the compound
is explained as 'gentle, because it sweetens the mind' in Apoll. Soph.; cf.
οἶνον εὔφρονα *Il.* 3.246.

77–8 ὕπνος . . . ἀώιος: the MSS of Stobaios have ἅμος (S), ἁμοσ (M)
and ἅμος (A), corrected by Blass. The corruption of ω to μ is more likely

to have occurred in majuscule than in minuscule. Sleep is sweetest before dawn, as Pindar says of Kyrene: 'while only briefly expending upon her eyelids that sweet bed-mate, the sleep that descends upon them toward dawn' (γλυκὺν . . . ὕπνον ἀναλίσκασα ῥέποντα πρὸς ἀῶ, P. 9.23–5), cf. [Eur.] Rhes. 554–6 and Moschos, Europa 2–4.

79 συμποσίων . . . βρίθοντ' ἀγυιαί   'the streets are laden with . . . feasts', cf. 3.16 βρύουσι φιλοξενίας ἀγυιαί. The verb means 'to be heavy with'; it takes either dative (Il. 8.304 μήκων . . . καρπῶι βριθομένη, PMG 994 Niobe is βλάσταις τε τέκνων βριθομένα) or genitive ([Hes.] Sc. 289–90 πέτηλα | βριθόμενα σταχύων, SH 982.7–8 εὐθενίης βαθυπλούτου βριθόμενος.

80 παιδικοί: with the exception of ethnic or geographical designations like Κρητικός, Ἀχαϊκός, ἀσμαρικός etc., adjectives in -ικός are very rare in early Greek poetry; Homer has only ὀρφανικός (Il. 6.432, 11.394), Aeschylus has ἀστικός (Supp. 501 and 618, Eum. 997), ἱππικός (Th. 245); παιδι[in Alkman PMG 3.83 (= 26 Calame) is very uncertain. However, the alternatives suggested by Maas (Resp. 1.23: λιπαροί, μαλακοί, ἱλαροί) are too general to be attractive: see the next note.

παιδικοί θ' ὕμνοι φλέγονται: hardly 'songs performed by boys' but 'lovesongs in praise of boys', as the verb suggests – the songs are 'burning' with passion; cf. Plato, Charm. 155d εἶδόν τε τὰ ἐντὸς τοῦ ἱματίου καὶ ἐφλεγόμην καὶ οὐκέτ' ἐν ἐμαυτοῦ ἦν, and similarly of homoerotic passion in hellenistic epigrams, e.g. AP 12.178 (Straton) and 46 (= Asklepiades 15 G.-P., discussed by Bonanno 1996: 155–9); cf. also AP 5.123.5–6 Σελήνη· | καὶ γὰρ σὴν ψυχὴν ἔφλεγεν Ἐνδυμίων (Poseidippos). On the origin of the metaphorical use of the verb see Braswell on Pind. P. 4.219b.

81–90   The last epode may have contained, as Maas (1932: 471 = Kl.Schr. 35) suggested, another invocation of Apollo, perhaps similar to the one in 58. In any case, there can be no doubt that Apollo was addressed at the beginning of this paean. The mythical narrative would then, if Maas' assumption is correct, have been punctuated by three addresses to the god.

FRAGMENTS 11 + 12: PROSODION

Fragments 11 and 12 are both transmitted in Stobaios' chapter 'On those who suffer unfairly' (περὶ τῶν παρ' ἀξίαν δυστυχούντων, 4.43.16 and 46 = Ioannis Stobaei Anthologium v pp.962 and 969 Wachsmuth-Hense) under the heading Βακχυλίδου προσοδίων, as is fr.13 in Stob. 4.34.24 (v p.833 W.-H., from 'On life being brief, paltry, and full of worries'). This ought to imply that the Alexandrian edition of the odes of B. contained a book of Προσόδια or 'Procession Songs'. *Prosodia* were defined as songs performed by male or female choirs in processions approaching an altar or a temple (schol. Lond. AE to Dionysius Thrax, p. 451.17 Hilgard: προσόδιόν ἐστι ποίημα ὑπὸ ἀρρένων ἢ παρθένων χοροῦ ἐν τῆι προσόδωι τῆι πρὸς τὸν θεὸν ἀιδόμενον, similarly schol. Ar. *Aves* 853 προσόδια τὰ εἰς πανηγύρεις τῶν θεῶν ποιήματα παρὰ τῶν λυρικῶν ποιητῶν). Inasmuch as they were composed for religious occasions, they were a sub-category of hymns, although according to Didymos they differed from hymns in that they were accompanied by oboes, not by the *kithara* (*EM* 690.33 προσόδια· παρὰ τὸ προσιόντας ναοῖς ἢ βωμοῖς πρὸς αὐλὸν ἀιδειν· ἴδια δὲ τῶν ὕμνων, ὅτι τοὺς ὕμνους πρὸς κιθάραν ἑστῶτες ἀιδουσιν. οὕτω Δίδυμος ἐν τῶι περὶ λυρικῶν ποιητῶν).

As regards frs.11 and 12 of B., Neue suggested long ago (*Bacchylidis Cei fragmenta*, p.26) that they belong to the same poem, in this order, and this is confirmed by the responsion of fr.12 with lines 3–5 of fr.11. Unfortunately, the surviving lines give no clue as to the identity of the goddess or god whom this procession song celebrated, or to the festival for which it was composed.

Fr. 11

1 εἷς ὅρος, μία . . . ὁδός: examples of words repeated for emphasis (emphatic anaphora) include Soph. fr. 591.1–2 ἓν φῦλον ἀνθρώπων, μί’ ἔδειξε πατρὸς | καὶ ματρὸς ἡμᾶς ἁμέρα τοὺς πάντας, Pind. *N.* 6.1–2 ἓν ἀνδρῶν, ἓν θεῶν γένος· ἐκ μιᾶς δὲ πνέομεν | ματρὸς ἀμφότεροι, *Il.* 2.204–5 εἷς κοίρανος ἔστω, | εἷς βασιλεύς, cf. Aesch. *Cho.* 725–6 and 1014, Hdt. 5.1.3, Pindar fr. 75.16. These and similar repetitions are discussed by Fehling, *Wiederholungsfiguren* 211–12, who classifies these verbal repetitions as 'strongly emphatic'.

ὅρος: the original meaning is 'boundary', 'boundary stone', as in *Il.* 21.405 (λίθον) τόν ῥ’ ἄνδρες πρότεροι θέσαν ἔμμεναι οὖρον ἀρούρης, cf. Solon 36.6; also in a temporal sense, 'time limit', see on B. 5.143–4 ζωᾶς ὅρον. Here B. seems to mean the 'limit' of happiness that mortals can attain, and the 'path' on which it is achieved (εὐτυχίας refers to both metaphors). This statement is a variation of a well-known *topos*, 'know your limits' or 'do not strive to become god', μὴ ματεύσηι θεὸς γενέσθαι Pind. *O.* 5.24, cf. *I.* 5.14 μὴ μάτευε Ζεὺς γενέσθαι and the passages discussed by Bundy 54–61.

Jebb, followed by LSJ, took ὅρος here to mean 'the canon, the rule or standard, by which true εὐτυχία is to be measured; ὁδός, the course to be followed'. This seems unlikely, because it is not before Plato that ὅρος is used in the sense of 'standard, rule'; in his discussion of wealth and oligarchic constitution in Book 8 of the *Republic*, he says that the 'standard' for being eligible for office in an oligarchy is wealth (ὅρον πολιτείας ὀλιγαρχικῆς ταξάμενοι πλῆθος χρημάτων, *Rep.* 551ab), a discussion to which Aristotle refers in *Pol.* 1294a10 ἀριστοκρατίας μὲν γὰρ ὅρος ἀρετή, ὀλιγαρχίας δὲ πλοῦτος, δήμου δὲ ἐλευθερία.

2–3 ἀπενθῆ . . . διατελεῖν βίον: cf. Alkman 1.37–9 ὁ δ' ὄλβιος, ὅστις εὔφρων | ἀμέραν [δι]απλέκει | ἄκλαυτος 'blessed is he who merrily weaves the day's pattern to its end, without a tear'. Maxims like this one, which give vent to a general desire for quiet happiness, are often found in cult songs such as *partheneia, prosodia, hyporchemata*, as well as in tragedy, cf. Soph. fr.593 'let any man procure as much pleasure as he can as he lives his daily life; but the morrow comes ever blind' (ζώοι τις ἀνθρώπων τὸ κατ' ἦμαρ ὅπως | ἥδιστα πορσύνων· τὸ δ' ἐς αὔριον αἰεὶ | τυφλὸν ἕρπει), also Eur. *Ba.* 902–11 (see Dodds ad loc.) and the passages listed by Dodds on Eur. *Ba.* 424–6. These general statements need not reflect the poet's personal views, although they would presumably not militate against them. They seem intentionally anodyne, so that everybody present, audience as well as chorus, would be able to subscribe to them. For the poet it was a means to engage the audience in the performance by enabling them to identify with fundamental ideas and sentiments voiced by the chorus, an essential element particularly in cult poetry, exemplified also in J. S. Bach's cantatas and the chorales of his *St. John Passion* and *St. Matthew Passion*.

3–4 ὃς δὲ μυρία μὲν ἀμφιπολεῖ φρενί 'but he who in his mind encompasses countless things', instead of concentrating his mind on what is attainable for mortals, will achieve nothing. A similar statement is offered by Pindar in *P.* 3.21–3 ἔστι δὲ φῦλον ἐν ἀνθρώποισι ματαιότατον, ὅστις αἰσχύνων ἐπιχώρια παπταίνει τὰ πόρσω, μεταμώνια θηρεύων ἀκράντοις ἐλπίσιν 'for there is among mankind a very foolish kind of person, who scorns what is at hand and peers at things far away, chasing the impossible with hopes unfulfilled'.

ἀμφιπολεῖ 'encompasses', 'surrounds' or 'takes hold of', as in Pind. *P.* 4.157–8 ἤδη με γηραιὸν μέρος ἁλικίας ἀμφιπολεῖ, explained by schol. ad loc. as περικυκλοῖ καὶ περιέχει, see Braswell ad loc.

5–7 τὸ δὲ παρ' ἆμαρ τε <καὶ> νύκτα . . . ἰάπτεται κέαρ   (Grotius: τὸ δὲ παρόμαρτε νύκτα MSS) 'but with this day and night . . . he torments his heart'. This usage of τὸ δέ or τό γε is well attested already in Homer: *Il.* 5.827 μήτε σύ γ' Ἄρηα τό γε δείδιθι, 14.191 κοτεσσαμένη τό γε θυμῶι. τὸ δέ is not used adverbially ('on the other hand'), but is the demonstrative pronoun in the accusative of respect, as often in Thukydides and Plato, cf. Plato, *Apol.* 23a τὸ δὲ κινδυνεύει . . . τῶι ὄντι ὁ θεὸς σοφὸς εἶναι ('in this respect'); on this usage see Miller 1908: 121–46 (on Pl. *Apol.* 23a: 144–5).

μελλόντων χάριν: it is useless to torment oneself 'for the sake of the future'. Pindar has a very similar statement: 'desires for various things stir in the minds of various men, and each one who wins what he strives for may gain the coveted object of his immediate concern, but there is no sure sign to foresee what a year may bring', *P.* 10.60–3; cf. Soph. fr. 590.

ἰάπτεται κέαρ: the verb seems to have attracted a variety of interpretations, as reflected in Hesych. 1 113 ἴαψε· προΰθηκεν . . . ἔπεμψεν. ἔβαλεν. ἔδωκεν. ἔδεισεν. ἔφθειρεν. ἐνίκησεν and 66 ἰάπτειν· σπαράσσειν. αἰκίζεσθαι . . . βλάπτειν, and so LSJ assume two distinct verbs, (a) = 'hurt, spoil' and (b) = 'send forth, shoot' (of missiles). This seems unnecessary, as the basic meaning seems to be 'to throw' (= βάλλειν), as in προΐαψεν *Il.* 1.3, hence – in analogy to βάλλειν – 'to hit, wound, damage', as in combination with κατά in *Od.* 2.376 and 4.749 and reflected in σπαράσσειν, αἰκίζεσθαι in Hesychios 1 66. The passive form also occurs in the very similar phrase ἰάπτομαι ἄλγεσιν ἦτορ in Moschos 4.39.

Fr. 12

1 τί γὰρ ἐλαφρὸν ἔτ' ἐστίν   'what relief is there any longer . . .?', a rhetorical question in the sense of βαρὺ γάρ or χαλεπὸν γάρ ἐστιν.

2–3 ἄπρακτ' ὀδυρόμενον: after *Il.* 24.524 οὐ γάρ τις πρῆξις πέλεται κρυεροῖο γόοιο, see on 5.162–4.

δονεῖν καρδίαν: the verb ('shaking, buffeting') is used of storms in the *Iliad* (12.157, 17.55) and in B. 5.65–7; its figurative usage is first found in Sappho 130 Ἔρος δηὖτέ μ' ὁ λυσιμέλης δόνει (cf. 47 Ἔρος δ' ἐτίναξέ μοι φρένας), parodied in Ar. *Eccl.* 954–5 πάνυ γάρ τις ἔρως με δονεῖ | τῶνδε τῶν σῶν βοστρύχων. Pindar, *P.* 4.219 also uses it of erotic passion, in *P.* 6.36 of panic in the face of death (cf. *N.* 6.56), B. 1.179 of κουφόταται μέριμναι ('lightweight ambitions'?). Here, ὀδυρόμενον may suggest some loss or bereavement.

FRAGMENTS 20A–D: ENKOMIA (?)

The title of the book, of which the papyri **P** and **Q** have preserved substantial fragments, is unfortunately not known. The first editors (Grenfell and Hunt, *P. Oxy.* xi p.66) thought of σκόλια or παροίνια 'drinking songs', Körte (1918: 137–8) suggested ἐγκώμια; none of these is attested as a book-title for B. Now, the songs frs. 20B and 20C were clearly composed to be sung at symposia, and this could well be true also of the other songs contained in this book. Even so, it does not seem likely that they would have been classified as σκόλια because those simple two-line and four-line songs which Athenaios 15.693f–696a (= *PMG* 884–908, = Fabbro, *Carmina convivialia* 1–25) quotes as examples of the old Attic drinking songs (σκόλια) are quite different in character and scope; they may well have been sung by guests at a symposion, one by one, in turns, and this would represent the second of the three types of *skolia* distinguished by Artemon (quoted in Athen. 15.694a): 'the songs sung in social gatherings; of these, the first kind was that which it was customary for all to sing in chorus; the second was sung by all, to be sure, but in a regular succession, one taking it up after another; and the third kind, which came last of all in order, was that no longer sung by all the company, but by those only who enjoyed the reputation of being specially skilled at it, and in whatever part of the room they happened to be' (τὰ περὶ τὰς συνουσίας ᾗν ἀιδόμενα, ὧν τὸ μὲν πρῶτον ᾗν ὃ δὴ πάντας ἄιδειν νόμος ᾗν, τὸ δὲ δεύτερον ὃ δὴ πάντες μὲν ᾗιδον, οὐ μὴν ἀλλά γε κατά τινα περίοδον ἐξ ὑποδοχῆς, τὸ τρίτον δὲ καὶ τὴν ἐπὶ πᾶσι τάξιν ἔχον, οὗ μετεῖχον οὐκέτι πάντες, ἀλλ'οἱ συνετοὶ δοκοῦντες εἶναι μόνοι καὶ καθ' ὅντινα τόπον ἀεὶ τύχοιεν ὄντες). This distinction, which seems to go back to Dikaiarchos (fr. 88 Wehrli = schol. Plat. *Gorg.* 451e), is still found in Plutarch, *Quaest. conv.* 1.1.5 (= *Mor.* 615b); cf. the testimonia collected by Fabbro, *Carmina convivialia* 3–15.

It seems to be the third of the three types outlined in these writers that is represented by Bacchylides' fragments 20A–D and by Pindar's fragments 118–28, i.e. the type of song not sung by all the guests but only by the 'experts' (οἱ συνετοὶ δοκοῦντες εἶναι μόνοι) who were able to offer a particularly attractive song that contained also good advice and useful information: 'they required all the trained singers in turn to offer a beautiful song for the common enjoyment. They believed that the beautiful song was the one which seemed to contain advice and counsel useful for the conduct of life' (ᾠδήν τινα καλὴν εἰς μέσον ἠξίουν προφέρειν. καλὴν δὲ ταύτην ἐνόμιζον τὴν παραίνεσίν τέ τινα καὶ γνώμην ἔχειν δοκοῦσαν χρησίμην εἰς τὸν βίον, Artemon in Athen. 15.694bc = *Carmina convivialia* 7–8). Of Pindar's fragments 118–28, three are explicitly quoted as σκόλια (frs. 122, 125 and 128), but the very similar fr. 118 as an ἐγκώμιον, so both terms evidently refer to the same kind of symposion song. The list of the seventeen books of Pindar's songs mentions only a book of ἐγκώμια (*vita Ambrosiana* 1.3 Drachm.), but the older biography of Pindar (*P. Oxy.* xxiii 2438.38) has ἐγκωμίων ᾱ ἐν [.] κα[, which has been convincingly restored to ἐν [ὧι] κα[ὶ σκόλιά τινα (Gallo, *Una nuova biografia di Pindaro* 73–7). This suggests that Aristophanes of Byzantium had called this book ἐγκώμια but included some songs which one would have called σκόλια, or 'drinking songs'. It therefore seems likely that Bacchylides' book partly preserved in the papyri **P** and **Q** also had this title, ἐγκώμια.

Enkomia, 'Songs of Praise', obviously suits the songs addressed to Alexander (fr. 20B) and Hieron (fr. 20C), but what about fr. 20A (Euenos and Marpessa) and fr. 20D (Niobe)? Both these songs contain 'negative' mythical examples which make it difficult to see how they could have served to praise the addressee. They must, however, have been relevant in some way to the person for whom they were composed, or to whom they were addressed; could it be, then, that fr. 20A was a kind of 'negative *enkomion*', as Snell 1952: 162 suggested, a song of censure or derision? As an example of this, Snell referred to Timokreon's song quoted by Plutarch (*Them.* 21 = *PMG* 727), which pretends to praise Aristeides but then turns out to be an invective against Themistokles. Its short stanzas in dactylo-epitrites are very similar to those of Pindar's *enkomia* and particularly of Bacchylides' fr. 20B and fr. 20C.

The idea of the ambivalence of *enkomia*, which can be 'negative' (blame or derision) as well as 'positive' (praise) may appear less surprising when one considers the hellenistic definitions of the term, preserved in the *etymologica*. The *Et. Gen.* AB (= *EM* 311.26) says ἐγκώμιον . . . ὕβριζον τὸν ἀδικοῦντα, to which *Et. Gud.* 158.23 Sturz = 395.5 Stef. adds τὴν γὰρ νύκτα ἤρχοντό τινες καὶ ἔλεγον ὅστις ἐποίει κακὰ πράγματα καὶ ἐκακολόγουν αὐτούς . . . ἐγκώμιον ὁ λόγος μεμπτικός· ἐνίοτε καὶ ἐπαινετικός. This last definition even appears to imply that invective, not praise, was the original function of the *enkomion*, because it originated from the κῶμος ('carousal') as the song of those revellers (κωμάζοντες), cf. Hesych. κ 4827 κωμάζει· κῶμον . . . ἄιδει· ὑβρίζει.

FR. 20A

In papyrus **P**, this song is followed by the praise songs for Alexander and Hieron (frs. 20B and 20C), but it is obviously very different in character. Snell (1952: 162–3) plausibly suggested that all three may have been classified as *enkomia* on the assumption that these could contain, as the ancient etymologica suggest, censure as well as praise, see above. On this basis, he interprets the story of Euenos and Marpessa as a warning example of what might happen to an obstinate father who jealously guards his daughter indoors, preventing her from getting married. The subject of 4 [κ]αθημένη and 7 ἰκ[ε]τεύει, at any rate, appears to be a daughter who is angry with her father (? ἄχθε]ται πατρί, 6) who keeps her isolated inside (μούνην ἔνδον ἔχω[ν, 11). The situation reflected in the first two stanzas involves real, not mythical, persons; whether father and daughter were in any way personally relevant to the poet, possibly recalling the relationship of Lykambes and his daughter Neobulē with Archilochos, must remain uncertain. On the story of Euenos, Marpessa and Idas see introduction to ode 20.

The number of lines missing from the beginning of this poem can be established with a reasonable degree of confidence. The following considerations suggest that fr. 19 of papyrus **P** contains remains of the first stanza of *this* poem (fr. 20A.1–6), preceded by the end of the penultimate line of the preceding poem: (1) The metrical pattern of fr. 20A consists of three short verses, followed by one long, one shorter and one long verse; (2) pap. **P** fr. 19 belongs to the foot of a column; the ends of its last three lines fit the metre of verses 4–6 of this poem; (3) if the last six lines of this column were preceded by another stanza of the same metrical structure, the seventh line from the bottom would be long, the preceding line short – but it is the other way round. Therefore, not more than one stanza of fr. 20A can have formed the bottom part of this column, i.e. only the first three short verses are lost before v.4 [κ]αθημενη, and the line-end preserved five lines above [κ]αθημενη must belong to a different poem.

4 κ]αθήμενη: as Lysistrate says, when a woman is past her prime, nobody wants to marry her and she sits, looking for omens (οὐδεὶς ἐθέλει γῆμαι ταύτην, ὀττευομένη δὲ κάθηται, Ar. *Lys.* 597).
5 If fr. 41 of pap. **P** has been correctly placed here, one could try something like αἰσχύ]νο[υ]σ᾽ [ἁπαλὸν δέ]μας, cf. Stesich. *SLG* 15 col.2.15–16 ὡς ὅκα μ[ά]κω[ν,] ἅτε καταισχύνοισ᾽ ἁπαλὸν [δέμας (suppl. Page); in Homer,

the verb is used to describe Achilles' reaction to the news of Patroklos' death: 'he took the dark dust and strewed it over his head and defiled his fair face . . . and with his own hands he tore and marred his hair', *Il.* 18.23–4 and 27.

6 ὑπέρ[μορ᾽ ἄχθε]ται πατρί: supplied by Snell, who referred to Hes. *Th.* 155 σφετέρωι δ᾽ἤχθοντο τοκῆϊ. The adverbial form ὑπέρμορα is found only in *Il.* 2.155, elsewhere always ὑπέρμορον or ὑπὲρ μόρον.

7–9 ἰκ[ε]τεύει . . . νιν τελ[έσαι: the construction (acc. + inf.) is similar to that in *Il.* 9.454–6, although there it is the father who invokes the Erinyes: κατηρᾶτο . . . | μή ποτε γούνασιν οἷσιν ἐφέσσεσθαι φίλον υἱὸν | . . . θεοὶ δ᾽ ἐτέλειον ἐπαράς. The same construction is used with λίσσεσθαι, cf. *Il.* 9.511–2 (the Λιταὶ) λίσσονται . . . Δία Κρονίωνα κιοῦσαι | τῶι Ἄτην ἅμ᾽ ἔπεσθαι and B. 11.69–72.

καμ[:   καμ[οῦσα (Snell) seems more likely than καμ[όντων (Maas), because there is no reason for the daughter to invoke the avenging spirits of the dead, as there is for Orestes (Aesch. *Cho.* 406 ἴδετε πολυκρατεῖς ἀραὶ φθινομένων); in her distress (καμ[οῦσα) she calls on the avenging spirits below, χ[θ]ονίας . . . [Ἀράς], cf. Aesch. *Eum.* 417 Ἀραὶ δ᾽ ἐν οἴκοις γῆς ὑπαί.

χ[θ]ονίας   'below the earth', cf. Soph. *OC* 1568 ὦ χθόνιαι θεαί, 1727 τὰν χθόνιον ἑστίαν; of the Titans: Hes. *Th.* 697; of Hades: Hes. *Th.* 767; of the entrance to Hades: Pindar, *P.* 4.43. Elsewhere in early poetry, compounds like ὑποχθόνιος (Hes. *Op.* 141) or καταχθόνιος (γῆρας *Il.* 9.457) are used.

9–10 ὀξ[ύ]τερον . . . καὶ κατάρᾶ[τον: (ϲτ[υ]γερόν cannot be read): Archilochos and Theognis use the comparative ὀξύτερος in the sense of 'vehement', 'uncontrolled' (Archil. 196a.37 ἡ δὲ μάλ᾽ ὀξυτέρη, Theognis 366 and 1030 of κραδίη), cf. ὀξύχολος Solon 13.26, ὀξυκάρδιος Aesch. *Sept.* 906. In B., however, it refers to γῆρας: the avenging spirits are to bring about a 'more painful old age' for the father. For ὀξύ in the sense of (physically) 'painful', see *Il.* 11.268–72, 16.518, Pind. *O.* 8.85, *P.* 3.97; in figurative sense in *Il.* 19.125 (ἄχος), *Od.* 19.517 (μελεδῶνες), Pind. *N.*1.53 (ἀνίαι), *N.*11.48 (ἀπροσίκτων δ᾽ ἐρώτων ὀξύτεραι μανίαι). In B., the comparative implies that old age, which is painful anyhow (ἀργαλέον, as Mimnermos insists, 1.20, 2.6, 5.2), shall be even more painful for the girl's father. Theognis, by contrast, complains from a father's perspective: 'The worst is . . . if someone has raised his sons and given them all they need, providing for them with much sacrifice, and then they hate their father, praying for his death' (τὸν πατέρ᾽ ἐχθαίρουσι, καταρῶνται δ᾽ ἀπολέσθαι᾽, Thgn. 271–8).

10–11 A change of subject has to be assumed before line 11, and probably after κατάρα[τον, after which one could supply ὅστ' εἴργει κόρη]ν . . . ἔνδον ἔχῳ[ν γάμων (Kapp) or ὅστ' εἴργει γάμῳ]ν . . . ἔχῳ[ν κόρην (Snell).

12 λε]υκαὶ δ' ἐν [κ]εφαλ[ῆι ‿ – ‿ – τ]ρίχες: whose hair? A marginal note, written on the right-hand side above τ]ρίχες, suggests that it refers to the girl's hair, τῆ]ς ὑπὸ πατρὸς ἐν [οἰκίαι κατεχομένης *vel sim.* The verb to be supplied may be γένοιντό οἱ, or (if this verse can end in ⸋ – ‿ –) γενήσονται or χνοάζουσι(ν), for which see Soph. *OT* 742 (Laios was χνοάζων λευκανθὲς κάρα) and Metagenes fr. 4 (*PCG* vii 6) ἄρτι χνοαζούσας αὐλητρίδας. The motif of the unmarried daughter growing old and grey-haired in the home recurs in Eur. *Hel.* 283 and *Andr.* 347–8 (Hermione), cf. Ap. Rhod. 1.672 (the Lemnians).

13 Ἄρ]εος χρυσολόφου: Euenos was the son of Ares and Demonike (Apollod. 1.7.7). The epithet, 'gold-crested', is also found in Anakreon (*PMG* 346 frs.11 + 3 + 6 line 18) and in the anonymous lemma in Hesych. χ 796 = *SH* 1118 χρυσόλοφοι δράκοντες. In ode 20.11, B. calls Euenos χρυσάσπιδος υἱό[ν Ἄρηος. At this point, the mythical narrative is introduced, asyndetically, as a precedent or parallel to the father and daughter referred to in the first two stanzas; on its possible relevance, see above, p. 240.

14 λέγουσι: B. presents the story as a traditional tale, as he does in ode 5.57 and 155.

χαλκ{ε}ομίτραν: Pindar gives this epithet to Kastor in *N.* 10.90; there, too, the MSS' unmetrical χαλκεο– has to be corrected.

14–18 The distribution of epithets in this stanza highlights the contrast between father and daughter, which culminates in [τοι]οῦτον; it is accentuated by the partly parallel and partly 'chiastic' (inverted) arrangement of nouns/names and epithets: first, two appositions (παῖ[δα] . . . χαλκομίτραν ↔ [τα]νυπέπλοιο κόρης, AabB), then names and epithets in parallel (AaaBb), highlighting the extreme contrast between the heavily armed, brutal and bloodthirsty father and his long-robed, flowerbud-faced daughter.

16 θρασύχειρα 'bold of hand', only here and ode 2.4, where it is said of a boxer or pancratiast.

μιαι[φόνο]ν 'blood-soiled'. The epithet, always said of Ares in Homer (*Il.* 5.31, 455, etc.), is here given to a son of Ares, who nailed the skulls of his daughter's defeated suitors to the wall of his house (schol. Pind. *I.* 4.92a; see introd. to ode 20: (above, p. 220).

17 καλυκώπιδος   'bud-eyed'; cf. Richardson on *h.Dem.* 8; see also B.17.95n. on λειρίων . . . ὀμμάτων.

18–20 χρόνος [ἐδά]μασσε κρατερά τ᾽ . . . ἀνάγκη   'time subdued him and strong avenging necessity'. 'Time' defeated him in the end, after he had murdered many, and 'Necessity', because Fate had so decided; in fact, Euenos committed suicide by throwing himself into the river Lykormas (which was thereafter renamed Euenos), because he had failed to catch up with Idas when he abducted his daughter, Marpessa, on his chariot with winged horses, cf. Apollod. 1.7.8. Bacchylides seems to have told this story in ode 20.

ἐκ[δόμεν ο]ὐ θέλοντ(α)   'unwilling to give her away'. The verb, ἐκδιδόναι, is standard in Greek marriage agreements (cf. Isaios 6.14; 8.8; Dem. *Or.* 59.122; *UPZ* 12.15), which state that the father 'gives' his daughter 'out' (sc. of his house).

22–3 Ποσειδαωνίας [ἵππους ὠκυδρόμ]ας   'the swift-running horses he had from Poseidon', who was Idas's divine father, according to 'many' (κατὰ πολλούς), as Apollod. 3.10.3 says.

24 ὄλβιον τέκος: Idas is 'fortunate' because he has won a beautiful bride. The motif is known from Sappho 112; it may have been a *topos* in wedding songs.

25 ἐθέλουσαν δ]ὲ κόρην: Maas's supplement is based on the two hexameters which Pausanias quotes in his description of the 'chest' of Kypselos (5.18.2): Ἴδας Μαρπήσσαν καλλίσφυρον, ἄν οἱ Ἀπόλλων | ἅρπασε, τὰν Εὐάνου ἄγει πάλιν οὐκ ἀέκουσαν 'Idas is bringing home Marpessa of beautiful ankles, whom Apollo snatched from him, Euenos' daughter, who was not unwilling'.

FR. 20B: FOR ALEXANDER, SON OF AMYNTAS

A substantial part (fr.1) of papyrus **P** overlaps with the quotation of lines 6–16 of the poem in Athenaios' *Epitome* 2.39e (1 p.92 Kaibel). Since the publication of pap. **P** by Grenfell and Hunt in 1915, eight more fragments of the same papyrus, most of them small scraps (frs. 2 + 3 + 22 + 39 + 25, 20 + 23, 26), have been placed within the same poem and partly joined to fr.1. The result has been that the first 16 lines are practically complete, lines 17–20 can be partly reconstructed, while lines 21–35 of the papyrus are still too fragmentary to yield any continuous sense and have therefore been omitted here. What remains of lines 33–5 appears to be in a different metre and probably represents the beginning of the next poem.

Fr. 20B, in four-line stanzas in dactylo-epitrites, fits the category of *enkomia* admirably, as do the remains of Pindar's song of praise for the same addressee, frs. 120 and 121. This Alexander is a Macedonian prince, son of king Amyntas I, who succeeded his father in about 495 BCE and ruled Macedonia for over forty years until his death in 452. His exact dates cannot be established with absolute certainty; Hammond and Griffith argue that he ascended the throne in *c*.495 (*History of Macedonia* II p.104). Alexander was later given the honorific title φιλέλλην ('friendly to Greeks') because during the Persian Wars, when his kingdom was a satellite of the Persian Empire, he repeatedly tried to mediate between the Greek states and Mardonios, the commander of Xerxes' army: see especially Hdt. 8.136–144 on the events in the spring of 479 BCE. Herodotos (5.17–22) also has a story about how young Alexander, when Persian nobles came to demand that his father Amyntas submit to Persian rule, had them murdered at a banquet given in their honour, but this story has the hallmarks of popular legend, 'designed to prove the patriotism of Alexander, the faithful friend of Athens' (How and Wells ad loc.). The fact is that Alexander remained a vassal of Dareios, paid tribute to the Persians and even gave his sister, Gygaia, to Bubares, the son of Dareios' general Megabazos, in marriage. 'Alexander was doubtless anxious to gain influence at the Persian court. It seems more likely that the marriage of his sister to a Persian grandee, which cast a slur on his phil-Hellenism, caused the invention of the tale that he murdered the envoys, than that the murder of the envoys was really hushed up by the marriage' (How and Wells on Hdt. 5.21).

More trustworthy is Herodotos' statement (5.22) that Alexander asked to compete in the Olympic Games, and when his Greek competitors objected on the grounds that only Hellenes were entitled to take part, he succeeded in convincing the judges of the Argive origin of his family. He was admitted and competed in the foot-race (στάδιον) which ended in a dead heat. He seems to have competed in another discipline as well, if we are to believe Justin 7.2.14 (*Olympio certamine vario ludicrorum genere contenderet*), perhaps in the pentathlon. As Pindar addresses him as παῖ θρασύμηδες (fr. 120.2), one might think of a discipline involving wrestling, boxing or pankration, probably in the 70th or 71st Olympic Games (500 or 496), before his accession, because it seems hardly credible that he would have competed in the games as ruling king of Macedonia (see Hammond and Griffith, *History of Macedonia* II 60). In fact, in both Bacchylides' poem (fr. 20B.17) and in Pindar's fr. 120 he is addressed with ὦ παῖ, and there are no indications in either poem that he was already then ruler of his country.

The implication must be that both poems belong to the period before *c*.495, Alexander's accession to the Macedonian throne, and that Bacchylides' fr. 20B and Pindar's fr. 120 are therefore among the earliest datable poems of either poet.

1–3 ὦ βάρβιτε . . . δεῦρ' ἐς ἐμὰς χέρας: B. addresses the instrument like a living creature. The anonymous singer of the Attic drinking song *PMG* 900 (= Fabbro, *Carmina convivialia* 17) often wishes to become a lyre himself: εἴθε λύρα καλὴ γενοίμην ἐλεφαντίνη | καί με καλοὶ παῖδες φέροιεν Διονύσιον ἐς χορόν. This instrument (ὁ βάρβιτος or τὸ βάρβιτον) was said to have been invented either by Anakreon or by Sappho; both are credited with its invention by Neanthes (? the historian from Kyzikos in the second century BCE), quoted in Athen. 4.175d (cf. *AP* 7.25 on Anakreon who βάρβιτον οὐδὲ θανὼν εὔνασεν εἰν Ἀΐδηι) and 4.182f = *PMG* 472. Pindar, however, claims that Terpander invented it, fr. 125. The instrument was narrower and longer than the lyra or kithara. On vases it is usually shown with seven strings, occasionally with more (see below on 2); it is already found on some black-figure vases, e.g. on a plate of *c*.510 BCE by the painter Psiax in the Käppeli collection, *ABV* 294.21 (Appendix No. 41); on an amphora in London: B214, *ABV* 141, Paquette 185 (B19); on an amphora of *c*.510–500 BCE in Munich: inv.1416, *ABV* 367.90 (Appendix no. 42); then very frequently on red-figure vases in the first half of the fifth century when it must have been very popular, more rarely after *c*.450; see West, *Ancient Greek music* 57–9; Michaelides, *Music* 48–9; Paquette, *L'instrument de musique* 173–85; Maas and McIntosh-Snyder, *Stringed instruments* 113–38.

1 πάσσαλον: B. may be thinking of Alkinoos' palace in *Od.* 8.67, where the lyre (φόρμιγξ) is appended on a peg in the wall, which can also be seen on vases; cf. also Pind. *O.* 1.17–18 and *PMG* 974.

2 ἑπτάτονον: Ion of Chios says (fr. 32 W.) that the lyre had seven strings in the old days, but eleven in his own time. For references to these instruments (lyre and barbiton) shown on vases see Wegner, *Musikleben* 222–6.

κάππαυε 'suppress, hold down', as if the instrument had a life of its own and an urge to sing which it finds hard to suppress. See above on 1–3.

3–4 τι . . . Μουσᾶν . . . πτερόν: the idea that a song has wings, because it travels over land and sea like a bird, is also familiar to Pindar, cf. *I.* 5.64

πτερόεντα νέον σύμπεμψον (i.e. together with the victor's crown) ὕμνον; Pindar even speaks of the 'wings of the Muses', *I.* 1.64–5 εἴη νιν (= the victor) εὐφώνων πτερύγεσσιν ἀερθέντ' ἀγλααῖς Πιερίδων; cf. Theognis 237–9 who says to Kyrnos: 'I have given you wings, on which to fly across the endless sea and all the earth with ease' (σοὶ μὲν ἐγὼ πτέρ' ἔδωκα, σὺν οἷς ἐπ' ἀπείρονα πόντον | πωτήσηι καὶ γῆν πᾶσαν ἀειρόμενος | ῥηϊδίως). The Muses' chariot is also winged, Pind. *Paean* 7b.13. Other parallels in Pindar have been discussed by Bundy 82.

3 ὁρμαίνω τι πέμπ[ειν: this is very similar to the opening stanza of fr. 20C; cf. also 5.9–16 and Pind. fr. 124ab. The 'willingness' motif provides a very obvious starting point for a poem of praise; Pindar, too, used it to begin his song for Theron of Akragas (fr. 118 Βούλομαι παίδεσσιν Ἑλλάνων [τι πέμψαι/δεῖξαι or the like), and may have done so also in his praise for the same Alexander, after the opening address (fr. 120).

5 συμποσ[ίαι]σιν (Maas) or -[ίοι]σιν (Grenfell & Hunt)? Pindar uses συμπόσιον only in the singular, but fem. συμποσίαι in the plural: *P.* 4.294 συμποσίας ἐφέπων, as in Alkaios 368.2. The καί links πτερόν and ἄγαλμα, not the datives.

[ἐν] εἰκάδες[σιν: Grenfell and Hunt refer to Plutarch, *Non posse suaviter vivi* 4 (*Mor.* 1089c): 'to gather as from an official journal statistics about . . . where they drank Thasian wine, <or> on what twentieth of the month they had the most sumptuous dinner' (ἐξ ἐφημερίδων ἀναλέγεσθαι . . . ποῦ Θάσιον ἔπιον <ἢ> ποίας εἰκάδος ἐδείπνησαν πολυτελέστατα) and to the testament of Epikouros in Diogenes Laertios 10.18: 'the meeting of all my School held every month on the twentieth day' (τὴν γενομένην σύνοδον ἑκάστου μηνὸς ταῖς εἰκάσι). These references suggest that the twentieth of each (?) month was popular as an occasion for private parties and festivities, but what exactly was being celebrated then we cannot tell. The twentieth day of the month may have had something to do with Apollon Eikadios, whose priestess was called Εἰκάς, *EM* 298.1; cf. Nilsson, *Gr. Rel.* 1 611 n.3.

6–7 ἁ[παλὸν] . . . θυμόν 'tender hearts'; the epithet ('soft, impressionable') has been supplied by Maas, cf. Archil. 191.3 κλέψας ἐκ στηθέων ἁπαλὰς φρένας. Maas had also thought of, and rejected, ἁ[ταλόν] – a child's, or a girl's, heart or mind (θυμός) may be ἀταλός, as is that of the boy Sogenes to whom Pindar's 7th *Nemean* is addressed, cf. lines 91–2 ἀταλὸν ἀμφέπων θυμὸν προγόνων. See also Denniston on Eur. *El.* 699.

γλυκεῖ' ἀνάγκα σευομενᾶν κυλίκων: 'constraint' is sweet because it is the 'compulsion of the speeding cups', as described by Kritias: ἔστ' ἂν

ὕδωρ οἴνωι συμμειγνύμενον κυλίκεσσιν | παῖς διαπομπεύηι προπόσεις
ἐπὶ δεξιὰ νωμῶν, fr. 8.6–7 (II p.98 G.-P.). Jebb, following Grenfell & Hunt,
took this to be an absolute genitive ('as the cups go swiftly round'). This
seems unlikely, because (a) the genitive absolute is much more common in
prose than in poetry (see Chantraine, *GH* II 324; K-G II 110–11; Schwyzer
II 398–401), and (b) it remains unclear why 'constraint' (ἀνάγκα) is 'sweet'.

6–8   Note the 'chiastic' inversion of the subjects (ἀνάγκα . . . κυλίκων ~
Κύπριδός τ' ἐλπίς) combined with the parallelism of the predicates
(θάλπησι θυμόν ~ δ<ι>αιθύσσηι φρένας). The third stanza of fr. 20A
has a similar structure; see there on line 14. The subjunctives after εὖτε are
generalizing or iterative, 'whenever' or 'each time'; a close parallel is *Od.*
7.202 ('the gods always appear to us, the Phaeacians') εὖτ' ἔρδωμεν ἀγακ-
λειτὰς ἑκατόμβας, and similar examples with ὅτε and ὁππότε are listed in
Chantraine, *GH* II 256; cf. Schwyzer II 649 and 660–6.

7   θάλπησι θυμόν   'warms their hearts', as in fr. 4.78 θάλπει κέαρ, instead
of the Homeric ἰαίνειν (θυμὸς ἰάνθη *Il.* 23.600 etc.) which B. adopts in
13.220 and 17.131. The spelling of the subjunctive ending is –ησι, correctly
preserved in the MSS of Athenaios; the papyrus has θαλπηισι, i.e. the first
iota was deleted by a corrector. See on 19.3–4.

8   Κύπριδός τ' ἐλπὶς δ<ι>αιθύσσηι: Athen. has Κύπριδος ἐλπὶς δ'
αἰθύσσει, but the papyrus adds τ(ε) after Κύπριδος, which makes the
subjunctive (-σσηι) necessary, in line with θάλπησι. The metre requires
– ◡ – ◡‒ ◡ – – –, so the line as quoted in Athen. omits one short syllable
after ἐλπίς: this, together with the odd δ', strongly suggests διαιθύσσηι
(διαιθύσσει Erfurdt, -σσηι Blass). The verb (mostly in compounds: ἀνα–,
δια–, κατα–, παρα–, see Braswell on Pind. *P.* 4.83a) is related to αἴθειν
'to kindle'; Chantraine, *Dict.* I 33 explains it as 'présent expressif comme
l'indique le suff. -ύσσω et qui s'emploie volontiers au figuré'. As to its
meaning, cf. Stanford, *Ambiguity* 132–6, esp. 134: 'The word . . . combines
two distinct perceptions, movement and light, quivering and glistening',
and 135 on Pind. *O.* 7.94–5 ἐν δὲ μιᾶι μοίραι χρόνου | ἄλλοτ' ἀλλοῖαι
διαιθύσσουσιν αὖραι: 'here more emphasis is on the movement than on
the light, but we may still detect a glint of Pindaric φέγγος in those veering
winds.' In B., being placed parallel to θάλπησι, the verb probably indicates
intensification, in the sense that wine 'warms' the heart, the thought of love
'glows' (rather than 'flashes') through the mind.

9–10   ἀμμειγνυμένα . . . ἀνδράσι δ':   Athenaios quotes ἀναμιγνυμένα
(ἀμμειγ- Dindorf)Διονυσίοισι δώροις. ἀνδράσι δ', but pap. **P** has ἃ

μειγνυμεν[. . . .]‖ ανδρασιν, which would make Κύπριδος ἐλπίς the subject not only of line 8, but of lines 9–16 as well; this seems very unlikely,
as the third stanza focusses on the gifts of Dionysos, not the hope for sex.
Besides, if ἀμμειγνυμένα is the original reading, it is more likely to have
been corrupted to αμειγ– (→ ἀ μειγ–) than the other way round. If, therefore, Athen. has preserved what is essentially the authentic reading, how
can the mistake in the papyrus-text be accounted for? Perhaps the scribe,
forgetting that a neuter plural noun (δῶρα) takes a verb in the singular,
failed to recognize the change of subject.

10 ὑψοτάτω: the drinker's thoughts soar up to heaven as the wine raises
his spirits; Ion of Chios (*PMG* 744) calls wine ἀερσίνοον ἀνθρώπων πρύ-
τανιν, 'the cheering master of men', and elegiac poets refer to the drinker's
κοῦφος νόος, e.g. Theognis 497–8 Ἄφρονος ἀνδρὸς ὁμῶς καὶ σώφρονος
οἶνος, ὅταν δὴ | πίνηι ὑπὲρ μέτρου, κοῦφον ἔθηκε νόον ('the witless and
the sound of wit alike turn empty-headed when they drink too deep'), see
van Groningen ad loc. The notion that tipsiness kindles the imagination,
sending ambitious dreams sky-high, also occurs in Pindar, with a slightly
different slant, fr. 124ab.5–11: 'When men's wearisome cares vanish from
their breasts, and on a sea of golden wealth we all alike sail to an illu-
sory shore; then the pauper is rich, while the wealthy . . . increase in their
minds, overcome by the arrows of the vine' (ἀνίκ' ἀνθρώπων καματώδεες
οἴχωνται μέριμναι | στηθέων ἔξω· πελάγει δ' ἐν πολυχρύσοιο πλούτου |
πάντες ἴσαι νέομεν ψευδῆ πρὸς ἀκτάν· | ὃς μὲν ἀχρήμων, ἀφνεὸς τότε,
τοὶ δ' αὖ πλουτέοντες . . . [dream of power and glory?, and all] ἀέξονται
φρένας ἀμπελίνοις τόξοις δαμέντες); on the likely sense of the lines missing
after line 8 see van Groningen, *Pindare au banquet* 97–9. The striking similarity between Pindar's song for Thrasyboulos and B.'s song for Alexander
suggests that both poets are employing *topoi* of sympotic poetry of the kind
which Aristophanes parodies in the *Knights*, where Demosthenes says to his
fellow slave (92–4) 'Do you see? When people drink, then they are rich,
successful, win their court-cases, are happy, help their friends' (ὁρᾶις; ὅταν
πίνωσιν ἄνθρωποι, τότε | πλουτοῦσι, διαπράττουσι, νικῶσιν δίκας,|
εὐδαιμονοῦσιν, ὠφελοῦσι τοὺς φίλους, quoted in Athen. 11.782c). Those
who believe (with Körte 1918: 130; Wilamowitz, *Pindaros* 319; van Groningen, *Pindare au banquet* 100–2) that B. is here imitating Pindar's *enkomion* for
Thrasyboulos ignore not only the probable early date of B.'s poem, which
makes their assumption almost impossible, but also the question of how one
poet could have known the other's poem if one was performed in Sicily

and the other in Macedonia; van Groningen does at least address this question, speculating that the audience, a 'public lettré', would have known the competitor's (i.e., Pindar's) poem because he would have circulated copies of it after its performance, and that other copies were also in circulation, in schools and in the hands of competing poets etc. There is not a shred of evidence for this; for the first decades, at least, of the fifth century BCE this kind of scenario seems utterly anachronistic.

11 πολίων κράδεμνα λύει: the image of the 'battlements of cities' is borrowed from Homer, cf. *Iliad* 16.100 Τροίης . . . κρήδεμνα λύωμεν, *Od.* 13.388 Τροίης λύομεν . . . κρήδεμνα, see also Richardson on *h.Dem.* 151. A similar metaphor is implied in the compound εὐστέφανος applied to cities, as in *Il.* 19.99 and Hes. *Th.* 978, see West ad loc.

λύει: in Homer, the present and imperfect forms have short υ, except in *Od.* 7.74 and *Il.* 23.513 for the sake of the metre, see Chantraine, *GH* I 372–3 and Wyatt, *Metrical lengthening* 209. It seems unnecessary to alter the verb to λύσειν (as Blass suggested).

12 ἀνθρώποις μοναρχήσειν: the verb is first found here and in Pindar, *Pae.* 4.29 and *P.* 4.165, but the noun, μοναρχία, is used by Alkaios 6.27, μούναρχος/μόναρχος by Solon 9.3 and Theognis 52.

13 ἐλέφαντι: B. may be thinking of Menelaos' palace, which impressed Telemachos by its wealth, *Od.* 4.71–5. Ever since Mycenean times, wealth had manifested itself through gold, silver and ivory (see Krzyszkowska, *Ivory*). In the *Odyssey*, for example, Odysseus' gift is made of bronze, silver and ivory (8.403–5), Penelope's chain is inlaid with ivory and silver (19.56), the bed with gold, silver and ivory (23.200); in the *Iliad*, cheek-pieces of a bridle, made of purple-stained ivory, are described as extremely precious (4.141–5, cf. 5.583); see also Sappho 44.8–10, Alkaios 350.1–2, Anakreon *PMG* 388.9–11; in a figurative sense, in Pindar, *N.* 7.78 (of the preciousness of his song).

14–16 πυροφόροι . . . πλοῦτον: the earliest explicit reference to merchants wishing to make a fortune from overseas trade is in Solon 13.43–4 ὁ μὲν κατὰ πλοῦτον ἀλᾶται | ἐν νηυσὶν χρῄζων οἴκαδε κέρδος ἄγειν, although references to treasures brought home from overseas are already found in the *Odyssey* (4.81–5), and Alkaios' brother Antimenidas brought back a precious scabbard of gold and ivory from Babylonia, fr. 350, on which see Page 1955: 223–4. Alkaios himself travelled to Egypt (fr. 432 = Strabo 1.37), as did Charaxos, Sappho's brother (Sappho frs. 5 + 15b, see Page 1955: 45–51), presumably on business, and Solon, who went there κατ' ἐμπορίαν ἅμα καὶ θεωρίαν according to Aristotle (*Ath. Pol.* 11.1). Greek merchants were allowed to settle at Naukratis, the colony founded in the Nile Delta by the Milesians in *c.*650 BCE, by Pharaoh Amasis (Amosis II Khnemibrê, 570–526 BCE), cf. Hdt. 2.177–82; see Lloyd on 2.178–9 with bibliography. Lucrative trade with Egypt may have been a motif in New Comedy (Philemon?): see Plautus, *Mostellaria* 440 where the merchant Theopropides is returning from Egypt. However, evidence for the grain trade between Egypt and Greece is scarce before the fourth century; see Roebuck 1950: 236–47.

14 αἰγλάεντα πόντον 'a dazzling sea'; the epithet is given to Mount Olympus by Homer (*Il.* 1.532 etc.) and Soph. *Ant.* 610, to the Golden Fleece by Pindar, *P.* 4.231, and Ap. Rhod. 4.1142, even to a horse's harness (Pind. *P.* 2.10), but never to the sea, although Homer once gives it a similar epithet, ἅλα μαρμαρέην (*Il.* 14.273).

16 ὡς πίνοντος ὁρμαίνει κέαρ: having first focussed on the young men who are thinking of sex (6–8), then on the various ambitions of adult men (10–16), the poet now brings the whole passage on 'high hopes, kindled by wine' to its conclusion. It is a variation on the Homeric formula ἧος ὁ ταῦθ' ὥρμαινε κατὰ φρένα καὶ κατὰ θυμόν (*Il.* 1.193 etc.), in that B. makes the heart subject: 'thus (i.e. with such thoughts) ponders the drinker's heart'; the verb is intransitive (the transitive form would be ὁρμᾶι, as in 18.41 and fr. 20D.3).

17 ᾧ π[α]ῖ : here the second part of the song seems to begin, starting with an address to the prince himself which is appropriate for a young man, hardly for a ruling king. Admittedly, Hieron is addressed by Pindar (*P.* 2.18–20) as ὦ Δεινομένειε παῖ, but then Pindar refers immediately to his power (διὰ τεὰν δύναμιν) as king of Syracuse.

μεγαλ[: the accents in the papyrus (μὲγὰλ[) show that this was part of a compound, such as μεγαλόκλεες (suggested by Snell, cf. 8.27 and fr. 62.10) or μεγαλοσθενές, which could refer to Alexander's athletic ambitions; cf. Pind. *P.* 6.21–3 μεγαλοσθενεῖ . . . Πηλεΐδαι (= Achilles).

Ἀμύντα: supplied by Maas; the address ὦ παῖ requires a patronymic, as in Pindar's song for Alexander, fr. 120.2 παῖ θρασύμηδες Ἀμύντα. Before the name, one might expect an epithet of three long syllables, such as ὑ[ψαυχέος (Snell) or ε]ὑ[ξείνοι' (Schadewaldt).

18 . . .]ϛ (or]Σ): there are few supplements that will produce a dactylic word (– ⏑ ⏑) ending in either ε (i.e. ε', if hiatus was avoided) or ϛ. One possibility is ἄιε]ϛ, which might suggest something like (18–19) [ἄιε]ϛ οὐ

π[ατέρων (π[ρογόνων ?) τοι]όν[δε κόμπον | ὃν σὺ] λάχ[ες· 'you have
not heard such praise of your ancestors as you yourself have received'; for
τοιόνδε . . . ὃν (instead of οἷον) one could compare *Od.* 4.826–7 τοίη γάρ
οἱ πομπὸς ἅμ᾽ ἔρχεται, ἥν τε καὶ ἄλλοι | ἀνέρες ἠρήσαντο, 2.286–7; cf.
Theognis 95–8; Soph. *Ant.* 691; also in prose: Plato, *Phd.* 92b.

19]λάχ[ον·]τί (]λάχ[. .]τι pap.):   Snell thought that the accent was put
to avoid confusion with λαχόντι, hence his supplement λάχ[ον·] which
would be a third person plural; but it is difficult to see what its subject
might be.

19–20 τί γάρ . . . κ[αλά 'for what greater gain is there for men than
to gratify one's heart with fine deeds?' This was Snell's tentative recon-
struction, based on B. 3.83–4 ὅσια δρῶν εὔφραινε θυμόν· τοῦτο γὰρ |
κερδέων ὑπέρτατον. For θυμῶι χαρίζεσθαι + acc., cf. Theognis 920, 1000,
1224 (θυμῶι δειλὰ χαριζομένη, sc. ὀργή: 'anger gratifies the heart with bad
things/consequences').

After this line, there seem to be remains of three more stanzas (12 lines)
before the next poem (in a different metre) begins – provided that Snell's
placements of frs. 2, 3, 20, 22, 23, 25, 26 and 39 of papyrus **P** are correct.
The remains are too scanty to allow reconstruction.

FR. 20C: FOR HIERON OF SYRACUSE

Papyrus **P** fr. 4 preserves parts of the first twenty lines of a column. It is the
beginning of a poem; its title is written to the left of its first line: [Ι]ερωνι
[Συ]ρακοσιωι (on Hieron, see the introduction to Ode 3, above p. 79).
Since its publication, a number of smaller fragments have been joined or
placed, nearly all of them by Snell, with the help of the metre and the
fibre structure. They represent more than forty lines in total, of which 24
form one column, which is followed by remains of another 14 lines of the
next column. Since the latter are extremely fragmentary, they have been
omitted here.

The poem preserved in this column of pap. **P** and most of the next fits
the pattern of *enkomia*, as does fr. 20B. It was destined to be performed at
a symposion (line 6), 'for Hieron and his chestnut horses' (lines 3–4). This
must be a reference to his victory in the chariot race, either at Delphi in 470
or at Olympia in 468, but as there seems to be no reference to the latter,
line 4 is likely to refer to Hieron's Pythian victory of 470, and the possible

date of this poem would seem to be not much later than 470. It is written in six (?) six-line stanzas in dactylo-epitrites.

1–2 Μήπω λιγυαχέ̣[α κοίμα] βάρβιτον·:   the papyrus has punctuation after βάρβιτον· In view of μήπω, the verb to be supplied in the gap can only be a subjunctive (παύσω Maas, Körte) or imperative. Maas (1919: 37–41 = *Kl.Schr.* 28–33), having examined similar self-exhortations in Pindar, concludes that (a) the first-person singular subjunctive is used only after imperatives like ἄγε, φέρε etc. or after particles with imperative meaning, such as δεῦρο or εἶα, and (b) that the first-person plural subjunctive, though possible, would be hard to accommodate in the short gap which could only admit a verb like ἀνῶμεν or ἐῶμεν, which would be stylistically unconvincing. This leaves only an imperative: Maas' supplement κοίμα 'put to sleep' is based on Pindar, *N.* 10.21 ἀλλ' ὅμως εὔχορδον ἔγειρε λύραν and *AP* 7.25 (Simonides?) βάρβιτον οὐδὲ θανὼν εὔνασεν, which both imply the notion of the instrument being 'asleep' while not being played; κρήμνα (Edmonds) or rather κρίμνα is also possible, 'do not yet hang up the barbitos . . .'

2 μέλλ[ω]:   cf. the very similar asyndeta ὁρμαίνω in fr. 20B.3 and ἐθέλει in ode 5.14.

3 ἄνθεμον Μουσᾶ[ν: for 'flower' as a metaphor for song or poem, see on fr. 4. 63.

5 ἱμ]ερόεν: the epithet is Homeric, cf. *Od.* 1.421 = 18.304 ἱμερόεσσαν ἀοιδήν, also 17.519, 23.144–5 etc.

7 Αἴ]τναν: Pindar's first *Pythian* was also sent to Aitna for Hieron's celebration of this Delphic victory with the chariot in 470. Pindar's victory ode focusses as much on the establishment of his son, Deinomenes, as ruler or governor of the newly renamed city of Aitna (= Κατάνη, Catania) as on Hieron's chariot victory. His residence remained, however, at Syracuse, so that the Alexandrian editors of Pindar's and B.'s odes had no problem in describing him as a Syracusan. His celebration may have been a political gesture, a message that the powerful ruler of Syracuse was also in control of the city of Katane. That city had been founded, as Strabo 6.2.3 records, by the 'Naxians' of Tauromenion (Taormina, founded in the eighth century by Chalkidians and Naxians). Hieron uprooted the local Ionian population and resettled them at Leontinoi, while recruiting 5000 Dorians from the Peloponnese and another 5000 from Syracuse to replace them at Katane, which he renamed Aitna. He imposed a Doric constitution on them, as schol. Pind. *P.* 1.118c (II p.20 Drachm.) states. The fullest account of this brutal act of 'ethnic cleansing', for which the original ('Naxian') Katanians later took their revenge, can be found in Diodoros 11.49, cf. Strabo 6.2.4.

ἐΰκτιτον: the conventional Homeric epithet appears particularly suggestive in this context, almost as a wish for good fortune; cf. Pind. *P.* 1.30–2 and 61–2.

7–8 εἰ κ[αὶ πρ]όσθεν 'if ever before', 'since'; for εἰ in causal sense (Lat. *si quidem* 'since'), cf. Pind. *O.* 1.18 and 9.26; B. 12.4; other examples are listed in LSJ *s.v.* B.VI.

8–10 τὸν . . . Φερ[ένικον . . .] . . . τε ν[ί]καν: whatever one might supply at the end of line 8 (ἐξευρόντα Πυθοῖ or ἐν Κίρραι θ' ἑλόντα Barrett, ἐν Δελφοῖς θ' ἑλόντα Snell), the τε in line 10 shows that *two* victories of Hieron's famous racehorse Pherenikos are referred to here, i.e. in addition to his Olympic victory in 476 (9–10 ἐπ' Ἀλ]φ[ε]ῶι) also a victory at Delphi, where Pherenikos had been successful in 478. For the supplement ἐξευρόντα one could quote Pind. *I.* 8.5 ἀέθλων . . . κράτος ἐξεῦρε, for ἑλόντα Pind. *P.* 3.74 στεφάνοις, τοὺς . . . Φερένικος ἕλεν Κίρραι ποτέ and *P.* 5.21 εὖχος . . . ἵπποις ἑλών.

10–13 The initial letters of these four lines are preserved in fr. 33 of pap. **P** which Snell placed here. The spacing in line 10 confirms that the papyrus had Ἀλ]φ[ε]ῶι, not -φ[ει]ωι (Pindar always uses the spelling with -φε-, except in *O.* 7.15 where the metre requires a long syllable; B. spells it -φε- except in 8.27 and 13.193). In the margin to the right of line 10 are remains of a note: φερε[

          τ[.]υς.[

which may have been Φερέ[νικος κέλης Ἱέρωνος

          τ[ο]ῦ Συ[ρακοσίων βασιλέως, or the like.

13–18 The gaps in the papyrus are too wide to make attempts at a reconstruction of these lines profitable. What seems reasonably probable is that τότε in line 13 ought to refer to a previous occasion (perhaps anticipated by εἰ κ[αὶ πρ]όσθεν in 7–8) when a song by B. had been performed in Hieron's honour; the 'maidens' (κοῦραι) may be the Muses, or there may be a choir of girls (and boys ?) who sang 'then' (τότε), perhaps at Olympia: this assumption is behind Snell's tentative suggestion σὺν] ἐμοὶ τότε κοῦραί [τ' ἠΐθεοι θ'] ὅσσοι Διὸς πάγχρυσον ἄλσος (= Olympia) | πᾶν βρύειν κώ]μο[ι]ς τίθεσαν 'then with me (came ? sang ?) maidens (and youths) who made the all-gold (sanctuary) of Zeus (loud with celebration)' ? The next three lines may, as [ὅστι]ς ἐπιχθονίων 17 would suggest, have contained a general statement leading on to the superlative praise for Hieron which follows in the fourth stanza.

14 πάγχρ[υσον: cf. Pind. *O.* 7.4 (a cup, φιάλη), *P.* 4.68 (the Golden Fleece).

19–20 τέχν]αι . . . ἅπᾳ[σαι | μυρία]ι: in choral lyric, this motif is often used as a foil leading up to a capping statement, as in B. 14.8–11 and 10.35–48, Pind. *O.* 11.7–10 (ἀφθόνητος δ᾽ αἶνος . . . ἐκ θεοῦ δ᾽ ἀνὴρ κτλ.), *N.* 1.25–30, *N.* 3.38–40, *O.* 9.107–12, *P.* 1.81–6. These and similar passages are discussed by Bundy 15–16, who states that 'a foil term may be subjective (or objective) when first introduced, but become objective (or subjective) before the capping term is reached . . . Although Bacch. frag. 20C.19f. are similarly ambiguous, I believe that the summary foil which they contain is subjective (at least with reference to the capping term introduced by σὺν θεῶι δέ in line 20), just as in 14.8ff. the summary foil μυρί]αι δ᾽ ἀνδρῶν ἀρε[ταὶ κτλ. is subjective with reference to νῦν χρή in line 20. The laudator means to say, "Though the resources of art are boundless, I shall abandon all device and say simply and with confidence that the sun never looked on a better man". But the audience, familiar with the conventions, will perceive the precise implication, "Whatever approach I take, I can't please everybody, for each will have his own vision of Hieron's greatness, but I know all will agree when I say . . .".'

20 σὺν θεῶι   'with god's help'; 'it contrasts inspirational with mechanical praise; the laudator will have recourse not to the devices of art . . . but to a natural and spontaneous enthusiasm that is divinely inspired', Bundy 16.

θ[α]ρσή[σας πιφαύσκω   (Maas, cf. B. 5.42, or θροήσω Schadewaldt): this kind of phrase often introduces a statement amounting to a superlative, as in B. 1.159–60; see also on B. 11.24.

21 οὔτι]ν᾽ . . . ἓ[τερον καθορᾶι: cf. Pind. *P.* 2.58–61 εἰ δέ τις . . . λέγει ἕτερόν τιν᾽ ἀν᾽ Ἑλλάδα . . . γενέσθαι ὑπέρτερον κτλ.; for other variations of the phrase 'the best/most beautiful etc. under the sun' cf. Sappho 56, Eur. *Hec.* 635–7, Kall. *h.* 3.249–50, and possibly Ibykos (?), *SLG* 166 fr.1.23–5.

23–24 τόσσ[ο]ν . . . φέγγος κατ᾽ ἀνθρώπ[ους φέρουσα: Snell's supplement links τόσσ[ο]ν with οὔτι]ν᾽ (21), 'no other man so great'. Maas suggested κατ᾽ ἀνθρώπ[ων χέοντα, which would make Hieron subject, τόσσ[ο]ν . . . φέγγος the object of χέοντα and a metaphor for 'blessing, joy': '(dawn) looks down at no other man who has showered mankind with so much light'. Although word-order would favour Maas's suggestion, it seems difficult to see in what sense Hieron could have 'showered *mankind*' with joy, glory, or benefactions: if this were what B. wanted to say, he would probably have said 'his people', or 'the Syracusans'. Snell's supplement may therefore be preferable, 'dawn that brings light to men never saw a greater man'.

FR. 20D

1. Text and metre

Of this poem, only about eleven lines are sufficiently well preserved to reveal their content. They are contained in two papyri, **P** and **Q**, though in divergent colometry; **P** fr. 36 overlaps with lines 10–12 (= **Q** col.ii 9–11), and **P** 'new fragment 2' (*P.Oxy.* 2081e. fr. 2) contains remains of two lines of text separated by five lines of a scholion which refers to line 6 of this poem, where the number of Niobe's children is given as ten sons and [ten] daughters: 6–7 δέκα τ᾽ ἠϊθέους δ[έκα τ᾽ εὐπλό]κου[ς ἅμα | κο<ύ>ρας, in agreement with a statement in Gellius, *N.A.* 20.7 *Homerus pueros puellasque eius* (= Niobe's) *bis senos dicit fuisse, Sappho bis novenos, Bacchylides et Pindarus bis denos.* With the supplements suggested by Lobel and Snell, this 'new fragment 2' can be reconstructed as follows:

]ΚΑΜΟΥ[
αντιλογι]α εστιν περι [του αριθμου
ομ ꟼη γ]εγενησθαι εξ [υιους και εξ
θυγατ]ερας, επτα και [επτα Ευ–
ριπιδ]ης, δεκα και δ[εκα Βακχυ–
λιδη]ς και Π[ιν]δαρος [
]ΤΕ[ ]ΡΟΜΕ[

The five lines of the scholion, in small script, occupy the space to the right of three lines of the main text, between two rather long lines. This cannot, however, be reconciled with the text as it stands in pap. **Q**; it seems therefore that the colometry in pap. **P** was different from that in pap. **Q** (this would not be a unique case; another example of divergent colometries is B. 24). W. S. Barrett, in a letter to B. Snell, suggested the following reconstruction of lines 6–10 in pap. **P**:

ΠΑΙΔΕΣΔΕΚΑΤΗΙΘΕΟΥΣΔΕΚΑΤΕΥΠΛΟ]ΚΆΜΟΥ[ΣΑΜΑ
ΚΟ<Υ>ΡΑΣΤΑΝΥΑΚΕΣΙΝΙΟΙΣ·
ΤΑΝΔΕΠΑΤΗΡΕΣΙΔωΝ
ΥΨΙΖΥΓΟΣΟΥΡΑΝΟΘΕΝ
ΖΕΥΣΕΛΕΗΣΕΝΑΝΑΚΕΣΤΟΙΣΚΑΤΑ]ΤΕ[Ι]ΡΟΜΕ[ΝΑΝ
ΑΧΕΣΙΝ κτλ.

Barrett also suggested altering εὔπλο]κάμου[ς to εὐπλόκους because
sequences of more than three dactyls are not found in choral lyric dactyloepitrites (for compounds of -πλόκος corrupted to -πλόκαμος in Pindaric
MSS, see *O.* 6.30 and *I.* 7.23), and εἰσιδών (8) to ἐσιδών. We would thus
get a strophe of 9 lines (against 8 as in **Q**):

– ◡ – – – ◡ ◡ –[◡ ◡ –(–)?	e – D(-)
– – ◡ – – – ◡ [– –	– E –
– – ◡ ◡ – ◡ ◡ – [◡ ◡ –] ◡ – [◡ ◡	– D d² ◡ e ‖
– – ◡ ◡ – ◡ ◡ – –	– D –
– ◡ ◡ – ◡ ◡ –	D
– – ◡ ◡ – ◡ [◡ –	– D
– ◡ ◡ – ◡ ◡ – –[– ◡ ◡] – ◡ ◡ –	D – D
◡ ◡ – – – ◡ ◡ – ◡ ◡ –[◡	d² – D – ‖
– – ◡ – – – ◡ – –[– ◡ – (–)	E – e (-) ‖‖

The punctuation after ἰοῖς· (7) seems to favour this colometry; it would also
provide space for a suitable participle in line 9 to accommodate ἄχεσιν (10).
All in all, Barrett's reconstruction of the colometry in pap. **P** has a good
chance of being correct.

2. The myth

From line 3 to line 11 the poet tells the sad story of Niobe and the death
of her children (on the function of this poem as a 'negative enkomion', see
above, p. 239). As this section begins with οὐδέ, and as there seems to be
no space for a verb at the end of line 4, Νιόβα [γενεάν (or Νιόβα[ς γενεά ?)
may be the subject (or object) of a verb in the preceding stanza (see below
on line 4), in which a story of a similar nature may have been told, possibly
about a 'good-looking wife' (εὐειδὴς ἄλοχος, 2). Who can she be? Lobel,
following the clue of ΟΙΝ[in the papyrus, initially thought of Oinone

(ἄλοχος Π[άριος, cf. Apollod. 3.12.6 and Diod. 4.34) who threw herself from a tower, according to Lykophron (*Alex.* 65–6), or hanged herself when she learned of Paris' death (Konon 23 = *FGrHist* 26 F 1; Parthenios 4, cf. Hellanikos *FGrHist* 4 F 29), or burned herself to death on Paris' funeral pyre (Quint. Smyrn. 10.466–8). On second thoughts, however, Lobel rejected this idea on the grounds that Oinone had nothing in common with Niobe; instead, he suggested Althaia, the wife of Oineus (ἄλοχος Οἰν[ῆος): 'The parallel will be between mothers who by their own action caused the death, the one of her son, the other of her whole family' (*Ox.Pap.* xxiii p.25).

Although this connection appears possible, an explicit reference to Althaia's beauty seems odd, not only because there is no other evidence for it, but above all because it would have no function in the context of the Meleager myth. There is, however, a third possibility which may deserve consideration: could she be Meleager's wife, the 'beautiful Kleopatra' (καλὴ Κλεοπάτρα, *Il.* 9.556), who urged him to go on his 'last path', i.e. into battle against the Kouretes (*Il.* 9.590–1 Μελέαγρον ἐΰζωνος παράκοιτις | λίσσετ' ὀδυρομένη), where he was to be killed by Apollo? Cf. [Hes.] fr. 25.12–13; 280.2; Minyas *PEG* fr.5 = Paus. 10.31.3; Ant. Lib. 2.5. In this case, ὤρμασεν would be transitive: 2–3 Μ[ελέαγρον] | λοισθίαν ὤρμασεν Οἰν[είδαν κέλευθον 'she drove Meleager, Oineus' son, onto his last path', cf. *Il.* 6.338–9 where Paris says to Hektor νῦν δέ με παρειποῦσ' ἄλοχος μαλακοῖς ἐπέεσσιν | ὤρμησ' ἐς πόλεμον. The link to the Niobe story would be that she unwittingly caused her husband's death, as Niobe caused the death of her children; both grieve unconsolably, Kleopatra hangs herself (Apollod. 1.8.3 and Ant. Lib. 2.5).

On the Niobe myth, see Barrett, *Niobe*.

2 .οθεν: of the first letter, only the foot of an upright remains which descends below the line; Lobel therefore suggested ὔ–]| ψοθεν (which he took to be a reference to hanging oneself, see above). But τ seems also possible (τόθεν): although τ does not normally descend below the level of the other letters, it does in fr. 6 of this papyrus (**Q**, see *Ox.Pap.* xxiii pl.5) at the beginning of a line.

3 λοισθίαν . . . [κέλευθον or ὁδόν? So (without article) Eur. *Alc.* 610 ὑστάτην ὁδόν, *Med.* 1067 τλημονεστάτην ὁδόν, *Ion* 1226 ἀθλίαν ὁδόν (with article: Soph. *Ant.* 807 τὰν νεάταν ὁδόν, *Tr.* 874–5 τὴν πανυστάτην | ὁδῶν ἁπασῶν).

ὥρμασεν Οἰν[είδαν   'she urged the son of Oineus on'?, cf. Ap.Rhod.
1.190–1 Οἰνεΐδης . . . ἀφορμηθεὶς Καλυδῶνος | ἀλκήεις Μελέαγρος, *SH* 970
= *P.Brux.* II col.ii 20 Οἰνεΐδης Μελέαγρος. For transitive ὁρμᾶν, cf. *Il.* 6.338
(quoted above), B. 18.41, Thuc. 1.87.2 ἐς τὸ πολεμεῖν . . . ὁρμῆσαι, 1.127
(Pericles) ἐς τὸν πόλεμον ὥρμα τοὺς Ἀθηναίους, 2.20.4 (the Acharnians)
ὁρμήσειν καὶ τοὺς πάντας ἐς μάχην.

4 τλαπενθής: not elsewhere attested, but cf. ταλαπενθής 5.157 and
16.26, and *Od.* 5.222 (Odysseus) τλήσομαι ἐν στήθεσσιν ἔχων ταλαπενθέα
θυμόν.

Νιόβα[‿‿–(–?):   in the next line, τὰν ὤλεσαν cannot refer to Niobe,
because Apollo and Artemis killed not her, but her children; Lobel therefore
suggested Νιόβα [γενεάν (or perhaps -ᾶς or -ᾱι, depending on the verb to
be supplied), rather than Νιόβα[ς γενεά, because τλαπενθής seems much
more suitable for Niobe herself than for her children. The verb may have
been something like 'she could not save', or 'she could not bear to see
destroyed': either would be suitable also for Kleopatra, see above.

5–6 Λατοῦς . . . παῖδες: ἀγαυός 'noble' is usually said of kings and
heroes, rarely of gods: Persephone in *Od.* 11.226, the Olympic gods in Hes.
Th. 461, the Titans in *Th.* 632, Lachesis in Isyllos' *Paean* 54 (*Coll. Alex.*
p.134 = Käppel, *Paian* 382 = Furley and Bremer II 183).

6–9   On the possibility of reconciling the text of pap. **Q** with that of pap.
P (*P.Oxy.* 2081e 'new fragment 2') see above, p. 255.

6 δέκα: in poetry and in the mythographers, the number of Niobe's
children varied from five to twenty. The lowest number, two + three, is
given by Herodoros, *FGrHist* 31 F 56 = Apollod. 3.5.6 δύο μὲν ἄρρενας,
τρεῖς δὲ θηλείας (but one MS has τέσσαρας μὲν ἄρρενας, apparently to
bring the numbers into line with those in Hellanikos, *FGrHist* 4 F 21: four
+ three); six + six *Il.* 24.603–4 and Pherekydes, *FGrHist* 3 F 126 (with
names), seven + seven Lasos, *PMG* 706 = Aelian, *V.H.* 12.36, Aesch. fr.
167b, Soph. fr. 446, Eur. fr. 453 (= schol. Eur. *Pho.* 159), Aristoph. fr. 294
(*PCG* III 2, p.166), Apollod. 3.5.6; nine + nine Sappho fr. 205 = Gellius, *N.A.*
20.7, ten + ten [Hes.] fr. 183, Mimnermos fr. 19, Pindar *Paian* 13 (cf. Aelian,
V.H. 12.36), and perhaps Alkman *PMG* 75 = 214 Calame (= Aelian, *V.H.*
12.36 Ἀλκμὰν δέκα φησί, which Barrett believes to be a misunderstanding
of 'ten sons' or 'ten daughters' as 'ten children', *Niobe* 227 n.130).

7 τανυάκεσιν ἰοῖς: τανυήκης/τανάηκης 'with long edge' is said of swords
or spears in Homer (*Il.* 14.385 etc., once of an axe: *Il.* 23.118, once also of
branches in a simile: *Il.* 16.765–9, which evokes the image of missiles flying

to and fro, 'a fine example of interaction between a simile's diction and its context', Janko ad loc.). Cf. τανυγλώχινας ὀϊστούς *Il.* 8.297 and *AP* 7.443 (Simonides), Quint. Smyrn. 6.463, Nonnos 22.324.

8 ὑψίζυγος 'high-throned' is a Homeric epithet of Zeus (*Il.* 14.166 etc.); also Hes. *Op.* 18, B. 1.155–6 and 11.2–3.

10–11 ὀκριόεντ[α] λᾶαν 'a jagged rock'; in Homer, the epithet is said of stones which kill (*Il.* 12.380, 16.735–9, *Od.* 9.499) or wound (*Il.* 8.327) fighters. In B. it seems designed to create compassion with Niobe. According to Pherekydes (*FGrHist* 3 F 38) and Apollod. 3.5.6, who may both reflect Sophocles' *Niobe* (see Barrett, *Niobe* 224), it was Niobe herself who prayed to be turned into stone; B. agrees with schol. A on *Il.* 24.602 θρηνοῦσαν οὖν τὴν Νιόβην τὸ τοιοῦτο δυστύχημα Ζεὺς ἐλεήσας εἰς λίθον μετέβαλεν κτλ. (the story is there attributed to Euphorion, but it is not certain that all of it comes from this source).

12 οὐδ[: another mythical example of a similar nature may have filled the next stanza.

APPENDIX: VASES REFERRED TO IN THE COMMENTARY

1 **Paris, Louvre G 197** (amphora by Myson); *ARV²* 238; *Para* 349; *Add.* 201; Boardman, *ARFV* fig.171; Simon, *Vasen* pll. 132–3

2 **Corinth, Mus. T.1144** (fragments of Attic hydria); *ARV²* 571.74; Beazley 1955 pl. 85

3 **Châtillon-sur-Seine, Musée** (bronze crater from Vix); Joffroy, *Le trésor de Vix*; Richter, *Handbook of Greek art* 215–16, figs. 302 and 303

4 **Florence, Mus. Arch. 4209** (volute crater, 'François Vase'); *ABV* 76.1; *Para* 29; *Add.* 21; Simon, *Vasen* pll. 52–7

5 **Bollingen** (Switzerland), **R. Blatter collection** (fr. of b/f dinos); R. Blatter, 'Dinosfragmente mit der kalydonischen Eberjagd', *AntK* 5 (1962) 45–7 pl.16.1 + 3; *Para* 42; Schefold, *Myth and legend* pl. 61b; *LIMC* vi 416 no.9

6 **Naples, Nat. Mus., Coll. Santangelo 99** (black-figure lekythos); Fairbanks, *Athenian lekythoi* 32 no.7 and pl. 2.1

7 **Rome, Vatican, Coll. Astarita A 565** (Corinthian crater); Amyx, *Corinthian vase-painting* I 264; II 576; III pll. 116 and 117; *LIMC* vii 837 no.3; 911 no.1; Beazley 1957: 233–44 and pll. 11–16; Schefold, *Myth and legend* 86 pl. 72

8 **Athens, Museum of the Argive Heraion** (fragments of early Attic dinos from the Heraion at Argos); J. M. Cook, *BSA* 35 (1934–5) 191; Brommer, *Vasenlisten* p. 156 (A.63); Brommer, *Herakles* II 51; C. Dugas, 'La mort du centaure Nessos', *RÉA* 45 (1943) 18–26 pl.19.3; Gentili, *Bacchilide* 51f.; March, *Creative poet* 53f. and pl. 20; *LIMC* vi 843 no. 89

9 **Cerveteri** (hydria from Caere, formerly in Rome, Villa Giulia); Hemelrijk 30–1 no.16 fig. 21 and pl.70; March, *Creative poet* 54 and pl.23a

10 **Paris, Louvre C 10228** (hydria from Caere); Hemelrijk 31–2 no.17 fig. 22 and pll. 72–3; Schefold, *Gods and heroes* 160 fig.197; March, *Creative poet* p.54 and pl. 23b

11 **Rome, Villa Giulia** (hydria from Caere); Hemelrijk p.36 no. 20B fig. 27 and pl.82; *LIMC* vi 842 no.80

12 **Basel, Antikenmuseum**, **Käppeli collection 601**
(relief-decorated amphora); Schefold, *Myth and legend* pl. 25a;
Brommer, *Theseus* pl.26; *LIMC* vi 576–7 no.33

13 **Paris, Louvre G 104** (r/f kylix); *ARV²* 318.1 + 1645; *Para* 358; *Add.*
214; Boardman, *ARFV* fig. 223; Brommer, *Theseus* 78f. and pl.22;
Neils no.15; *LIMC* i 730 no.75

14 **New York, MMA 53.11.4** (r/f kylix); *ARV²* 406.7; Neils no.59
(fig.48 on pl.10); *LIMC* i 730 no.76

15 **Zürich, University Archaeol. collection L5** (amphora); *ARV²*
1656.2bis; C. Isler-Kerenyi, *Lieblinge der Meermädchen* (Zürich 1977)
fig. 1b, 7a, 8ab; J. M. Barringer, *Divine escorts* 174 no.14 and
pll.150–5

16 **Paris**, Bibliothèque Nationale, **Cabinet des Médailles 418**
(calyx crater); *ARV²* 260.2; *Add.* 204; Neils no.47 (fig.40 pl.9);
Brommer, *Theseus* 80 fig.12; *LIMC* i 730 no.77; vi 815 no.426; vii 939
no.221

17 **Cambridge/Mass.**, Harvard University, **Fogg Art Museum
1960.339** (column crater); *ARV²* 274.39; *Add.* 207; Neils no.48 (fig.41
pl.9); *LIMC* i 730 no.78

18 **Copenhagen, Ny Carlsberg Glyptotek 2695** (pelike); *ARV²*
362.19; *Add.* 222; Brommer, *Theseus* pl.23a; Neils no.65; *LIMC* i 730
no.78a; vii 939 no.222

19 **Bologna, Museo Civico 303**; *ARV²* 1184.6; *Para* 460; *Add.* 341;
Brommer, *Theseus* pl.23b; Neils no.143; *LIMC* i 731 no.79

20 **Paris, Louvre MNC 675** (Boiotian skyphos); Dugas, *REG* 56
(1943) 6–7 and fig.4; Dugas and Flacelière, *Thésée* pl.1; *LIMC* iii 1055
no.35

21 **Athens, Nat. Mus. 15499** (dinos by Sophilos); *ABV* 39.16;
Boardman, *BFVA* fig.26; Schefold, *Myth and legend* 90 and pl.vi;
G. Bakır, *Sophilos* 65 (A.3, fig.10 pl.6); Simon, *Vasen* pl.50

22 **Madrid, Mus. Arqueol. 11265** (kylix); *ARV²* 174.1; *Add.* 339;
Brommer, *Theseus* pll.15ab, 16ab, 48b; Simon, *Vasen* pll.221–223;
Neils no.129 (figs.82–4 pl.17); *LIMC* vii 928 no.52 (outside), 941
no.240 (inside)

23 **Athens**, Nat. Mus., **Akropolis Museum 1280** (b/f skyphos);
ABL 249.1; Neils no.29; *LIMC* vii 929 no.62 (= 931 no.99; 947
no.308)

24 Toledo/Ohio 63.27 (b/f skyphos); *Para* 257; *Add.* 129f.; Boardman, *BFVA* fig.245.1–2; *LIMC* VII 931 no.97

25 Laon, Musée 37.996 (b/f skyphos); *ABL* 249.2; *Para* 255.2; *LIMC* VII 931 no.98

26 London, BM, E 36 (r/f kylix); *ARV²* 115.3; Brommer, *Theseus* pl.8a; Neils no.4 (figs.12–13 pl.3); *LIMC* VII 926 no.34

27 London, BM, E 48 (r/f kylix); *ARV²* 431.47; Brommer, *Theseus* pl.9ab; Neils no.55 (figs.43–5 pl.9); *LIMC* VII 927 no.39

28 Oxford, Ashmol. Mus. 1937.983 (calyx crater); *ARV²* 1153.13; *Para* 457; *Add.* 336; Brommer, *Theseus* pl.34; Schefold, *Göttersage* 88 fig.112; *LIMC* VII 928 no.50

29 Munich 2565 (r/f kantharos); *ARV²* 889.169; *Add.* 302; Neils no.97; *CVA* 2 (Germany 6) pl.93.3–4

30 Sydney 49.64 (bell crater); Pryce (1936) pl.5

31 Munich 585 (north-ionian amphora); Schefold, *Gods and heroes* 25 fig.19; Steinhart, *Das Motiv des Auges* 121 and pl.46; Yalouris, *Le mythe d'Io* no.2 fig.2; *LIMC* V 667 no.31

32 London, BM 1848.6–19.4 (amphora); *ABV* 148.2; *Add.* 41; Boardman, *BFVA* fig.107; Schefold, *Gods and heroes* 26 fig.20

33 Paris, Louvre G 229 (pelike); *ARV²* 289.3; *Add.* 210; Yalouris, *Le mythe d'Io* no.9 fig.6; *LIMC* V 666 no.25

34 Vienna, Kunsthist. Mus. IV 3729 (stamnos); *ARV²* 288.1; *Add.* 209; March, *Dict.* 216 fig.77; Yalouris, *Le mythe d'Io* no.8 fig.5; *LIMC* V 665 no.13

35 Naples, Nat. Mus., ex Spinelli 2041 (pelike); *ARV²* 1122; *Add.* 332; Yalouris, *Le mythe d'Io* no.14 fig.8; *LIMC* V 669 no.62

36 Palermo, Fond. Mormino 178 (skyphos); *ARV²* 1689; *LIMC* V 667–8 no. 39

37 Boston, MFA 1901.562 (Lucanian jug); Trendall, *The red-figured vases of Lucania, Campania and Sicily* (1967) 16.9; Yalouris no.13 fig.17; *LIMC* V 667.33

38 Munich 2417 (psykter); *ARV²* 556.101 *Para* 387.188; *Add.* 258; Schefold, *Göttersage* 189 figs.253–4; Boardman, *ARFV* fig.338.1–2; March, *Dict.* 213 fig.76; *LIMC* VI 365 no.2

39 Florence, Mus. Arch. 19B 41 + Paris, Louvre C 10834 (stamnos); *ARV²* 191.100 + 361.3; *Add.* 222; *LIMC* VI 365 no.3

40 London, BM 95.10–31.1 (amphora); *ARV²* 583.1

41 **Basel, Antikenmuseum, Käppeli collection 421** (b/f plate by Psiax); *ABV* 294.21; *Para* 128; *Add.* 77; Paquette, *L'instrument de musique* 185 (B19)

42 **Munich 1416** (amphora); *ABV* 367.90; *Add.* 98; Wegner, *Musikleben* pl.9; Paquette, *L'instrument de musique* 203B

WORKS CITED

CITATIONS OF FRAGMENTS OF GREEK POETRY

Fragments of Greek epic poetry are cited from *PEG* (see below); of elegiac and iambic poetry from *IEG*; of lyric poetry (other than that of Sappho, Alcaeus, and Pindar) from *PMG*, *PMGF* or *SLG*; of Sappho and Alcaeus from *PLF*; of Pindar, from *Pindarus, Pars II* (ed. H. Maehler, Leipzig 1989); of comedy, from *PCG*; of tragedy, from *TrGF*, except fragments of Euripides' plays, which are cited from *Tragicorum graecorum fragmenta* rec. A. Nauck (2nd edn., Leipzig 1889, = N²); those of Antimachos from *Antimachi Colophonii reliquiae* ed. B. Wyss (Berlin 1936); those of mimes from *Herodae mimiambi* ed. I. C. Cunningham (Leipzig 1987).

Most of the translations are taken (with some slight modifications) from M. L. West, *Greek lyric poetry* (Oxford 1993) and from the Loeb editions of D. A. Campbell, *Greek lyric*, vols. I–V (1982–93), and W. H. Race, *Pindar*, vols. I–II (1997).

BOOKS AND ARTICLES REFERRED TO BY AUTHOR'S NAME

Adamesteanu, D. *La Basilicata antica: storia e monumenti* (Cava dei Tirreni 1974)

Amandry, P. 'Trépieds de Delphes', *BCH* III (1987) 81–92

Amyx, D. A. *Corinthian vase-painting of the archaic period*, 3 vols. (Berkeley 1988)

Andronikos, M. 'Totenkult' 9 = *Archaeologia Homerica* III W (Göttingen 1968)

Bakır, G. *Sophilos* (Mainz 1981)

Barrett, W. S. 'Bacchylides, Asine and Apollo Pythaieus', *Hermes* 82 (1954) 421–44

'Dactylo-epitrites in Bacchylides', *Hermes* 84 (1956) 248–53

Euripides: Hippolytos (Oxford 1964)

Niobe, in R. Carden, *The papyrus fragments of Sophocles* (Berlin 1974) 171–235

Barringer, J. M. *Divine escorts: Nereids in archaic and classical Greek art* (Ann Arbor 1995)

Barron, J. P. 'Ibycus: To Polycrates', *BICS* 16 (1969), 119–49

'Bacchylides, Theseus and a woolly cloak', *BICS* 27 (1980) 1–8

Bean, G. E. *Aegean Turkey* (London 1966)

Beazley, J. D. 'Hydria-fragments in Corinth', *Hesperia* 24 (1955) 305–19 and pl.85

'ΕΛΕΝΗΣ ΑΠΑΙΤΗΣΙΣ', *Proceedings of the British Academy* 43 (1957) 233–44

Boardman, J. *Black figured vases in Athens* (London 1974)

Athenian red-figured vases: The archaic period (London 1975)

Greek sculpture: The archaic period (London 1978)

Bonanno, M. G. 'Asklep. xv G.-P. (= AP xii 46),2 φλέγετε', *Eikasmos* 7 (1996) 155–9

Bothmer, D. von *Amazons in Greek art* (Oxford 1957)

Bowra, C. M. *Greek lyric poetry*, 2nd edn. (Oxford 1961)

On Greek margins (Oxford 1970)

Braswell, B. K. *A commentary on the fourth Pythian Ode of Pindar* (Berlin 1988)

Brommer, F. *Vasenlisten zur griechischen Heldensage*, 3rd ed. (Marburg 1973)

Theseus (Darmstadt 1982)

Bundy, E. L. *Studia Pindarica* (Berkeley-Los Angeles 1962)

Burkert, W. 'Jason, Hypsipyle and the new fire at Lemnos', *CQ* 20 (1970) 1–16

Greek religion (Cambridge, Mass. 1985)

Burnett, A. P. *The art of Bacchylides* (Cambridge, Mass. 1985)

Calame, C. *Les chœurs de jeunes filles en Grèce archaïque*, I *Morphologie, fonction religieuse et sociale*, II *Alcman* (Rome 1977)

Campbell, M. Review of Vian and Delage, *Apollonios de Rhodes* vol. iii, *CR* 32 (1982) 16

Carey, C. 'Bacchylides experiments: Ode 11', *Mnemosyne* 33 (1980) 225–43

Carter, J. C. 'Sanctuaries in the *Chora* of Metaponto', in S. E. Alcock and R. Osborne (eds.), *Placing the gods: Sanctuaries and sacred space in ancient Greece* (Oxford 1994) 161–98

Cartledge, P. 'The Greek religious festivals', in P. E. Easterling and J. V. Muir, *Greek religion and society* (Cambridge 1985) 98–127

Caskey, L. D. 'Archaeological notes', *AJA* 41 (1937) 525–7

Chamoux, F. 'L'aurige', *Fouilles de Delphes* iv 5 (Paris 1955) 51–82

Chantraine, P. *Morphologie historique du grec* (2nd edn., Paris 1961)

Grammaire homérique, I *Phonétique et morphologie* (Paris 1958), II *Syntaxe* (Paris 1963)

Dictionnaire étymologique de la langue grecque, 2 vols. (Paris 1968–80)

Christ, W. 'Zu den neuaufgefundenen Gedichten des Bakchylides', *Sitzungsberichte der Bayrischen Akademie* (Munich 1898)

Combellack, F. M. 'Agamemnon's black heart', *Grazer Beiträge* 4 (1975) 81–7

Constantinidou, S. 'Dionysiac elements in Spartan cult dances', *Phoenix* 52
      (1998) 15–30

Courby, M. F. 'La terrasse du temple', *Fouilles de Delphes* ii 2 (Paris 1927)

Cozzoli, A.-T. *Euripide: Cretesi* (Pisa-Rome 2001)

Crum, W. *A Coptic dictionary* (Oxford 1939)

Crusius, O. 'Aus den Dichtungen des Bakchylides', *Philologus* 57 (1898) 150–
      83 and 352

D' Angour, A. 'How the dithyramb got its shape', *CQ* n.s. 47 (1997) 331–51

Davies, J. K. *Athenian propertied families* (Oxford 1971)

Davies, M. I. 'The reclamation of Helen', *AntK* 20 (1977) 73–85 and pl.17

Denniston, J. D. *Euripides: Electra* (Oxford 1939)
      The Greek particles, 2nd edn. (Oxford 1954)

Dodds, E. R. *Euripides: Bacchae*, 2nd edn. (Oxford 1960)

Dugas, C. 'L'évolution de la légende de Thésée', *RÉG* 56 (1943) 1–24 and
      pll.1–4

Dugas, C. and Flacelière, R. *Thésée: Images et récits* (Paris 1958)

Easterling, P. E. *Sophocles: Trachiniae* (Cambridge 1982)

Ebert, J. *Griechische Epigramme auf Sieger an gymnischen und hippischen Agonen*
      (Berlin 1972)

      (ed.), *Olympia: Mythos und Geschichte moderner Wettkämpfe* (Vienna 1980)

Edmonds, J. M. *CR* 36 (1922) 159–61

Erichsen, W. *Demotisches Glossar* (Copenhagen 1954)

Fabbro, H. *Carmina convivialia attica* (Rome 1995)

Fagles, R. *Bacchylides: Complete poems* (New Haven 1961)

Fairbanks, A. *Athenian Lekythoi* (New York 1907)

Farnell, L. W. *The cults of the Greek states* (Oxford 1896–1909)

Fatouros, G. S. 'Bakchylides der Flötenspieler, nicht Bakchylides der
      Dichter', *Philologus* 105 (1961) 147–9

Fehling, D. *Die Wiederholungsfiguren und ihr Gebrauch bei den Griechen vor Gorgias*
      (Berlin 1969)

Foltiny, S. 'Schwert, Dolch und Messer', in H. G. Buchholz, *Archaeologia
      homerica E2: Kriegswesen* (Göttingen 1980)

Fraenkel, E. *Aeschylus: Agamemnon*, 3 vols. (Oxford 1950)

Fränkel, H. *Early Greek poetry and philosophy* (Oxford 1975)

Fraser, P. M. *Ptolemaic Alexandria*, 3 vols. (Oxford 1972)

Frisk, H. *Griechisches etymologisches Wörterbuch* (Heidelberg 1960)

Frödin, O. and Persson, A. W. *Asine: Results of the Swedish excavations* (Stock-
      holm 1938)

Führer, R. *Formproblem-Untersuchungen zu den Reden in der frühgriechischen Lyrik* (Munich 1967)

Furley, W. D. and Bremer, J. M. *Greek hymns*, I *The texts in translation*, II *Greek texts and commentary* (Tübingen 2001)

Galiart, L. H. *Beiträge zur Mythologie bei Bakchylides* (Freiburg/Fribourg 1910)

Gallavotti, C. 'Studi sulla lirica greca', *RFIC* 22 (1944) 1–15

Gallo, I. *Una nuova biografia di Pindaro* (Salerno 1968)

Gentili, B. *Bacchilide: Studi* (Urbino 1958)

  Poetry and its public in ancient Greece (Baltimore 1988)

  'Il ditirambo XVIISn. di Bacchilide e il cratere Tricase di Ruvo', *ArchClass* 6 (1954) 121–5

Gerber D. E., 'The gifts of Aphrodite (Bacchylides 17.10)', *Phoenix* 19 (1965) 212–13

  'Bacchylides 17.124–9', *ZPE* 49 (1982) 3–5

Gercke, H.-J. 'Ephebeia', *Der Neue Pauly* III (Stuttgart 1997) 1071–5

Gomme, A. W. *A historical commentary on Thucydides*, 5 vols. (Oxford 1959–81)

Goodwin, W. W. *Syntax of the moods and tenses of the Greek verb* (London 1889)

Gow, A. S. F. *Theocritus*, 2 vols. (Cambridge 1950)

Graf, F. 'Dionysian and Orphic eschatology', in T. H. Carpenter and C. A. Faraone (eds.), *Masks of Dionysos* (Ithaca 1993) 239–58

Grenfell, B. P. and Hunt, A. S. *The Oxyrhynchus Papyri* XI (1915) 65–83 and pl.3 (no.1361)

Griffith, M. *Aeschylus: Prometheus Bound* (Cambridge 1983)

Groningen, B. A. van *La composition littéraire archaïque grecque* (2nd edn., Amsterdam 1960)

  Pindare au banquet (Leiden 1960)

  Théognis: Le premier livre (Amsterdam 1966)

Hammond, N. G. L. and Griffith, G. T. *History of Macedonia*, 3 vols. (Oxford 1972–88)

Hanfmann, G. M. A. 'On the palace of Croesus', in U. Höckmann and A. Krug (eds.), *Festschrift F. Brommer* (Mainz 1977) 145–54 and pl. 41

  Sardis from prehistoric to Roman times (Cambridge, Mass. 1983)

Headlam, W. in A. D. Knox (ed.), *Herodas: The mimes and fragments* (Cambridge 1922)

Heitsch, E. 'Die nicht-philosophische ἀλήθεια', *Hermes* 90 (1962) 26–33

  Die griechischen Dichterfragmente der römischen Kaiserzeit, I–II (Göttingen 1963–4)

Hemelrijk, J. M. *Caeretan hydriae* (Mainz 1984)

Hignett, C. *Athenian constitution to the end of the fifth century BC* (Oxford 1952)

Hoey, T. F. 'The date of the *Trachiniae*', *Phoenix* 33 (1979) 210–32

Homolle, T. 'Le trépied de Gelon', *BCH* 21, 1897, 588–90

Hooker, J. T. 'Arion and the dolphin', *Greece and Rome* 36 (1989) 141–6

How, W. W. and Wells, J. *A commentary on Herodotus*, 2 vols. (Oxford 1912)

Hunt, A. S. *The Oxyrhynchus Papyri* XVII (1927) 79–80 (no. 2081e)

Hunter, R. L. *Theocritus and the archaeology of Greek poetry* (Cambridge 1996)

Ieranò, G. 'Osservazioni sul Teseo di Bacchilide', *Acme* 40 (1987) 87–103

    Il ditirambo di Dioniso: Le testimonianze antiche (Rome 1997)

Immerwahr, H. *Attic script* (Oxford 1990)

Irigoin, J. *Histoire du texte de Pindare* (Paris 1952)

Irwin, E. *Colour terms in Greek poetry* (Toronto 1974)

Isler-Kerenyi, C. *Lieblinge der Meermädchen* (Zürich 1977)

Janko, R. *The Iliad: A commentary*, vol. 4: Books 13–16 (Cambridge 1992)

Jeffery, L. H. *The local scripts of archaic Greece*, 2nd edn. revised by A. W. Johnston (Oxford 1990)

Joffroy, R. 'Le trésor de Vix', *Monuments Piot* 48.1 (Paris 1954)

Jörgensen, O. 'Das Auftreten der Götter in den Büchern ι–μ der Odyssee', *Hermes* 39 (1904) 357–82

Jost, M. *Sanctuaires et cultes d'Arcadie* (Paris 1985)

Kamerbeek, J. C. *The plays of Sophocles*, vol. II (Leiden 1959)

Käppel, L. *Paian: Studien zur Geschichte einer Gattung* (Berlin 1992)

Kearns, E. *The heroes of Attica* (London 1989)

Kirchner, J. *Prosopographia attica* (Berlin 1901–3)

Kirk, G. S. *The Iliad: A commentary*, vol. 1: Books 1–4 (Cambridge 1985)

Körte, A. 'Bacchylidea', *Hermes* 53 (1918) 113–47

Kron, U. *Die zehn attischen Phylenheroen* (Berlin 1976)

Krumeich, R. 'Zu den goldenen Dreifüßen der Deinomeniden in Delphi', *JdI* 106 (1991) 37–62.

Krzyszkowska, O. *Ivory and related materials* (London 1990)

Kuiper, W. E. J. 'De Bacchylidis carmine xv', *Mnemosyne* 53 (1925) 343–50

    'De Bacchylidis carmine XVIII', *Mnemosyne* 56 (1928) 55–9

Latte, K. 'Randbemerkungen', *Philologus* 87 (1932) 265–76

    'Zur griechischen Wortforschung', *Glotta* 34 (1955) 190–202

Leaf, W. *The Iliad*, 2 vols. (London 1900 and 1902)

Lee, H. M. *The program and schedule of the ancient Olympic Games* (Hildesheim 2001)

Leumann, M. *Homerische Wörter* (Basel 1950)

Lloyd, A. B. *Herodotus: Book* ii, 3 vols. (Leiden 1975–88)

Lloyd-Jones, H. [*Review Ox.Pap.* xxiii ed. E. Lobel] *CR* n.s.8 (1958) 16–22

Lobel, E. Σαπφοῦς μέλη (Oxford 1925)

Löffler, I. *Die Melampodie* (Meisenheim 1963)

Lorenzoni, A. 'Simon. Cei fragm. novum', *MusCrit* 15–17 (1980–82) 51

Ludwich, A. [review of Kenyon] *Vorlesungsverzeichnis Königsberg, Sommer 1898*, 12–13

Maas, M. and McIntosh-Snyder, J. *Stringed instruments of ancient Greece* (New Haven 1989)

Maas, P. *Die neuen Responsionsfreiheiten bei Bakchylides und Pindar*, i–ii (Berlin 1914 and 1921)

    'Zu den neuen Bruchstücken des Bakchylides', *Jahresberichte des Philologischen Vereins Berlin* 45 (1919) 37–41 [reprinted in *Kleine Schriften* 28–33]

    'Zu dem Paean des Bakchylides', *Hermes* 67 (1932) 469–71 [reprinted in *Kleine Schriften* 33–5]

    Greek Metre (Oxford 1962)

    Kleine Schriften (Munich 1973)

Maehler, H. *Die Lieder des Bakchylides.* i *Die Siegeslieder,* ii *Die Dithyramben und Fragmente* (Leiden 1982 and 1997)

    'Bemerkungen zum Gebrauch des Satz-Asyndetons bei Bakchylides und Pindar', in *Poesia e religione in Grecia: Studi in onore di G. A. Privitera*, (Naples 2000) 421–30

    'Bakchylides and the Polyzalos inscription', *ZPE* 139 (2002) 19–21

March, J. R. *The creative poet* (London 1987)

    Cassell dictionary of classical mythology (London 1998)

Merkelbach, R. 'ἀγλαόθρονος', *ZPE* 11 (1973) 160

    'Der Theseus des Bakchylides', *ZPE* 12 (1973) 56–62

    'Die goldenen Totenpässe: ägyptisch, orphisch, bakchisch', *ZPE* 128 (1999), 1–13

Merkelbach, R. and West, M. L. (eds.), *Fragmenta Hesiodea* (Oxford 1967)

Michaelides, S. *The music of ancient Greece* (London 1978)

Miller, C. W. E. 'On τὸ δέ "whereas" ', *TAPA* 39 (1908) 121–46

Mitsopoulos-Leon, V. 'The statue of Artemis at Lousoi', in O. Palagia and W. Coulson (eds.), *Sculpture from Arcadia and Laconia* (Oxford 1993) 33–9

Moretti, L. *Iscrizioni agonistiche greche* (Rome 1953)

Neils, J. *The youthful deeds of Theseus* (Rome 1987)

Neue, C. F. *Bacchylidis Cei fragmenta* (Berlin 1822)

Newhall, A. E. 'The Corinthian Kerameikos', *AJA* 35 (1931) 1–30

Nilsson, M. P. *Geschichte der griechischen Religion*, 2 vols. (Munich 1941)

O'Brian-Moore, A. *Madness in ancient literature* (Weimar 1924)

Page, D. 'Simonidea', *JHS* 71 (1951) 140–2

    Sappho and Alcaeus (Oxford 1955)

    'An early tragedy on the fall of Croesus?', *PCPS* 188 (1962) 47–9

    Epigrammata graeca (Oxford 1975)

Paquette, D. *L'instrument de musique dans la céramique de la Grèce antique* (Paris 1984)

Peek, W. *Der Isis-Hymnus von Andros und verwandte Texte* (Berlin 1930)

Pelekidis, C. *Histoire de l'éphébie attique* (Paris 1962)

Pfeiffer, R. *History of classical scholarship*, vol. 1 (Oxford 1968)

Pfeijffer, I. L. *Three Aeginetan odes of Pindar* (Leiden 1999)

Pickard-Cambridge, A. W. *Dithyramb, tragedy and comedy*, 2nd edn. (Oxford 1962)

    The dramatic festivals of Athens, 2nd edn. (Oxford 1968)

Platt, A. 'Notes on Bacchylides', *CR* 12 (1898) 58–64

Pryce, F. N. 'An illustration of Bacchylides', *JHS* 56 (1936) 77–8

Race, W. H. *Style and rhetoric in Pindar's Odes* (Atlanta 1990)

Radt, S. L. *Pindars zweiter und sechster Paian* (Amsterdam 1958)

Reichel, W. and Wilhelm, A. 'Das Heiligtum der Artemis zu Lusoi', *ÖJh.* 4 (1901) 1–89

Richards, H. 'Notes on Bacchylides', *CR* 12 (1898) 76–7

Richardson, N. J. *The Homeric hymn to Demeter* (Oxford 1974)

Richter, G. M. A. *A Handbook of Greek Art* (Oxford 1959)

Risch, E. 'θρόνος, θρόνα und die Komposita vom Typus χρυσόθρονος', *Studii Clasice* 14 (1972) 17–25

Roebuck, C. 'The grain trade between Greece and Egypt', *CPh* 45 (1950) 236–47

Ruijgh, C. J. *Autour de TE épique* (Amsterdam 1971)

Rutherford, I. *Pindar's paeans* (Oxford 2001)

Sachs, C. *History of musical instruments* (New York 1940)

Schefold, K. *Gods and heroes in late archaic Greek art* (Cambridge 1992)

    Die Göttersage in der klassischen und hellenistischen Kunst (Munich 1981)

    Myth and legend in early Greek art (London 1966)

Schmidt, D. 'An unusual victory list from Keos: *IG* xii 5, 608 and the dating of Bakchylides', *JHS* 119 (1999) 67–85

Schwinge, E. R. *Die Stellung der 'Trachinierinnen' im Werk des Sophokles* (Göttingen 1962)

Schwyzer, E. *Griechische Grammatik*, vols. I–III (Munich 1953–60)

Scodel, R. 'The irony of fate in Bacchylides 17', *Hermes* 112 (1984) 137–43

Segal, C. 'Croesus on the pyre: Herodotus and Bacchylides', *WS* 84 (1971) 39–51

    'Bacchylides reconsidered: epithets and the dynamic of lyric narrative', *QUCC* 22 (1976) 99–130

Severyns, A. *Bacchylide, essai biographique* (Liège 1933)

Shapiro, H. A. *Personifications in Greek art* (Kilchberg/Zürich 1993)

Siewert, P. 'The ephebic oath in fifth-century Athens', *JHS* 97 (1977) 102–11

Simon, E. *Die griechischen Vasen* (Munich 1976)

Simonini, L. 'Il ditirambo XVI di Bacchilide', *Acme* 30 (1977) 485–99

Sinn, U. 'The sacred herd of Artemis at Lousoi', in R. Hägg (ed.), *The iconography of Greek cult* (Athens/Liège 1992 = *Kernos* Suppl. 1) 177–87

Slater, W. 'Futures in Pindar', *CQ* 19 (1969) 86–94

Slings, S. R. 'Bacchylides XVIII 41–2', *ZPE* 80 (1990) 9–10

Snell, B. 'Das Bruchstück eines Paians von Bakchylides', *Hermes* 67 (1932) 1–13

    The discovery of the mind (Cambridge, Mass. 1953)

    'Bakchylides' Marpessa-Gedicht (Fr.20A)', *Hermes* 80 (1952) 156–63 [reprinted in *Gesammelte Schriften* (Göttingen 1966) 105–11]

    Bacchylides, 10th edn. rev. by H. Maehler (Leipzig 1970)

    'Gyges und Kroisos als Tragödien-Figuren', *ZPE* 12 (1973) 197–205

Snodgrass, A. M. *Early Greek armour and weapons* (Edinburgh 1964)

    Arms and armour of the Greeks (London 1967)

    Narration and illusion in archaic Greek art (London 1982)

Sordi, M. (ed.), *La pace nel mondo antico* (Milano 1985)

Stanford, W. B. *Ambiguity in Greek literature: Studies in theory and practice* (Oxford 1939)

Steinhart, M. *Das Motiv des Auges in der griechischen Bildkunst* (Mainz 1995)

Stern, J. 'Bestial imagery in Bacchylides' ode 11', *GRBS* 6 (1965) 275–82

Strid, O. *Die Dryoper: Eine Untersuchung der Überlieferung* (Uppsala 1999)

Swaddling, J. *The ancient Olympic Games* (London 1980)

Taccone, A. *Bacchilide* (Turin 1923)

Tausend, K. 'Zur Bedeutung von Lusoi in archaischer Zeit', *ÖJh.* 62 (1993) Beiblatt 13–26

Thesleff, H. *Studies on intensification in early and classical Greek* (Helsinki 1954)

Thummer, E. *Pindar: Die isthmischen Gedichte*, 2 vols. (Heidelberg 1968–9)

Townsend, E. D. *Bacchylides and lyric style* (PhD thesis, Bryn Mawr College 1956)

Turyn, A. 'Lyrica graeca', *Eos* 27 (1924) 110–12

Verdenius, W. J. *Commentaries on Pindar* i–ii (Leiden 1987–8)

Vian, F. *La guerre des géants: Le mythe avant l'époque hellénistique* (Paris 1952)
    Répertoire des Gigantomachies figurées dans l'art grec et romain (Paris 1951)

Wackernagel, J. 'Zu Bakchylides', *Hermes* 40 (1905) 154
    Vorlesungen über Syntax i–ii (2nd edn. Basel 1926–8)
    Kleine Schriften (Göttingen 1953)

Walker, R. J. *Athenaeum* (18.12.1897)

Wegner, M. *Das Musikleben der Griechen* (Berlin 1949)

Weiden, M. J. H. van der, *The dithyrambs of Pindar* (Amsterdam 1991)

Weniger, L. 'Das Hochfest des Zeus in Olympia', *Klio* 4 (1904) 125–51

West, M. L. *Hesiod: Theogony* (Oxford 1966)
    Hesiod: Works and Days (Oxford 1978)
    Greek metre (Oxford 1982)
    The Hesiodic Catalogue of Women (Oxford 1987)
    Ancient Greek music (Oxford 1992)
    'Greek lyric 4' [rev. of D. A. Campbell], *CR* n.s. 43 (1993) 236–8
    'Eumelos: a Corinthian epic cycle?', *JHS* 122 (2002) 109–33

West, S. *A commentary on Homer's Odyssey*, vol. i by A. Heubeck, S. West, J. B. Hainsworth (Oxford 1988)

Wilamowitz-Moellendorf, U. von, *Pindaros* (Berlin 1922)

Wilcken, U. *Grundzüge und Chrestomathie der Papyruskunde* (Leipzig 1912)

Williger, E. *Untersuchungen zu den Komposita der griechischen Dichter des 5. Jahrhunderts* (Göttingen 1928)

Wyatt, W. F. *Metrical lengthening in Homer* (Rome 1969)

Yalouris, N. *Le mythe d'Io: Les transformations d'Io dans l'iconographie et la littérature grecques*, in *BCH Supplément* 14 (1986) 3–23

Zampaglione, G. *The idea of peace in antiquity* (Notre Dame 1973)

Zuntz, G. *Persephone: Three essays on religion and thought in Magna Graecia* (Oxford 1971)

INDEXES

1. SUBJECTS AND NAMES

Achaians 133, 138, 155, 156
Acheloios 107
adaptation 22, 126, 161
Admetos 83, 84, 95, 98
Aeolic 11, 12, 111, 139
    see also metre
Aeschylus 18, 86, 120, 193, 208, 213,
    216, 226
Agelaos 122
Aigeus 189, 191, 192, 193, 200
Aithra 180
Aitna 100, 252
Akousilaos 135, 146, 206
Akrisios 145, 148, 226
Alexander the Great 232
Alexandrian library 26, 27
    see also Mouseion
Alexandros, son of Amyntas 9, 244,
    246
Alkaios 15, 164, 165, 249
Alkman 1, 2, 11, 18, 211, 221, 236
alliteration 215
Althaia 120, 123, 124, 257
Amazons 192
Amphitrite 173, 174, 176, 185
anaclasis 16
Anakreon 15, 245
anaphora 235
Anaxilas of Rhegion 15
anceps 15, 17
Ankaios 122
Antenor 157
anthology 28, 160, 223
anticipated apposition 91
antistrophe 14, 83
Anyte 233
Aphrodite 5, 176, 186
apocopē 12
Apollo 7, 8, 81, 83, 84, 106, 164, 168,
    172, 220, 223, 228, 234

Apollonia 3, 4, 25, 172
Archilochos 1, 5, 211, 240
archives 25
Ares 222
Argos (giant) 205, 206, 207
Argos (town) 135, 137, 145
Ariadne 173, 175, 177
Arion 6, 183, 184
Aristarchos 7, 26, 27, 29, 173
Aristonoos 189
Aristophanes 25, 225, 248
Aristophanes of Byzantion 10, 14, 26,
    27
Artemis 121, 133, 135, 136, 138, 144,
    154, 156, 219
asyndetic pairs of epithets 215
asyndeton 23, 92, 96, 113, 131, 141,
    163, 164, 186, 187, 211, 212, 242,
    252
Athena 157, 174
Augustus 227

baccheus 16
brevis in longo 14

catalexis 16
centaur 166
    see also Nessos
choriambic dimeter 17
classification 6, 27, 173
clausula 16, 209, 222
cock 103
cola 14
colometry 14, 27, 30, 255
colour 19, 122
colour compounds 19, 121, 127, 153
compounds 12, 26, 86, 103, 104, 117,
    125, 159
conditional clause 104, 121, 123, 142
consecutive infinitive 87, 231

contrast 20, 92, 93, 105, 109, 113, 117, 127, 144, 164, 171, 214, 242
convivial poetry 25, 248
coronis 27
correption 13, 170
cretic 16, 17, 209
cult songs 2, 3, 25
Cyclopes 151

dactyloepitrite 15, 17, 85, 209, 244, 252, 256
Danaos 151
dancing 7, 155, 185, 219, 220
Dante 113
Deianeira 107, 166
Deinomenes, son of Hieron 79, 100, 106, 252
Delia: *see* Apollonia
Demokritos 225, 226
Dickens 126
Didymos 25, 27, 173
digamma 13, 119, 221
Dike 105, 225
Dionysos 5, 6, 135, 147, 165, 205, 208, 217, 248
dissimilation 118
dithyramb 2, 3, 5, 6, 23, 25, 157, 165
dolphin 184
Doric 11, 12, 13, 18, 111
dramatic climax 21, 23, 92, 94, 137, 164, 187
dramatic tension 176, 181
Dryopes 223, 227
dual 201

eagle 113, 114
Egypt 249
Eirene 225
see also peace
élitism 3, 111
elliptical narrative 22
emotional appeal 20, 21, 23, 125, 145, 214
see also pathos
encomiologicum 15

enkomion 239, 240, 244, 251
see also negative *e.*
Epaphos 208, 217
ephebe 189, 191, 203, 205
epic flavour 161
epic forms 11
epic lengthening 13
epic poetry 18
Epicharmos 22, 96
epithets 19, 20, 145
epode 14, 84, 138
Eriboia 176, 179
etymology 23, 91, 99, 112, 114, 121, 155, 211, 224, 229
Euenos, son of Ares 219, 220, 240, 242
Eumelos 11
Eunomia 163, 225
Euphronios 174, 178
Euripides 92, 225, 231, 232
Eurystheus 107

flowers 98, 168, 172, 217, 231, 252
formal structure 22, 24, 83, 109, 130, 136, 145, 193
François Vase 108, 122, 174, 176
future 99

Gelon, son of Deinomenes 89, 115
generosity 88
Giants 157, 164
glyconic 14, 16, 209
gnomai 24, 84, 85, 96, 97, 109, 117, 186, 188, 236
gold 97, 139, 180, 214
Graces 23, 162
Gyges 82, 91

Helen 5, 157, 158, 164
hellanodikai 8
see also judges
hemiepes 14, 209
Hera 120, 134, 137, 146, 205, 214
Herakleides Pontikos 193
Herakles 107, 117, 166, 191, 223
herald 24, 100, 158, 191
Hermes 205, 206, 215, 217, 220

Herodotos 6, 81, 226, 244
Hesiod 128, 135, 142, 147, 163, 205,
   211, 225
hiatus 13, 94, 98, 189
Hieron, son of Deinomenes 4, 9, 22,
   27, 79, 100, 106, 195, 226, 250, 251
Hipparchos, son of Peisistratos 9
Hippodameia 220
Homeric compounds 19
Homeric forms 19
Homeric vocabulary 19
Horace 28
horses 87, 106, 115, 116, 184, 220, 243,
   251
   see Pherenikos
Hybris 163
Hyperboreans 82, 84, 94, 164

iambic: see metre
Ibykos 5, 18, 96, 113
Idas 219, 220, 243
imperfect of attempted action 150
intertextual reference 96, 126, 162
   see also 'quotation'
intrusive gloss 170, 171, 180, 232
Io 205, 207
Iole 171
Ionians 193, 232
Ionic 11, 13
ionic dimeter 16
irony 119, 171, 191, 195, 200, 204, 214,
   217
ivory 249

judges 8, 142, 244
   see also hellanodikai

Kalamis 79, 107
Kallimachos 7, 25, 26, 27, 29, 173
Kalydonian Boar 108, 121
Kerberos 107, 118
Kerkyon 197
Keyx 224, 227
Kimon 190, 202
Kleio 83, 86
Kleopatra 257

Kroisos 21, 80, 226
Kypria 158, 161, 176
Kyros 81, 92

Lasos of Hermione 5
lekythion 16, 17
'Lemnian fire' 203
linen 218
'link-syllable' 15, 17, 209
literary models 22, 110, 126
   see also intertextual reference
Longos 201
lost victory 141, 142, 143
love-charm 166, 167
lyric poetry 1

Maas's Bridge 112
Marpessa 219, 220, 240, 243
Melampous, son of Amythaon 134,
   135, 147, 230
Meleagros 107, 118, 257
Menelaos 6, 157, 158, 226
metre: aeolic 16, 85, 209
   iambic 15, 16, 85
   trochaic 15
   see dactyloepitrite
Mikon 176
Milton 114, 118
mimesis 173
Minos 173, 175
Minotauros 173, 175, 192
Mnasalkas 233
Moira 179
Mouseion 26
Muses 23, 83, 86, 96, 162, 185, 208,
   210, 211, 217
   see also Kleio, Ourania
muta cum liquida 12
Myson 80, 82, 93

name-cap 96, 98, 204
negative *enkomion* 239, 256
negative superlative 94
Nereids 176, 185, 188
Nessos 166
nightingale 96, 100

Nika, Nike 138, 139, 140
Niobe 147, 255, 256
Nostoi 133

Odysseus 158, 226
Oichalia 169
Oinomaos 174, 220
Onatas 79, 107
Onesimos 25, 174, 178
oral poetry 1, 136
oratory 215
Orphic eschatology 83
Ourania 103, 112, 132
Ovid 214, 217

paean 2, 3, 5, 25, 164, 223
paeon 16, 17
Paktolos 92
Panathenaia 4, 157, 189
Panhellenic festivals 7
paragraphos 27, 30
Parmenides 127
pathos 21, 92, 121, 123, 125, 170
Pausanias 28, 133, 176, 229
peace 5, 129, 150, 163, 225, 231,
    233
Peisistratos 4, 191
Pelops 220
Pergamon 26
period 14
Pherekydes 134, 135, 146, 152
Pherenikos 79, 101, 107, 253
Phoronis 136
Phrynichos 108, 123, 148
Pindar 2, 6, 9, 17, 25, 79, 86, 94, 97,
    100, 106, 107, 111, 116, 127, 128,
    130, 131, 139, 140, 155, 181, 187,
    188, 197, 210, 211, 225, 230, 231,
    234, 236, 237, 238, 244, 245, 246,
    248, 250, 252
Plato 25, 227, 228, 232, 236
Plutarch 28, 178, 192, 197
Polykrates of Samos 4, 96
Polypemon 197
Polyzalos, son of Deinomenes 101,
    105

Poseidon 7, 176, 182, 184, 185, 196, 220
'programme' 24, 83
Proitos 21, 134, 137, 145, 148, 226
Prokoptas (Prokroustes) 197
prolepsis 84, 145, 154, 170, 180
Prometheus 93, 126
prosodion 235
Ptolemy I Soter 26
pun 129, 130, 179, 185
purple 146, 202

quotation 22, 28, 85, 96, 125, 128,
    162

repetition 24, 85, 98, 117, 235
responsion 14, 27, 102, 168, 170
'ring-composition' 24, 137, 138, 148

Sappho 245
Sardis 92
self-address 212
self-confidence 113
self-exhortation 252
self-presentation 100
    see also sphragis
silence 98
sillybos 30, 157
simile 109, 113, 115, 118, 126
Simonides 9, 11, 15, 18, 25, 128, 130,
    132, 178, 192, 194, 220
Sinis 196
Skiron 197
skolion 238
Solon 81, 91, 157, 163, 249
song as 'path' 23
Sophocles 18, 123, 166, 167, 170,
    259
sphragis 85
statues 2, 115
Stesichoros 18, 94, 108, 109, 122
Strabo 28
strophe 14, 27, 83, 138
Styx 139
superlative 106, 111, 116, 141, 195, 212,
    254
    negative s. 94

swan 165, 168
symmetry 24, 25, 84, 85, 109, 137, 138,
 148, 204
synekphonesis 90

Terpander 245
Theano 157
Themis 163
Theognis 226
Theokritos 232
Theseus 173, 189
'Throne of Amyklai' 207
Tibullus 233
Timokreon 239
Tiryns 135, 137, 145, 148, 151
titles 6, 28, 29, 30, 157, 175, 205, 238,
 251
tragedy 4, 6, 18, 20, 81, 92, 146, 170,
 171, 191, 200, 205, 236

tragic plot 167
transition 83, 84, 85, 115, 117, 127, 137,
 138, 140
triad 14, 27
tricolon 121, 139, 195
tripods 89, 98, 115, 165
trochaic *see* metre
trumpet 194, 233

verbal correspondence 130
verbal echo 137, 149
Virgil 119

willingness-motif 109, 110, 113, 128,
 129, 246
wings 245

zeugma 231
Zeus 7, 84, 88, 104, 127, 132

2. GREEK WORDS

ἅ 171
ἁβροβάτας 93
ἀγάθεος 94
ἄγαλμα 111
ἀγαυός 258
Ἀγλαΐα 87
ἀγυιαί 89, 148
ἀδίαντος 187
ἀελλοδρόμας 115
ἄθεος 154
αἰγλάεις 250
αἰολόπρυμνος 26
αἰών 186
ἄλαστος 91
ἀλήθεια 99
ἄλοχος 171
ἀλυκτάζειν 152
ἀμαιμάκετος 149
ἀμείβειν 196
ἀμετρόδικος 150
ἀμύσσειν 195
ἀμφιβάλλειν 195
ἀμφιπολεῖν 236

ἀναιδομάχας 121
ἀναπάλλεσθαι 149
ἀργεϊφόντης 205
ἀρετή 3
ἀτάρβακτος 123
ἄτρυτος 114
αὐδάεις 161
αὐλοί 1
αὐχεῖν 179

βάρβιτος 245, 252
βαρύς 180
βλέφαρον 141
βοῶπις 153
βρίθεσθαι 234
βρύειν 89, 132, 218

γε μέν 98
γελανοῦν 119
γνῶμαι 2

δαίμων 170, 171, 172, 180
δαΐφρων 122

δέρκειν 182
διαιθύσσειν 247
Δίκα 163, 179
δίκαι 200
δίκη 163
δοιάζειν 152
δονεῖν 237
δυσπαίπαλος 114

ἐγκώμιον 2, 239
εἰ in causal sense (= siquidem) 253
εἰκάς 246
ἐκδιδόναι 243
ἐλεφαντόκωπος 201
ἐνδυκέως 122, 123
ἐντύειν (ἐντύνειν) 228
ἐπίνικος 2
ἐρατός 145
εὐθύδικος 111
εὔμοιρος 110
εὔοχθος 228

ἦ 112, 199, 213, 216
ἦρα + genitive 141

θελημός 183
θρῆνος 2

ἰάπτειν 237
ἱπποδίνητος 110
ἴσχειν 180
ἰσχυρός 199

καλά 99
κέλευθος 23, 210, 257
κοινοῦν 162
κρατεῖν 132
κῦδος 3
κυνέα 201
κῶμος 239

λάσκειν 104
λείριος 184

μαρμαρυγαί 89
μεγάλαυχος 179
μελαμφαρής 88

μέλας 179
μελίφρων 233
μέλος 1
μέριμνα 212, 216
μήδεσθαι 105

Νίκα 137
νωμᾶν 114

ξανθός 115
ξένος (adjective) 151

ὀλολύζειν 188
ὀξύτερος 241
ὁρμᾶν 257
ὅρος 235
ὀρσίμαχος 159
ὅσιος 179
οὔλιος 203

παιανίζειν 188
παλίντροπος 147
πανδερκής 182
πανόπτης 207
πίπτειν 178
πλείσταρχος 88
ποδάνεμος 132
πολύπλαγκτος 143
που 120
πρίν + subjunctive 168
πρόδομος 130, 132

σοεῖν 184
στολά 198
σφραγίς 100
σχάζειν 187

τανυάκης 258
τε 139, 203, 211
τίκτειν 231
τὸ δέ (demonstrative pronoun) 237
τυγχάνειν 155
τύχα: σὺν τύχαι 155

ὑγρός 185
υἱός 118

ὕμνος 112, 211
ὑφαίνειν 112, 211
ὑψιδαίδαλτος 90

φᾶρος 178
φθόνος 95, 128, 156
φιλεῖν 102
φλέγειν 234
φραδαί 214
φυλλοβολία 104, 141

χάρις 85, 99, 211
χθόνιος 241
χλαμύς 203
χρέος 128
χρή 128
χρυσάορος 91
χρυσηλάκατος 144
χρυσοκόμας 102

ψυχή 146